Hey! You're Reading in the Wrong Direction!

This is the end of this graphic novel!

To properly enjoy this VIZ graphic novel, please turn it around and begin reading from right to left. Unlike English, Japanese is read right to left, so Japanese comics are read in reverse order from the way English comics are typically read.

This book has been printed in the original Japanese format in order to preserve the orientation of the original artwork. Have fun with it!

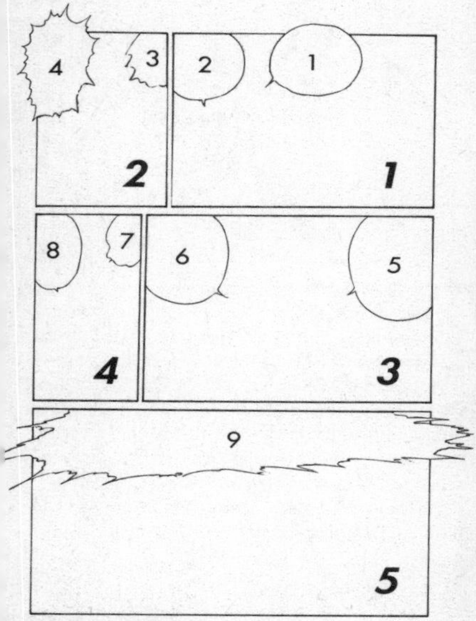
1
2
1
3
4
2
5
6
3
7
8
4
9
5

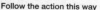

Follow the action this way

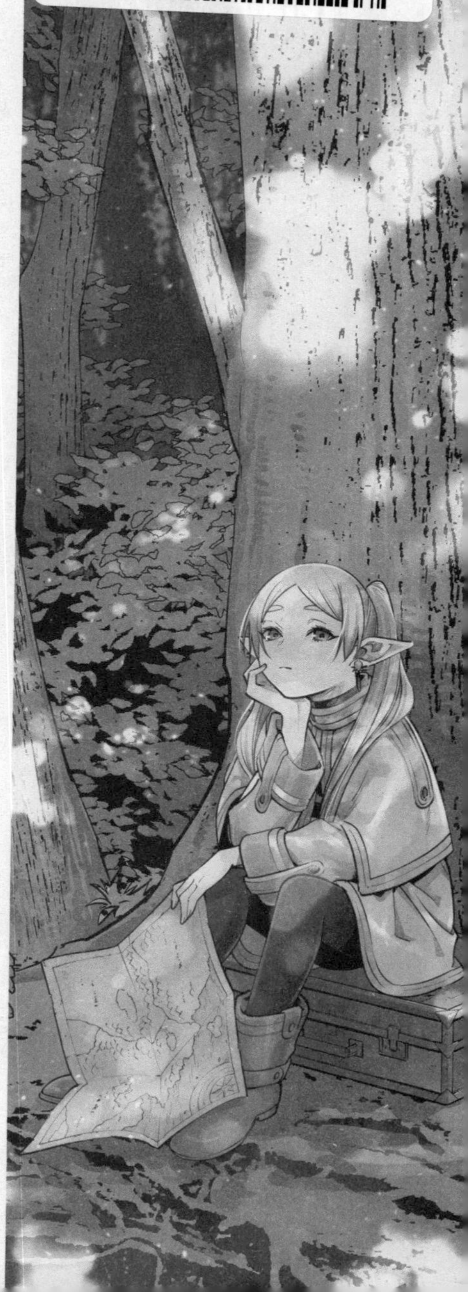

Kidnapped by the Demon King and imprisoned in his castle, Princess Syalis is...bored.

SLEEPY PRINCESS IN THE DEMON CASTLE

Story & Art by
KAGIJI KUMANOMATA

Captured princess Syalis decides to while away her hours in the Demon Castle by sleeping, but getting a good night's rest turns out to be a lot of work! She begins by fashioning a DIY pillow out of the fur of her Teddy Demon guards and an "air mattress" from the magical Shield of the Wind. Things go from bad to worse—for her captors—when some of Princess Syalis's schemes end in her untimely— if temporary—demise and she chooses the Forbidden Grimoire for her bedtime reading...

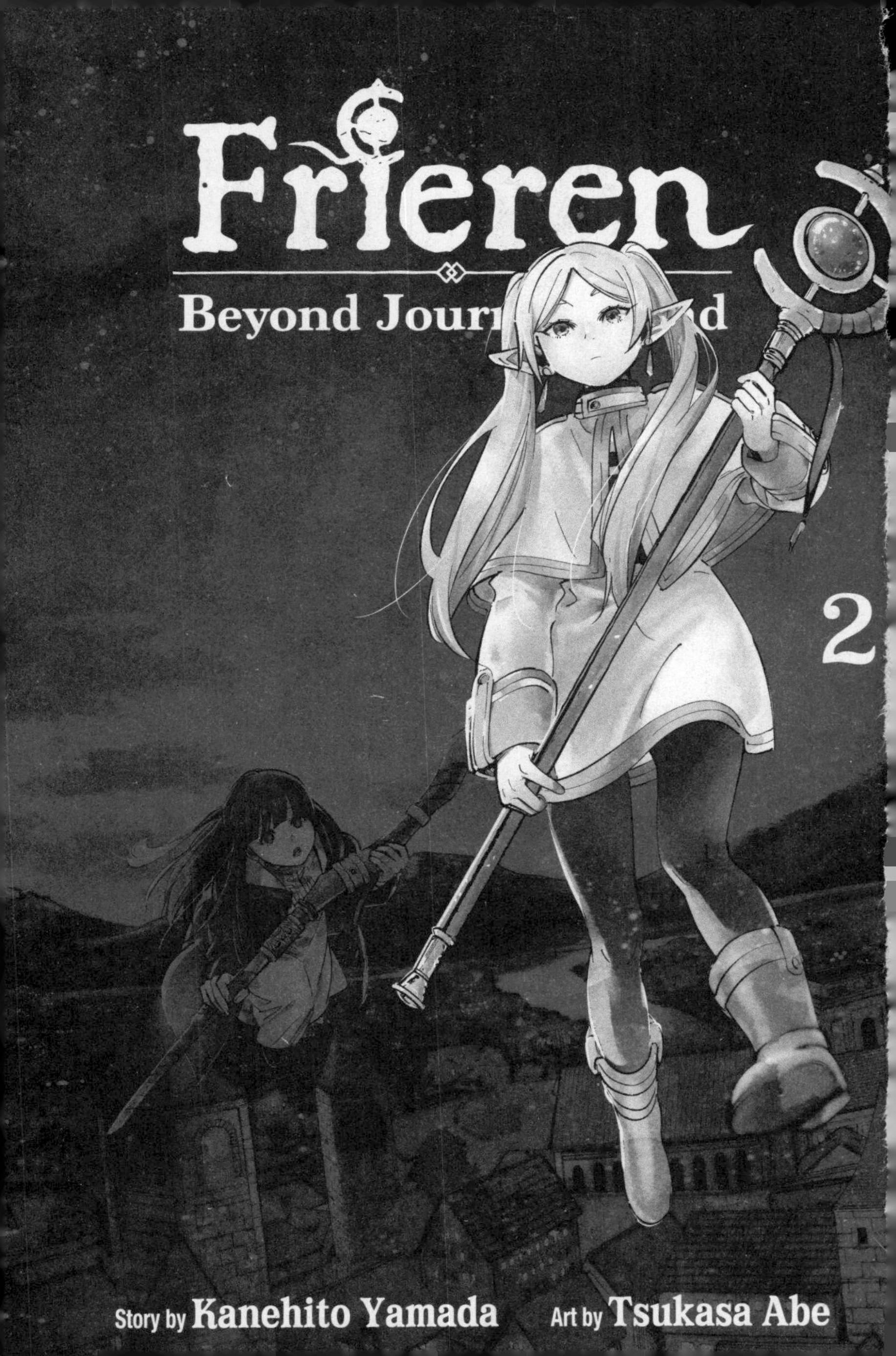
Frieren
Beyond Journ nd
2
Story by Kanehito Yamada
Art by Tsukasa Abe

CONTENTS

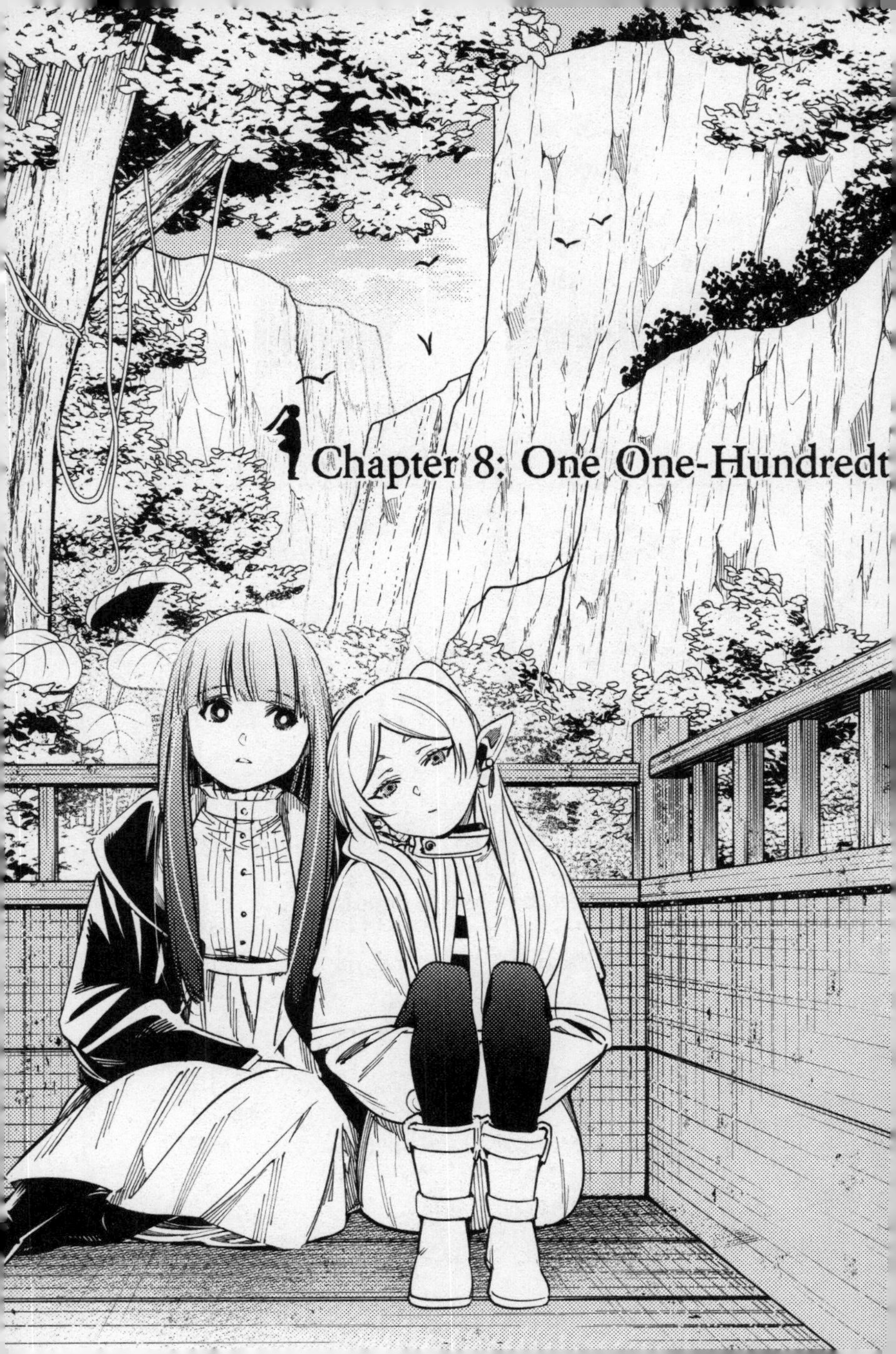
Chapter 8: One One-Hundredt

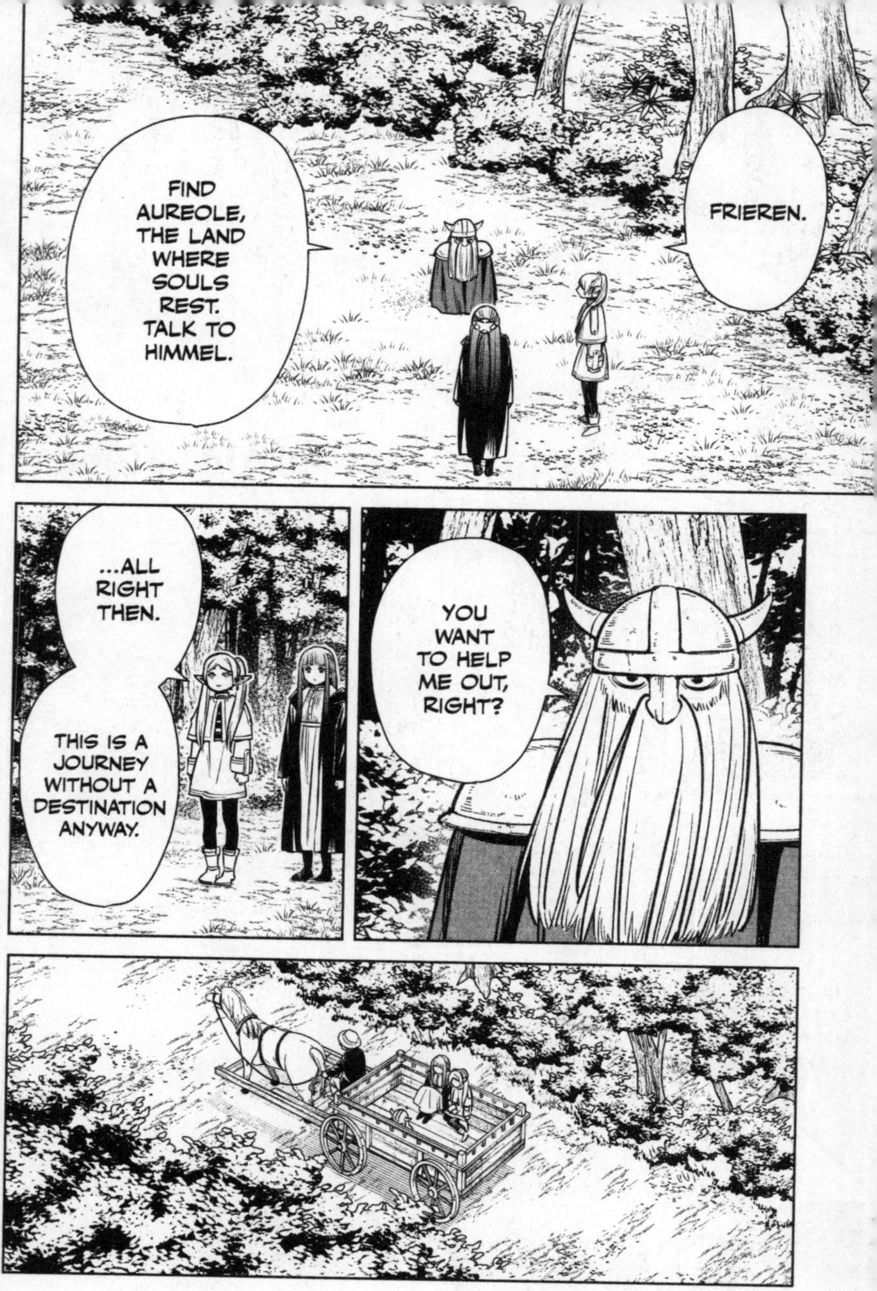
FRIEREN.
FIND AUREOLE, THE LAND WHERE SOULS REST. TALK TO HIMMEL.
YOU WANT TO HELP ME OUT, RIGHT?
...ALL RIGHT THEN.
THIS IS A JOURNEY WITHOUT A DESTINATION ANYWAY.

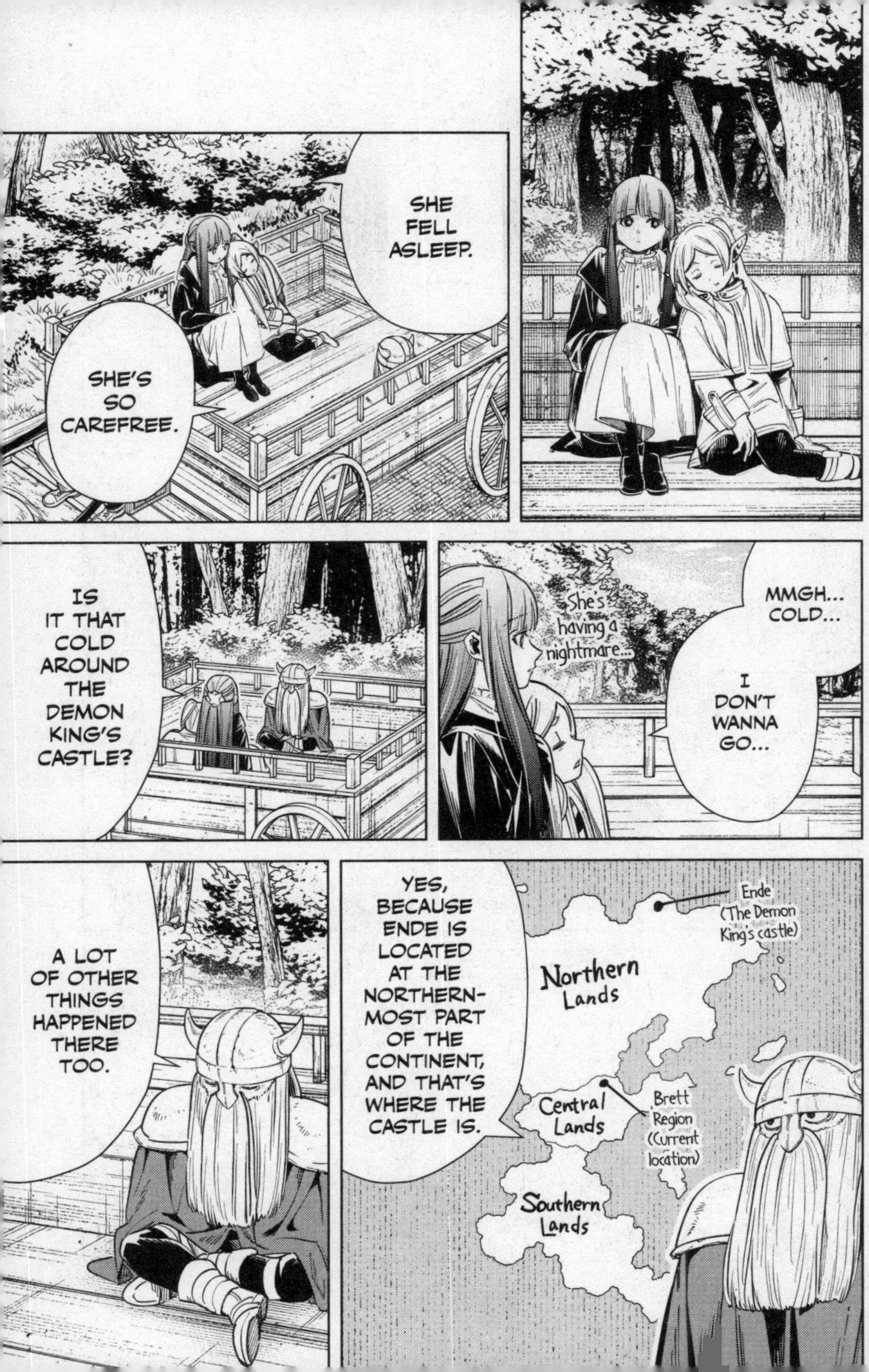
SHE FELL ASLEEP.
SHE'S SO CAREFREE.
MMGH... COLD...
I DON'T WANNA GO...
She's having a nightmare...
IS IT THAT COLD AROUND THE DEMON KING'S CASTLE?
YES, BECAUSE ENDE IS LOCATED AT THE NORTHERN-MOST PART OF THE CONTINENT, AND THAT'S WHERE THE CASTLE IS.
Ende (The Demon King's castle)
Northern Lands
Central Lands
Brett Region (Current location)
Southern Lands
A LOT OF OTHER THINGS HAPPENED THERE TOO.

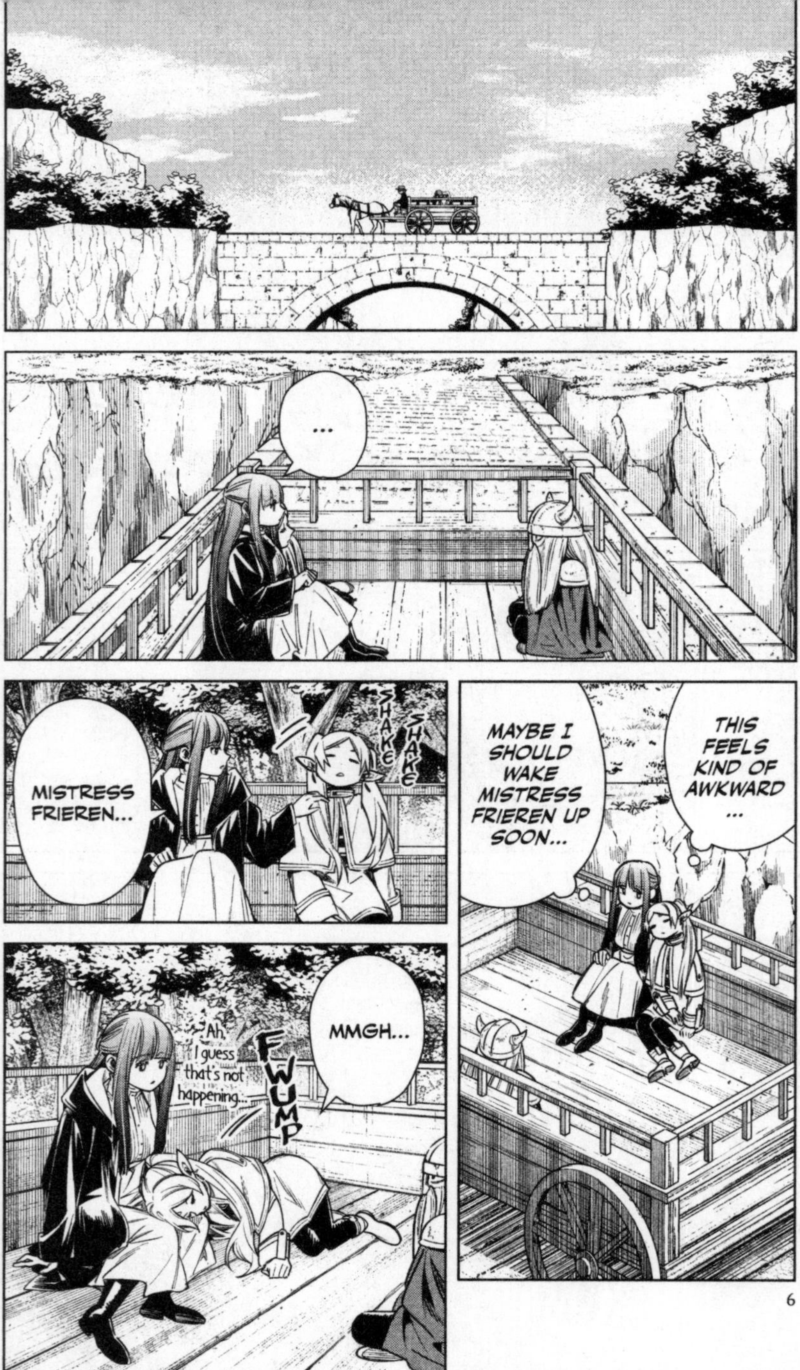
...
THIS FEELS KIND OF AWKWARD...
MAYBE I SHOULD WAKE MISTRESS FRIEREN UP SOON...
SHAKE SHAKE
MISTRESS FRIEREN...
MMGH...
FWUMP
Ah, I guess that's not happening...

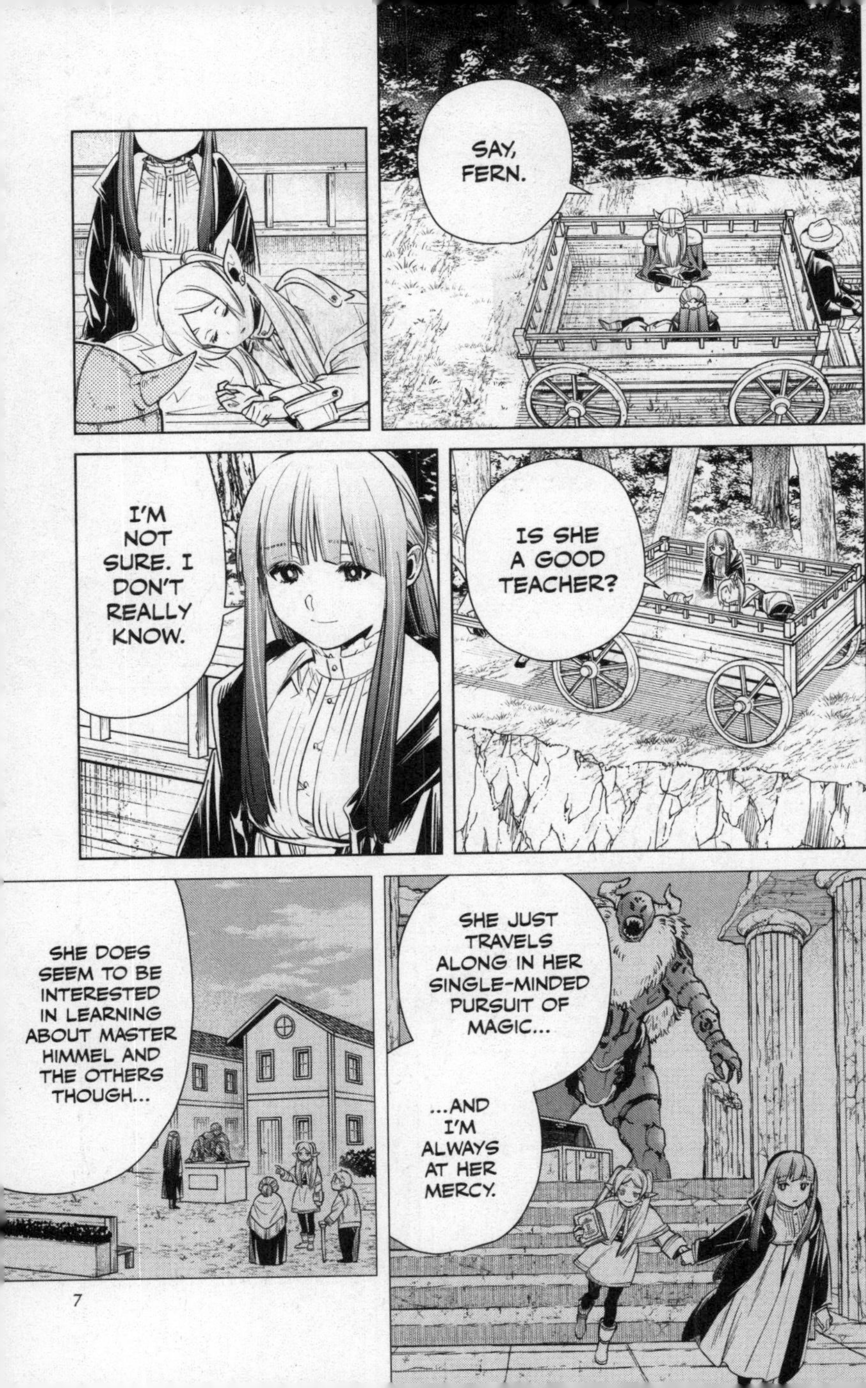
SAY, FERN.
IS SHE A GOOD TEACHER?
I'M NOT SURE. I DON'T REALLY KNOW.
SHE JUST TRAVELS ALONG IN HER SINGLE-MINDED PURSUIT OF MAGIC...
...AND I'M ALWAYS AT HER MERCY.
SHE DOES SEEM TO BE INTERESTED IN LEARNING ABOUT MASTER HIMMEL AND THE OTHERS THOUGH...

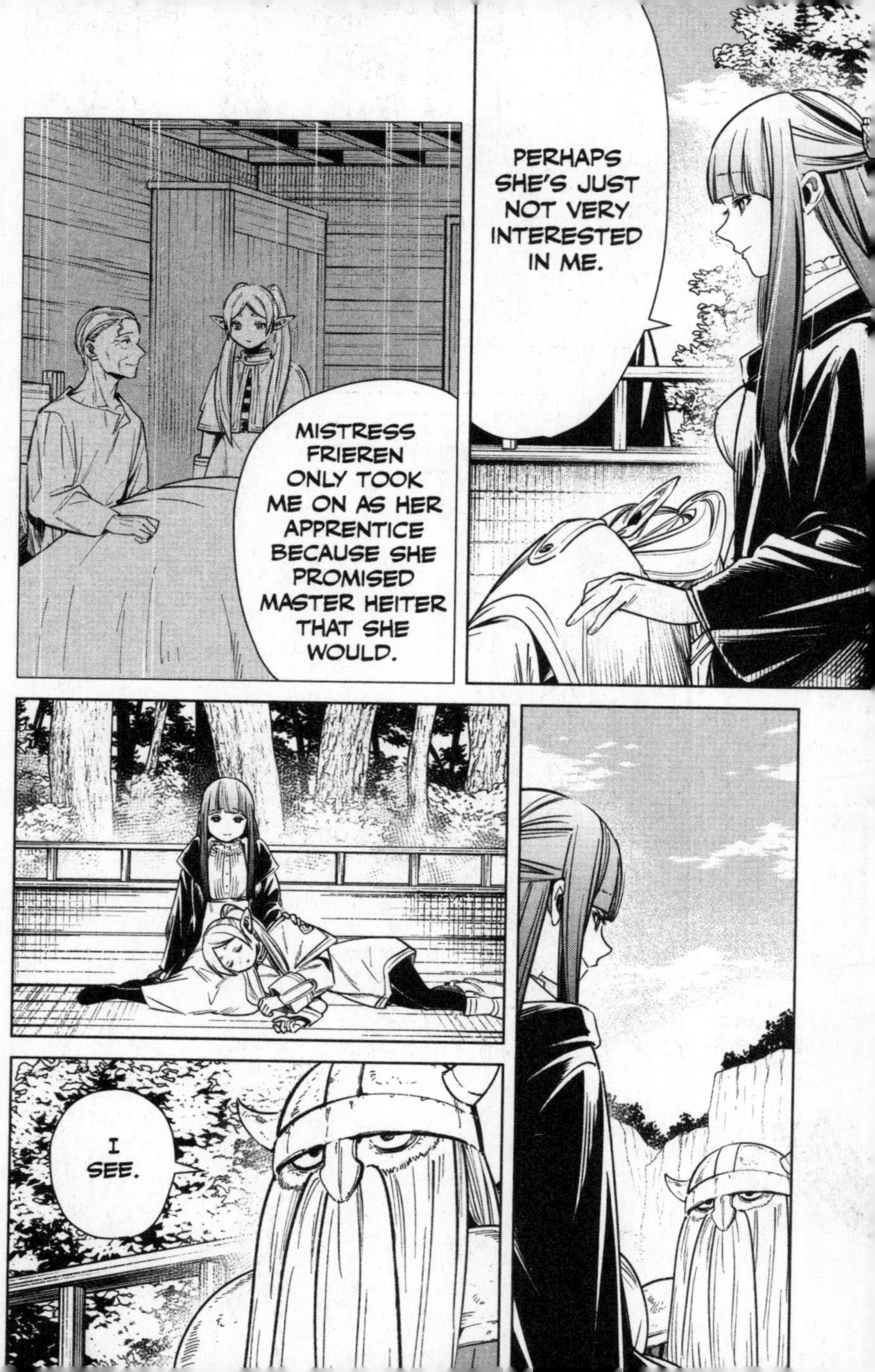
PERHAPS SHE'S JUST NOT VERY INTERESTED IN ME.
MISTRESS FRIEREN ONLY TOOK ME ON AS HER APPRENTICE BECAUSE SHE PROMISED MASTER HEITER THAT SHE WOULD.
I SEE.

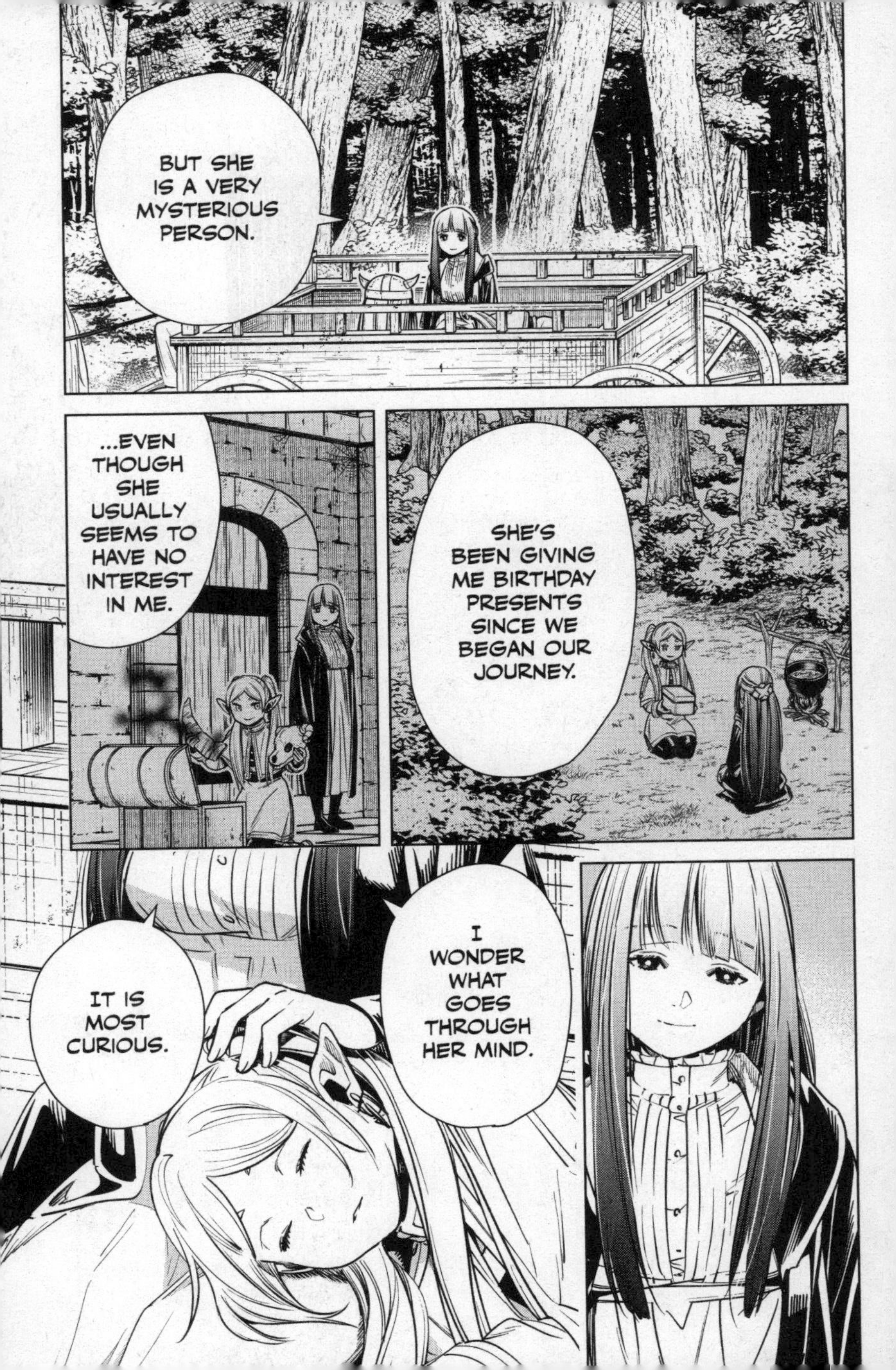
BUT SHE IS A VERY MYSTERIOUS PERSON.
SHE'S BEEN GIVING ME BIRTHDAY PRESENTS SINCE WE BEGAN OUR JOURNEY.
...EVEN THOUGH SHE USUALLY SEEMS TO HAVE NO INTEREST IN ME.
I WONDER WHAT GOES THROUGH HER MIND.
IT IS MOST CURIOUS.

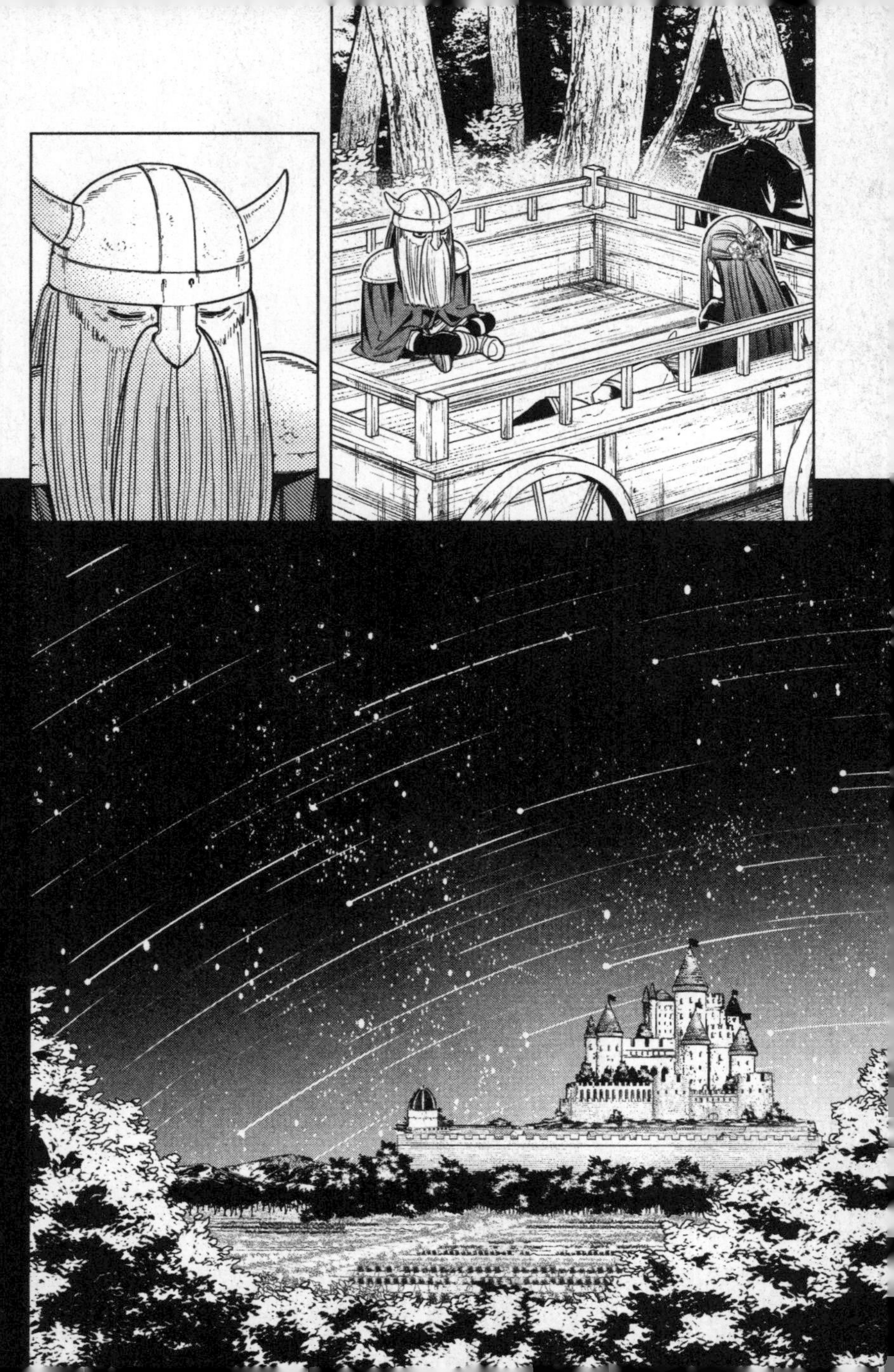

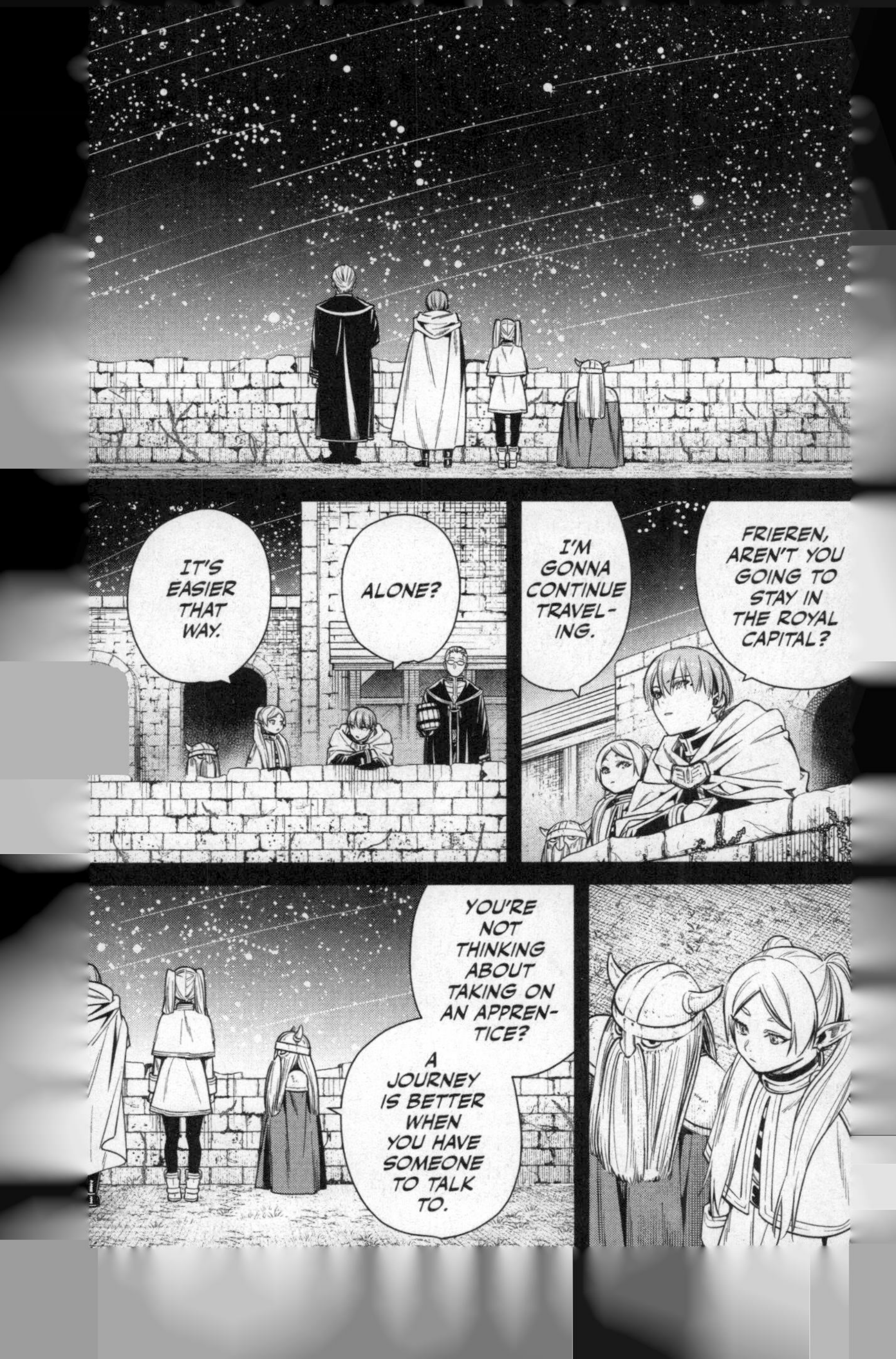
FRIEREN, AREN'T YOU GOING TO STAY IN THE ROYAL CAPITAL?
I'M GONNA CONTINUE TRAVEL-ING.
ALONE?
IT'S EASIER THAT WAY.
YOU'RE NOT THINKING ABOUT TAKING ON AN APPREN-TICE?
A JOURNEY IS BETTER WHEN YOU HAVE SOMEONE TO TALK TO.

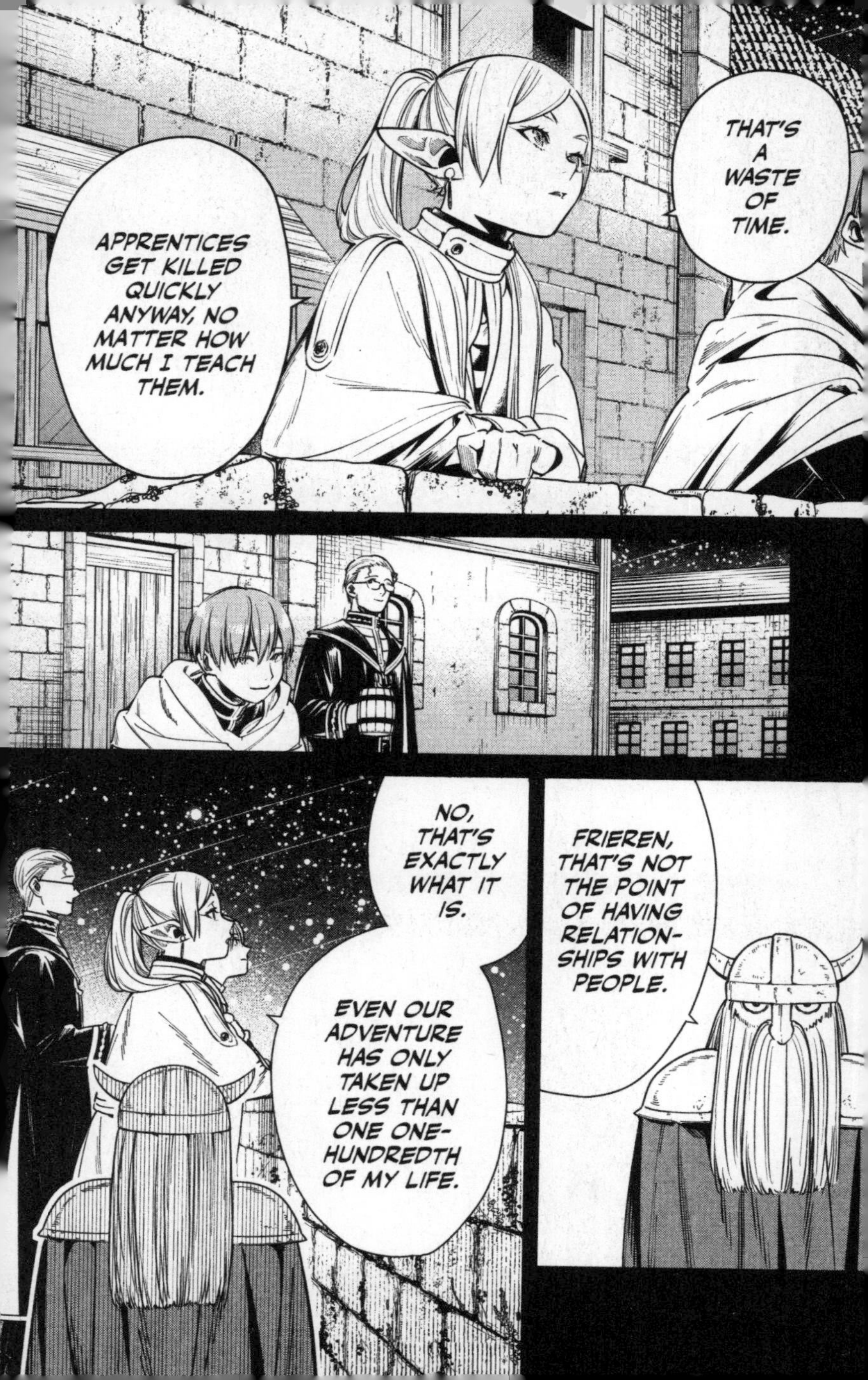
THAT'S A WASTE OF TIME.
APPRENTICES GET KILLED QUICKLY ANYWAY, NO MATTER HOW MUCH I TEACH THEM.
FRIEREN, THAT'S NOT THE POINT OF HAVING RELATION-SHIPS WITH PEOPLE.
NO, THAT'S EXACTLY WHAT IT IS.
EVEN OUR ADVENTURE HAS ONLY TAKEN UP LESS THAN ONE ONE-HUNDREDTH OF MY LIFE.

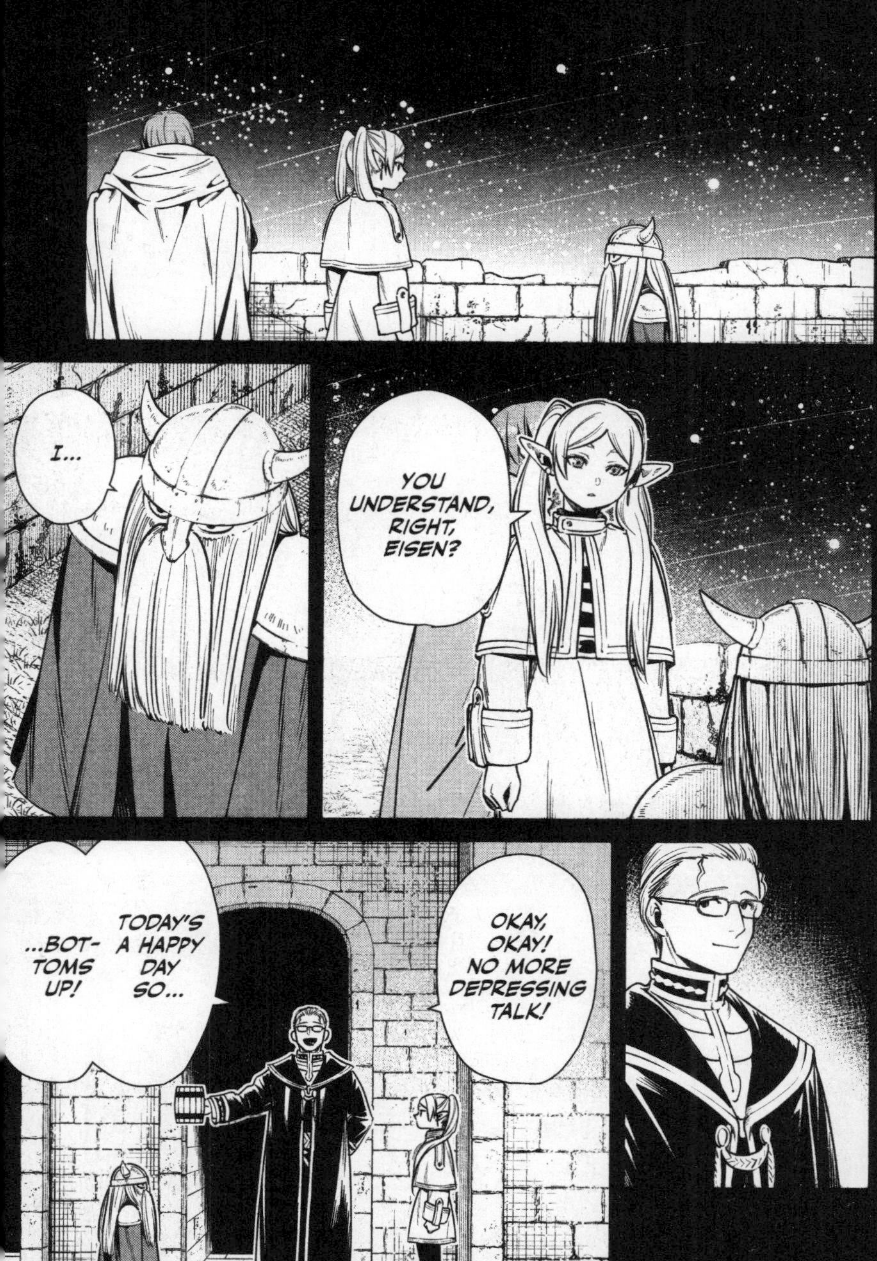
YOU UNDERSTAND, RIGHT, EISEN?
I...
OKAY, OKAY! NO MORE DEPRESSING TALK!
TODAY'S A HAPPY DAY SO...
...BOT-TOMS UP!

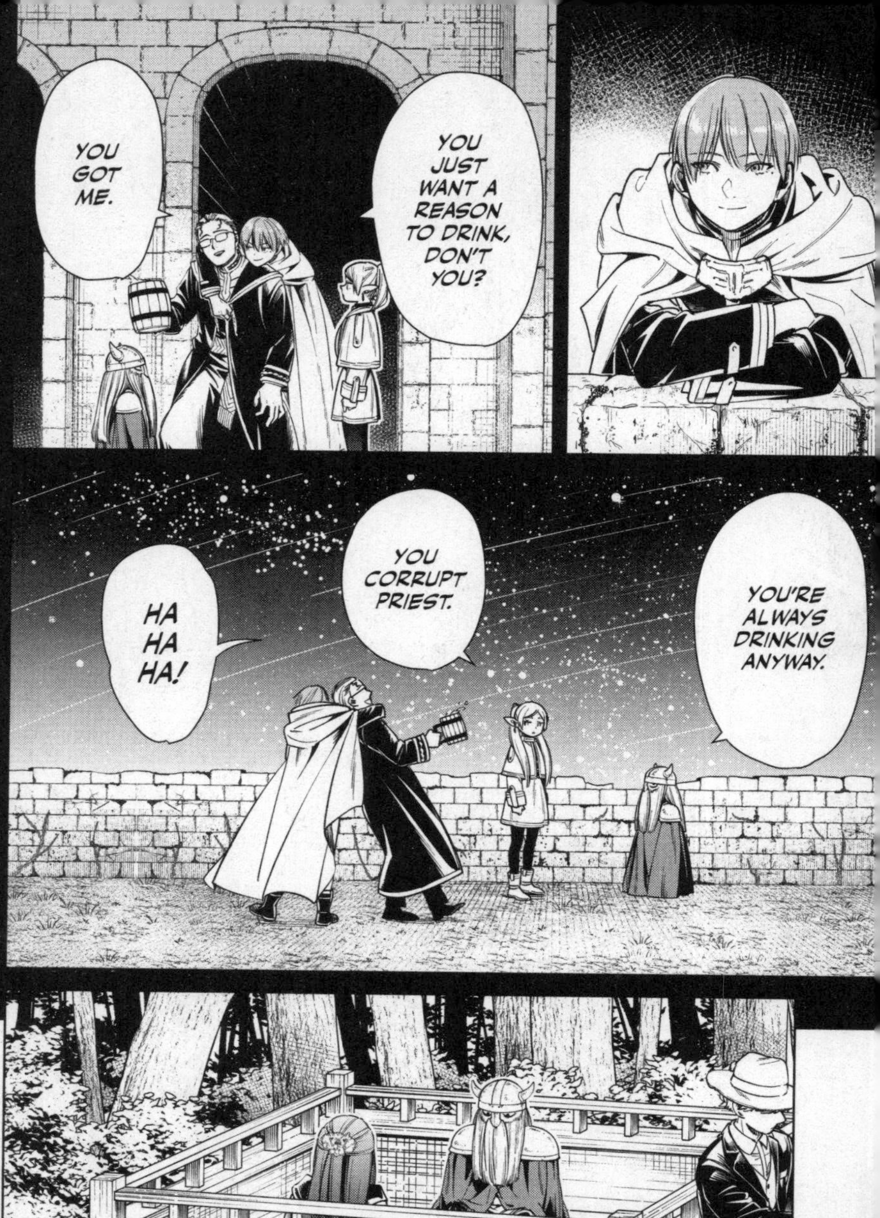
YOU JUST WANT A REASON TO DRINK, DON'T YOU?
YOU GOT ME.
YOU'RE ALWAYS DRINKING ANYWAY.
YOU CORRUPT PRIEST.
HA HA HA!

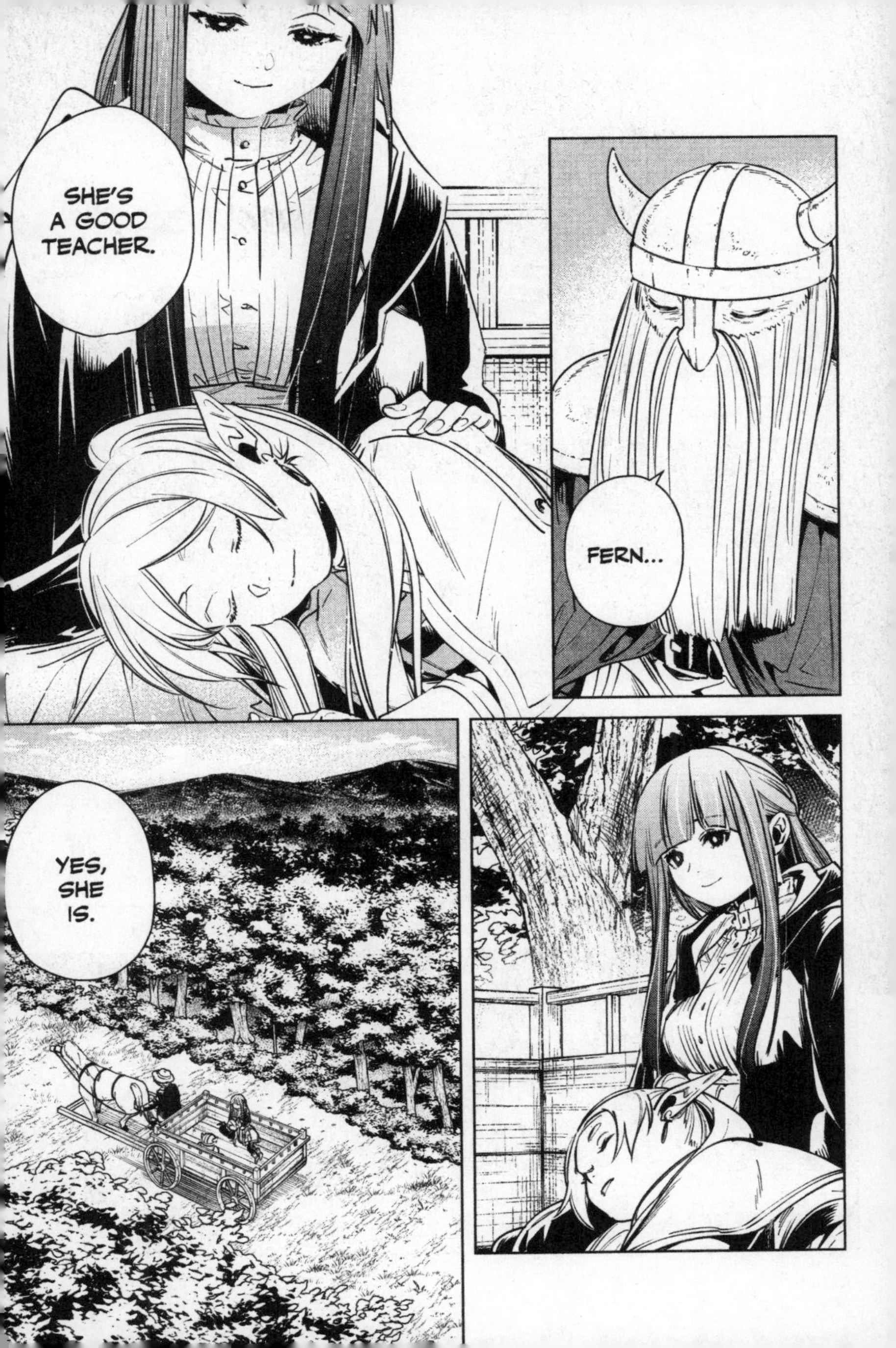
FERN...
SHE'S A GOOD TEACHER.
YES, SHE IS.

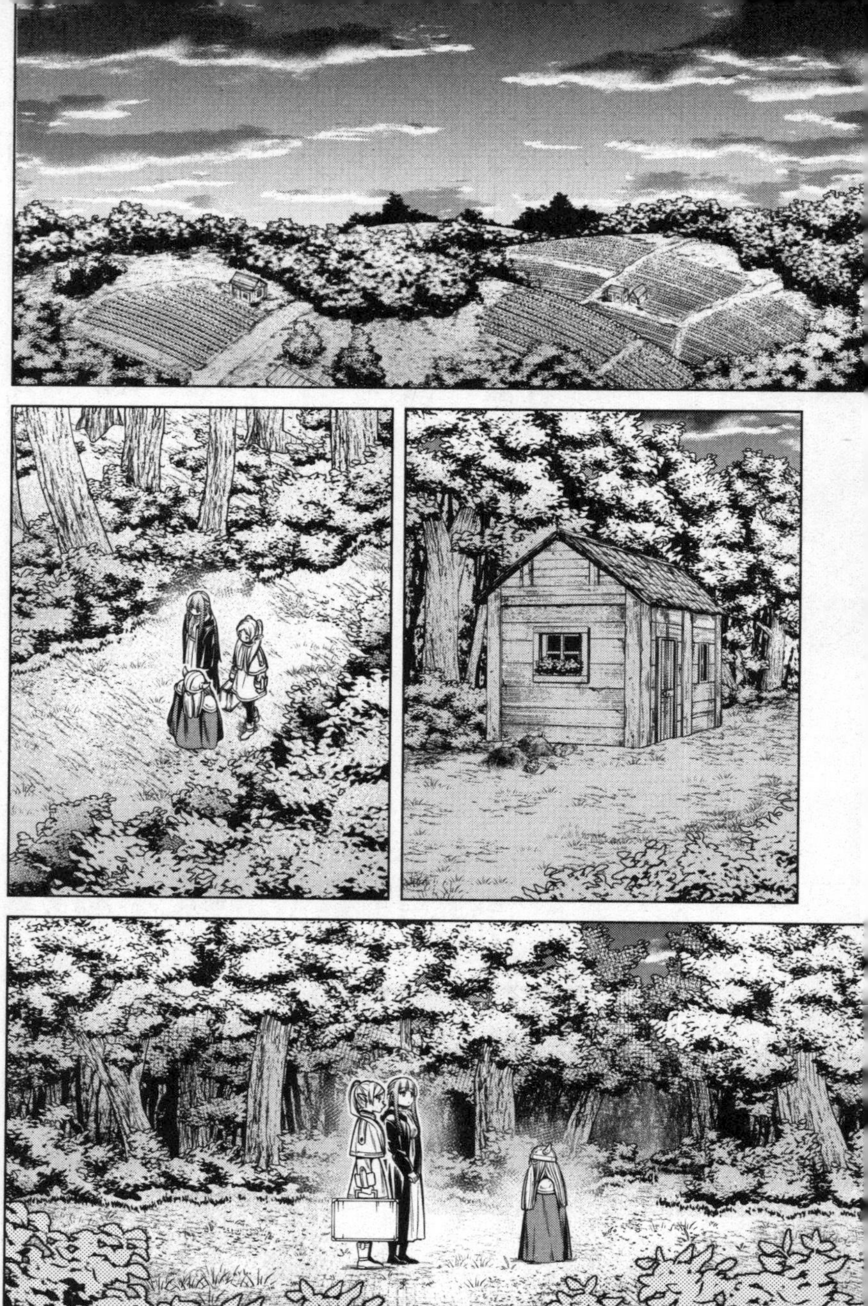

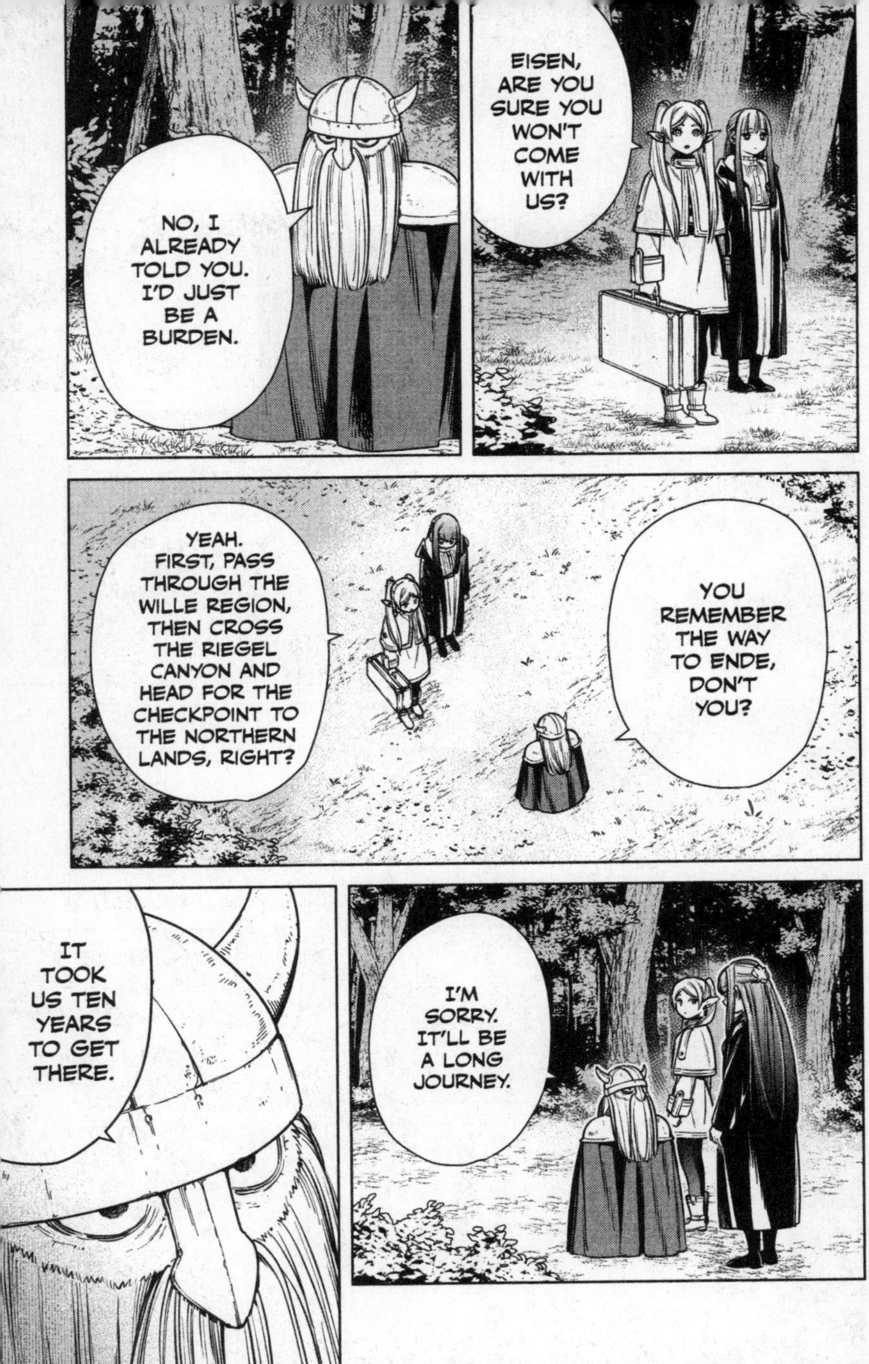
EISEN, ARE YOU SURE YOU WON'T COME WITH US?
NO, I ALREADY TOLD YOU. I'D JUST BE A BURDEN.
YOU REMEMBER THE WAY TO ENDE, DON'T YOU?
YEAH. FIRST, PASS THROUGH THE WILLE REGION, THEN CROSS THE RIEGEL CANYON AND HEAD FOR THE CHECKPOINT TO THE NORTHERN LANDS, RIGHT?
I'M SORRY. IT'LL BE A LONG JOURNEY.
IT TOOK US TEN YEARS TO GET THERE.

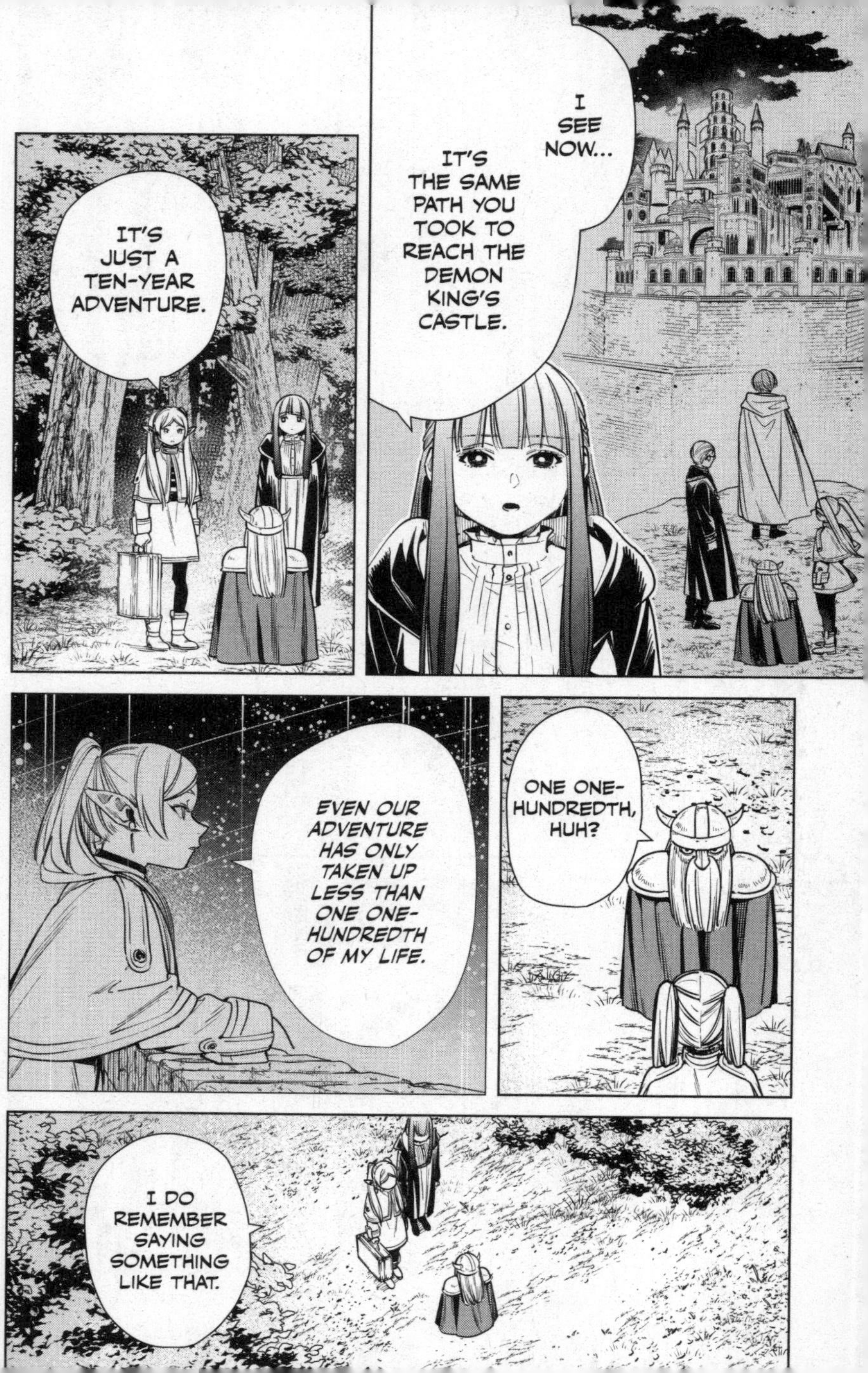
I SEE NOW...
IT'S THE SAME PATH YOU TOOK TO REACH THE DEMON KING'S CASTLE.
IT'S JUST A TEN-YEAR ADVENTURE.
ONE ONE-HUNDREDTH, HUH?
EVEN OUR ADVENTURE HAS ONLY TAKEN UP LESS THAN ONE ONE-HUNDREDTH OF MY LIFE.
I DO REMEMBER SAYING SOMETHING LIKE THAT.

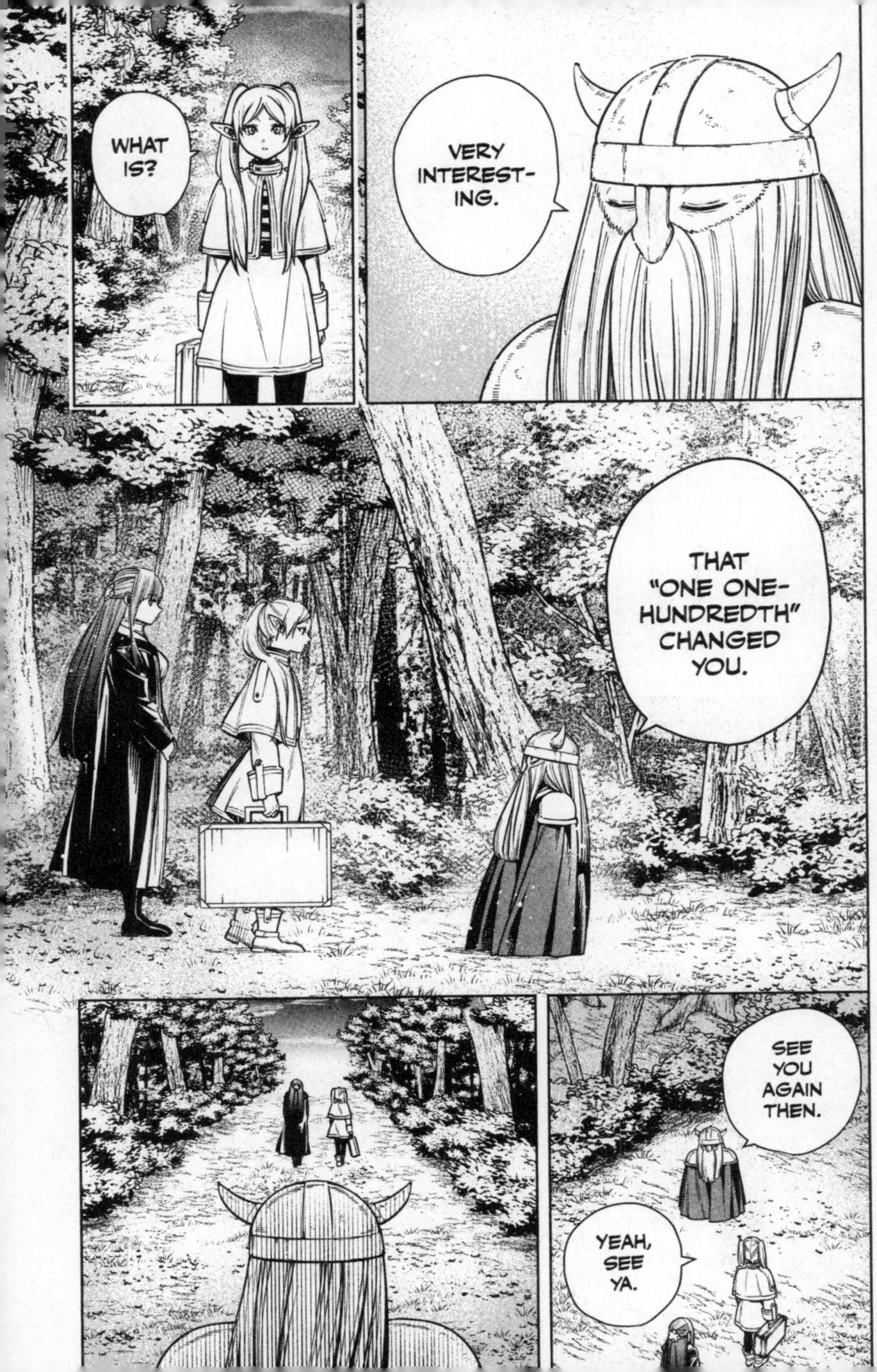
VERY INTEREST-ING.
WHAT IS?
THAT "ONE ONE-HUNDREDTH" CHANGED YOU.
SEE YOU AGAIN THEN.
YEAH, SEE YA.

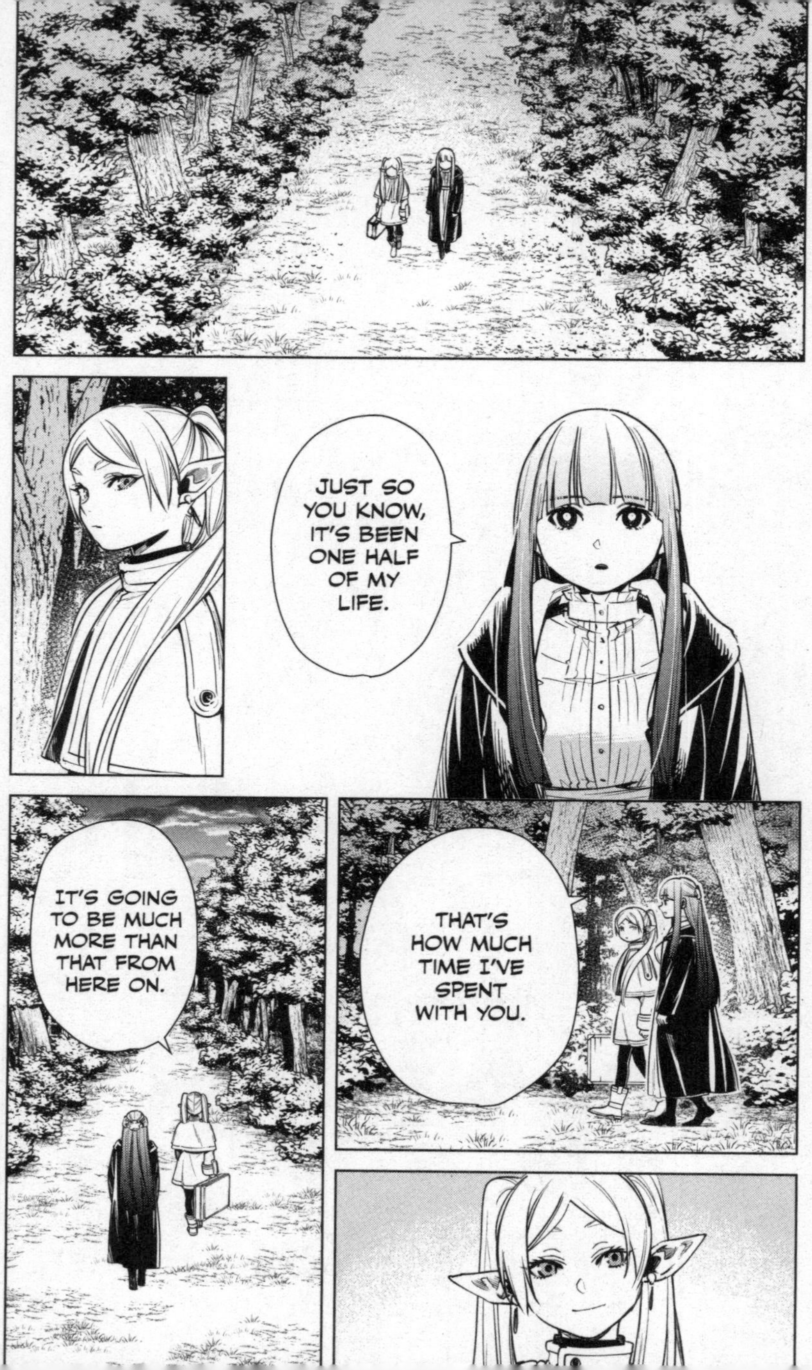
JUST SO YOU KNOW, IT'S BEEN ONE HALF OF MY LIFE.
THAT'S HOW MUCH TIME I'VE SPENT WITH YOU.
IT'S GOING TO BE MUCH MORE THAN THAT FROM HERE ON.

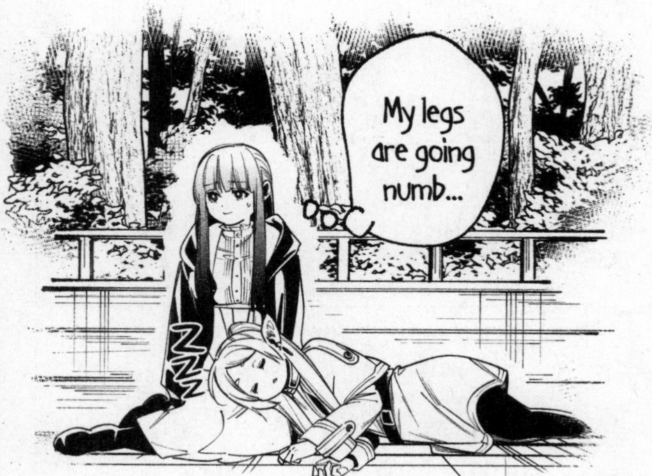
My legs are going numb...
ZZZ

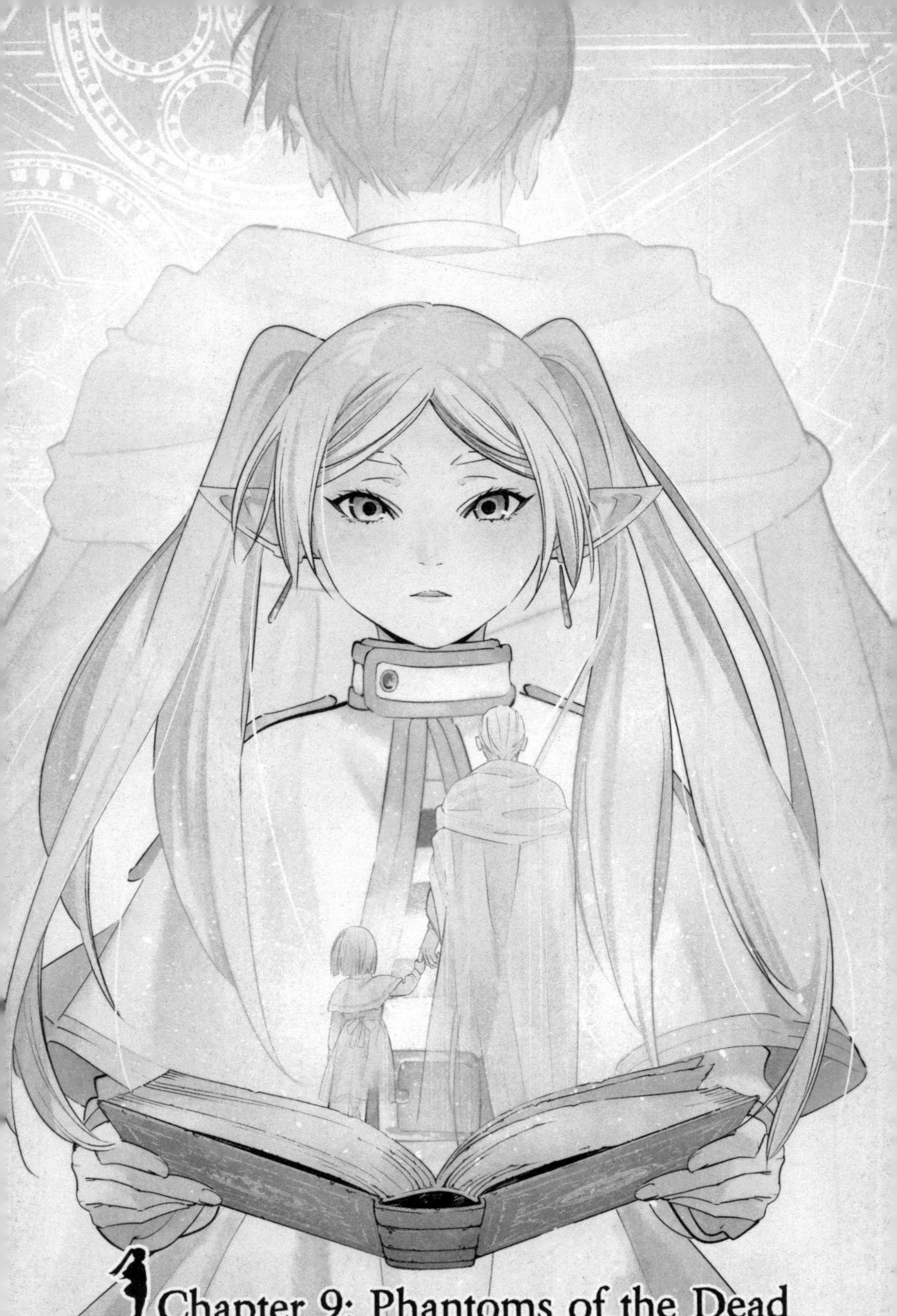

Chapter 9: Phantoms of the Dead

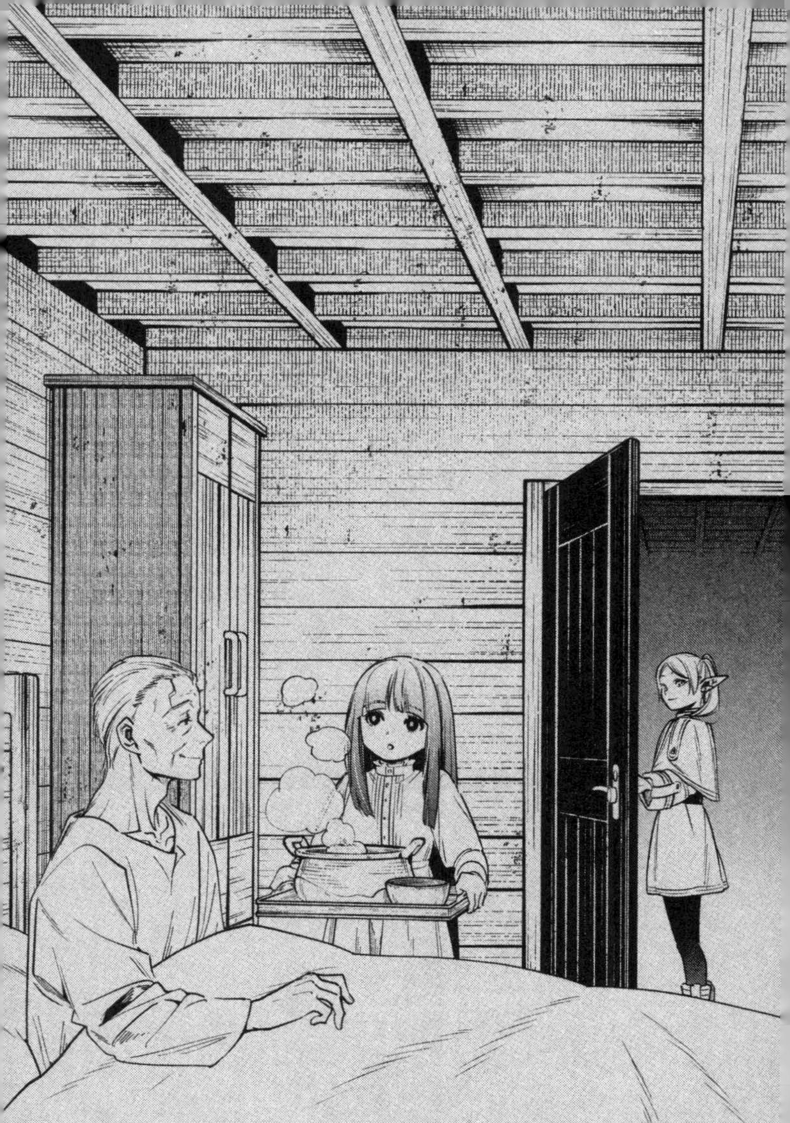

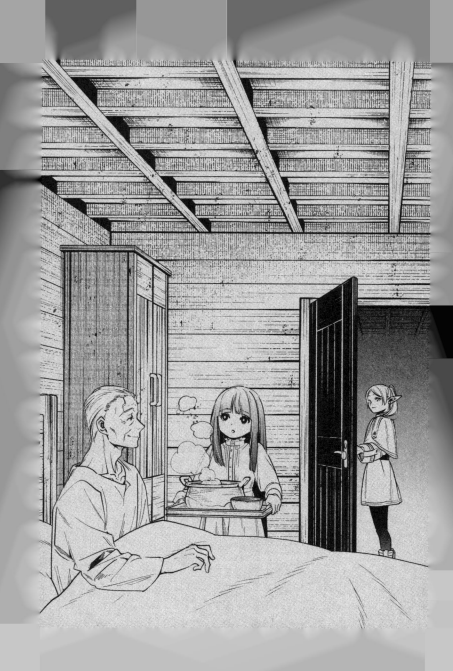

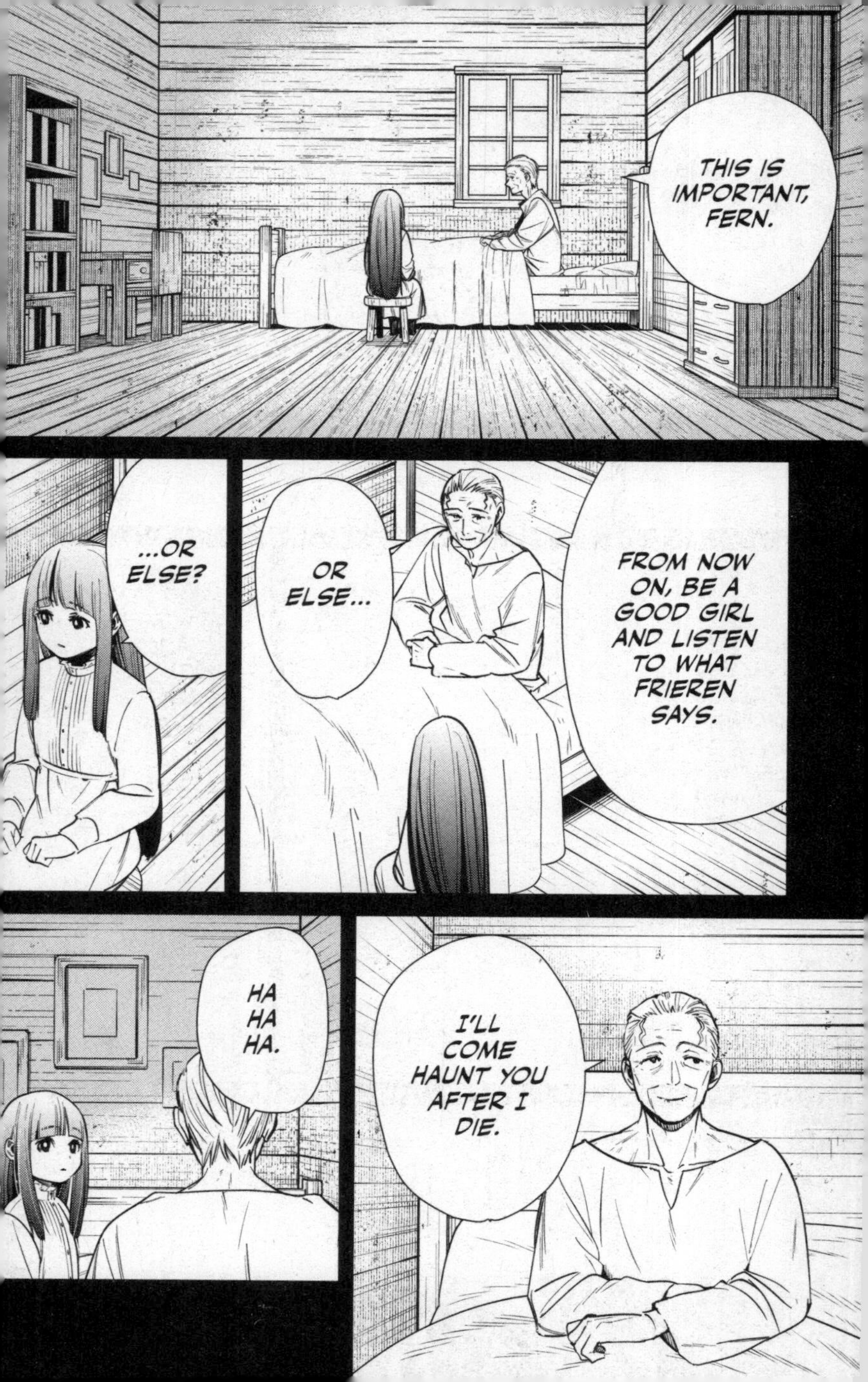
THIS IS IMPORTANT, FERN.
FROM NOW ON, BE A GOOD GIRL AND LISTEN TO WHAT FRIEREN SAYS.
OR ELSE...
...OR ELSE?
I'LL COME HAUNT YOU AFTER I DIE.
HA HA HA.

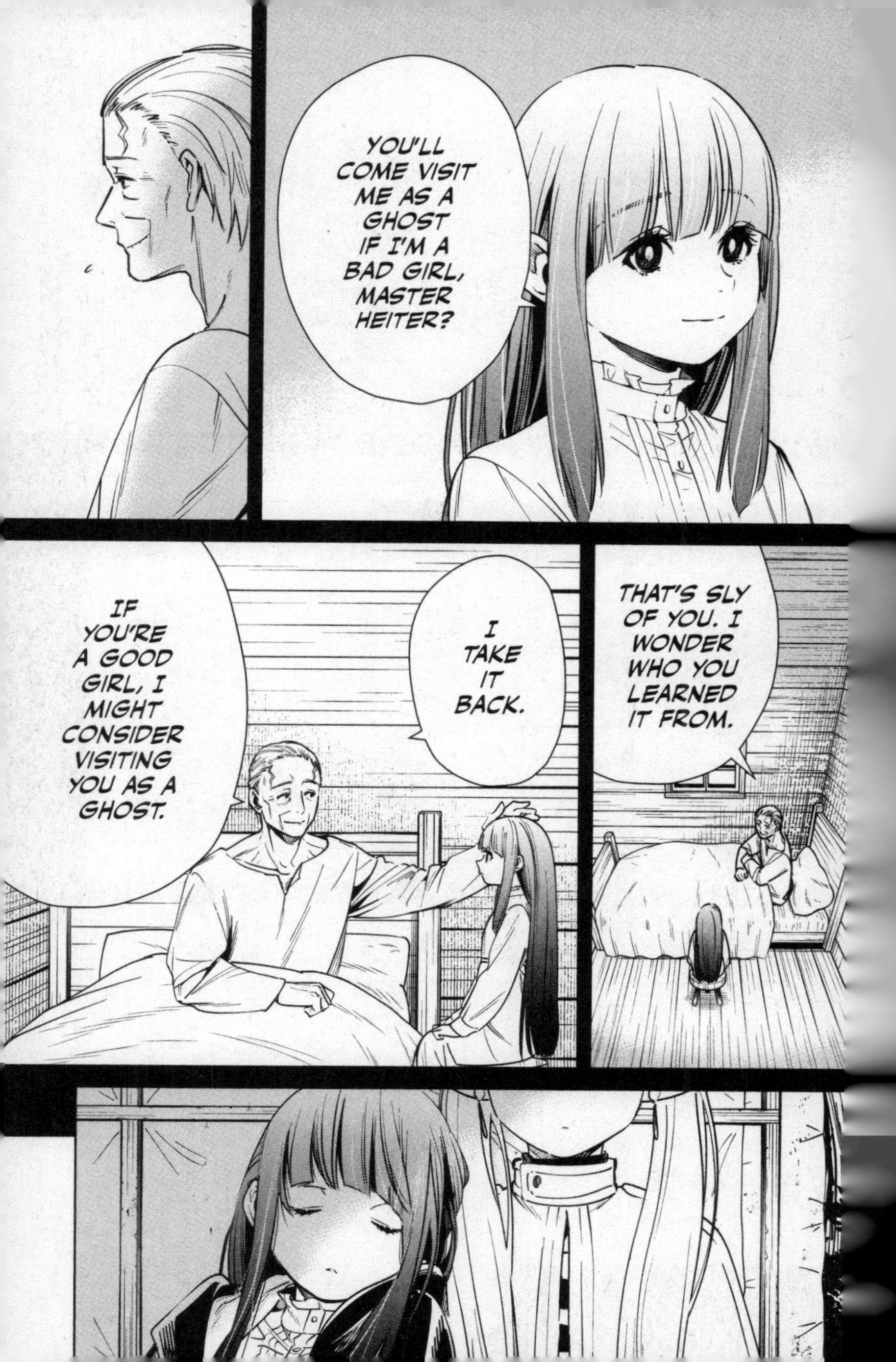
YOU'LL COME VISIT ME AS A GHOST IF I'M A BAD GIRL, MASTER HEITER?
THAT'S SLY OF YOU. I WONDER WHO YOU LEARNED IT FROM.
I TAKE IT BACK.
IF YOU'RE A GOOD GIRL, I MIGHT CONSIDER VISITING YOU AS A GHOST.

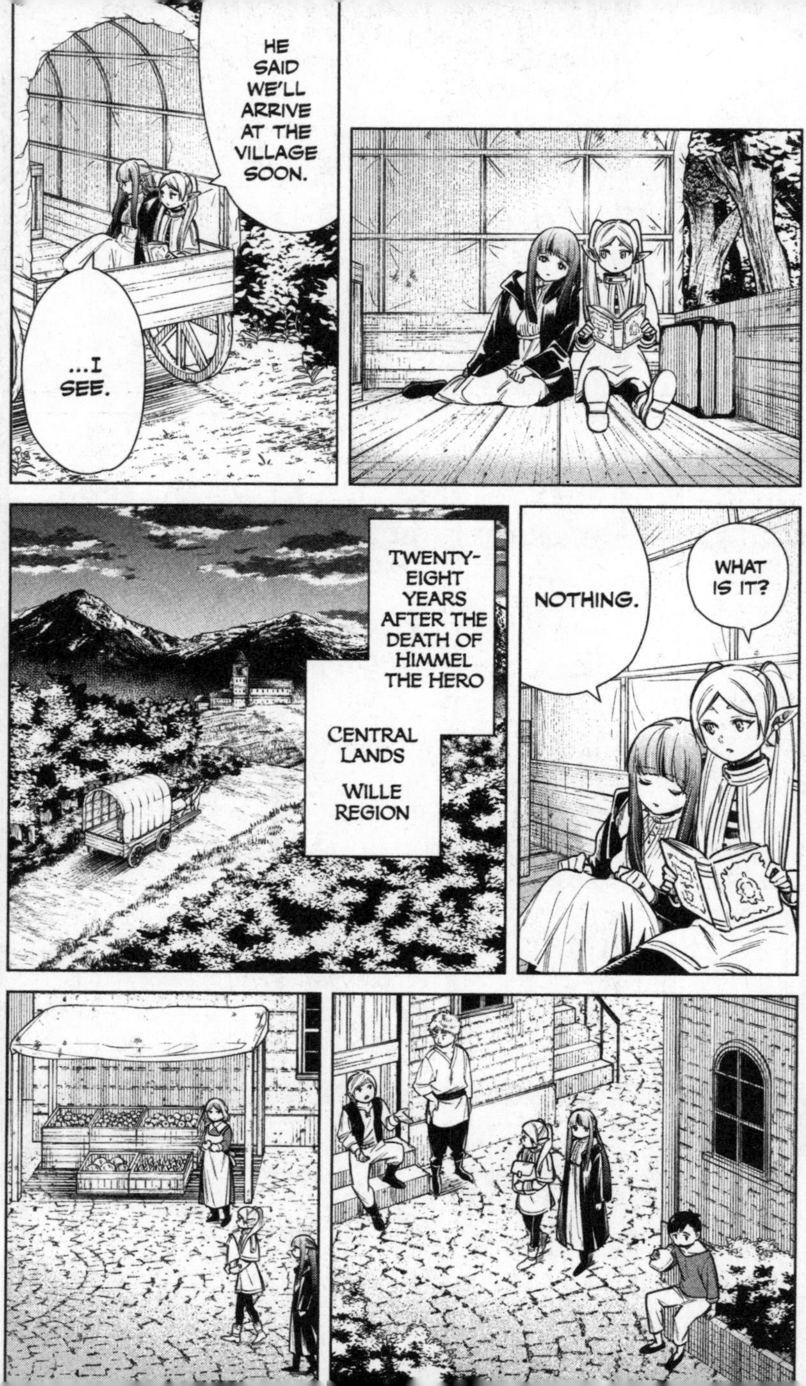
HE SAID WE'LL ARRIVE AT THE VILLAGE SOON.
...I SEE.
WHAT IS IT?
NOTHING.
TWENTY-EIGHT YEARS AFTER THE DEATH OF HIMMEL THE HERO
CENTRAL LANDS
WILLE REGION

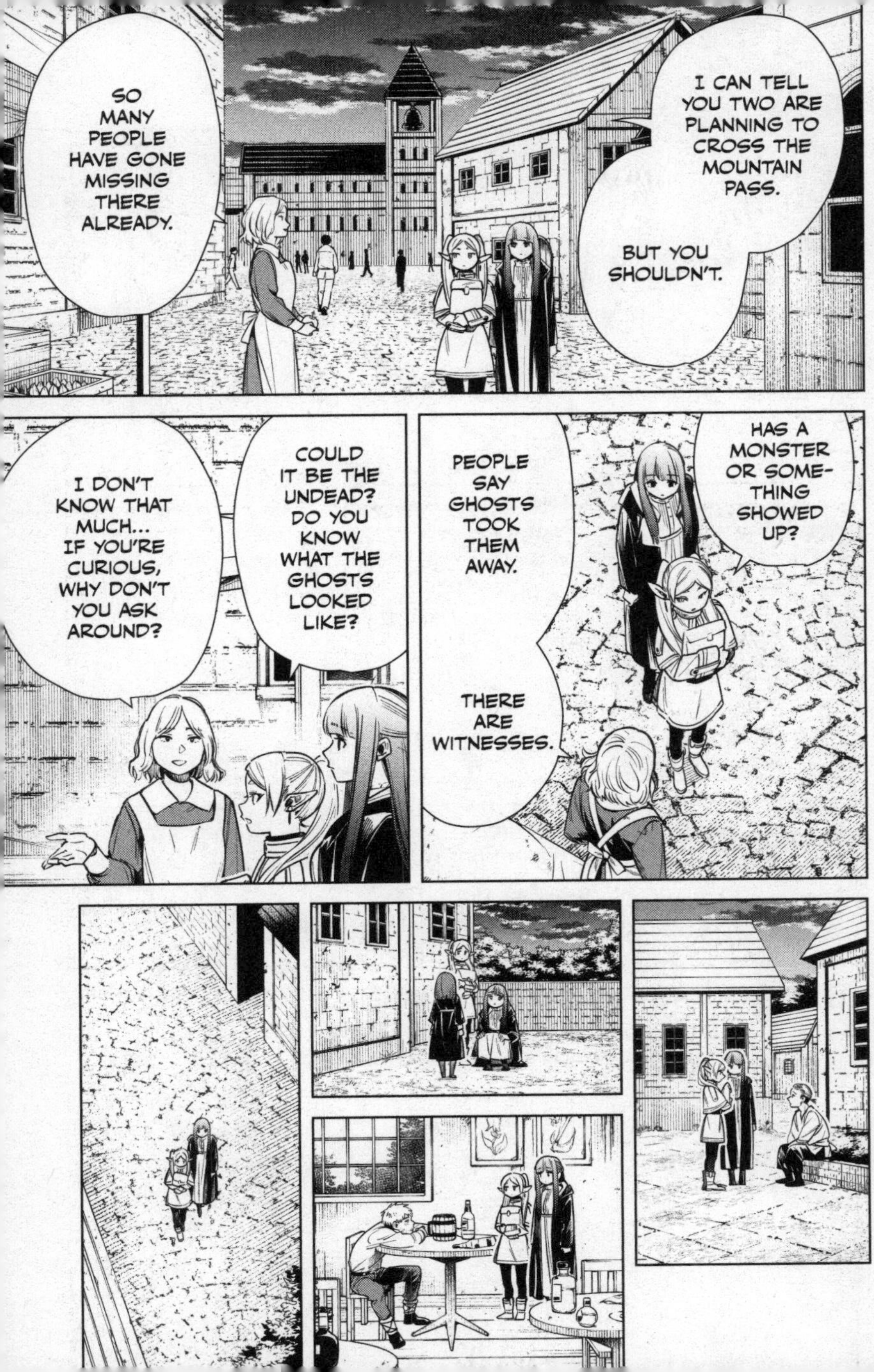
I CAN TELL YOU TWO ARE PLANNING TO CROSS THE MOUNTAIN PASS.
BUT YOU SHOULDN'T.
SO MANY PEOPLE HAVE GONE MISSING THERE ALREADY.
HAS A MONSTER OR SOME-THING SHOWED UP?
PEOPLE SAY GHOSTS TOOK THEM AWAY.
THERE ARE WITNESSES.
COULD IT BE THE UNDEAD? DO YOU KNOW WHAT THE GHOSTS LOOKED LIKE?
I DON'T KNOW THAT MUCH... IF YOU'RE CURIOUS, WHY DON'T YOU ASK AROUND?

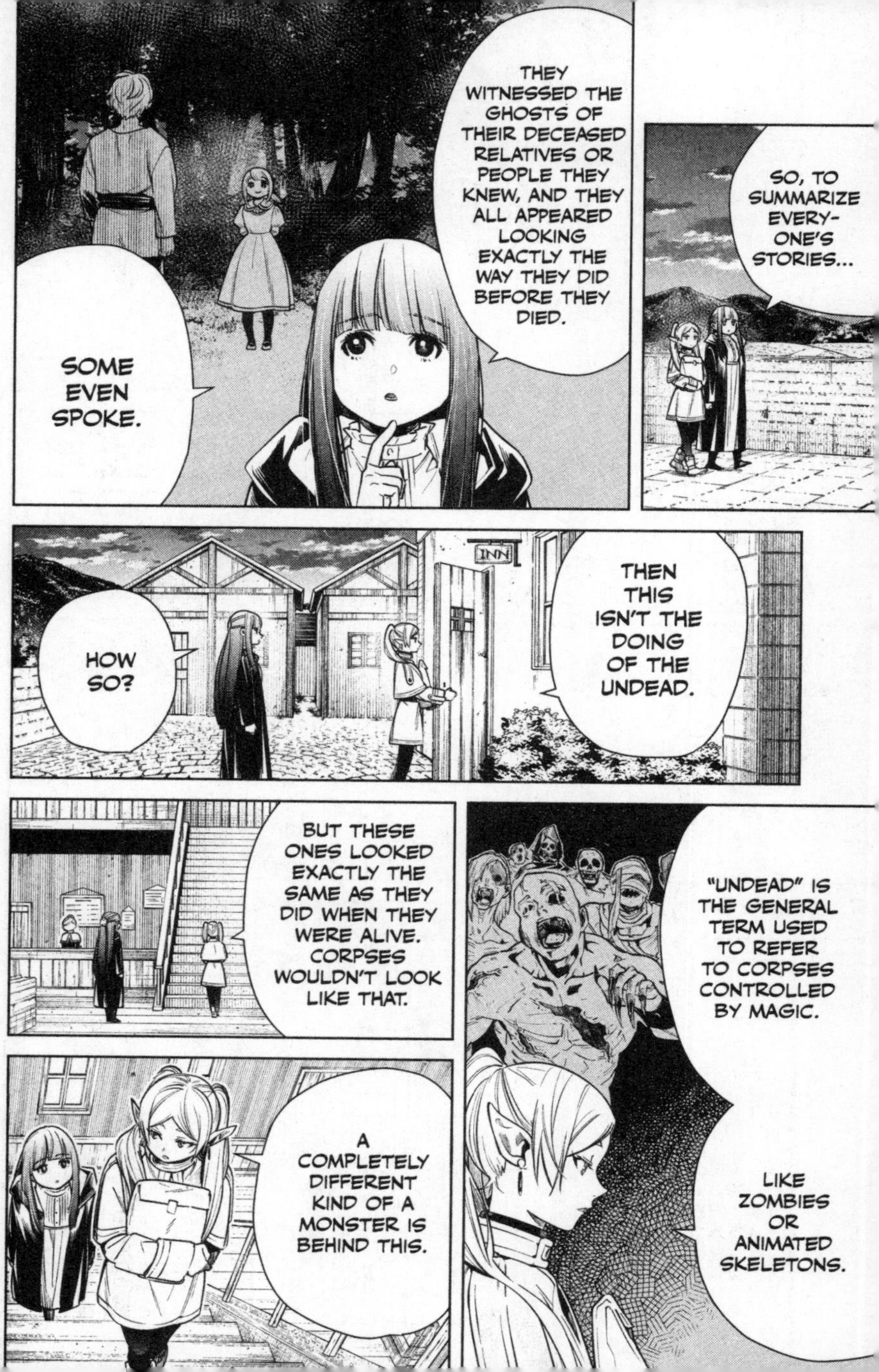
SO, TO SUMMARIZE EVERY-ONE'S STORIES...
THEY WITNESSED THE GHOSTS OF THEIR DECEASED RELATIVES OR PEOPLE THEY KNEW, AND THEY ALL APPEARED LOOKING EXACTLY THE WAY THEY DID BEFORE THEY DIED.
SOME EVEN SPOKE.
THEN THIS ISN'T THE DOING OF THE UNDEAD.
INN
HOW SO?
"UNDEAD" IS THE GENERAL TERM USED TO REFER TO CORPSES CONTROLLED BY MAGIC.
LIKE ZOMBIES OR ANIMATED SKELETONS.
BUT THESE ONES LOOKED EXACTLY THE SAME AS THEY DID WHEN THEY WERE ALIVE. CORPSES WOULDN'T LOOK LIKE THAT.
A COMPLETELY DIFFERENT KIND OF A MONSTER IS BEHIND THIS.

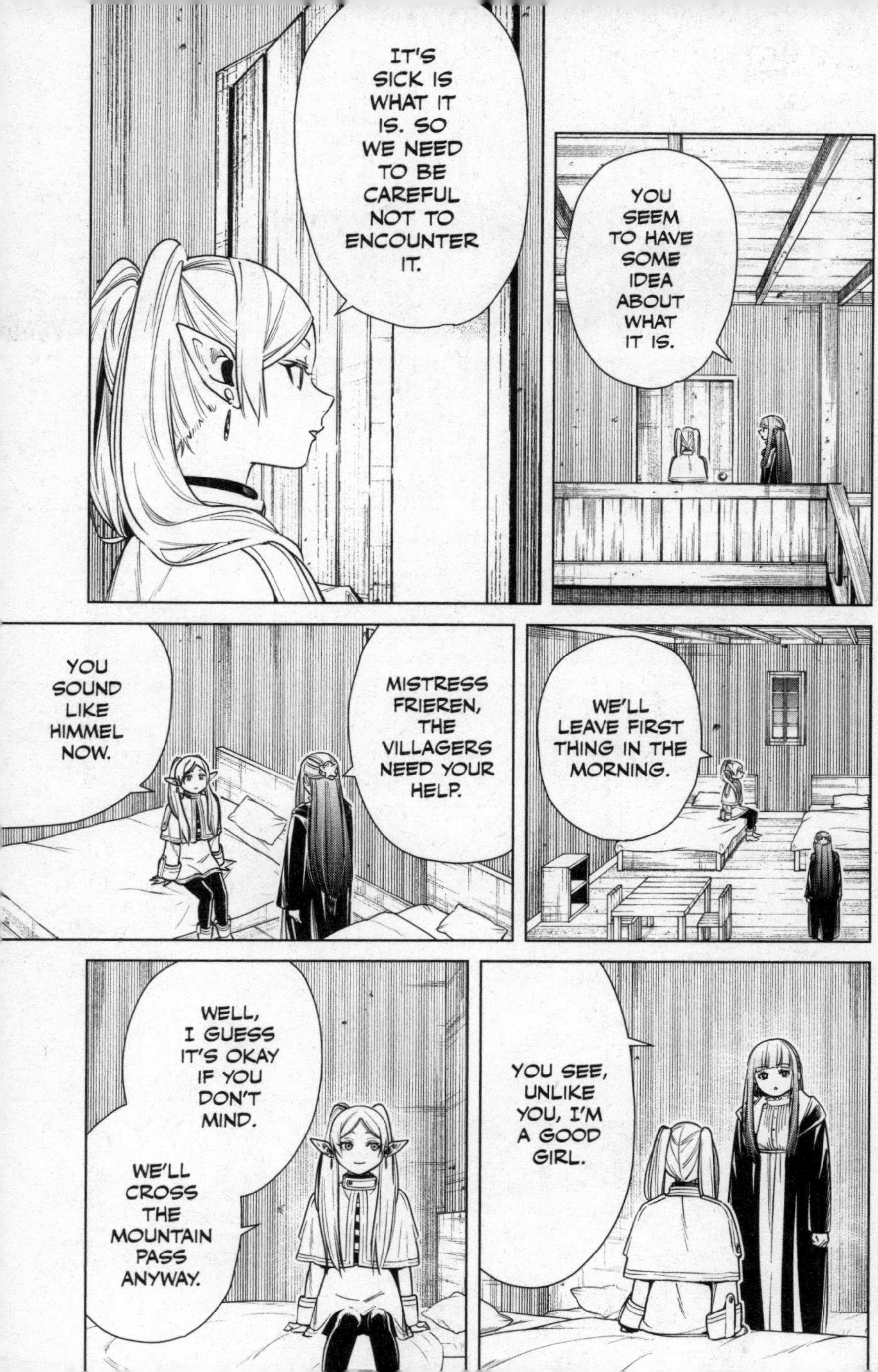
YOU SEEM TO HAVE SOME IDEA ABOUT WHAT IT IS.
IT'S SICK IS WHAT IT IS. SO WE NEED TO BE CAREFUL NOT TO ENCOUNTER IT.
WE'LL LEAVE FIRST THING IN THE MORNING.
MISTRESS FRIEREN, THE VILLAGERS NEED YOUR HELP.
YOU SOUND LIKE HIMMEL NOW.
YOU SEE, UNLIKE YOU, I'M A GOOD GIRL.
WELL, I GUESS IT'S OKAY IF YOU DON'T MIND.
WE'LL CROSS THE MOUNTAIN PASS ANYWAY.

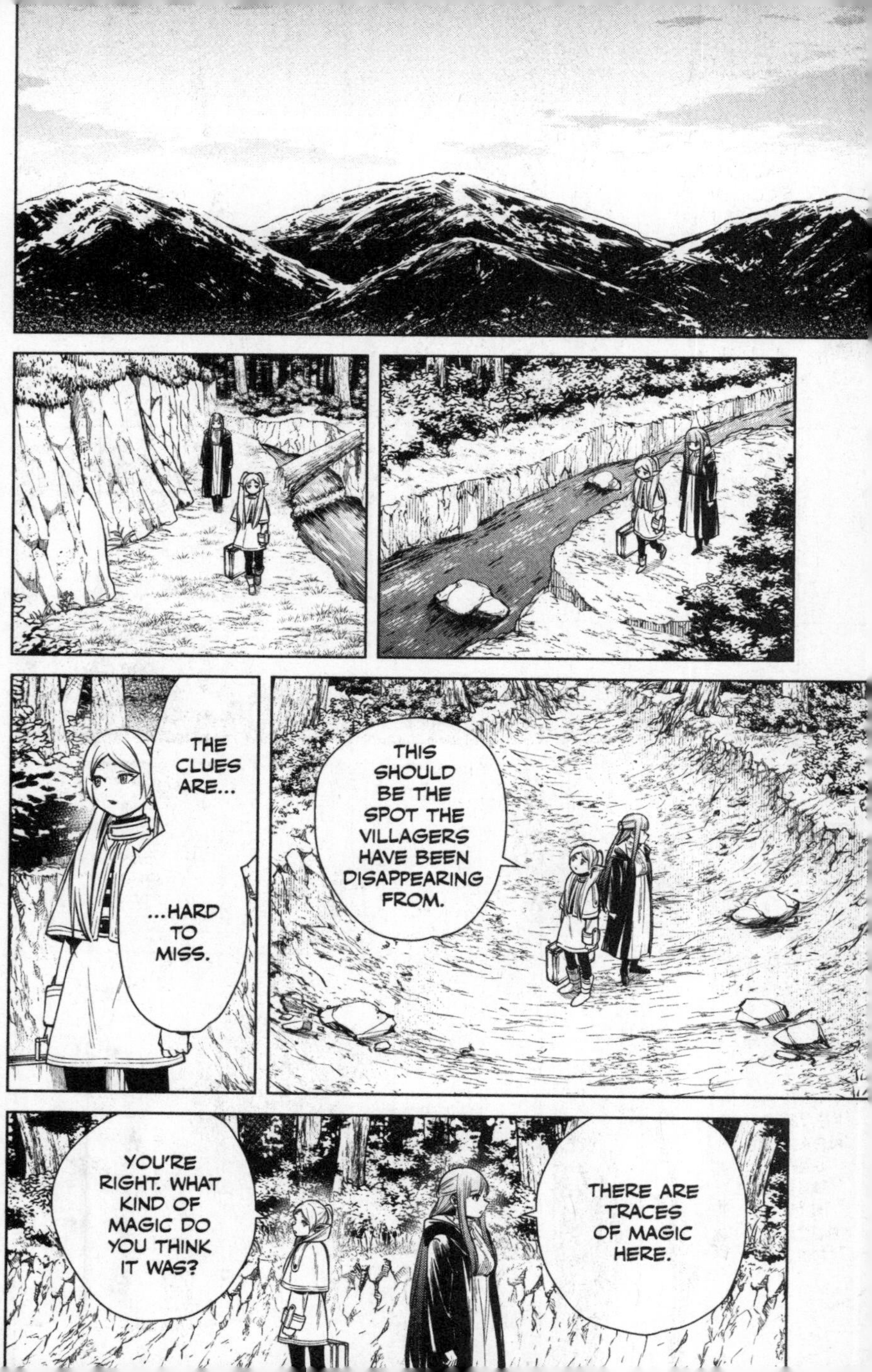
THIS SHOULD BE THE SPOT THE VILLAGERS HAVE BEEN DISAPPEARING FROM.
THE CLUES ARE...
...HARD TO MISS.
THERE ARE TRACES OF MAGIC HERE.
YOU'RE RIGHT. WHAT KIND OF MAGIC DO YOU THINK IT WAS?

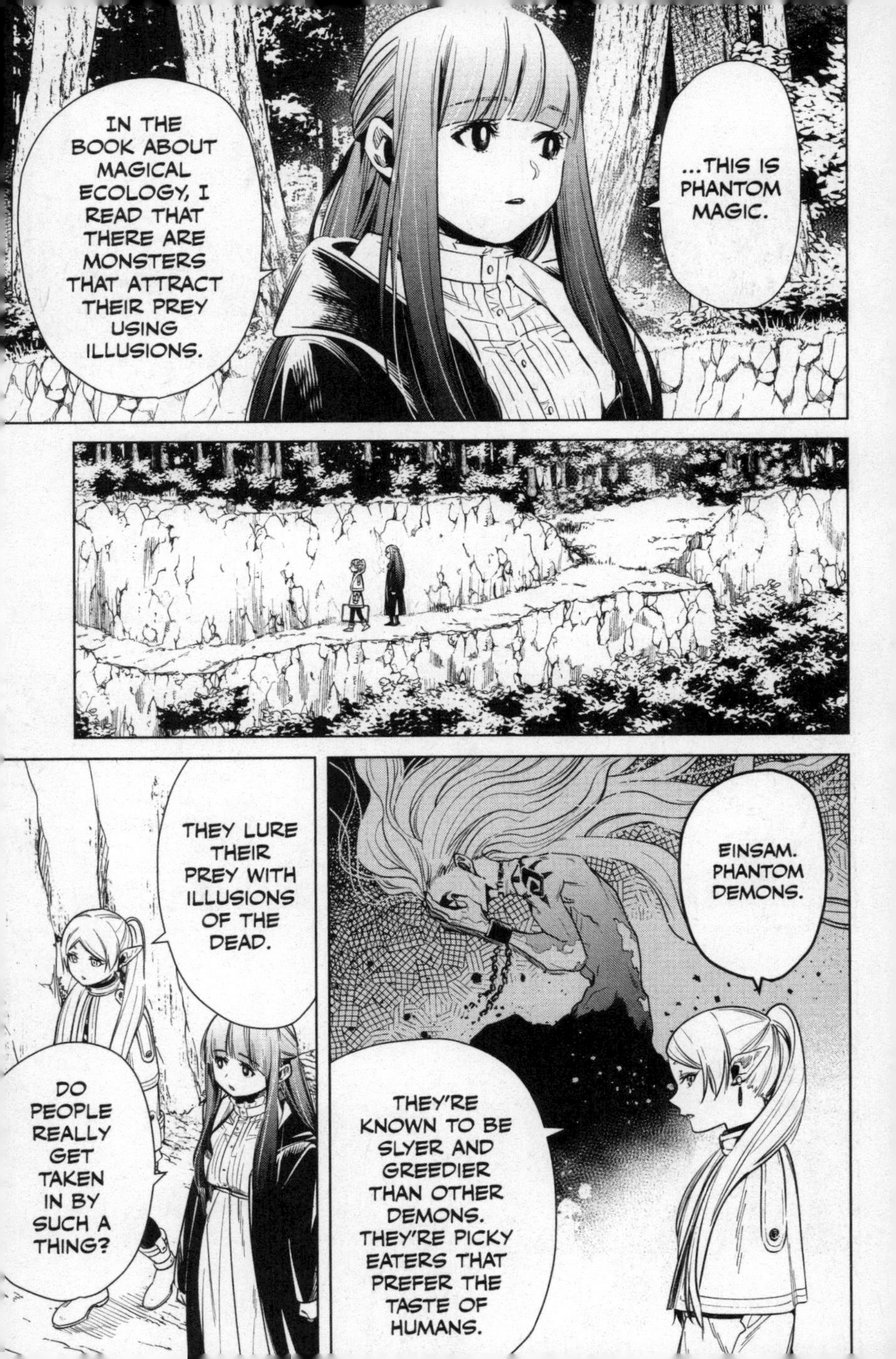
...THIS IS PHANTOM MAGIC.
IN THE BOOK ABOUT MAGICAL ECOLOGY, I READ THAT THERE ARE MONSTERS THAT ATTRACT THEIR PREY USING ILLUSIONS.
EINSAM. PHANTOM DEMONS.
THEY'RE KNOWN TO BE SLYER AND GREEDIER THAN OTHER DEMONS. THEY'RE PICKY EATERS THAT PREFER THE TASTE OF HUMANS.
THEY LURE THEIR PREY WITH ILLUSIONS OF THE DEAD.
DO PEOPLE REALLY GET TAKEN IN BY SUCH A THING?

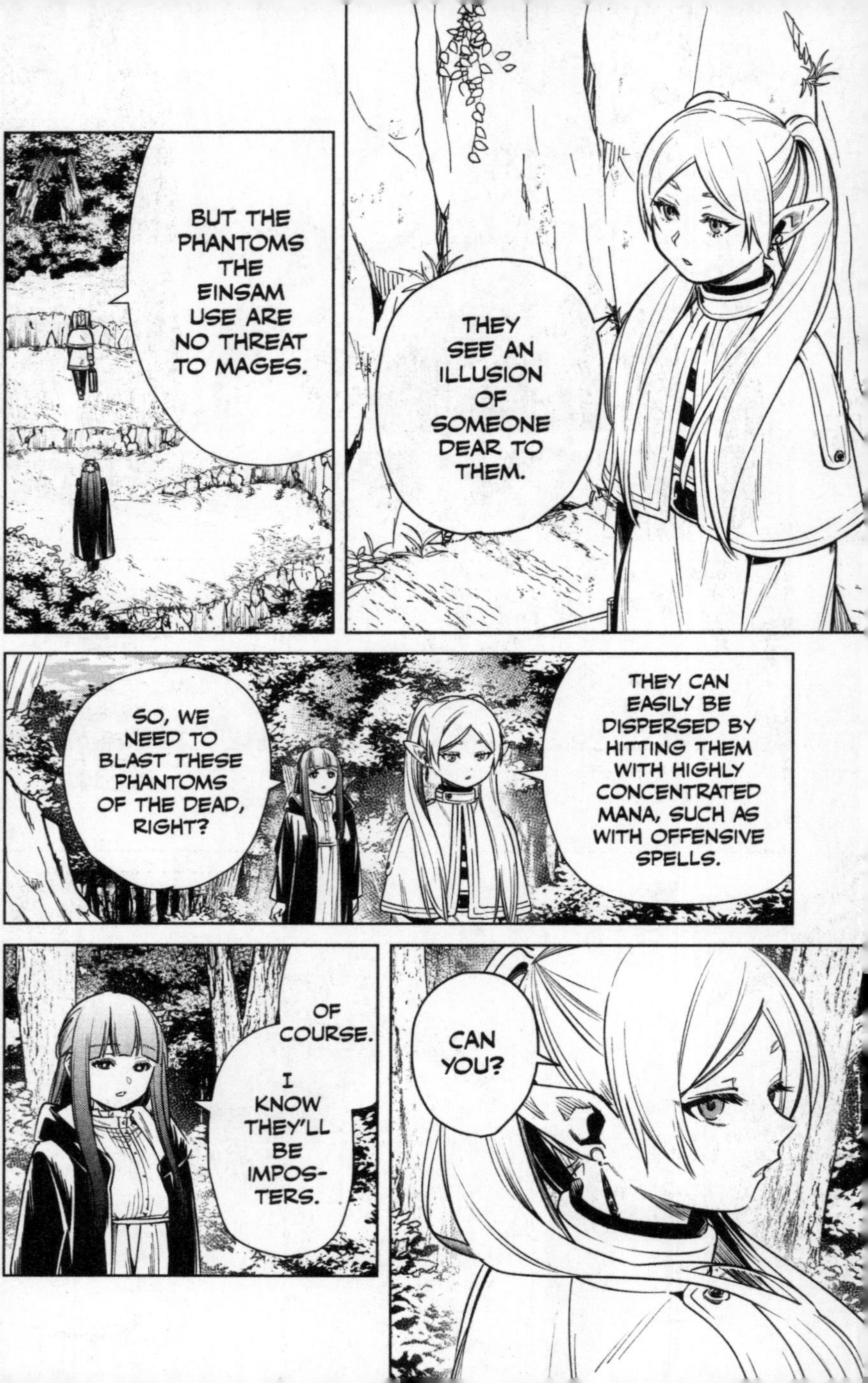
THEY SEE AN ILLUSION OF SOMEONE DEAR TO THEM.
BUT THE PHANTOMS THE EINSAM USE ARE NO THREAT TO MAGES.
THEY CAN EASILY BE DISPERSED BY HITTING THEM WITH HIGHLY CONCENTRATED MANA, SUCH AS WITH OFFENSIVE SPELLS.
SO, WE NEED TO BLAST THESE PHANTOMS OF THE DEAD, RIGHT?
CAN YOU?
OF COURSE.
I KNOW THEY'LL BE IMPOSTERS.

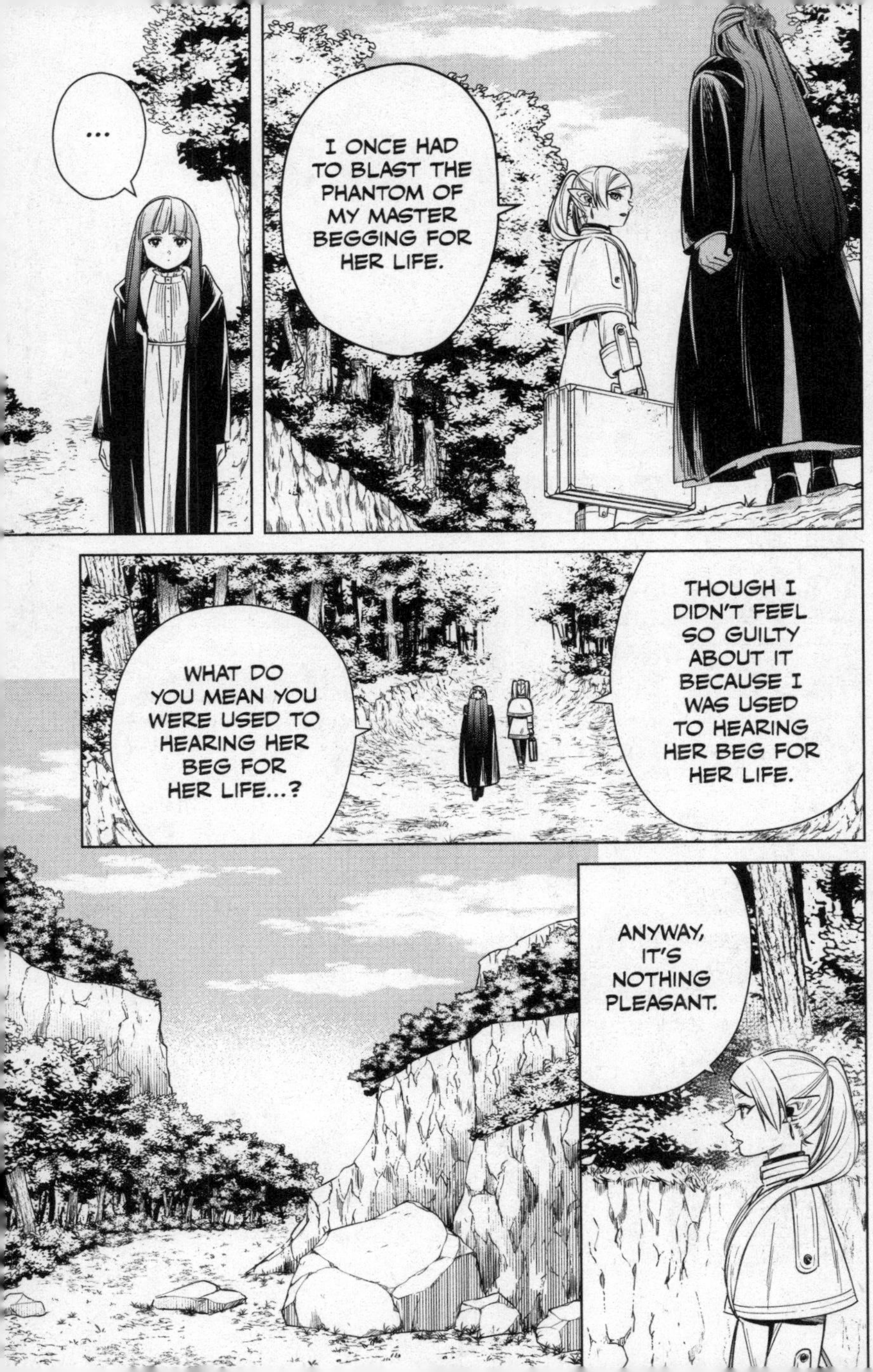
I ONCE HAD TO BLAST THE PHANTOM OF MY MASTER BEGGING FOR HER LIFE.
...
THOUGH I DIDN'T FEEL SO GUILTY ABOUT IT BECAUSE I WAS USED TO HEARING HER BEG FOR HER LIFE.
WHAT DO YOU MEAN YOU WERE USED TO HEARING HER BEG FOR HER LIFE...?
ANYWAY, IT'S NOTHING PLEASANT.

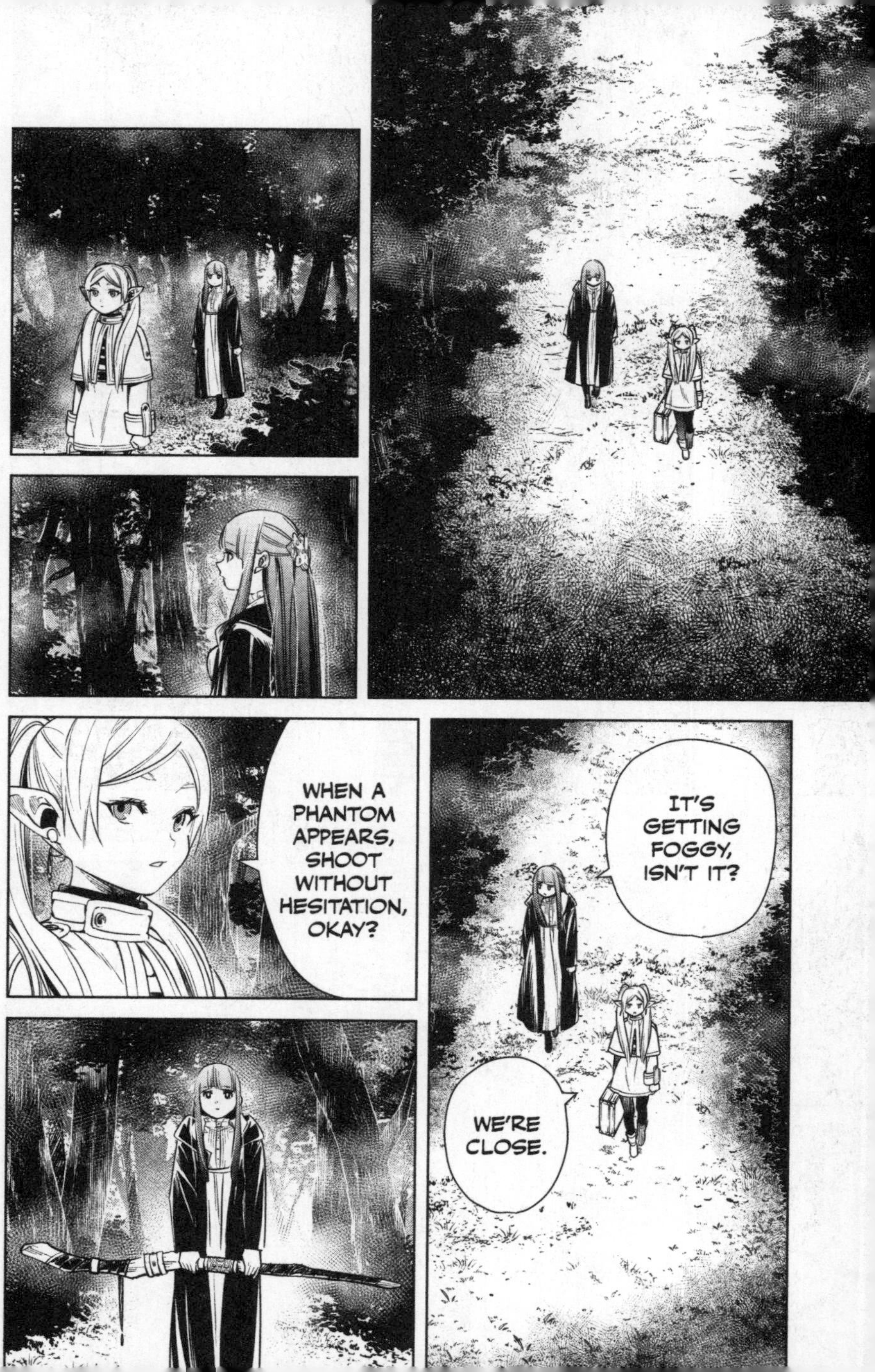
IT'S GETTING FOGGY, ISN'T IT?
WE'RE CLOSE.
WHEN A PHANTOM APPEARS, SHOOT WITHOUT HESITATION, OKAY?

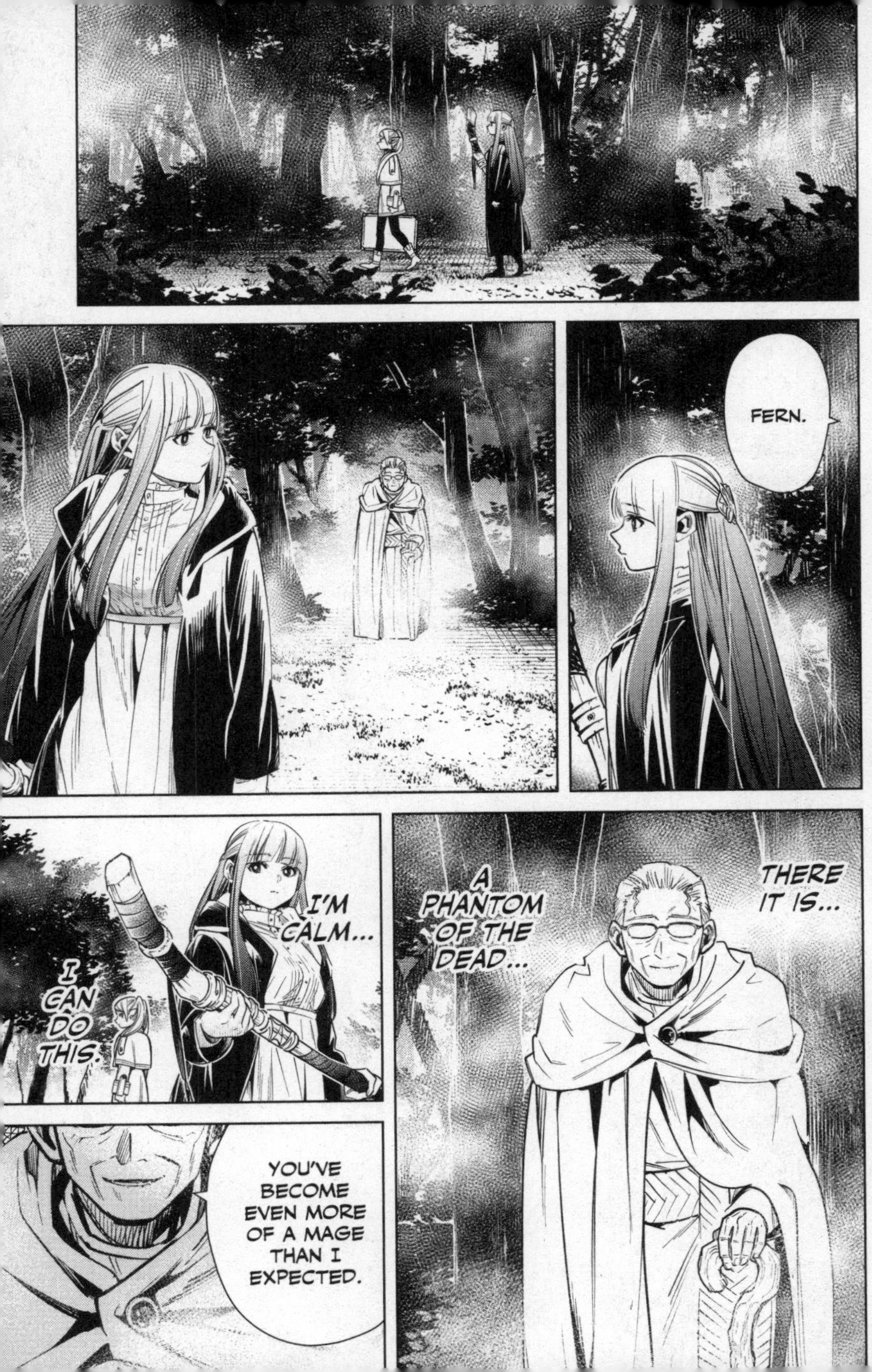
FERN.
THERE IT IS...
A PHANTOM OF THE DEAD...
I'M CALM...
I CAN DO THIS.
YOU'VE BECOME EVEN MORE OF A MAGE THAN I EXPECTED.

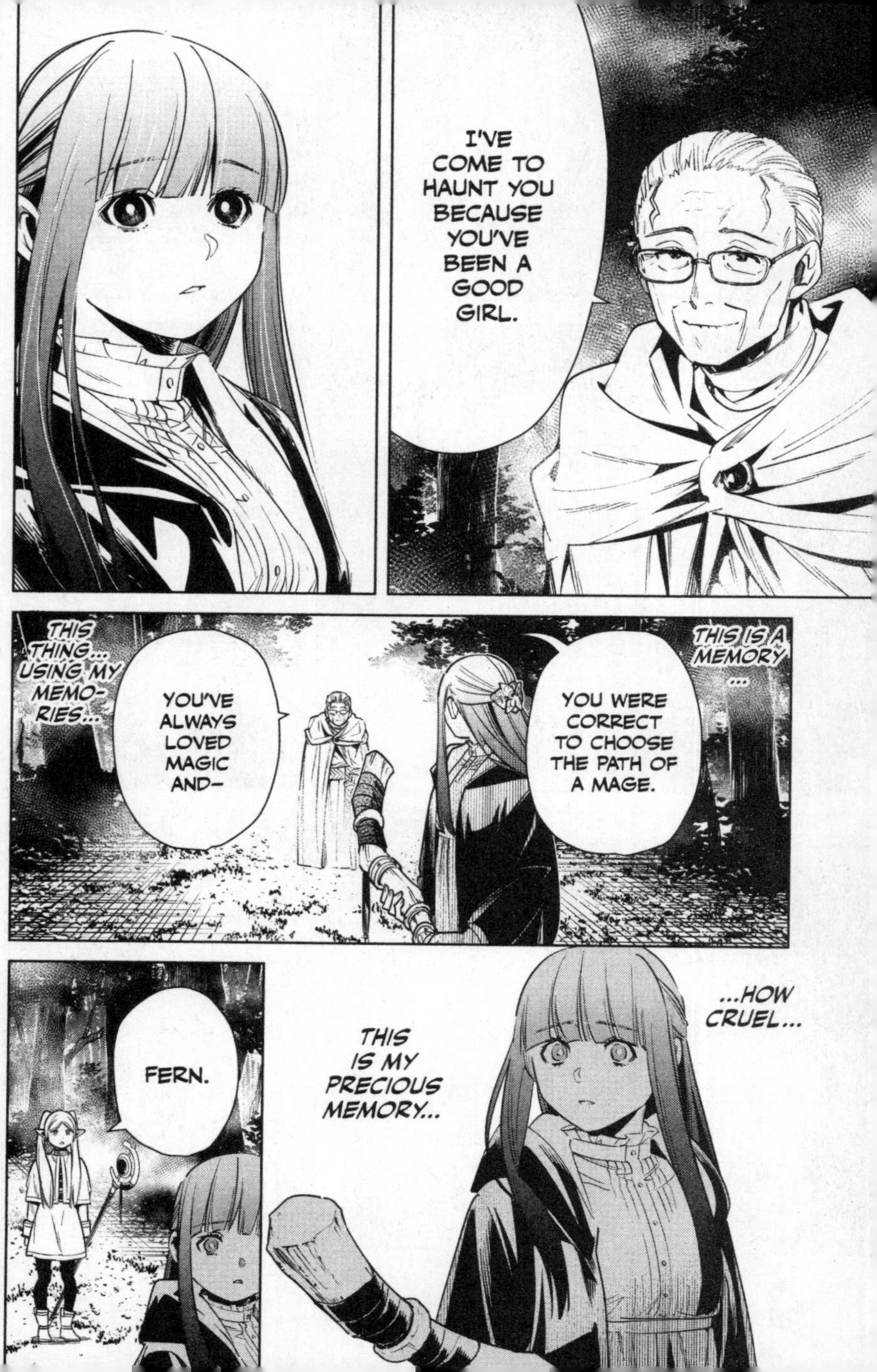
I'VE COME TO HAUNT YOU BECAUSE YOU'VE BEEN A GOOD GIRL.
THIS IS A MEMORY...
YOU WERE CORRECT TO CHOOSE THE PATH OF A MAGE.
YOU'VE ALWAYS LOVED MAGIC AND–
THIS THING... USING MY MEMORIES...
...HOW CRUEL...
THIS IS MY PRECIOUS MEMORY...
FERN.

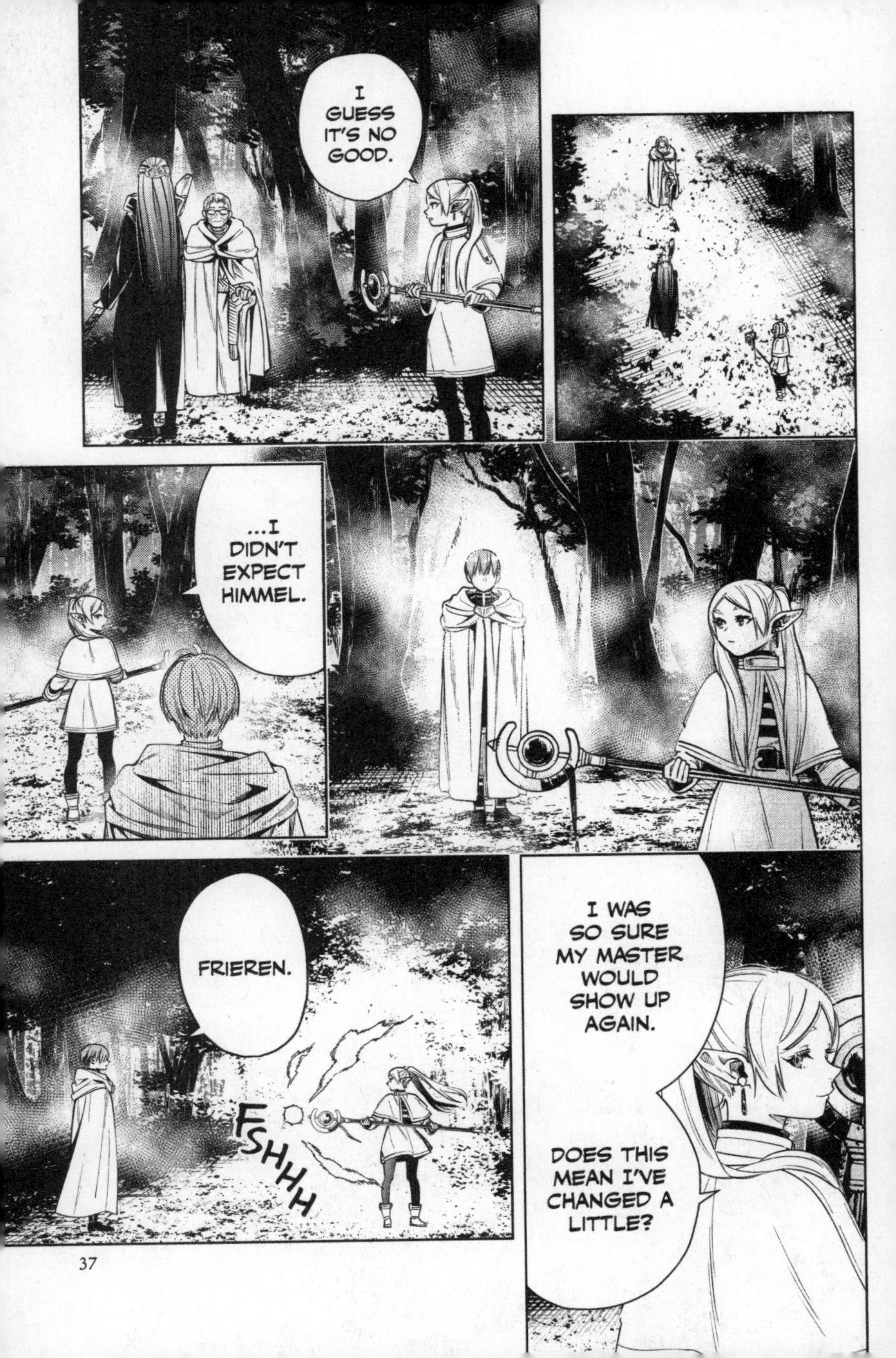
I GUESS IT'S NO GOOD.
...I DIDN'T EXPECT HIMMEL.
I WAS SO SURE MY MASTER WOULD SHOW UP AGAIN.
DOES THIS MEAN I'VE CHANGED A LITTLE?
FRIEREN.
FSHHH

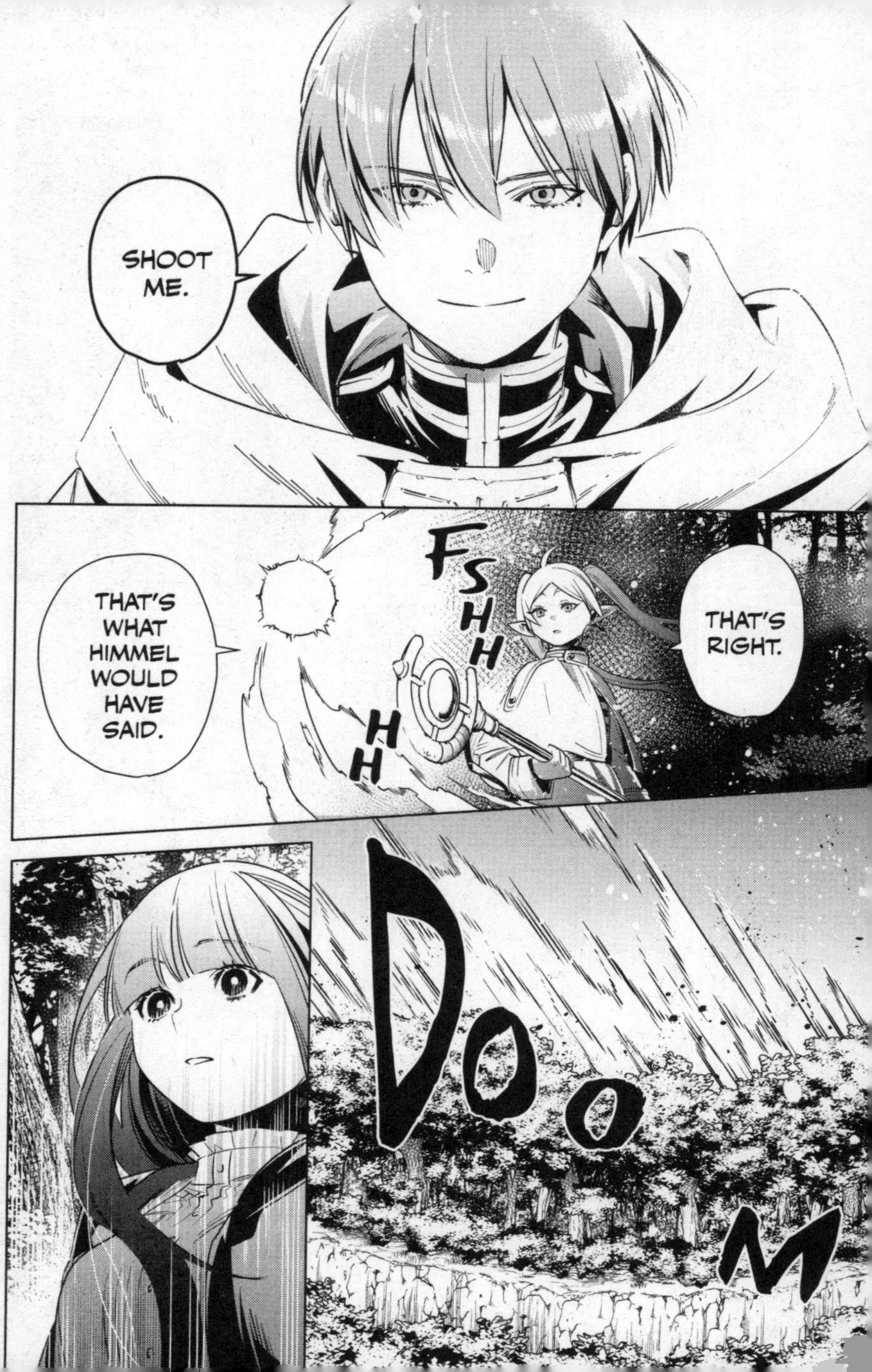
SHOOT ME.
THAT'S RIGHT.
FSHHHH
THAT'S WHAT HIMMEL WOULD HAVE SAID.
DOOOM

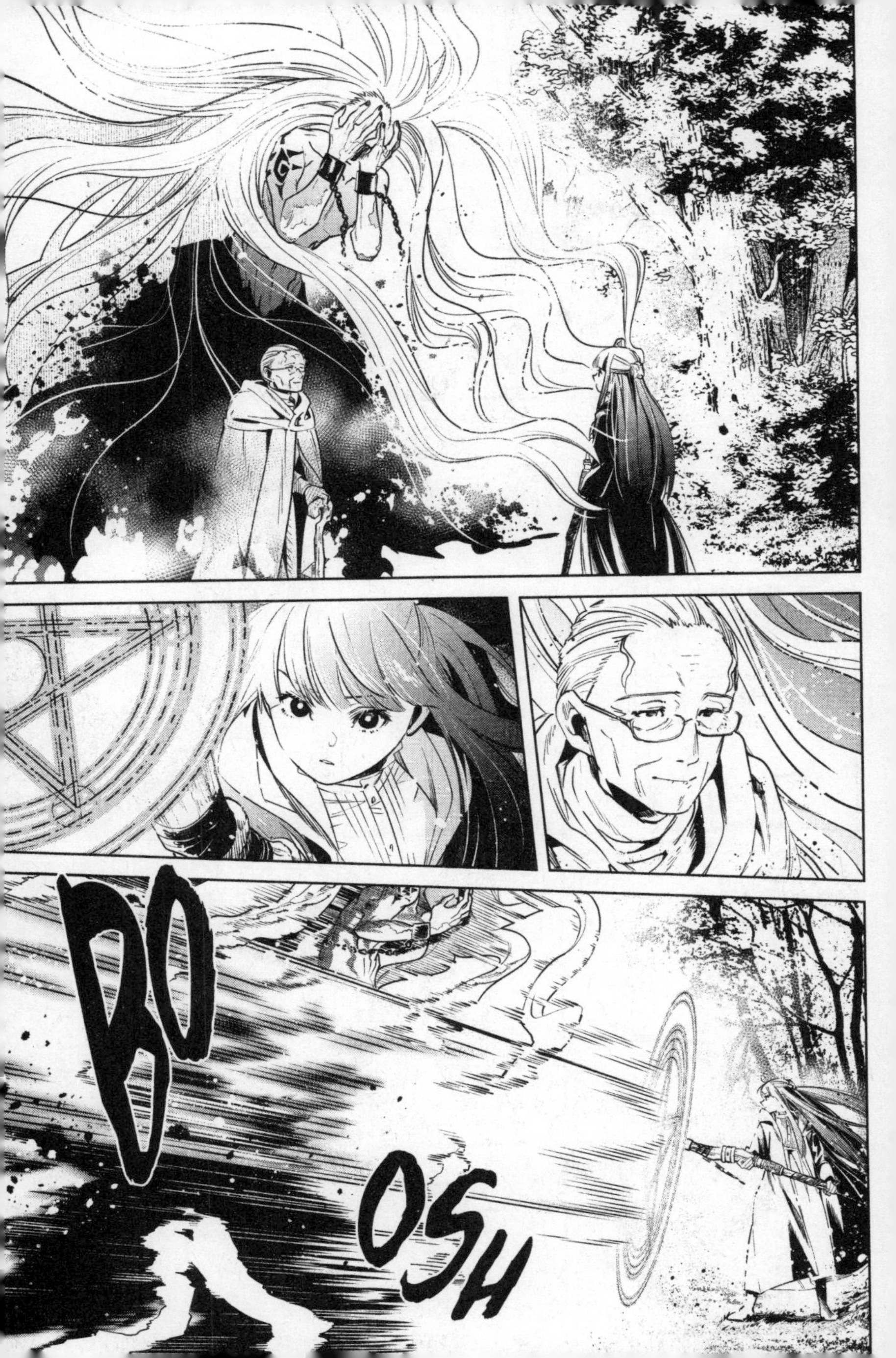
BOOSH

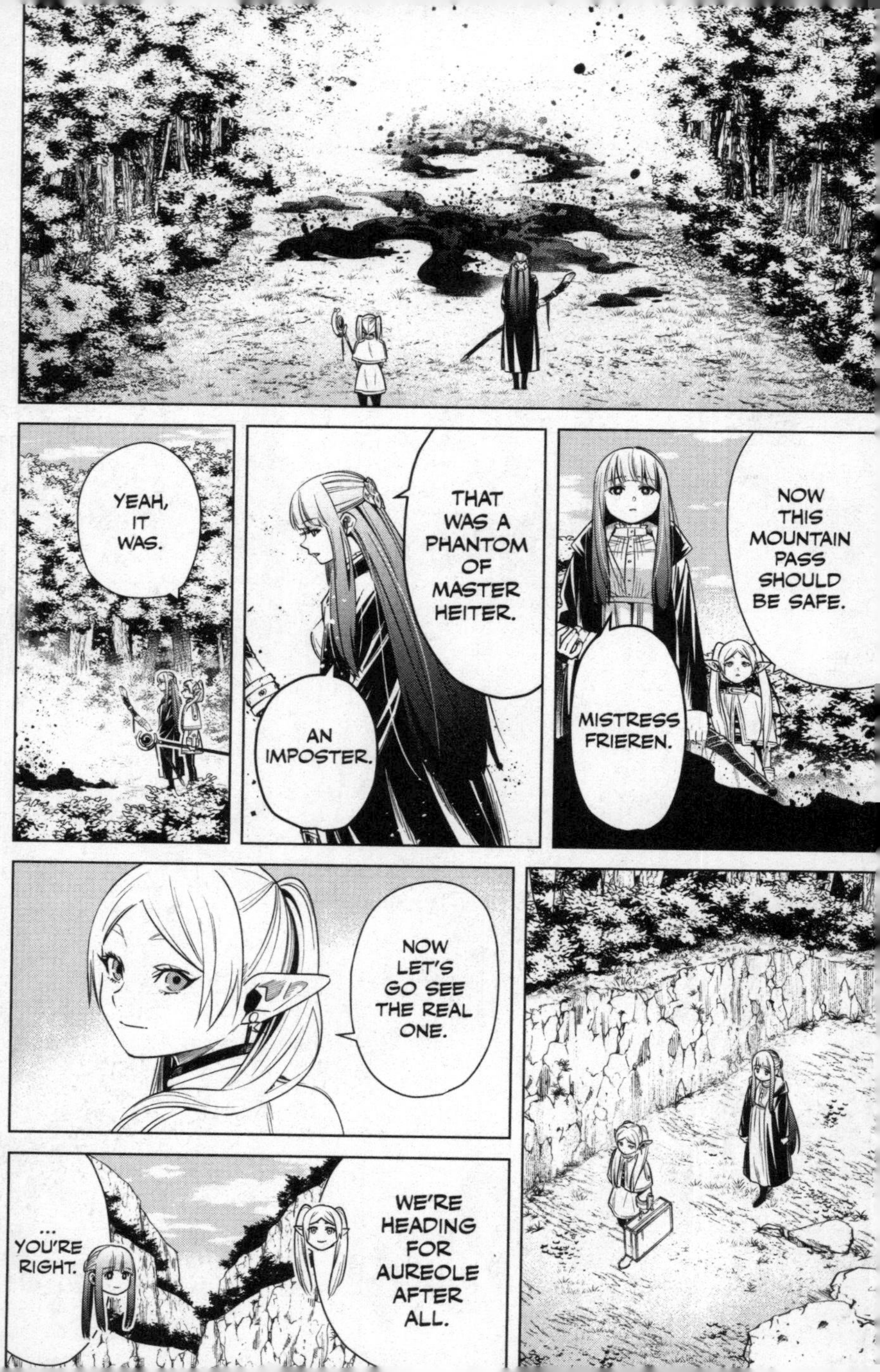
NOW THIS MOUNTAIN PASS SHOULD BE SAFE.
MISTRESS FRIEREN.
THAT WAS A PHANTOM OF MASTER HEITER.
AN IMPOSTER.
YEAH, IT WAS.
NOW LET'S GO SEE THE REAL ONE.
WE'RE HEADING FOR AUREOLE AFTER ALL.
... YOU'RE RIGHT.

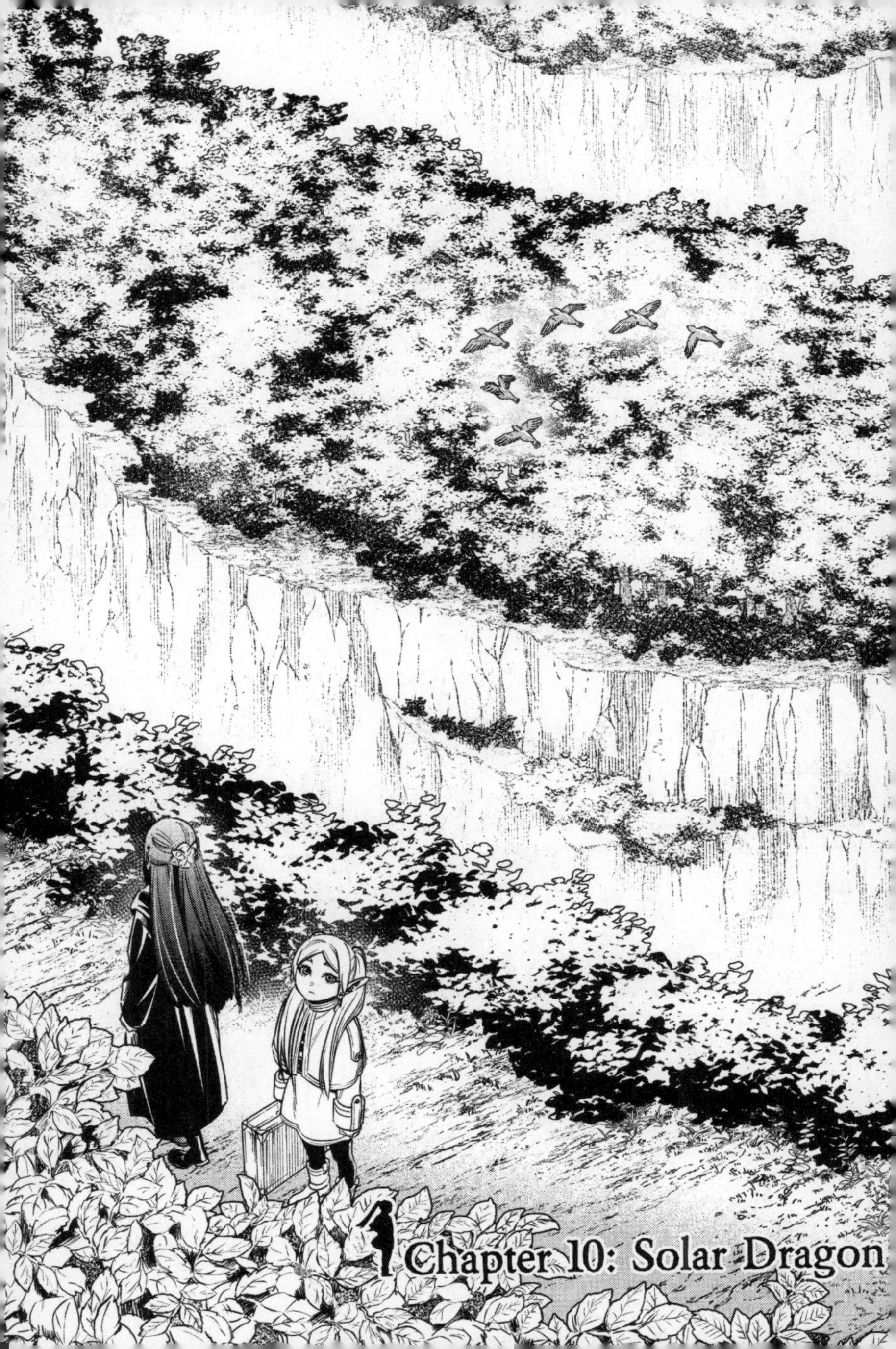
Chapter 10: Solar Dragon

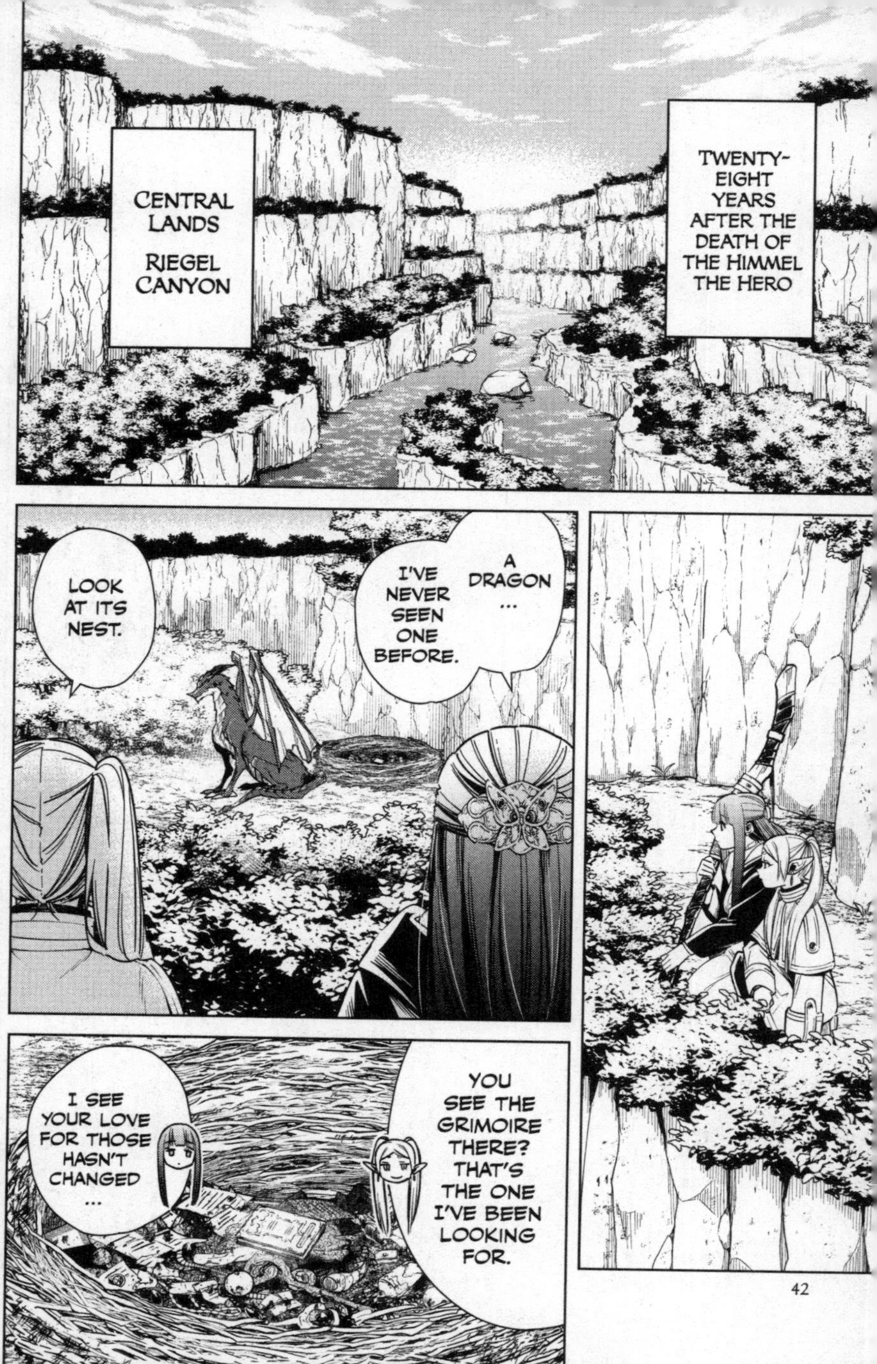
TWENTY-EIGHT YEARS AFTER THE DEATH OF THE HIMMEL THE HERO
CENTRAL LANDS
RIEGEL CANYON
A DRAGON ... I'VE NEVER SEEN ONE BEFORE.
LOOK AT ITS NEST.
YOU SEE THE GRIMOIRE THERE? THAT'S THE ONE I'VE BEEN LOOKING FOR.
I SEE YOUR LOVE FOR THOSE HASN'T CHANGED ...

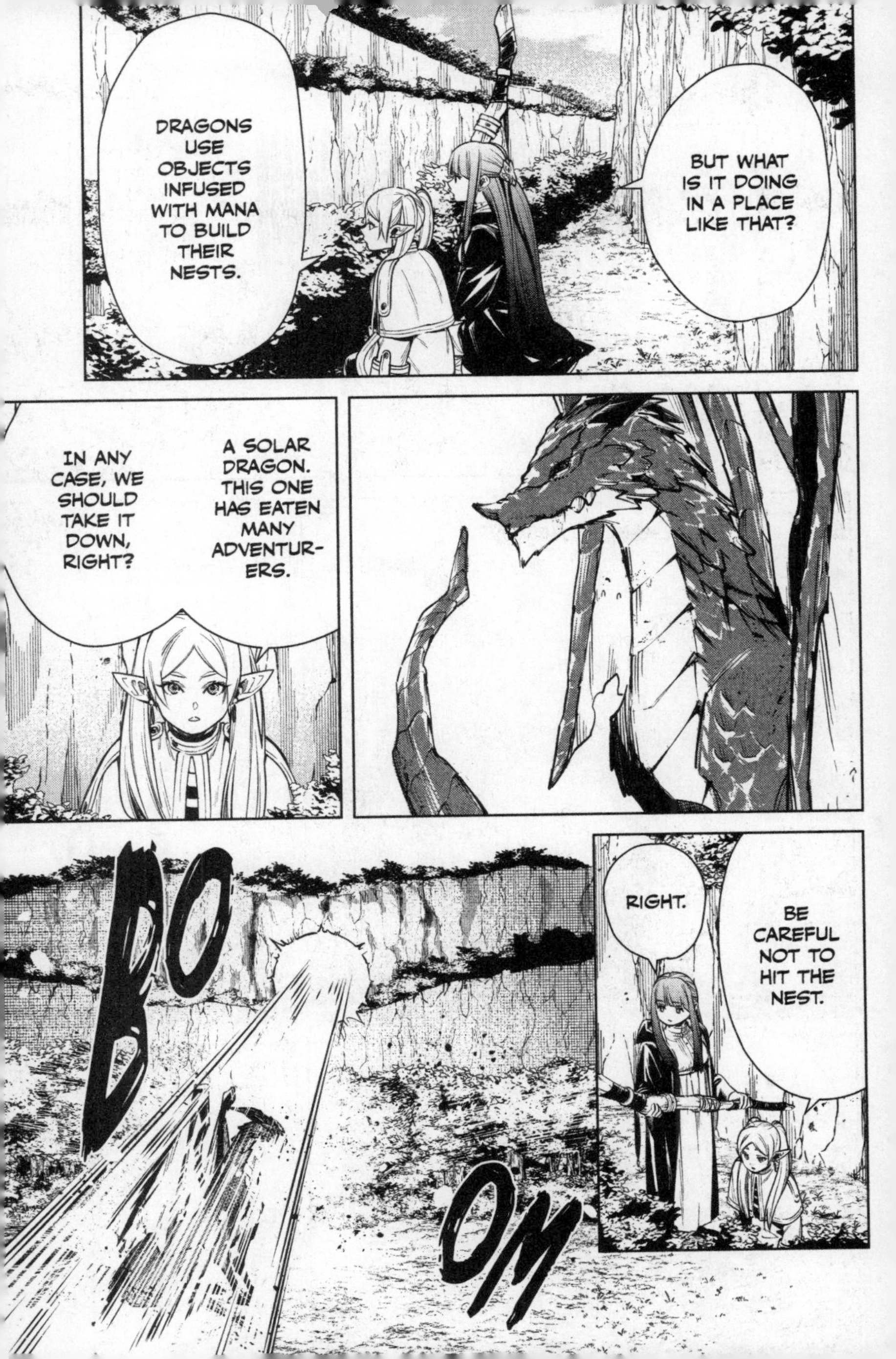
BUT WHAT IS IT DOING IN A PLACE LIKE THAT?
DRAGONS USE OBJECTS INFUSED WITH MANA TO BUILD THEIR NESTS.
A SOLAR DRAGON. THIS ONE HAS EATEN MANY ADVENTURERS.
IN ANY CASE, WE SHOULD TAKE IT DOWN, RIGHT?
BE CAREFUL NOT TO HIT THE NEST.
RIGHT.
BOOM

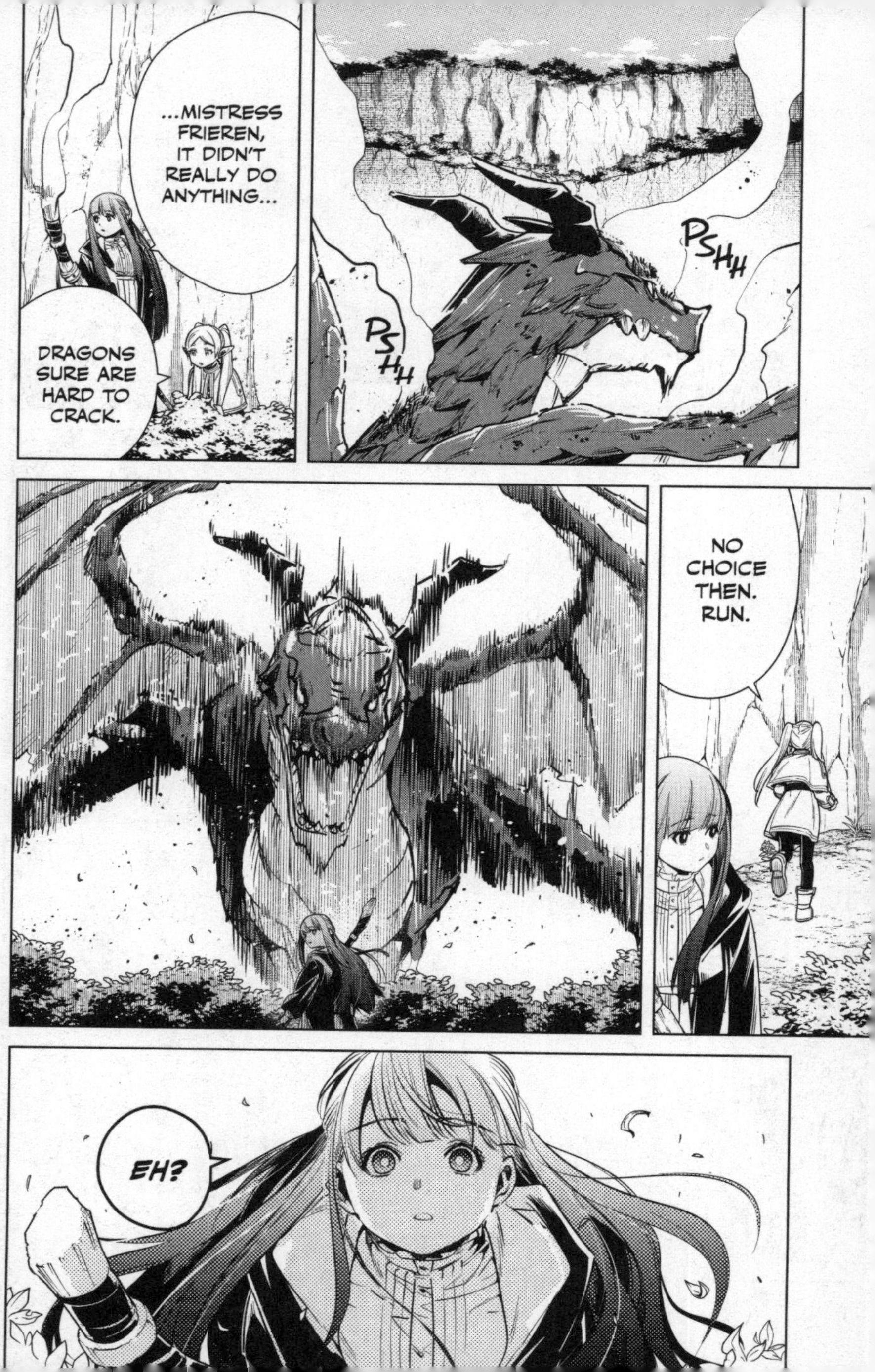
PSHH
PSHH
...MISTRESS FRIEREN, IT DIDN'T REALLY DO ANYTHING...
DRAGONS SURE ARE HARD TO CRACK.
NO CHOICE THEN. RUN.
EH?

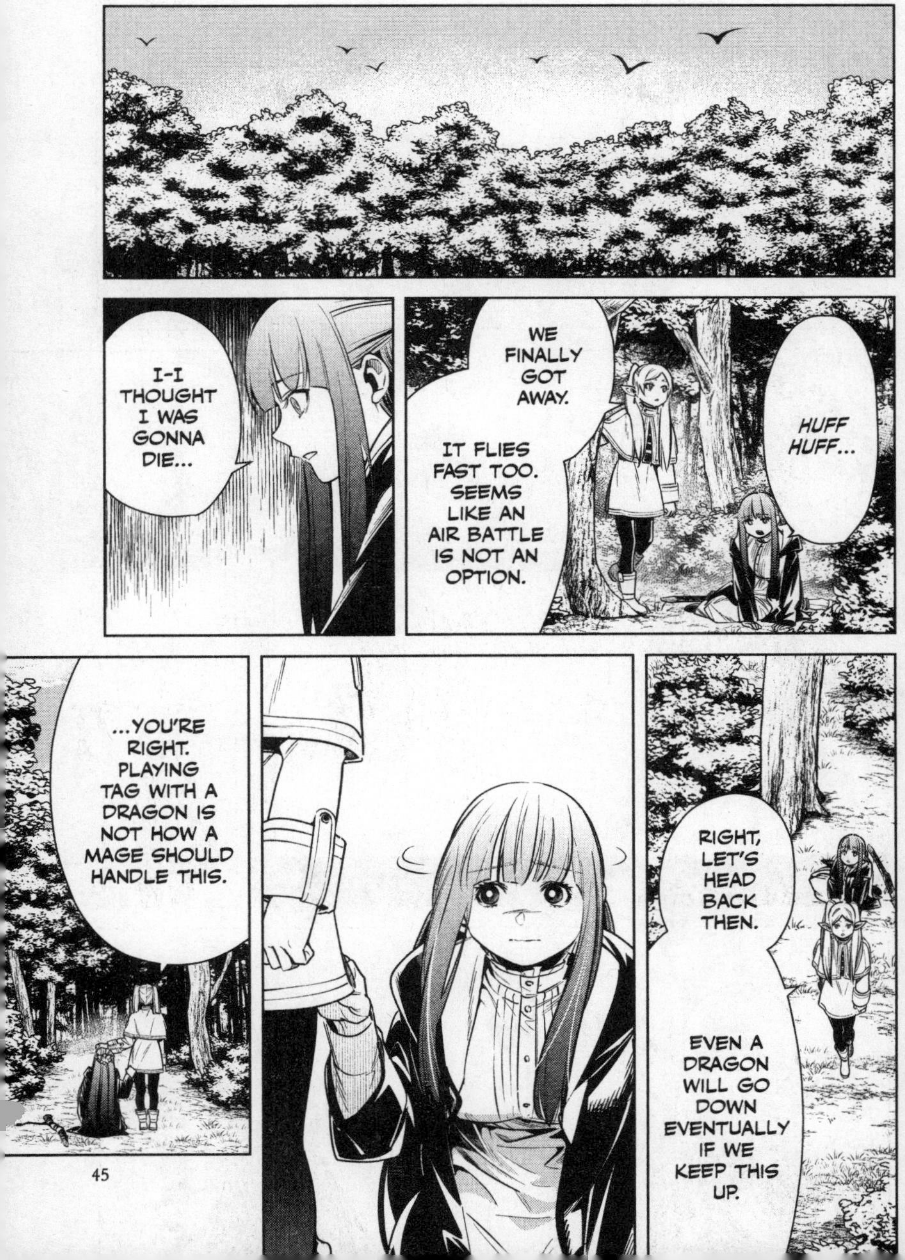
HUFF HUFF...
WE FINALLY GOT AWAY.
IT FLIES FAST TOO. SEEMS LIKE AN AIR BATTLE IS NOT AN OPTION.
I-I THOUGHT I WAS GONNA DIE...
RIGHT, LET'S HEAD BACK THEN.
EVEN A DRAGON WILL GO DOWN EVENTUALLY IF WE KEEP THIS UP.
...YOU'RE RIGHT. PLAYING TAG WITH A DRAGON IS NOT HOW A MAGE SHOULD HANDLE THIS.

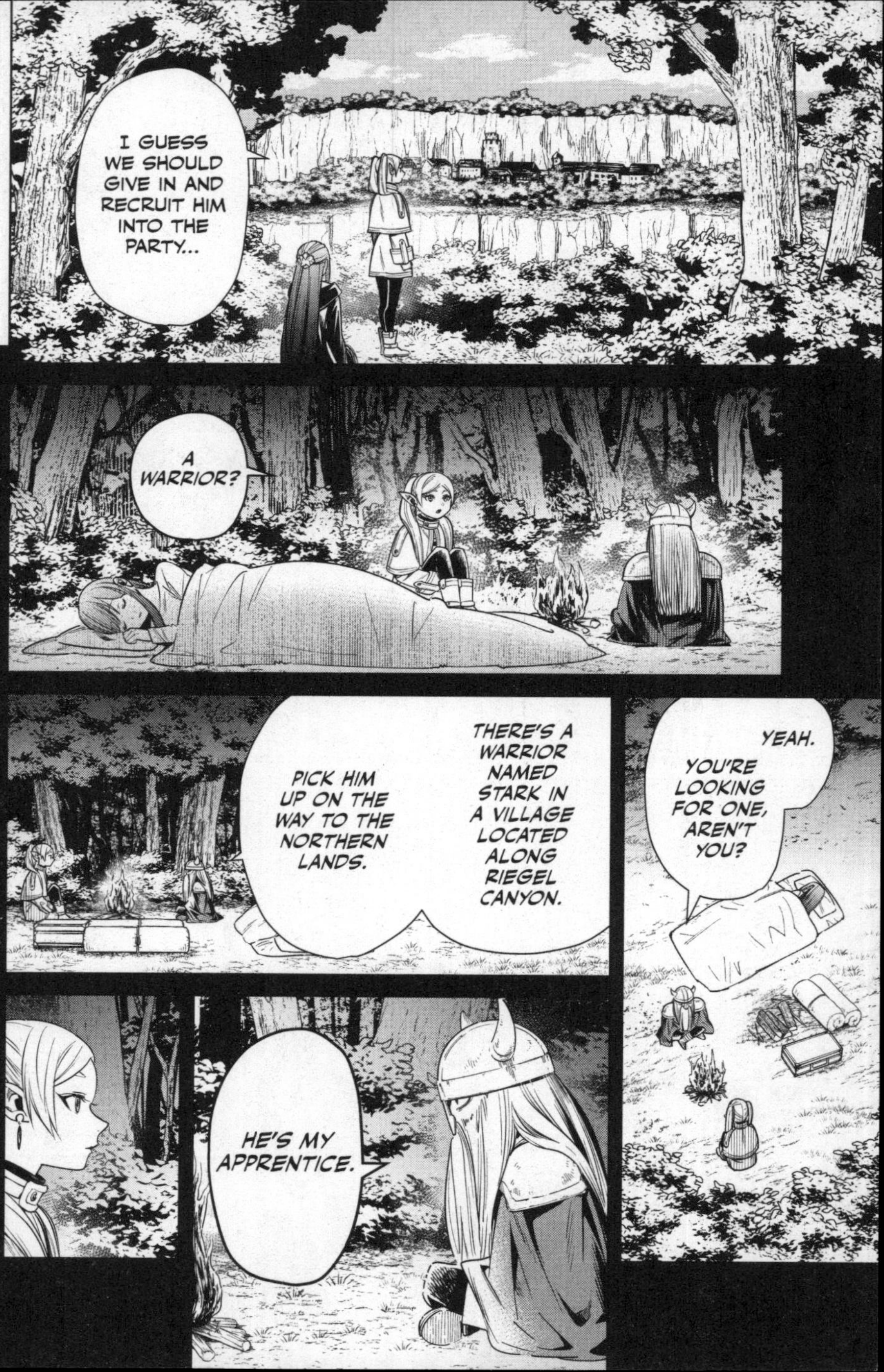
I GUESS WE SHOULD GIVE IN AND RECRUIT HIM INTO THE PARTY...
A WARRIOR?
YEAH.
YOU'RE LOOKING FOR ONE, AREN'T YOU?
THERE'S A WARRIOR NAMED STARK IN A VILLAGE LOCATED ALONG RIEGEL CANYON.
PICK HIM UP ON THE WAY TO THE NORTHERN LANDS.
HE'S MY APPRENTICE.

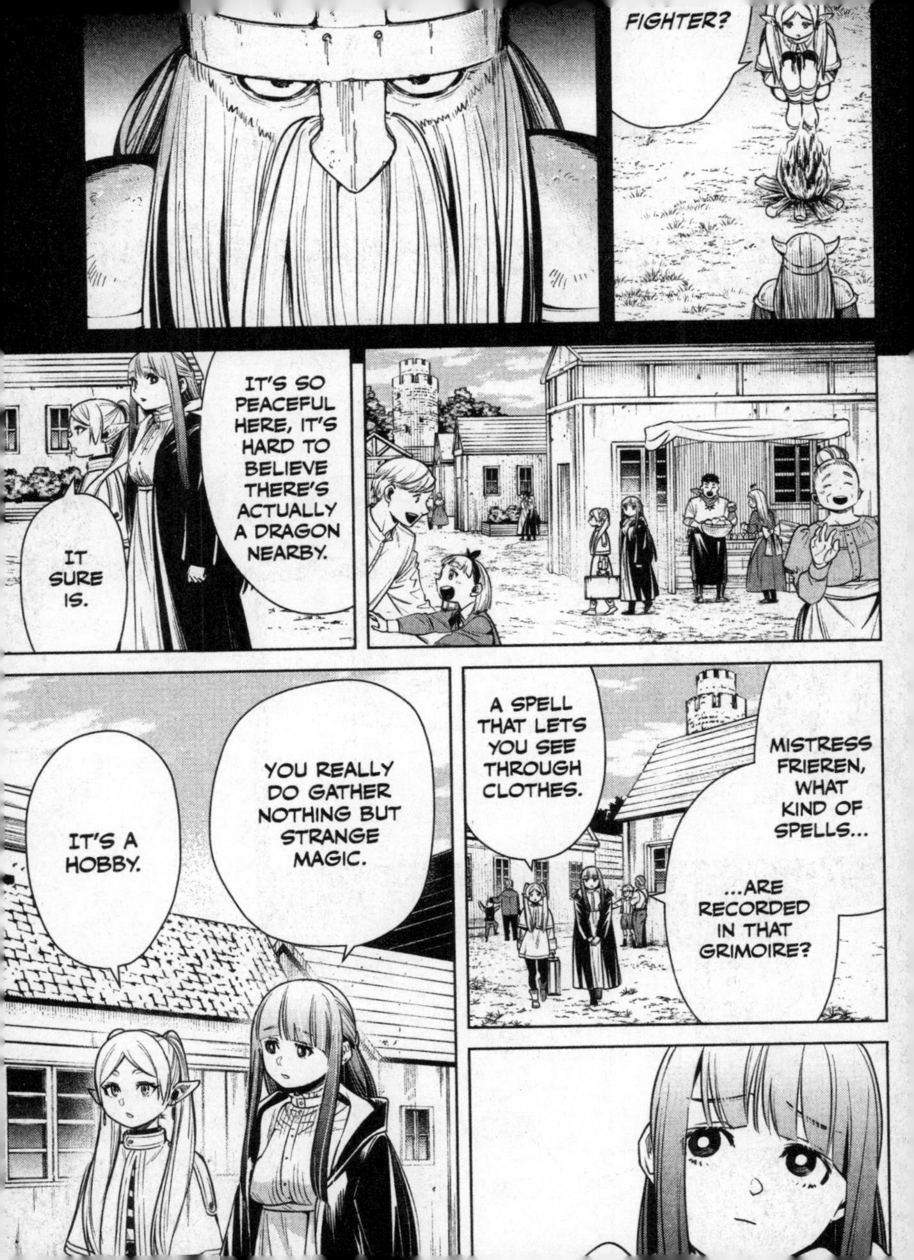
FIGHTER?
IT'S SO PEACEFUL HERE, IT'S HARD TO BELIEVE THERE'S ACTUALLY A DRAGON NEARBY.
IT SURE IS.
MISTRESS FRIEREN, WHAT KIND OF SPELLS...
...ARE RECORDED IN THAT GRIMOIRE?
A SPELL THAT LETS YOU SEE THROUGH CLOTHES.
YOU REALLY DO GATHER NOTHING BUT STRANGE MAGIC.
IT'S A HOBBY.

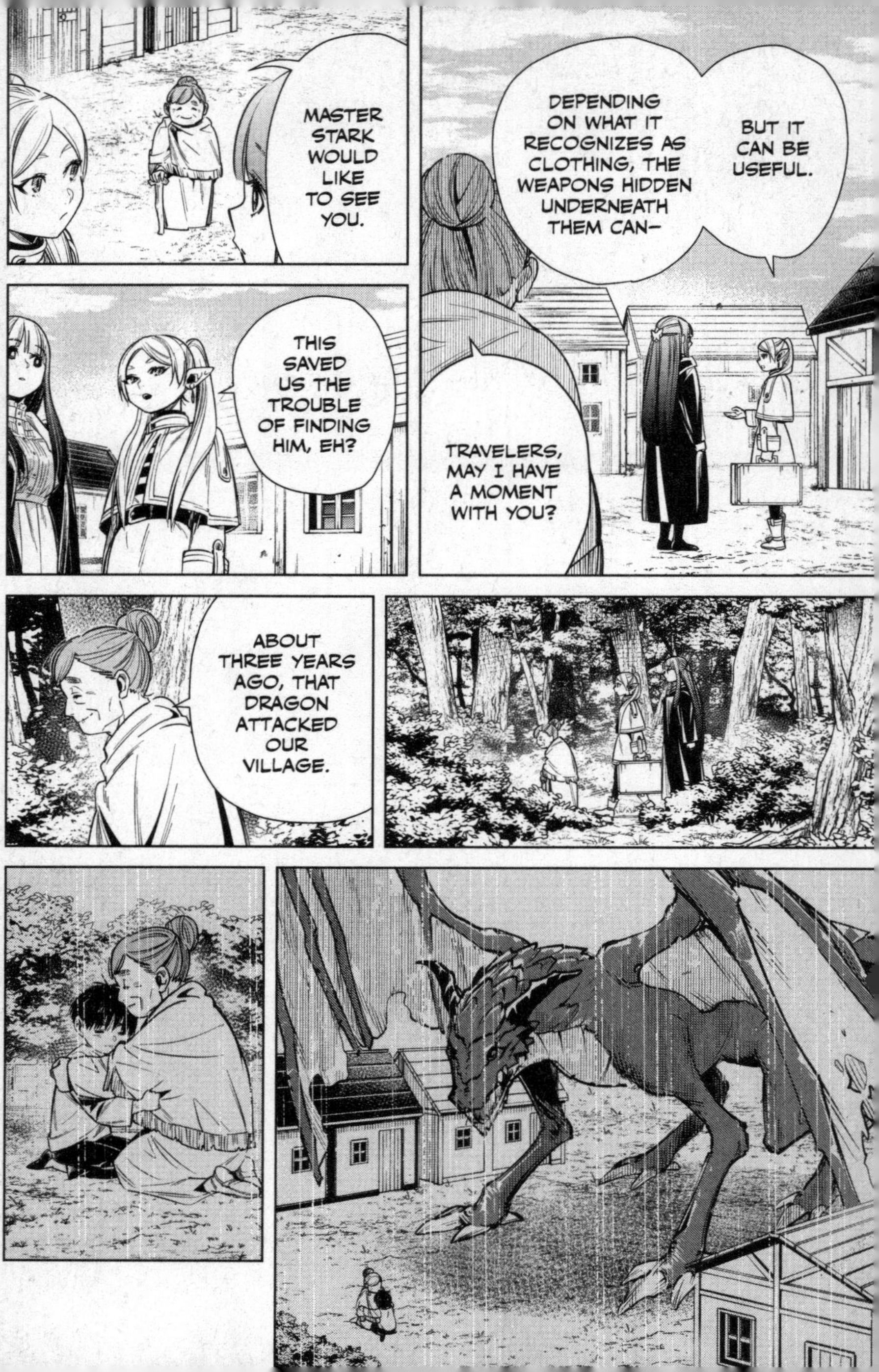
BUT IT CAN BE USEFUL.
DEPENDING ON WHAT IT RECOGNIZES AS CLOTHING, THE WEAPONS HIDDEN UNDERNEATH THEM CAN–
TRAVELERS, MAY I HAVE A MOMENT WITH YOU?
MASTER STARK WOULD LIKE TO SEE YOU.
THIS SAVED US THE TROUBLE OF FINDING HIM, EH?
ABOUT THREE YEARS AGO, THAT DRAGON ATTACKED OUR VILLAGE.

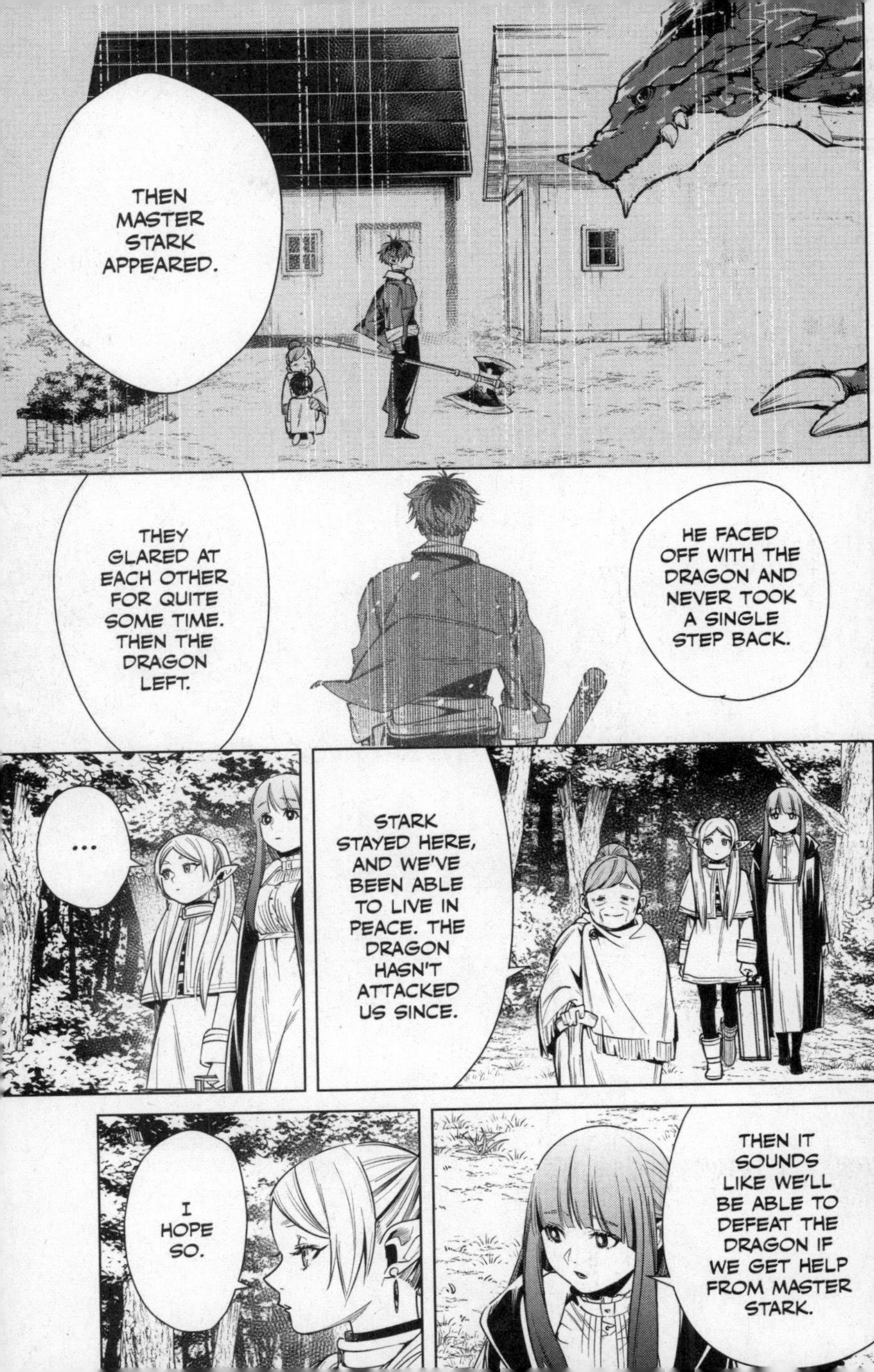
THEN MASTER STARK APPEARED.
HE FACED OFF WITH THE DRAGON AND NEVER TOOK A SINGLE STEP BACK.
THEY GLARED AT EACH OTHER FOR QUITE SOME TIME. THEN THE DRAGON LEFT.
STARK STAYED HERE, AND WE'VE BEEN ABLE TO LIVE IN PEACE. THE DRAGON HASN'T ATTACKED US SINCE.
...
THEN IT SOUNDS LIKE WE'LL BE ABLE TO DEFEAT THE DRAGON IF WE GET HELP FROM MASTER STARK.
I HOPE SO.

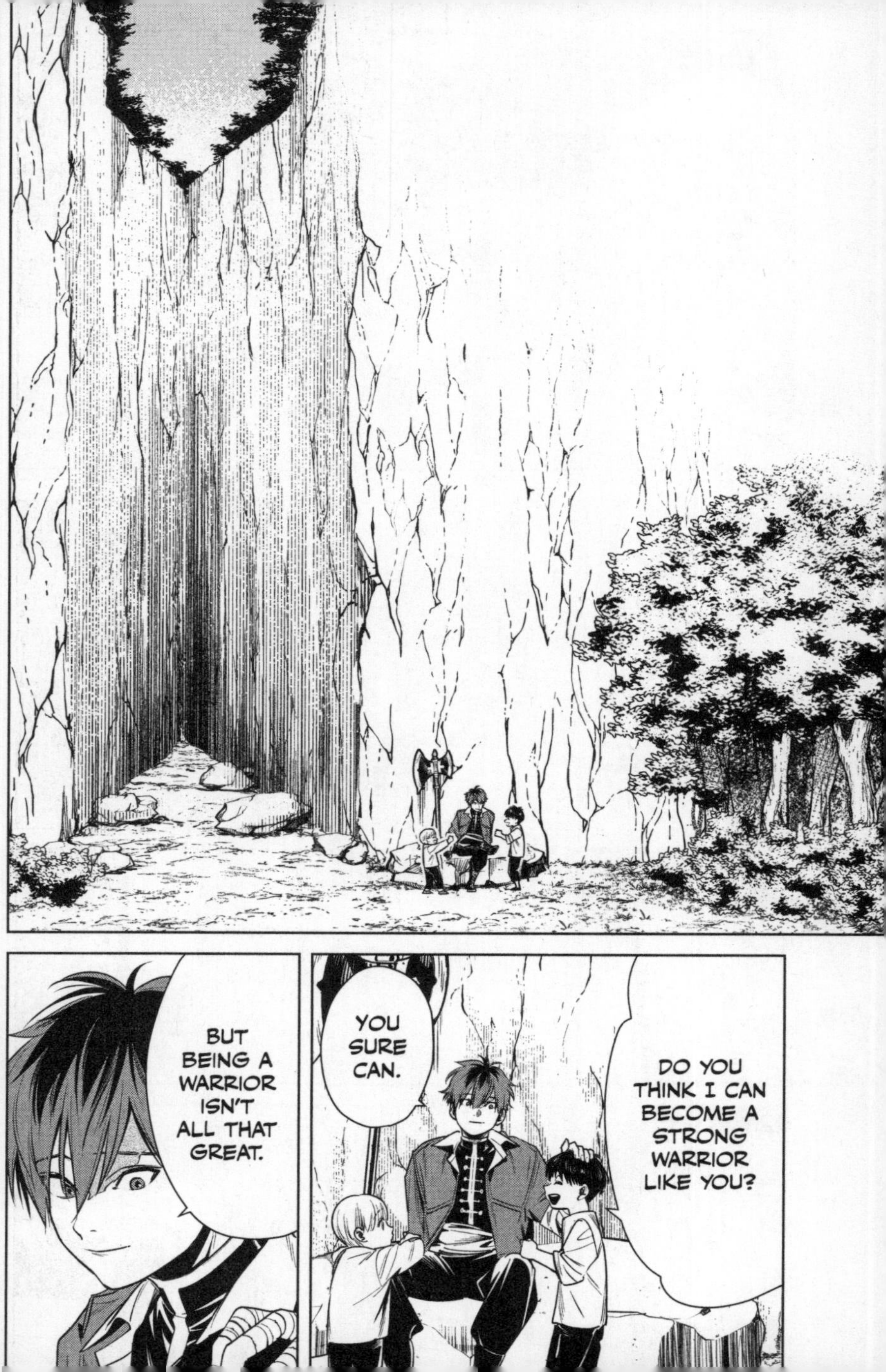
DO YOU THINK I CAN BECOME A STRONG WARRIOR LIKE YOU?
YOU SURE CAN.
BUT BEING A WARRIOR ISN'T ALL THAT GREAT.

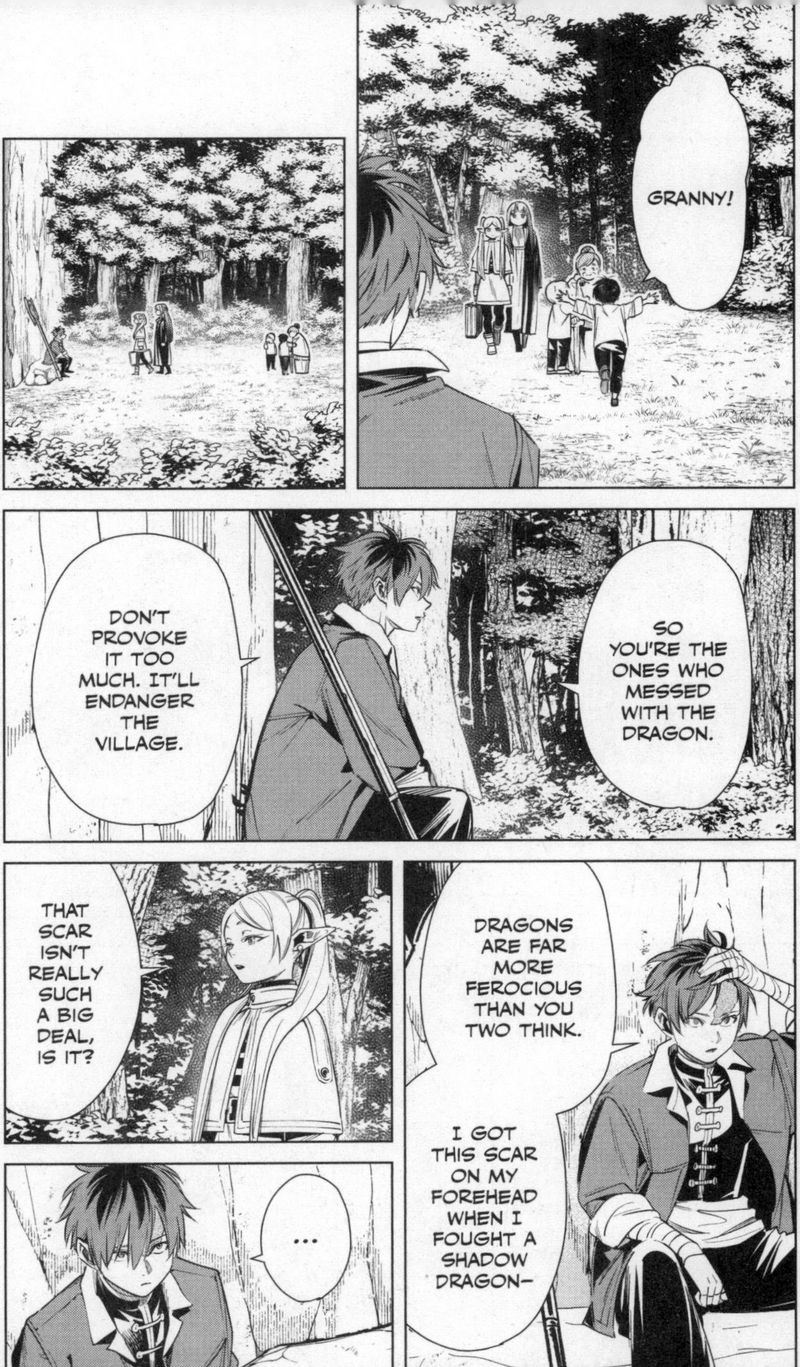
GRANNY!
SO YOU'RE THE ONES WHO MESSED WITH THE DRAGON.
DON'T PROVOKE IT TOO MUCH. IT'LL ENDANGER THE VILLAGE.
DRAGONS ARE FAR MORE FEROCIOUS THAN YOU TWO THINK.
I GOT THIS SCAR ON MY FOREHEAD WHEN I FOUGHT A SHADOW DRAGON—
THAT SCAR ISN'T REALLY SUCH A BIG DEAL, IS IT?
...

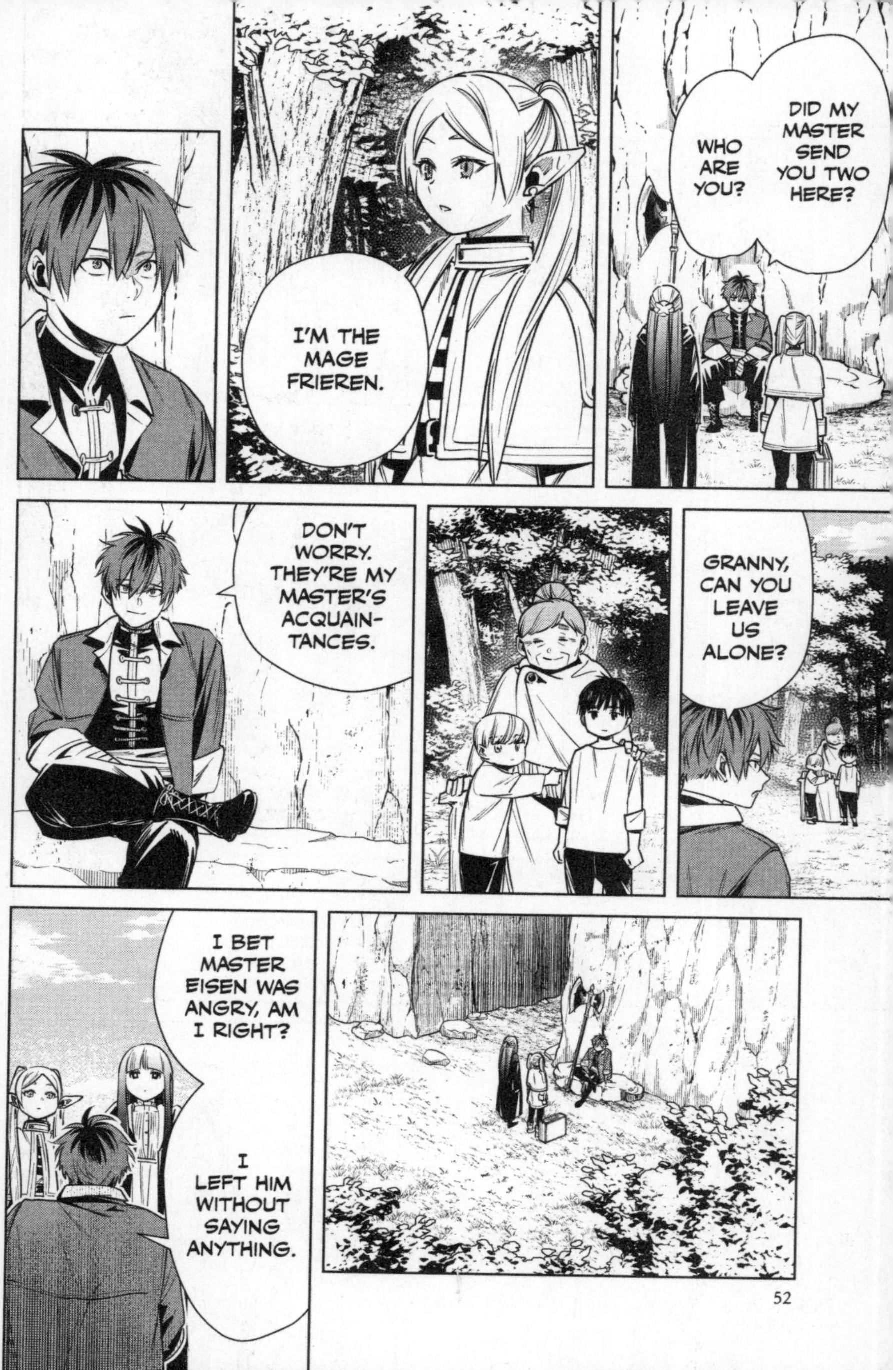
DID MY MASTER SEND YOU TWO HERE?
WHO ARE YOU?
I'M THE MAGE FRIEREN.
GRANNY, CAN YOU LEAVE US ALONE?
DON'T WORRY. THEY'RE MY MASTER'S ACQUAIN-TANCES.
I BET MASTER EISEN WAS ANGRY, AM I RIGHT?
I LEFT HIM WITHOUT SAYING ANYTHING.

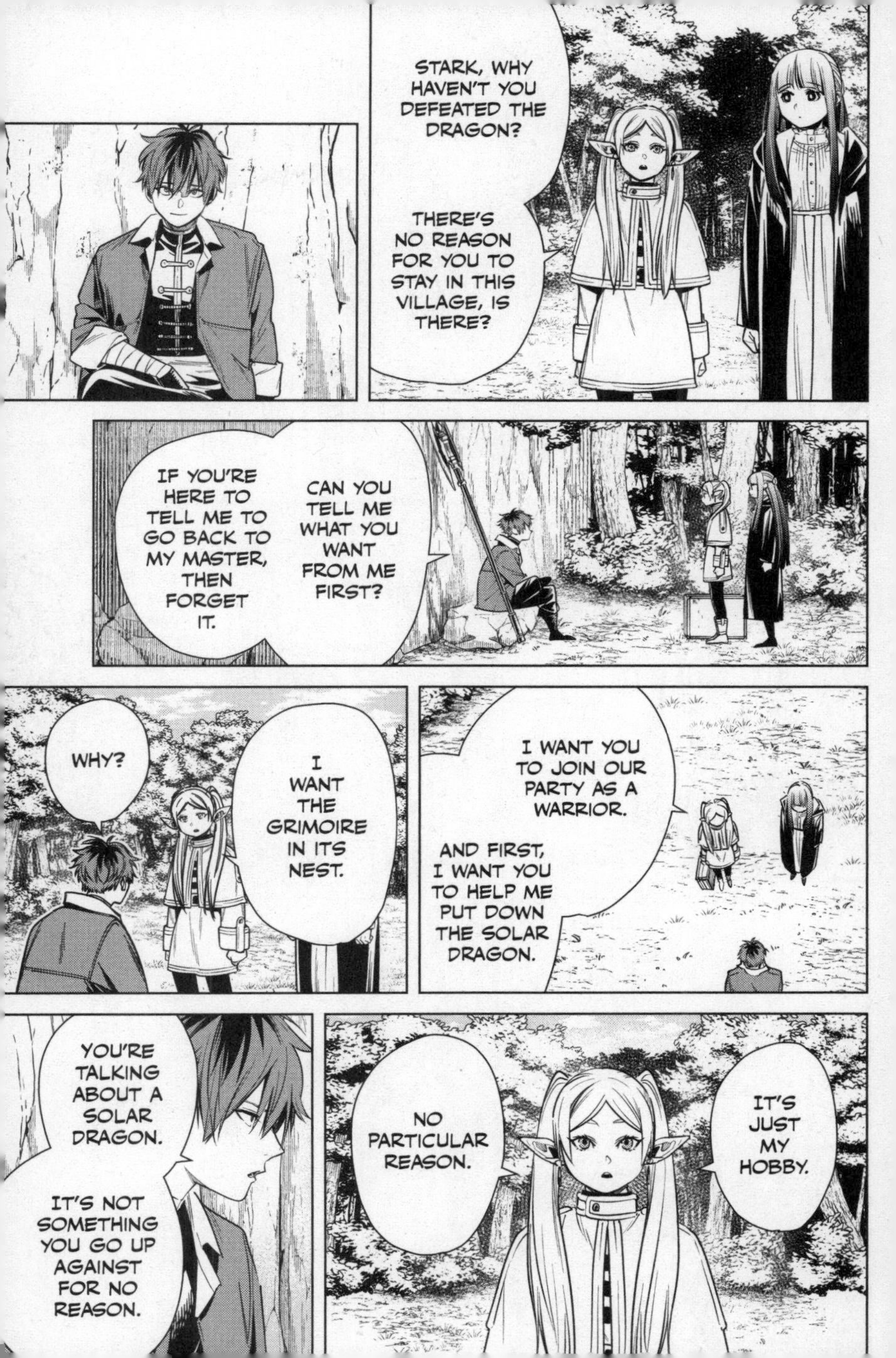
STARK, WHY HAVEN'T YOU DEFEATED THE DRAGON?
THERE'S NO REASON FOR YOU TO STAY IN THIS VILLAGE, IS THERE?
CAN YOU TELL ME WHAT YOU WANT FROM ME FIRST?
IF YOU'RE HERE TO TELL ME TO GO BACK TO MY MASTER, THEN FORGET IT.
I WANT YOU TO JOIN OUR PARTY AS A WARRIOR.
AND FIRST, I WANT YOU TO HELP ME PUT DOWN THE SOLAR DRAGON.
WHY?
I WANT THE GRIMOIRE IN ITS NEST.
IT'S JUST MY HOBBY.
NO PARTICULAR REASON.
YOU'RE TALKING ABOUT A SOLAR DRAGON.
IT'S NOT SOMETHING YOU GO UP AGAINST FOR NO REASON.

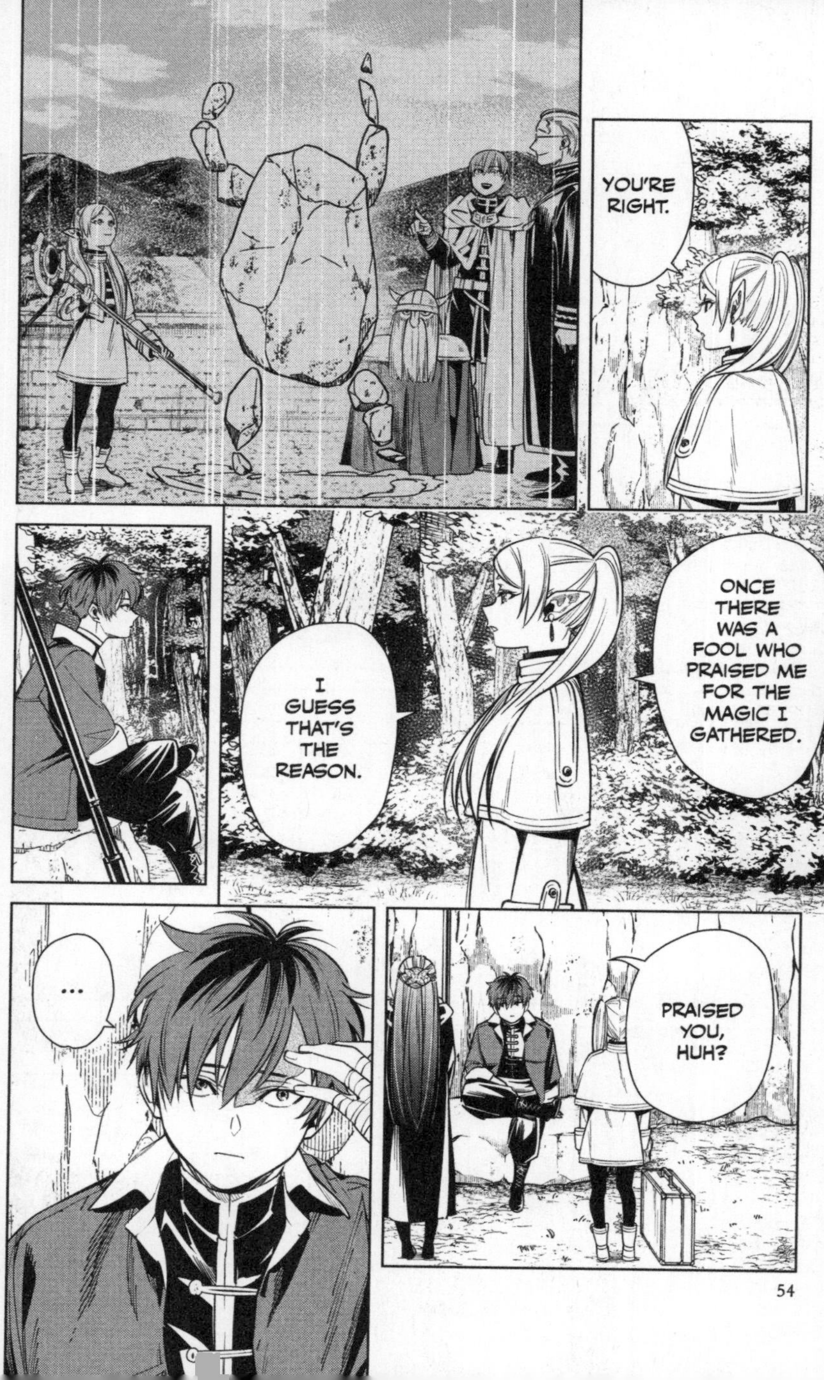
YOU'RE RIGHT.
ONCE THERE WAS A FOOL WHO PRAISED ME FOR THE MAGIC I GATHERED.
I GUESS THAT'S THE REASON.
PRAISED YOU, HUH?
...

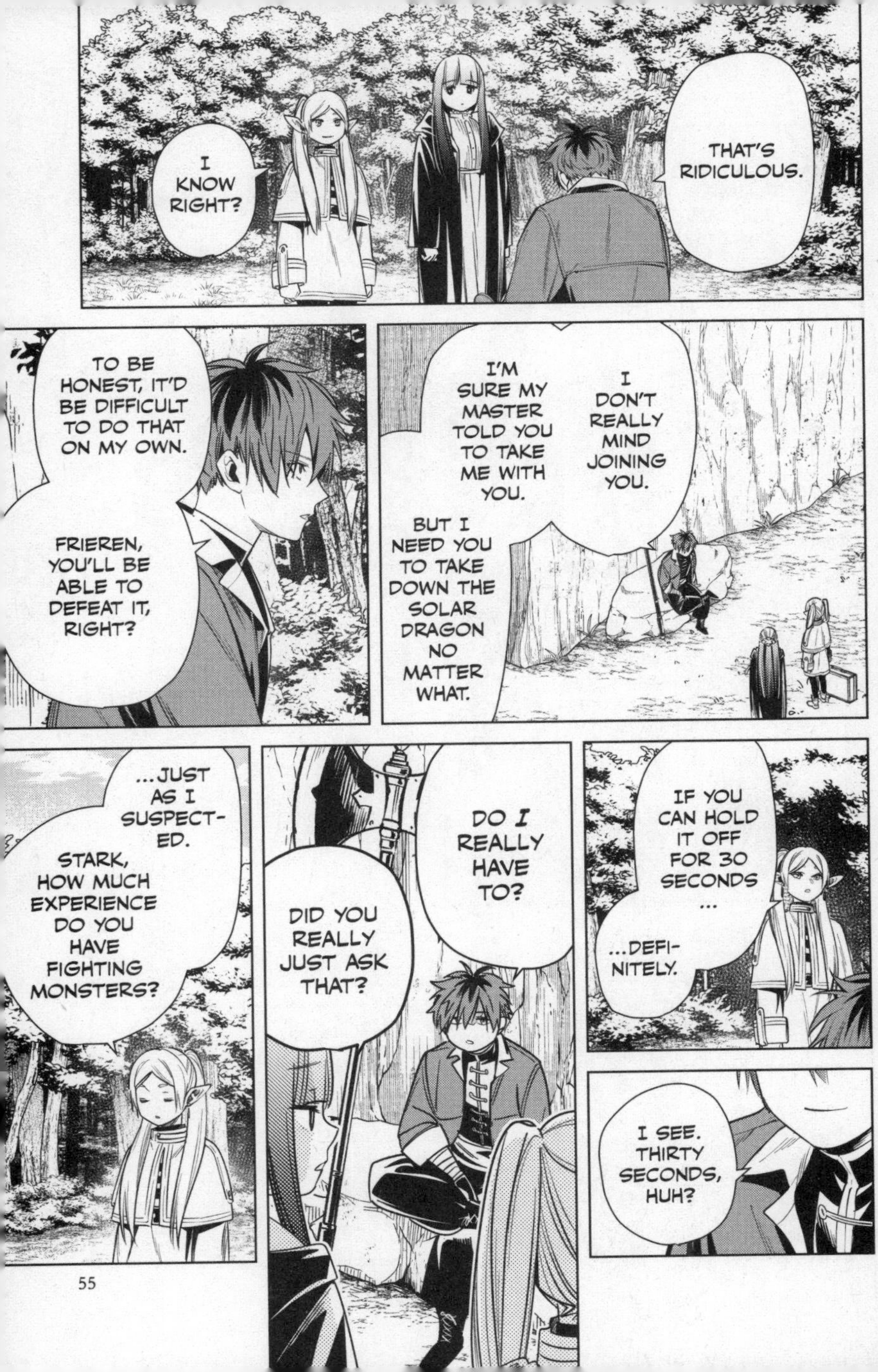
THAT'S RIDICULOUS.
I KNOW RIGHT?
I DON'T REALLY MIND JOINING YOU.
I'M SURE MY MASTER TOLD YOU TO TAKE ME WITH YOU.
BUT I NEED YOU TO TAKE DOWN THE SOLAR DRAGON NO MATTER WHAT.
TO BE HONEST, IT'D BE DIFFICULT TO DO THAT ON MY OWN.
FRIEREN, YOU'LL BE ABLE TO DEFEAT IT, RIGHT?
IF YOU CAN HOLD IT OFF FOR 30 SECONDS ...
...DEFI- NITELY.
I SEE. THIRTY SECONDS, HUH?
DO *I* REALLY HAVE TO?
DID YOU REALLY JUST ASK THAT?
...JUST AS I SUSPECT- ED.
STARK, HOW MUCH EXPERIENCE DO YOU HAVE FIGHTING MONSTERS?

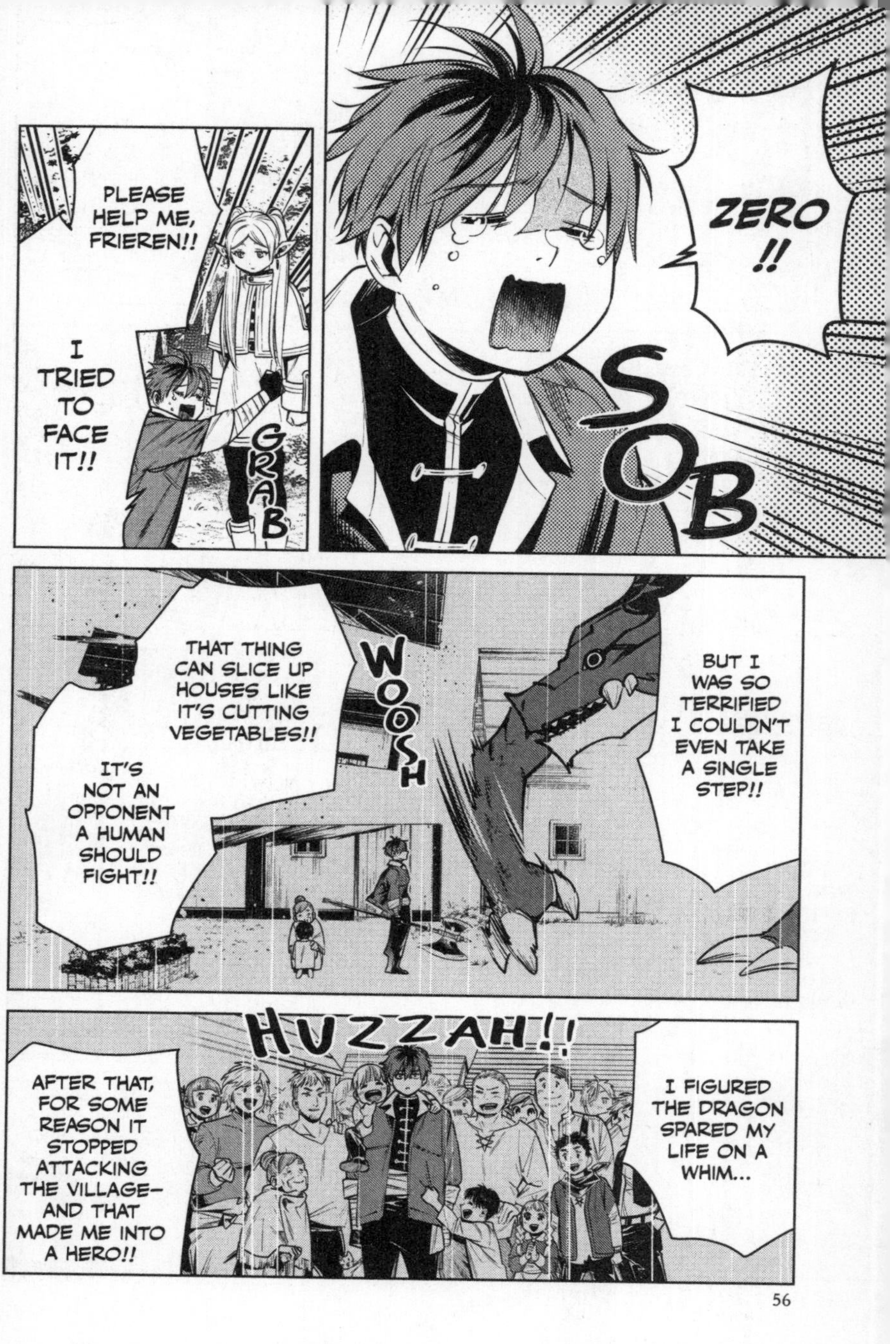
ZERO!!
SOB
PLEASE HELP ME, FRIEREN!!
I TRIED TO FACE IT!!
GRAB
BUT I WAS SO TERRIFIED I COULDN'T EVEN TAKE A SINGLE STEP!!
WOOSH
THAT THING CAN SLICE UP HOUSES LIKE IT'S CUTTING VEGETABLES!!
IT'S NOT AN OPPONENT A HUMAN SHOULD FIGHT!!
HUZZAH!!
I FIGURED THE DRAGON SPARED MY LIFE ON A WHIM...
AFTER THAT, FOR SOME REASON IT STOPPED ATTACKING THE VILLAGE—AND THAT MADE ME INTO A HERO!!

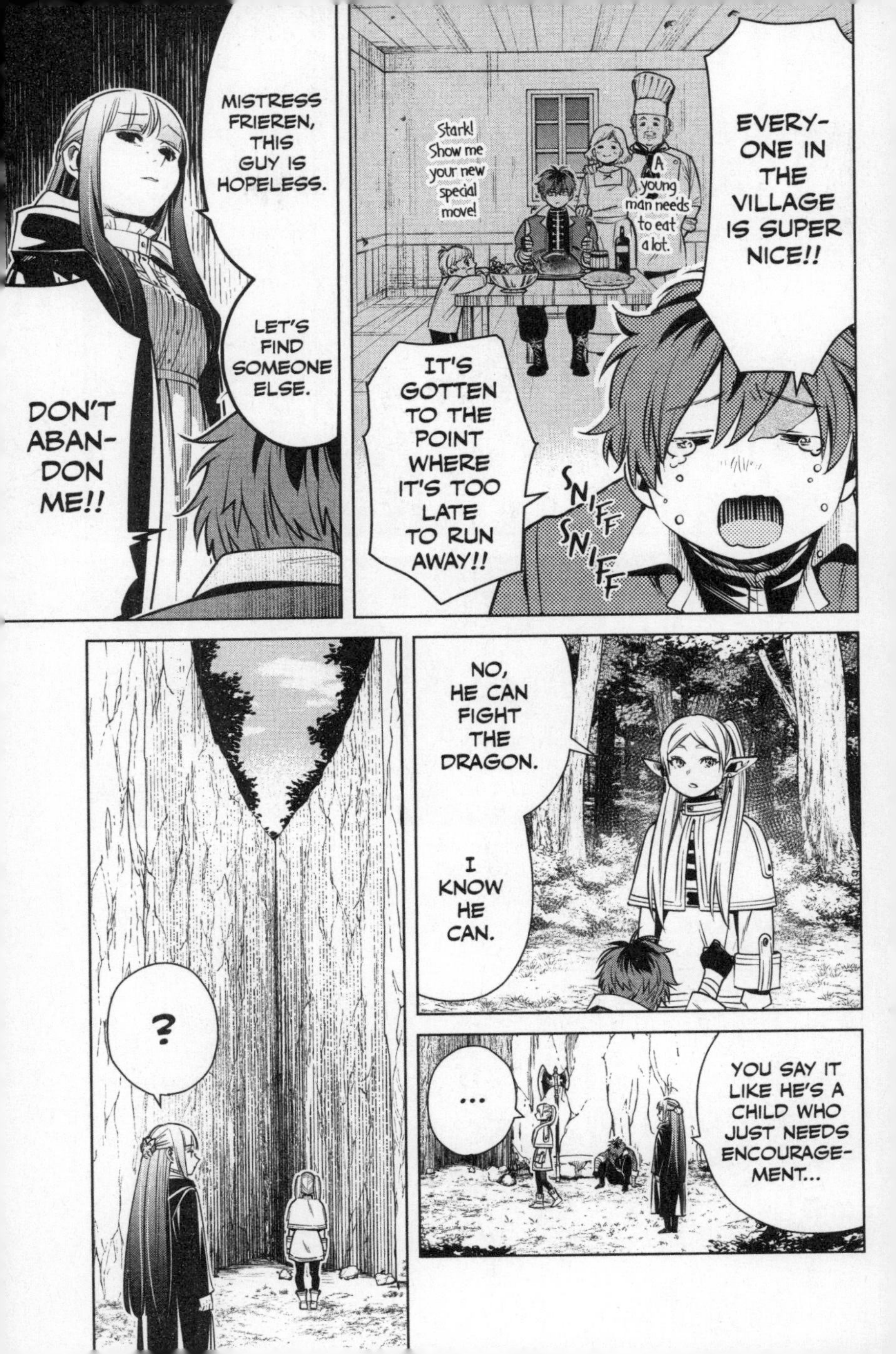
EVERY-ONE IN THE VILLAGE IS SUPER NICE!!
Stark! Show me your new special move!
A young man needs to eat a lot.
IT'S GOTTEN TO THE POINT WHERE IT'S TOO LATE TO RUN AWAY!!
SNIFF SNIFF
MISTRESS FRIEREN, THIS GUY IS HOPELESS.
LET'S FIND SOMEONE ELSE.
DON'T ABAN-DON ME!!
NO, HE CAN FIGHT THE DRAGON.
I KNOW HE CAN.
YOU SAY IT LIKE HE'S A CHILD WHO JUST NEEDS ENCOURAGE-MENT...
...
?

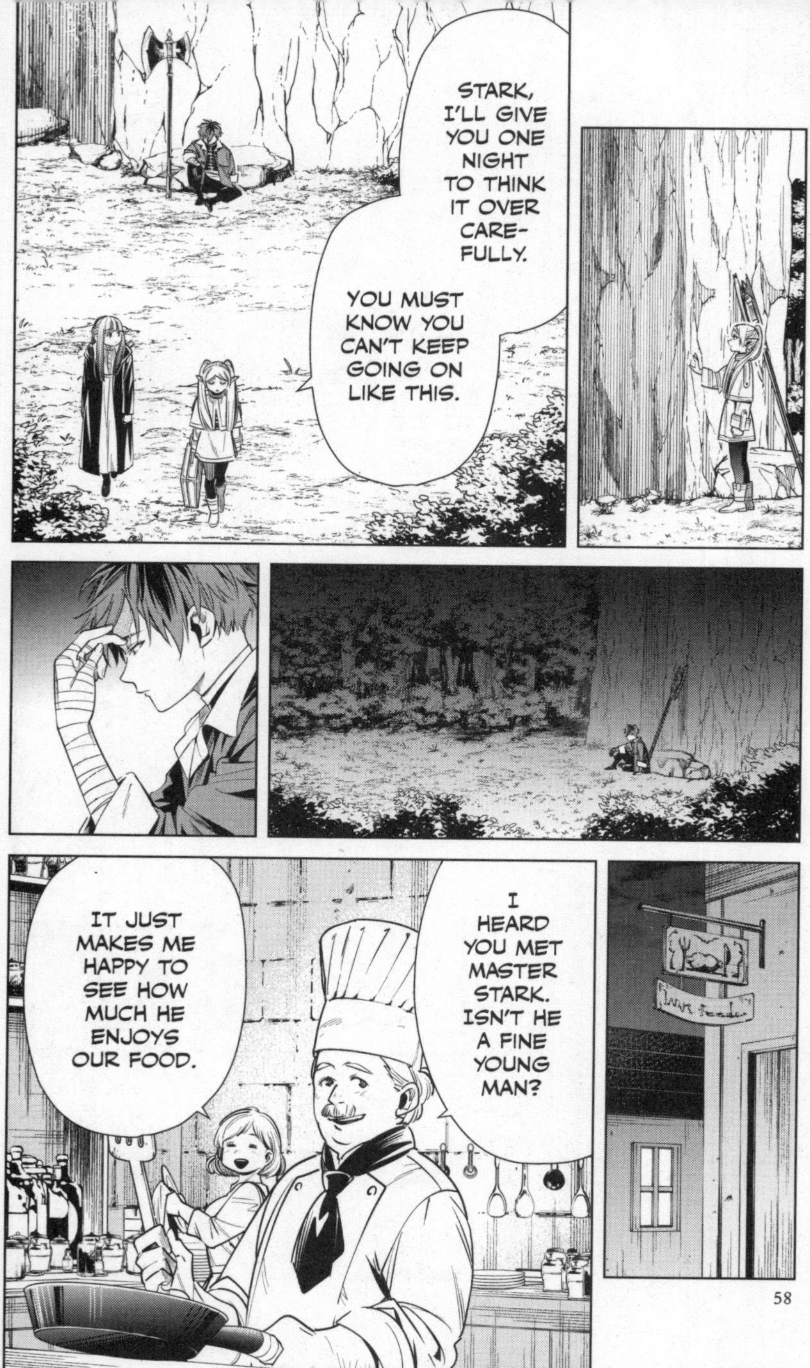
STARK, I'LL GIVE YOU ONE NIGHT TO THINK IT OVER CARE-FULLY.
YOU MUST KNOW YOU CAN'T KEEP GOING ON LIKE THIS.
I HEARD YOU MET MASTER STARK. ISN'T HE A FINE YOUNG MAN?
IT JUST MAKES ME HAPPY TO SEE HOW MUCH HE ENJOYS OUR FOOD.

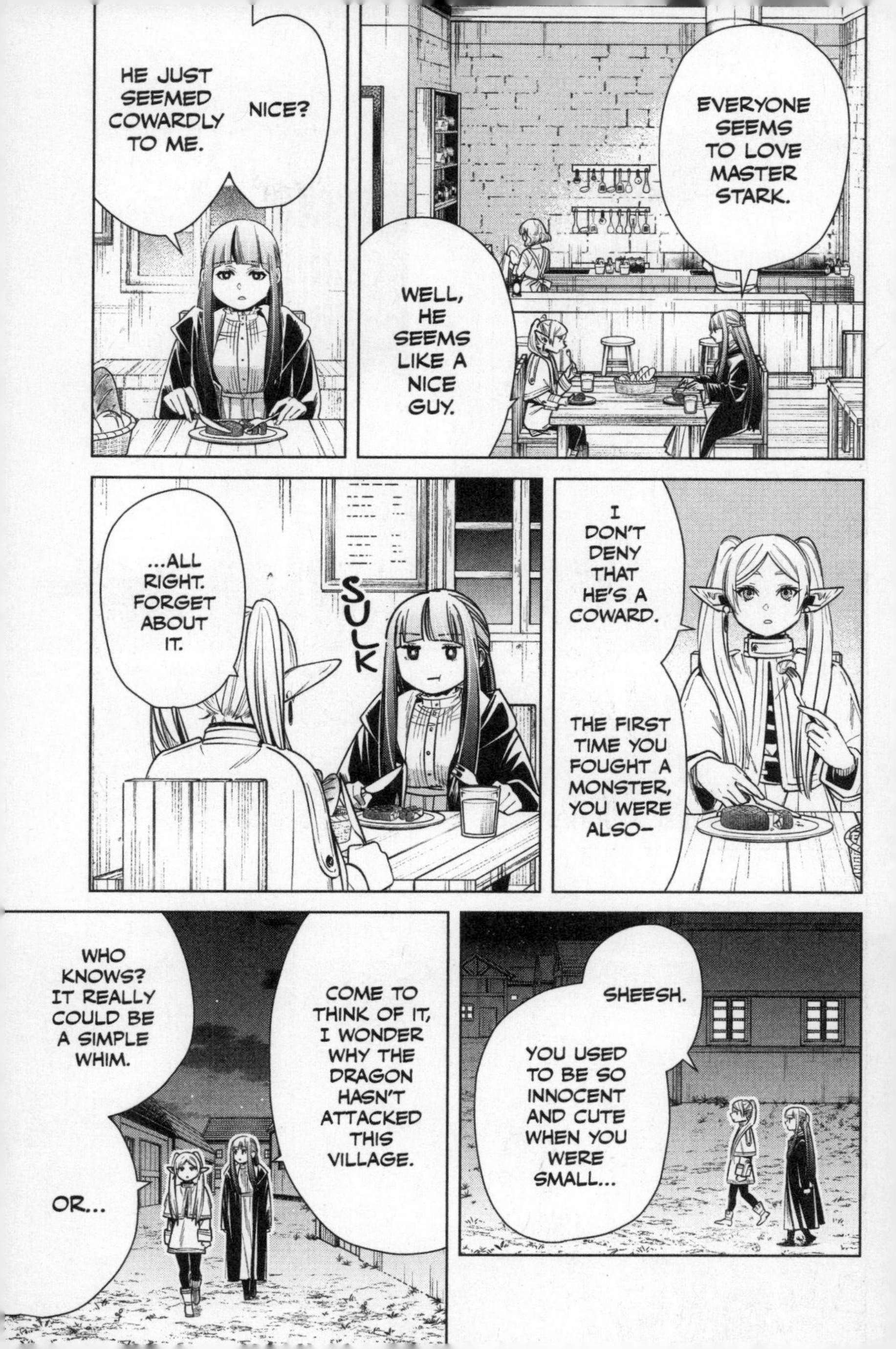
EVERYONE SEEMS TO LOVE MASTER STARK.
WELL, HE SEEMS LIKE A NICE GUY.
NICE?
HE JUST SEEMED COWARDLY TO ME.
I DON'T DENY THAT HE'S A COWARD.
THE FIRST TIME YOU FOUGHT A MONSTER, YOU WERE ALSO—
SULK
...ALL RIGHT. FORGET ABOUT IT.
SHEESH.
YOU USED TO BE SO INNOCENT AND CUTE WHEN YOU WERE SMALL...
COME TO THINK OF IT, I WONDER WHY THE DRAGON HASN'T ATTACKED THIS VILLAGE.
WHO KNOWS? IT REALLY COULD BE A SIMPLE WHIM.
OR...

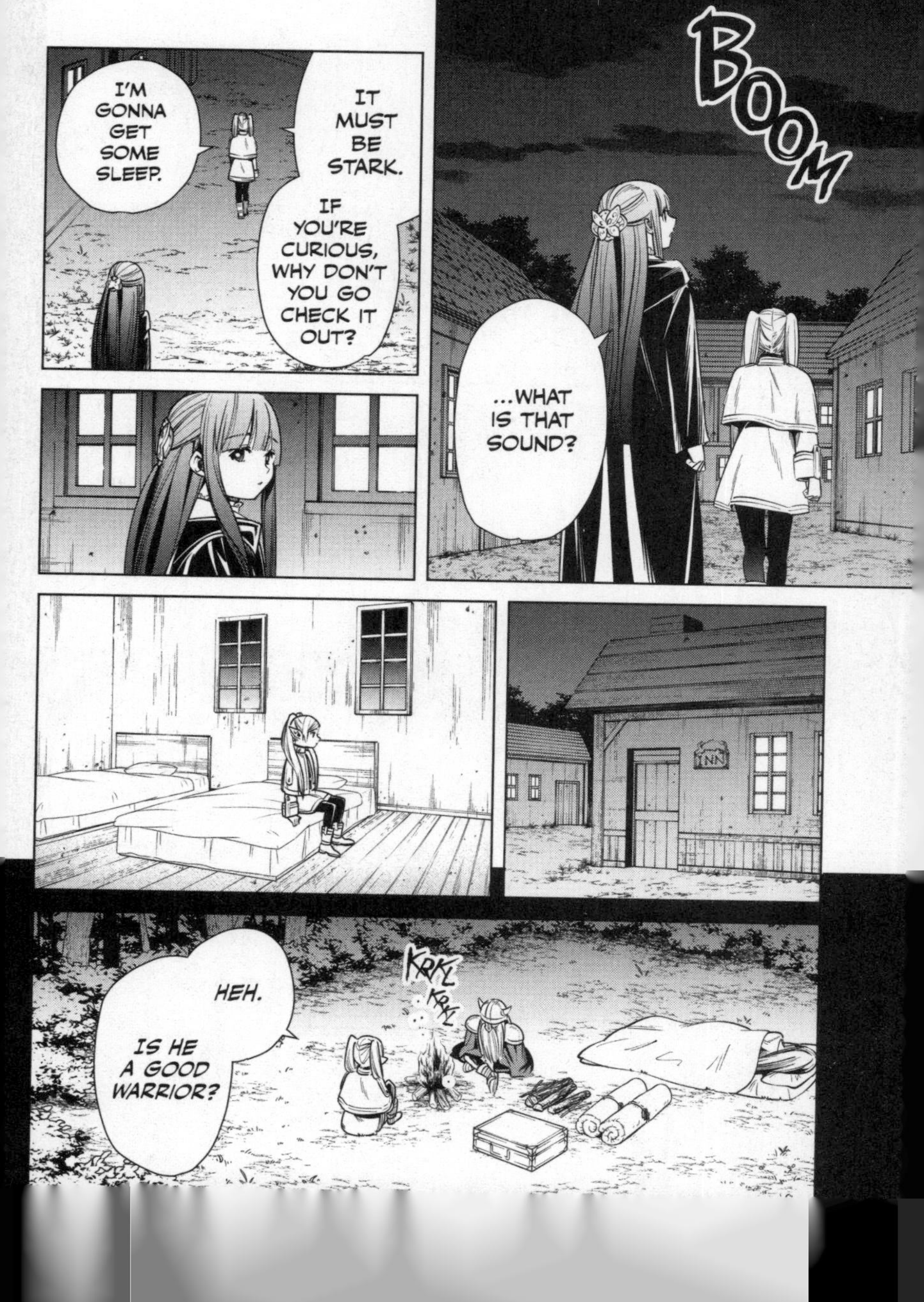
BOOM
...WHAT IS THAT SOUND?
IT MUST BE STARK.
IF YOU'RE CURIOUS, WHY DON'T YOU GO CHECK IT OUT?
I'M GONNA GET SOME SLEEP.
INN
KRKL KRKL
HEH.
IS HE A GOOD WARRIOR?

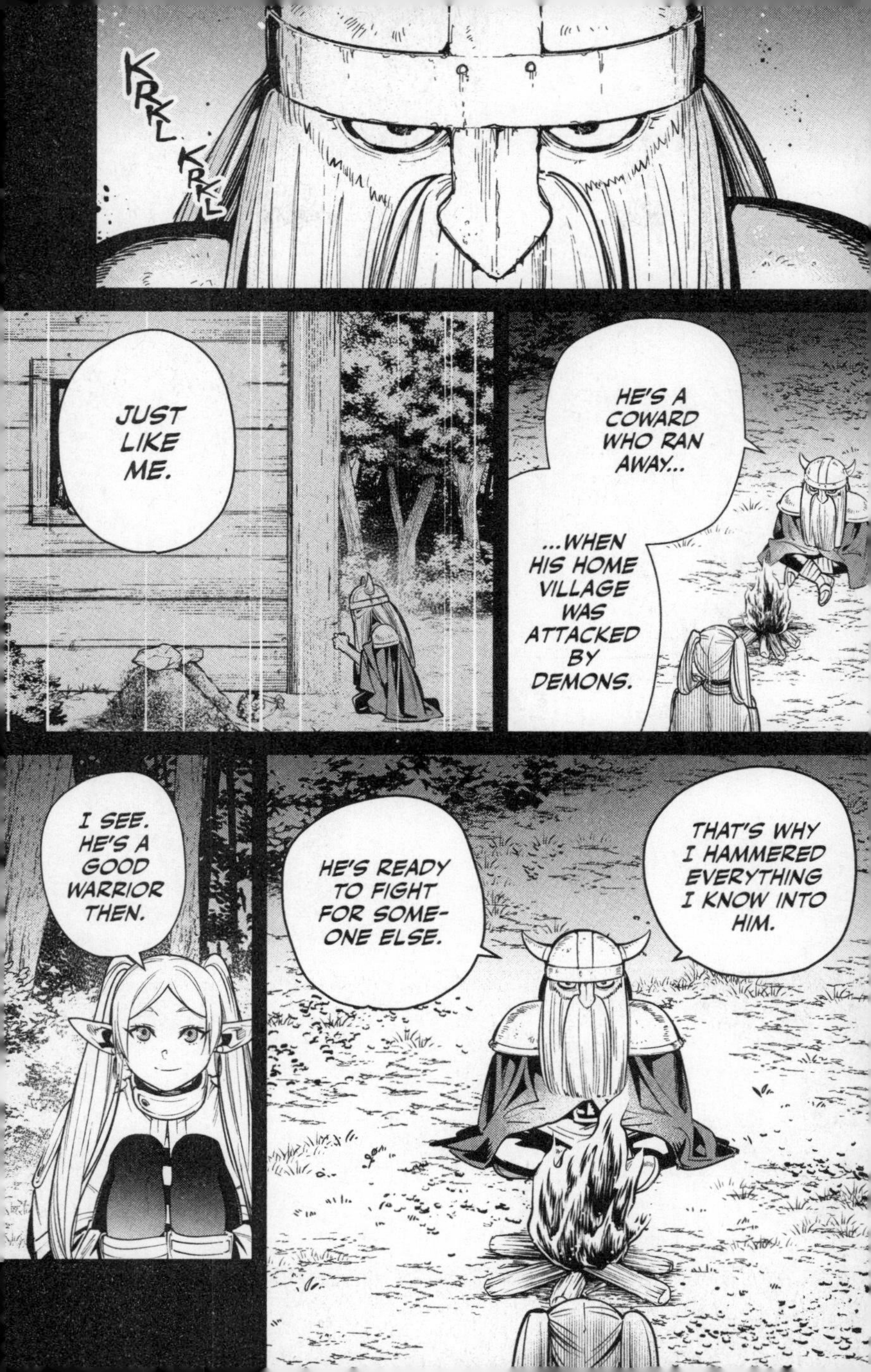
KRKL KRKL
HE'S A COWARD WHO RAN AWAY...
...WHEN HIS HOME VILLAGE WAS ATTACKED BY DEMONS.
JUST LIKE ME.
THAT'S WHY I HAMMERED EVERYTHING I KNOW INTO HIM.
HE'S READY TO FIGHT FOR SOME-ONE ELSE.
I SEE. HE'S A GOOD WARRIOR THEN.

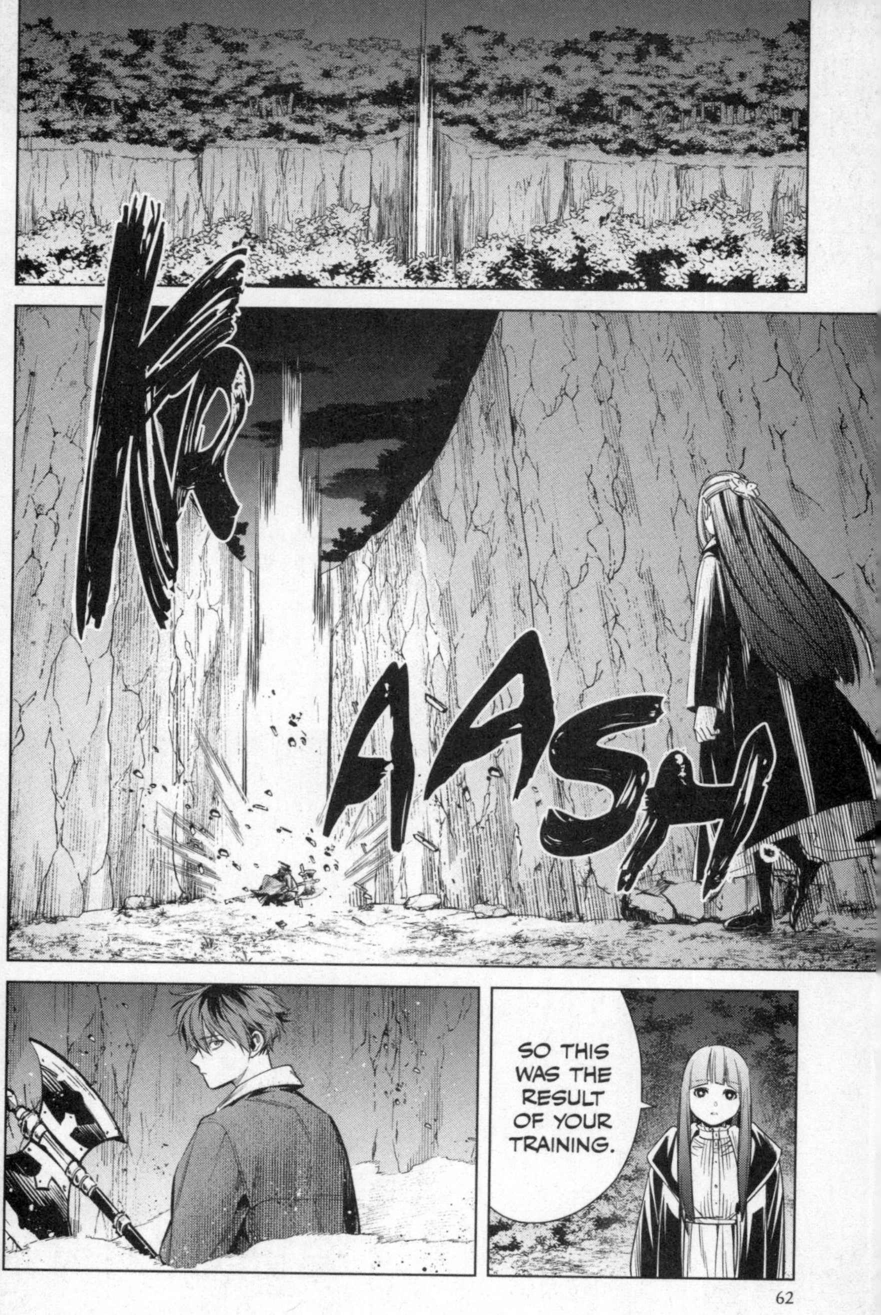
KRAASH
SO THIS WAS THE RESULT OF YOUR TRAINING.

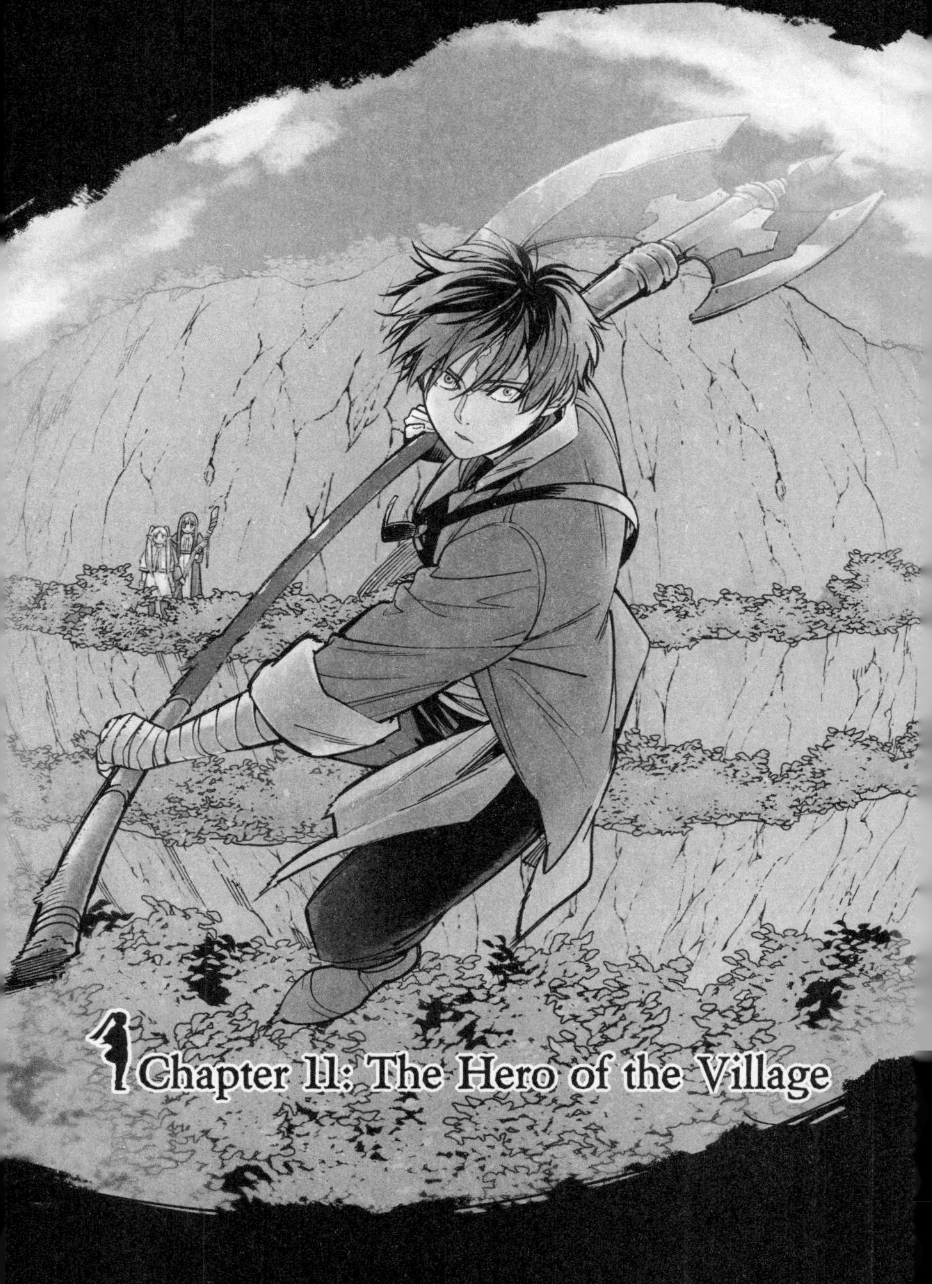

Chapter 11: The Hero of the Village

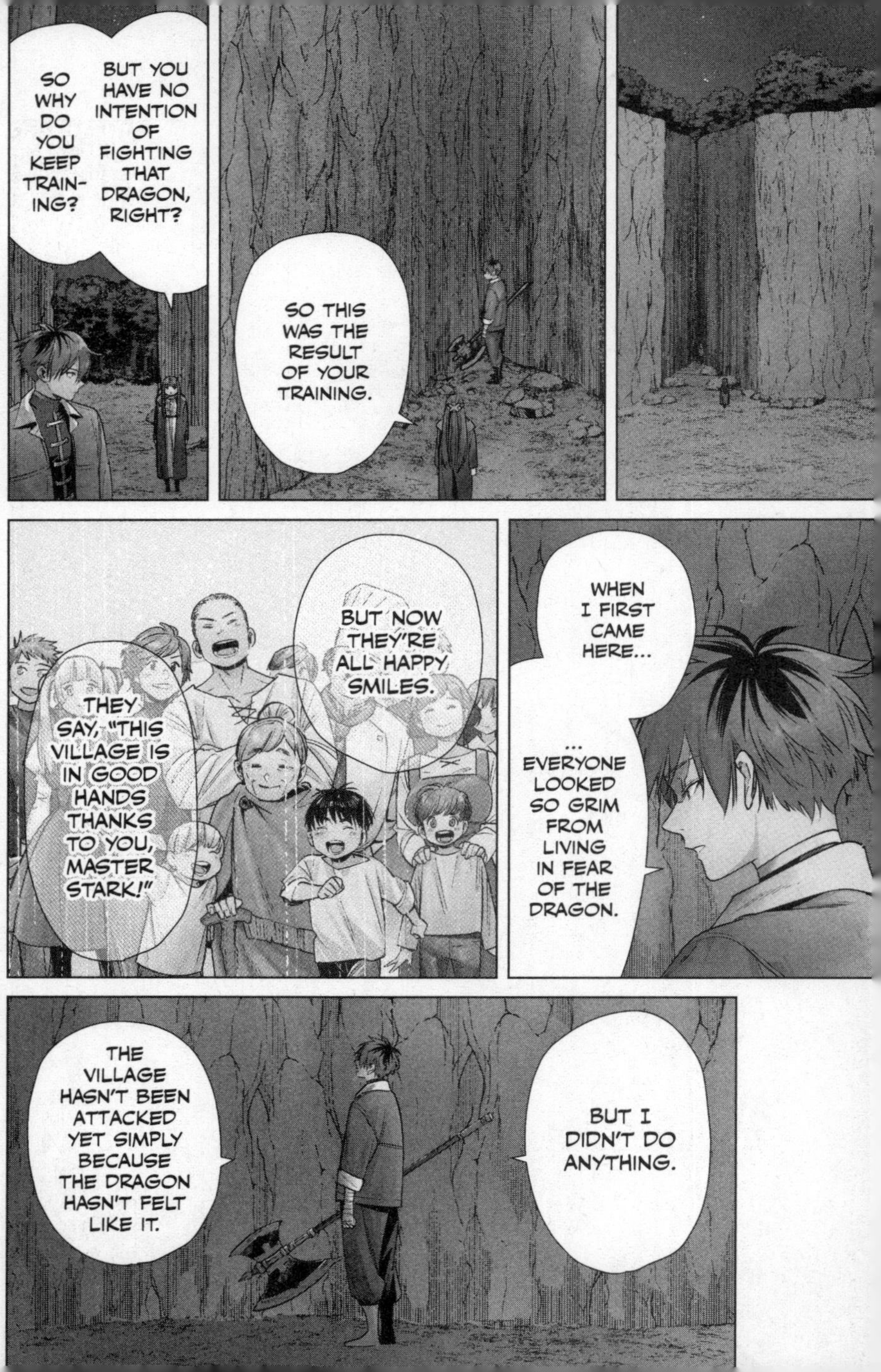
SO THIS WAS THE RESULT OF YOUR TRAINING.
BUT YOU HAVE NO INTENTION OF FIGHTING THAT DRAGON, RIGHT?
SO WHY DO YOU KEEP TRAIN-ING?
WHEN I FIRST CAME HERE...
...EVERYONE LOOKED SO GRIM FROM LIVING IN FEAR OF THE DRAGON.
BUT NOW THEY'RE ALL HAPPY SMILES.
THEY SAY, "THIS VILLAGE IS IN GOOD HANDS THANKS TO YOU, MASTER STARK!"
BUT I DIDN'T DO ANYTHING.
THE VILLAGE HASN'T BEEN ATTACKED YET SIMPLY BECAUSE THE DRAGON HASN'T FELT LIKE IT.

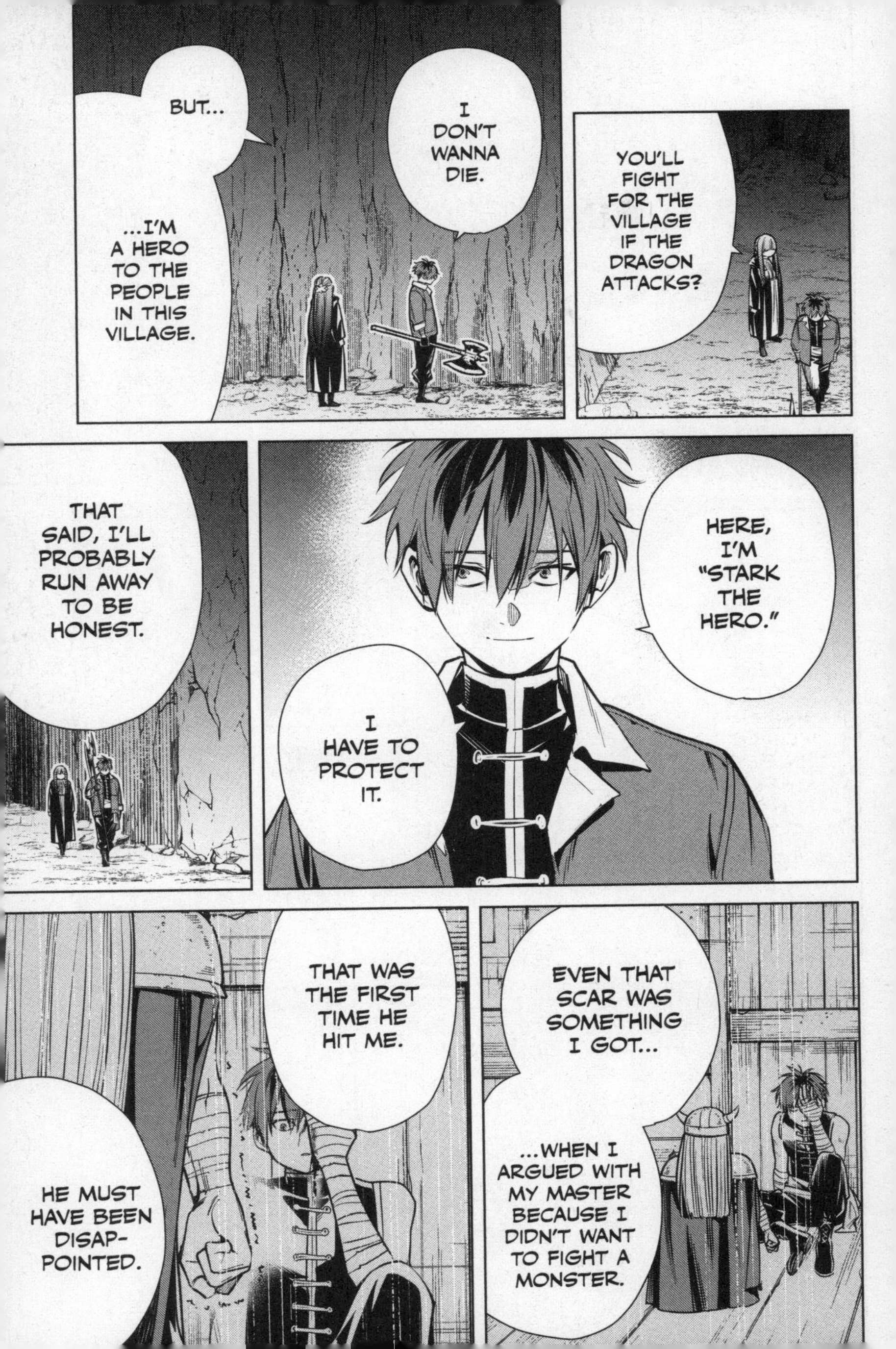
YOU'LL FIGHT FOR THE VILLAGE IF THE DRAGON ATTACKS?
I DON'T WANNA DIE.
BUT...
...I'M A HERO TO THE PEOPLE IN THIS VILLAGE.
HERE, I'M "STARK THE HERO."
I HAVE TO PROTECT IT.
THAT SAID, I'LL PROBABLY RUN AWAY TO BE HONEST.
EVEN THAT SCAR WAS SOMETHING I GOT...
...WHEN I ARGUED WITH MY MASTER BECAUSE I DIDN'T WANT TO FIGHT A MONSTER.
THAT WAS THE FIRST TIME HE HIT ME.
HE MUST HAVE BEEN DISAP-POINTED.

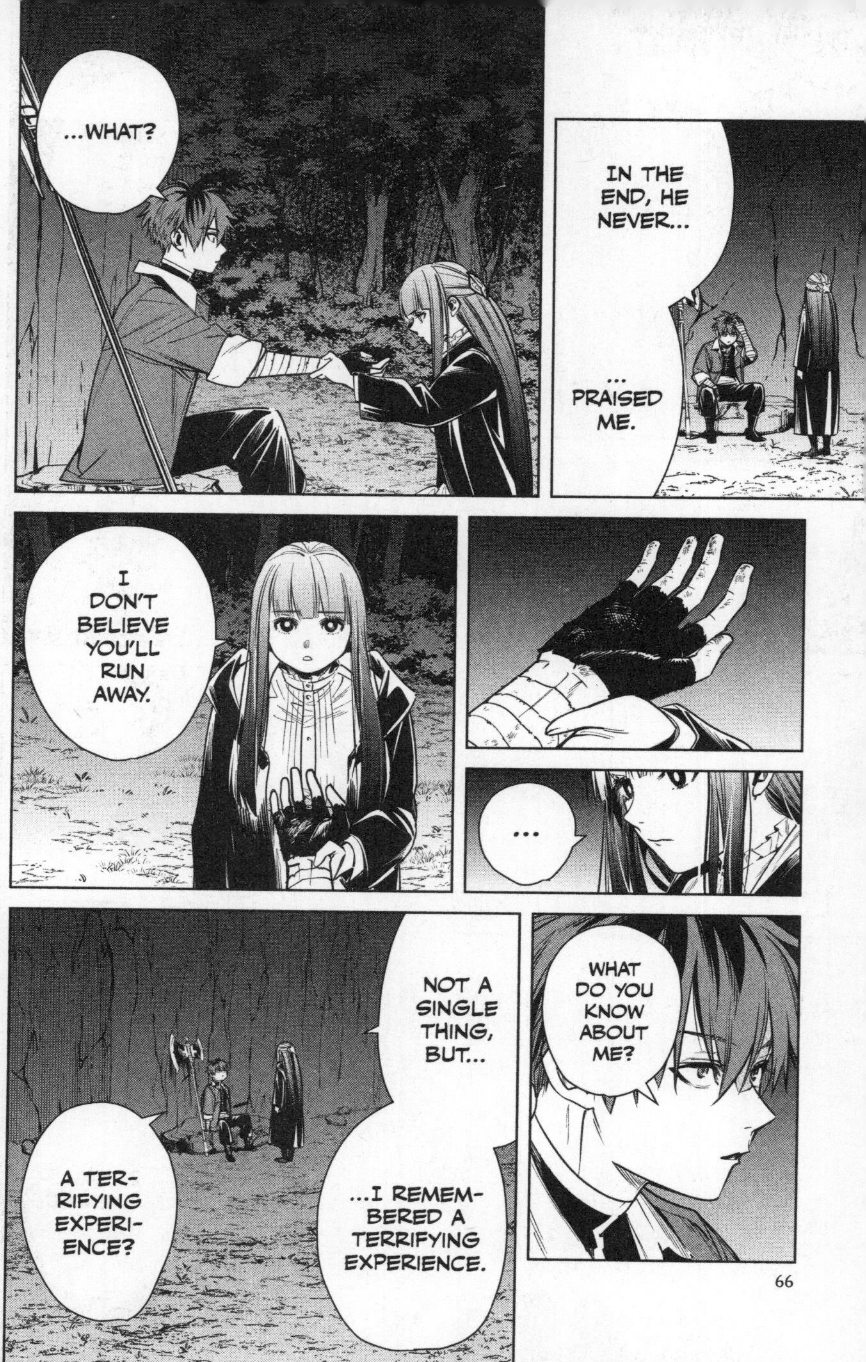
IN THE END, HE NEVER...
...PRAISED ME.
...WHAT?
...
I DON'T BELIEVE YOU'LL RUN AWAY.
WHAT DO YOU KNOW ABOUT ME?
NOT A SINGLE THING, BUT...
...I REMEMBERED A TERRIFYING EXPERIENCE.
A TERRIFYING EXPERIENCE?

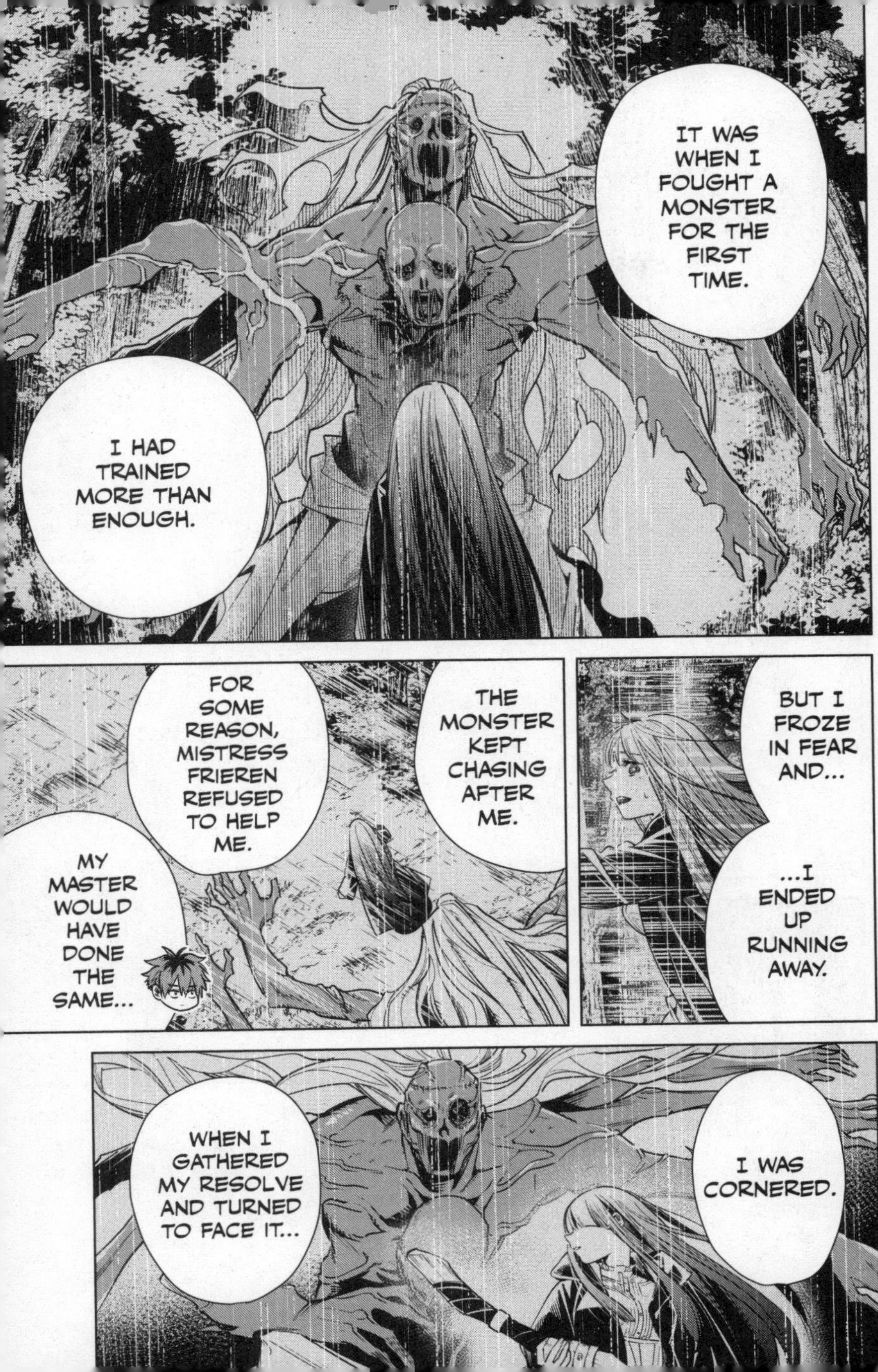
IT WAS WHEN I FOUGHT A MONSTER FOR THE FIRST TIME.
I HAD TRAINED MORE THAN ENOUGH.
BUT I FROZE IN FEAR AND...
...I ENDED UP RUNNING AWAY.
THE MONSTER KEPT CHASING AFTER ME.
FOR SOME REASON, MISTRESS FRIEREN REFUSED TO HELP ME.
MY MASTER WOULD HAVE DONE THE SAME...
I WAS CORNERED.
WHEN I GATHERED MY RESOLVE AND TURNED TO FACE IT...

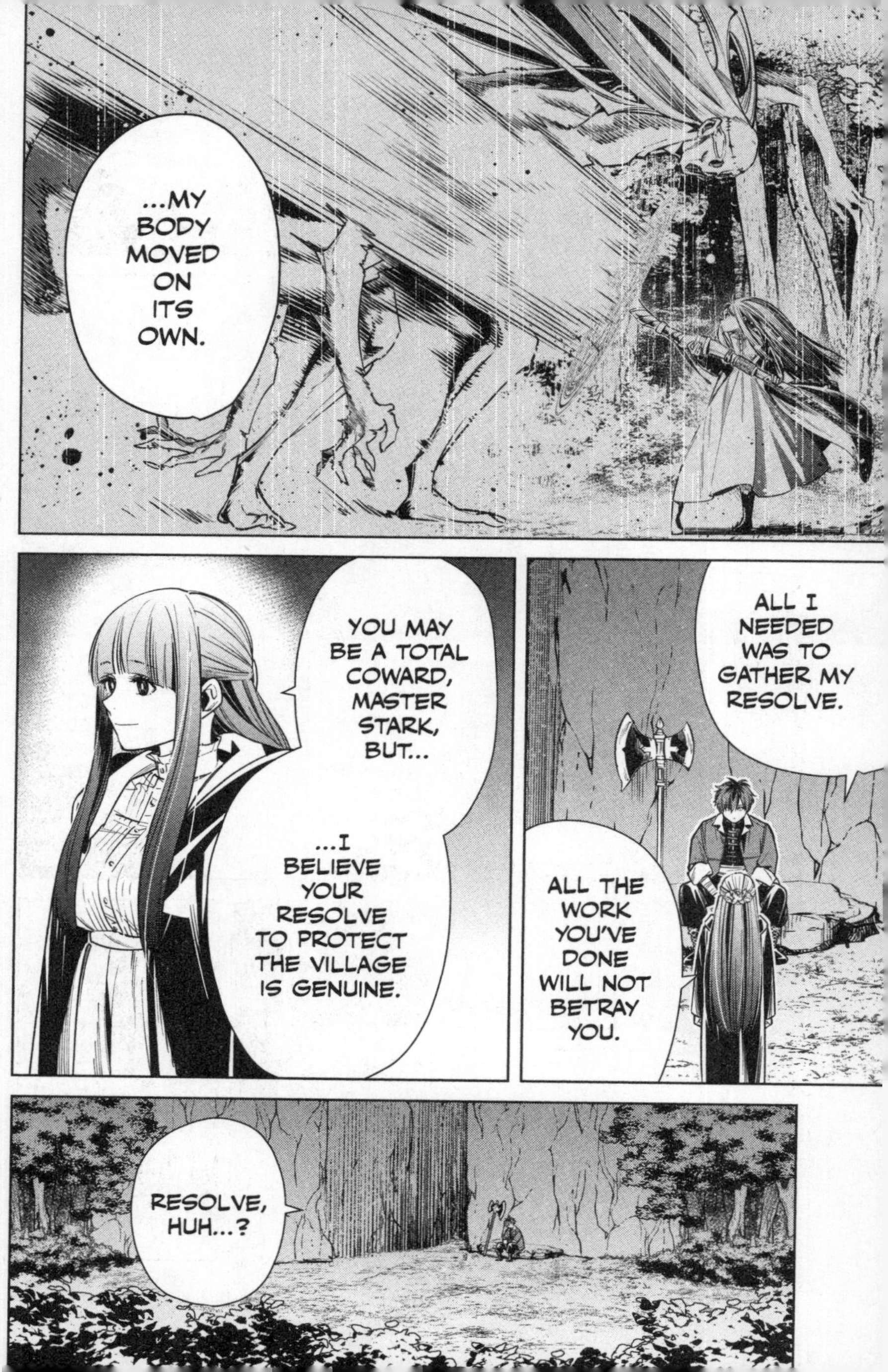
...MY BODY MOVED ON ITS OWN.
ALL I NEEDED WAS TO GATHER MY RESOLVE.
ALL THE WORK YOU'VE DONE WILL NOT BETRAY YOU.
YOU MAY BE A TOTAL COWARD, MASTER STARK, BUT...
...I BELIEVE YOUR RESOLVE TO PROTECT THE VILLAGE IS GENUINE.
RESOLVE, HUH...?

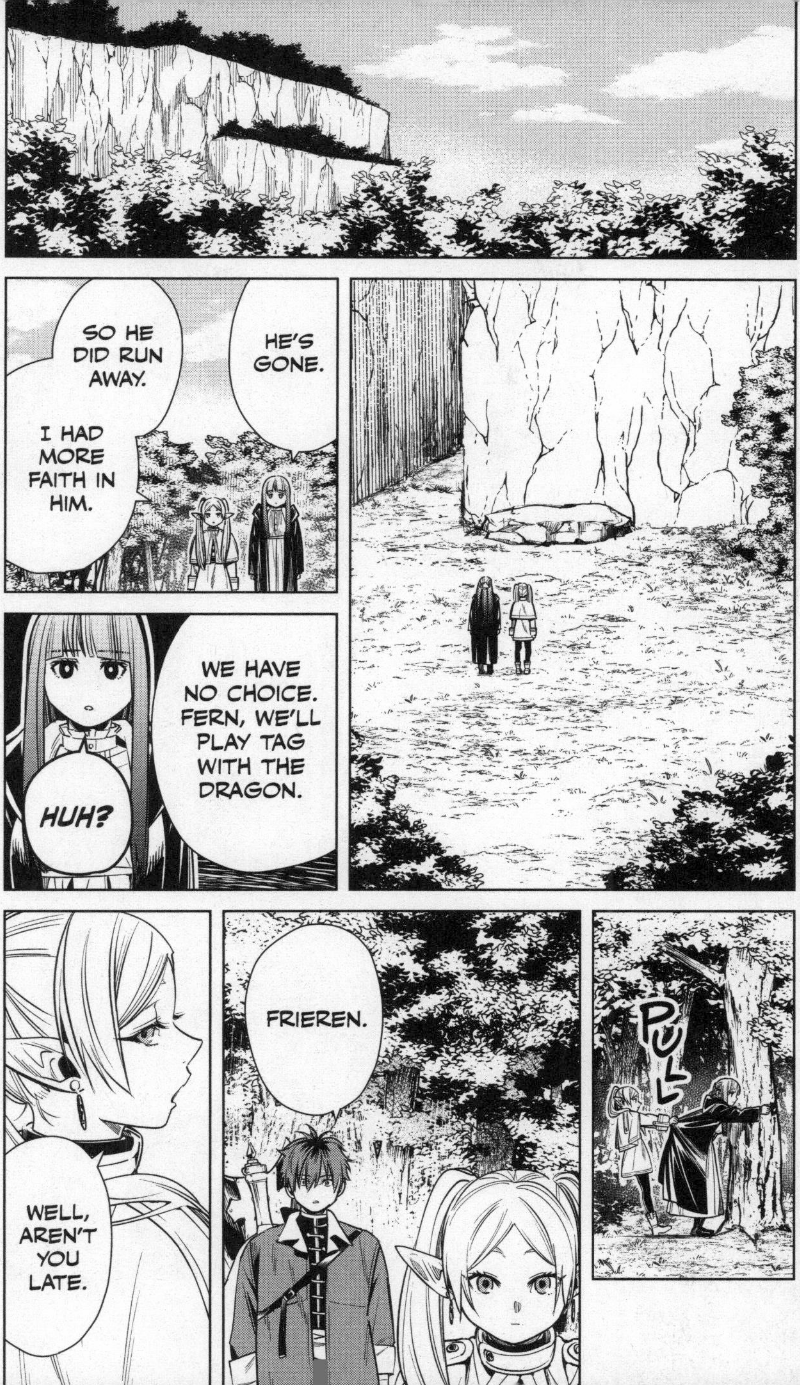
HE'S GONE.
SO HE DID RUN AWAY.
I HAD MORE FAITH IN HIM.
WE HAVE NO CHOICE. FERN, WE'LL PLAY TAG WITH THE DRAGON.
HUH?
PULL
FRIEREN.
WELL, AREN'T YOU LATE.

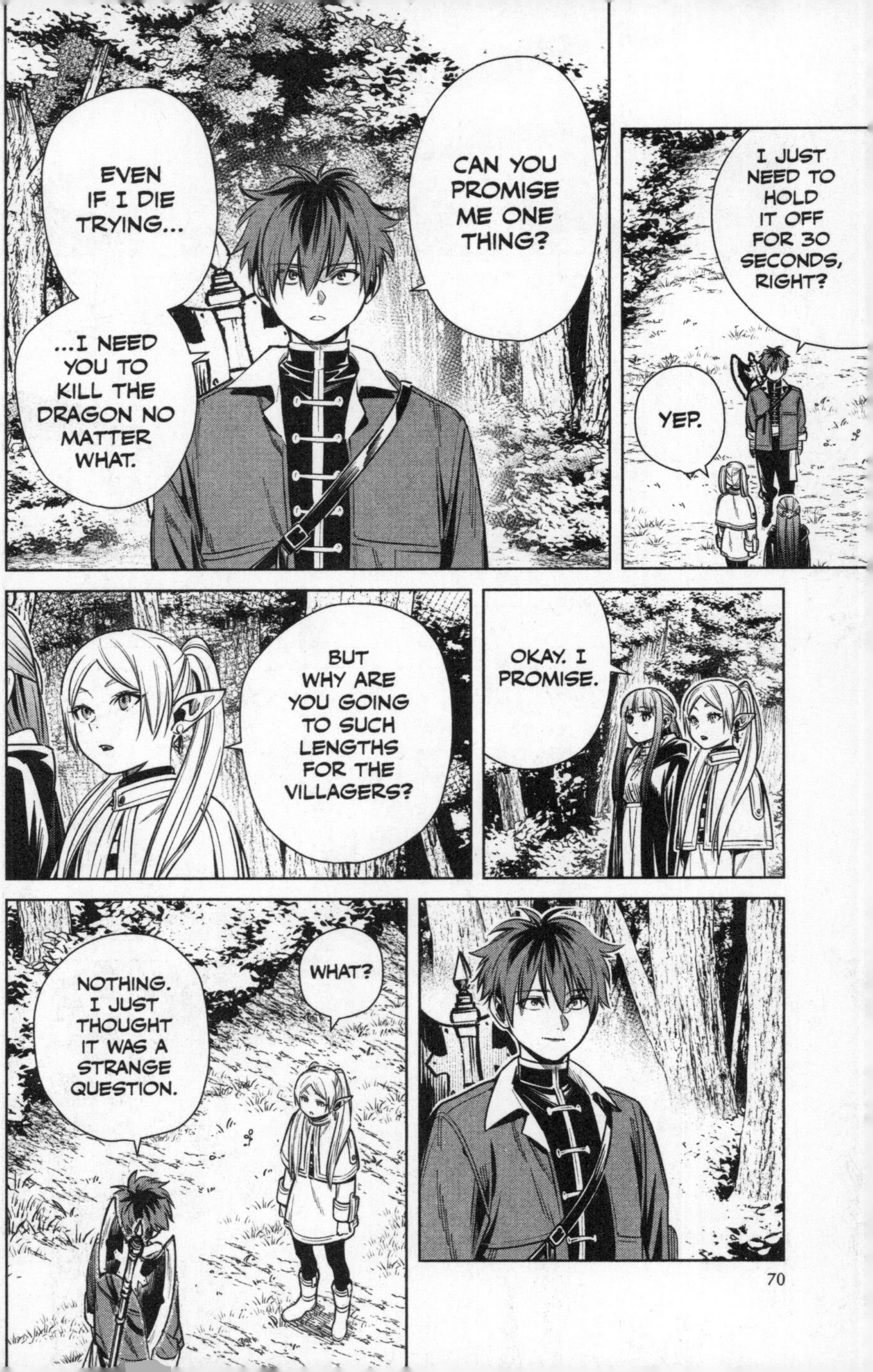
I JUST NEED TO HOLD IT OFF FOR 30 SECONDS, RIGHT?
YEP.
CAN YOU PROMISE ME ONE THING?
EVEN IF I DIE TRYING...
...I NEED YOU TO KILL THE DRAGON NO MATTER WHAT.
OKAY. I PROMISE.
BUT WHY ARE YOU GOING TO SUCH LENGTHS FOR THE VILLAGERS?
WHAT?
NOTHING. I JUST THOUGHT IT WAS A STRANGE QUESTION.

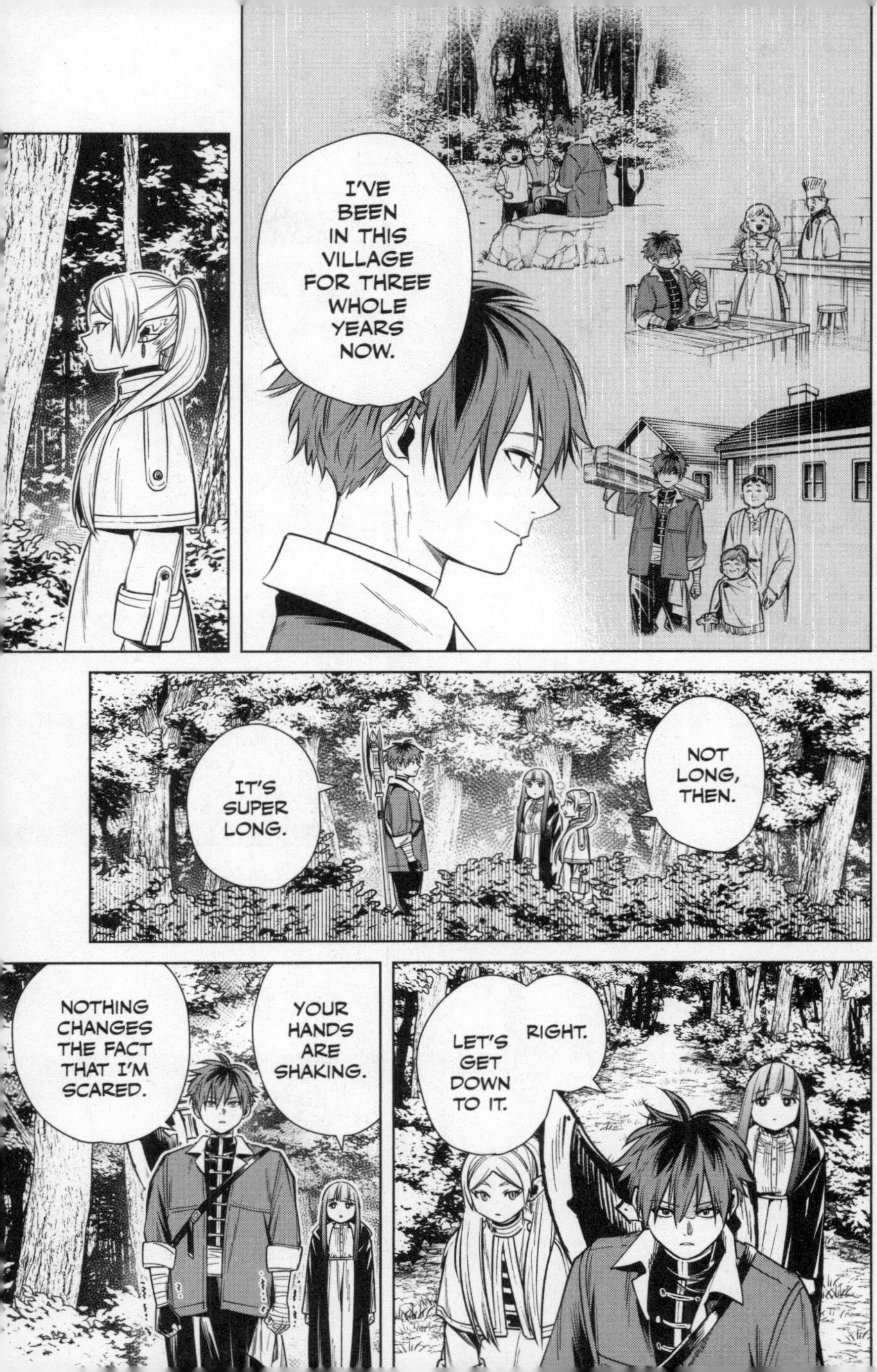
I'VE BEEN IN THIS VILLAGE FOR THREE WHOLE YEARS NOW.
NOT LONG, THEN.
IT'S SUPER LONG.
RIGHT.
LET'S GET DOWN TO IT.
YOUR HANDS ARE SHAKING.
NOTHING CHANGES THE FACT THAT I'M SCARED.

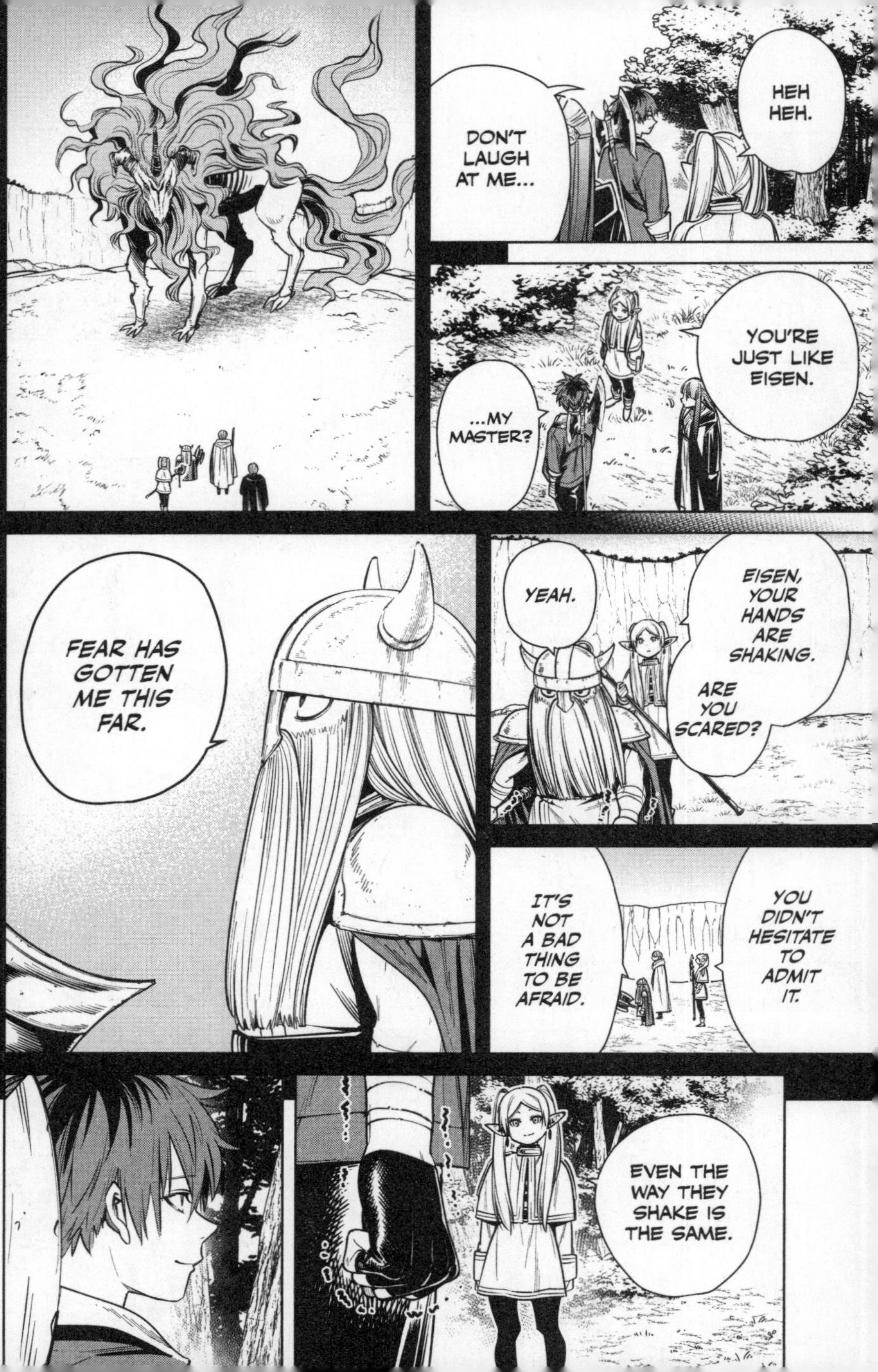
HEH HEH.
DON'T LAUGH AT ME...
YOU'RE JUST LIKE EISEN.
...MY MASTER?
EISEN, YOUR HANDS ARE SHAKING.
ARE YOU SCARED?
YEAH.
YOU DIDN'T HESITATE TO ADMIT IT.
IT'S NOT A BAD THING TO BE AFRAID.
FEAR HAS GOTTEN ME THIS FAR.
EVEN THE WAY THEY SHAKE IS THE SAME.

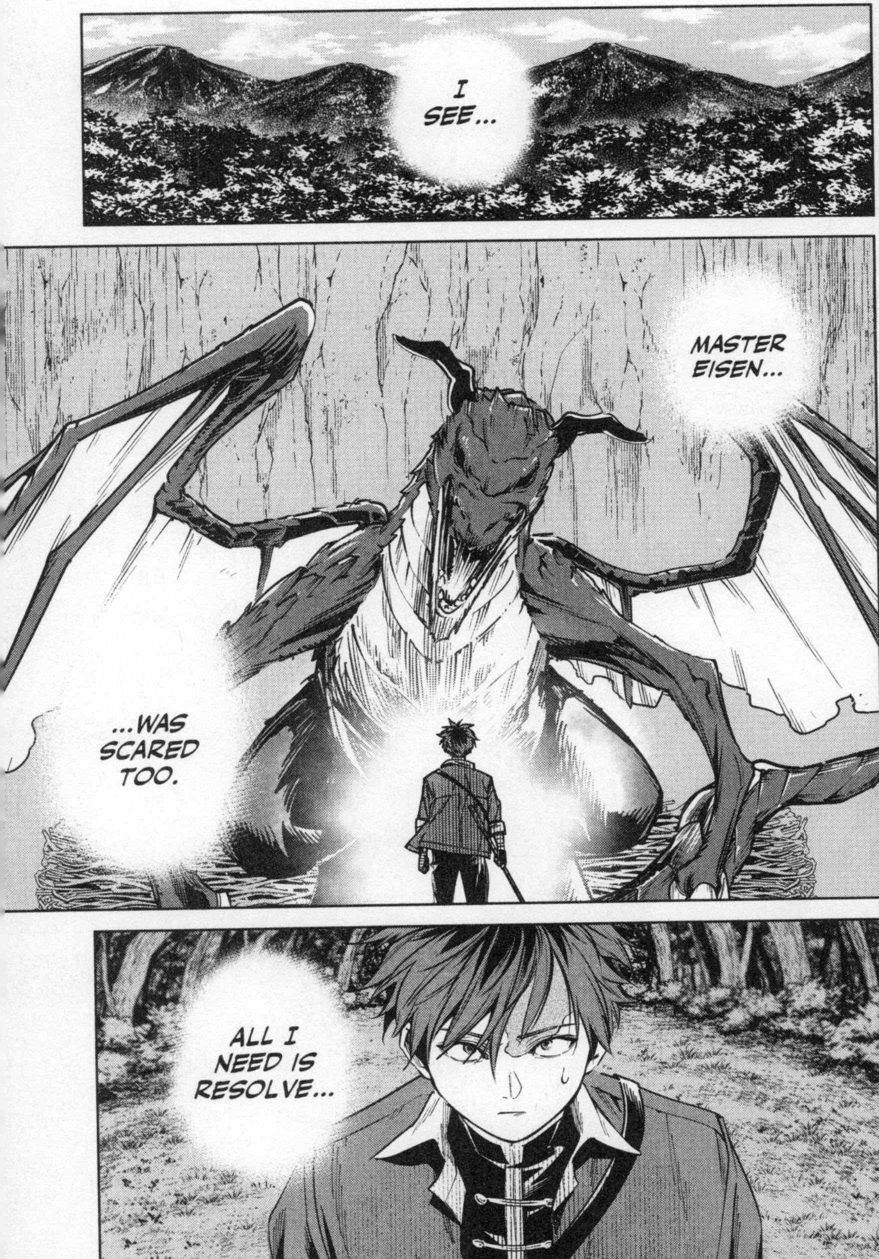
I SEE...
MASTER EISEN...
...WAS SCARED TOO.
ALL I NEED IS RESOLVE...

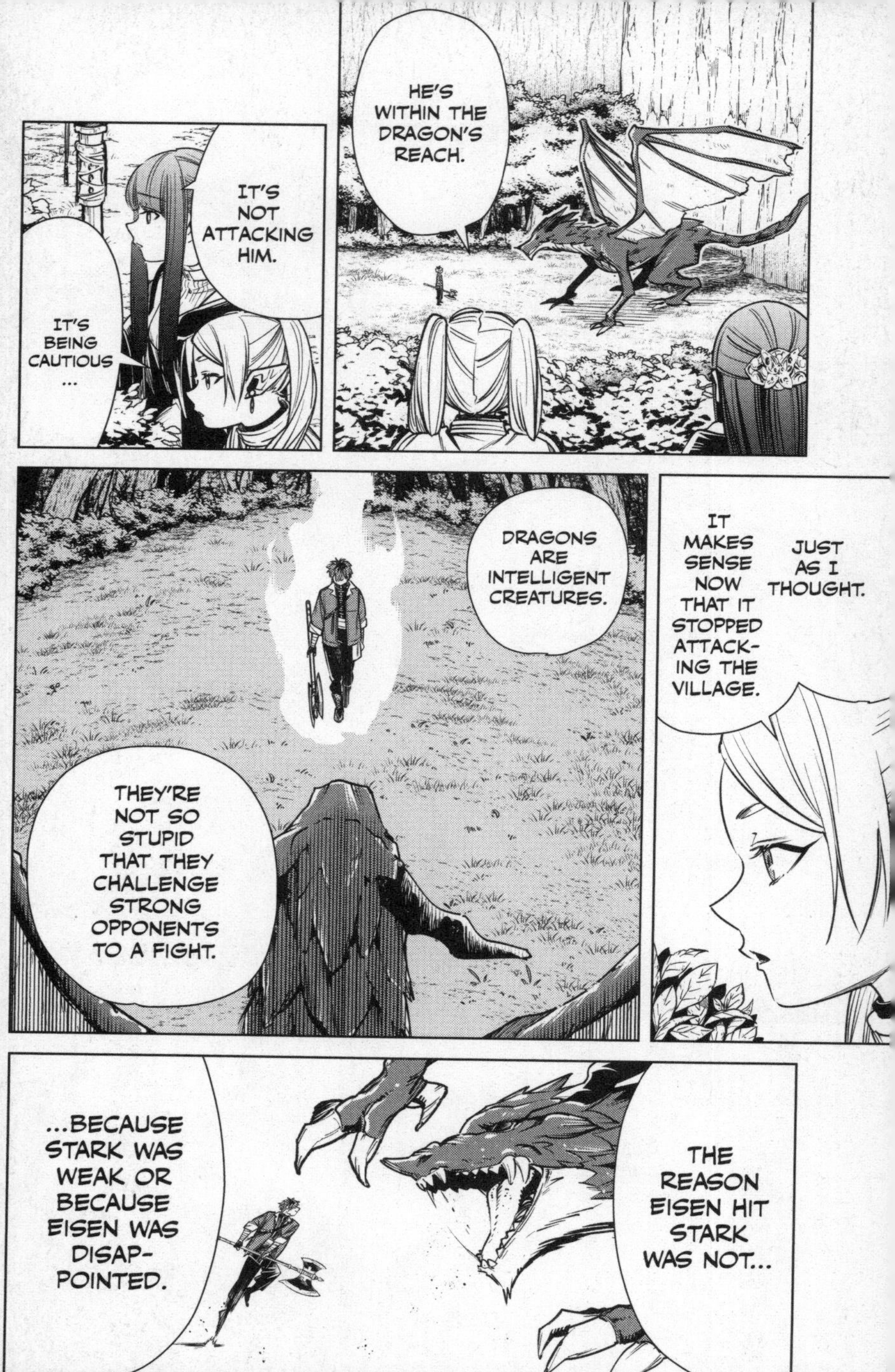
HE'S WITHIN THE DRAGON'S REACH.
IT'S NOT ATTACKING HIM.
IT'S BEING CAUTIOUS ...
JUST AS I THOUGHT.
IT MAKES SENSE NOW THAT IT STOPPED ATTACK-ING THE VILLAGE.
DRAGONS ARE INTELLIGENT CREATURES.
THEY'RE NOT SO STUPID THAT THEY CHALLENGE STRONG OPPONENTS TO A FIGHT.
THE REASON EISEN HIT STARK WAS NOT...
...BECAUSE STARK WAS WEAK OR BECAUSE EISEN WAS DISAP-POINTED.

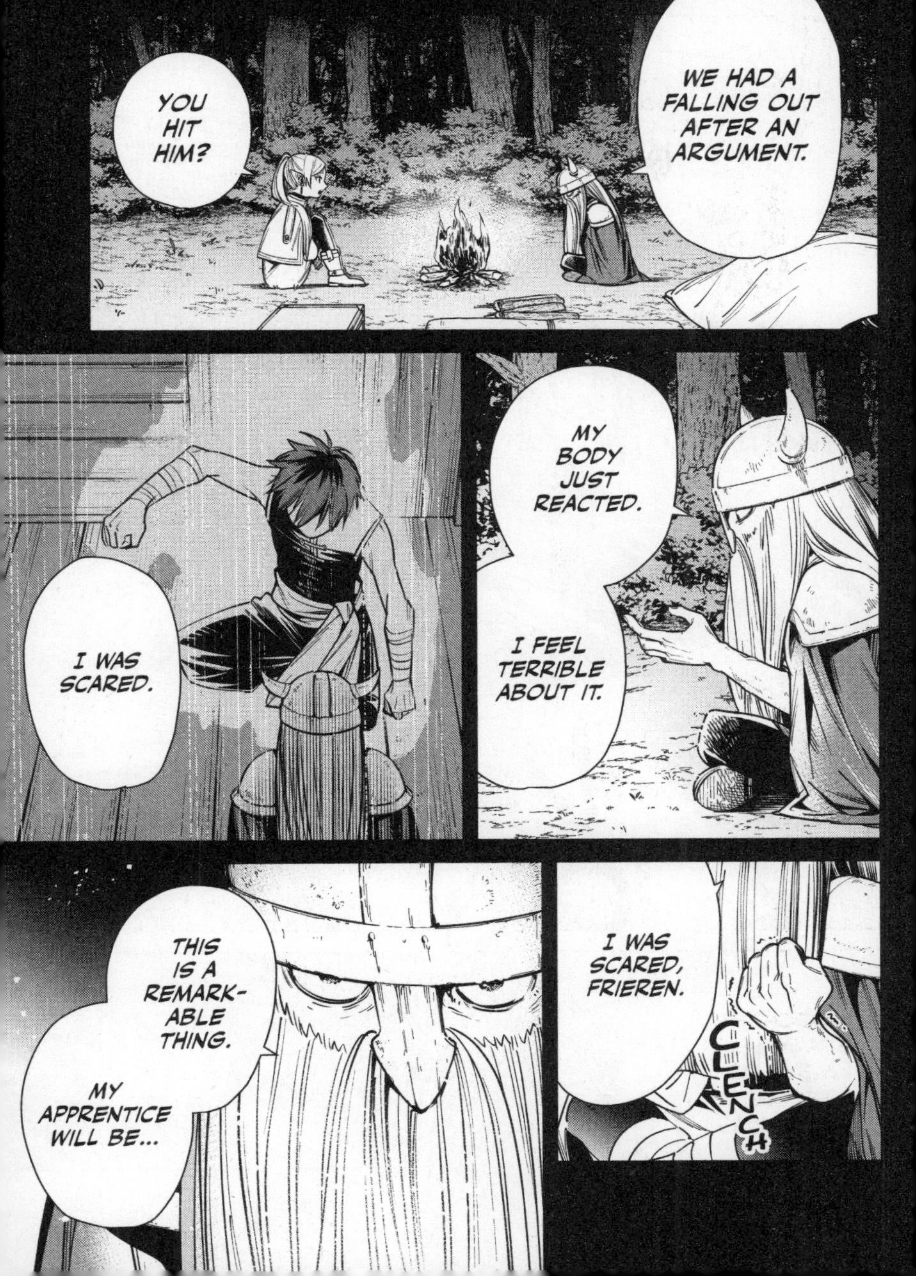
WE HAD A FALLING OUT AFTER AN ARGUMENT.
YOU HIT HIM?
MY BODY JUST REACTED.
I FEEL TERRIBLE ABOUT IT.
I WAS SCARED.
I WAS SCARED, FRIEREN.
CLENCH
THIS IS A REMARKABLE THING.
MY APPRENTICE WILL BE...

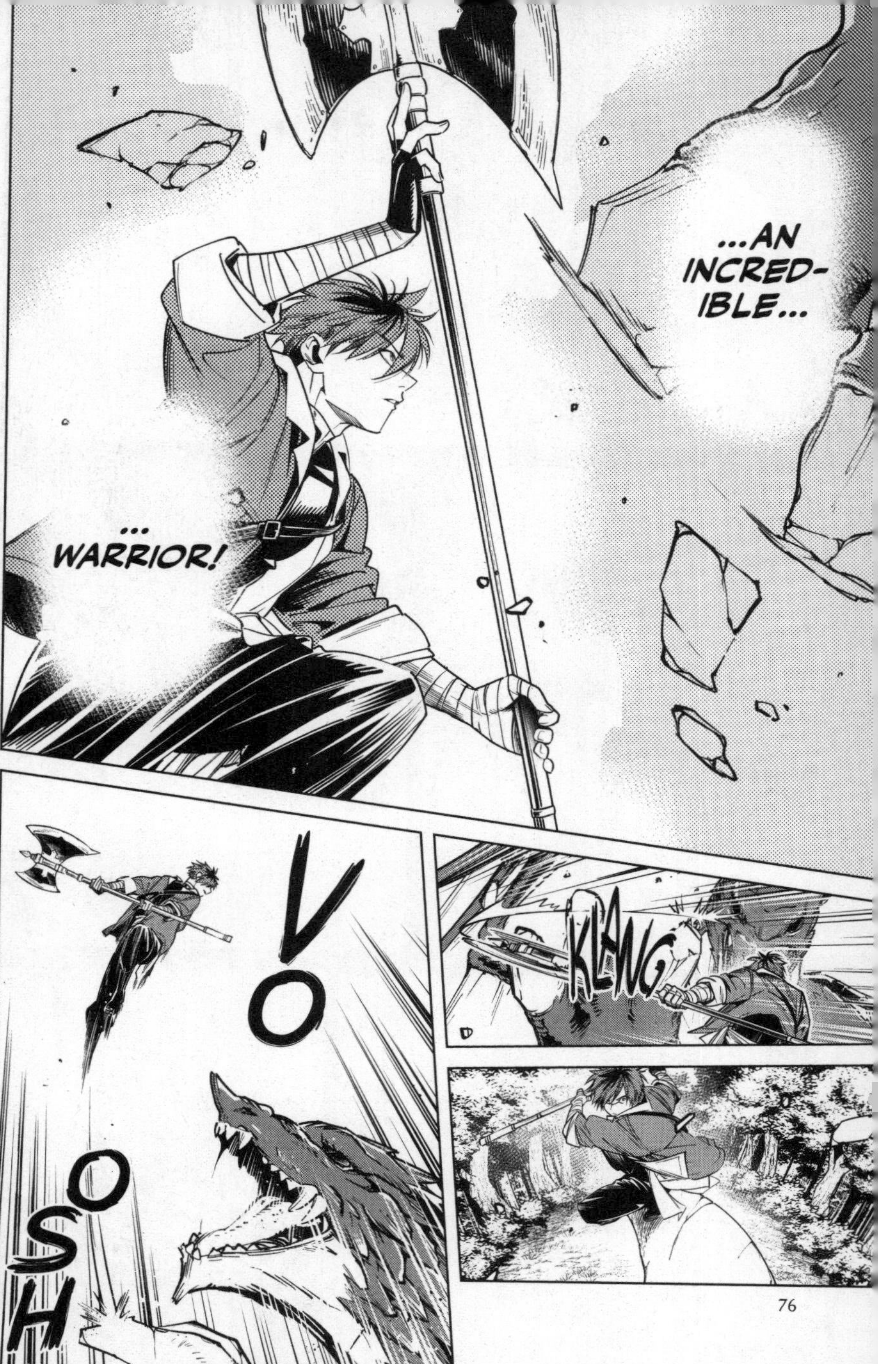
...AN INCREDIBLE...
...WARRIOR!
KLANG
VOOSH

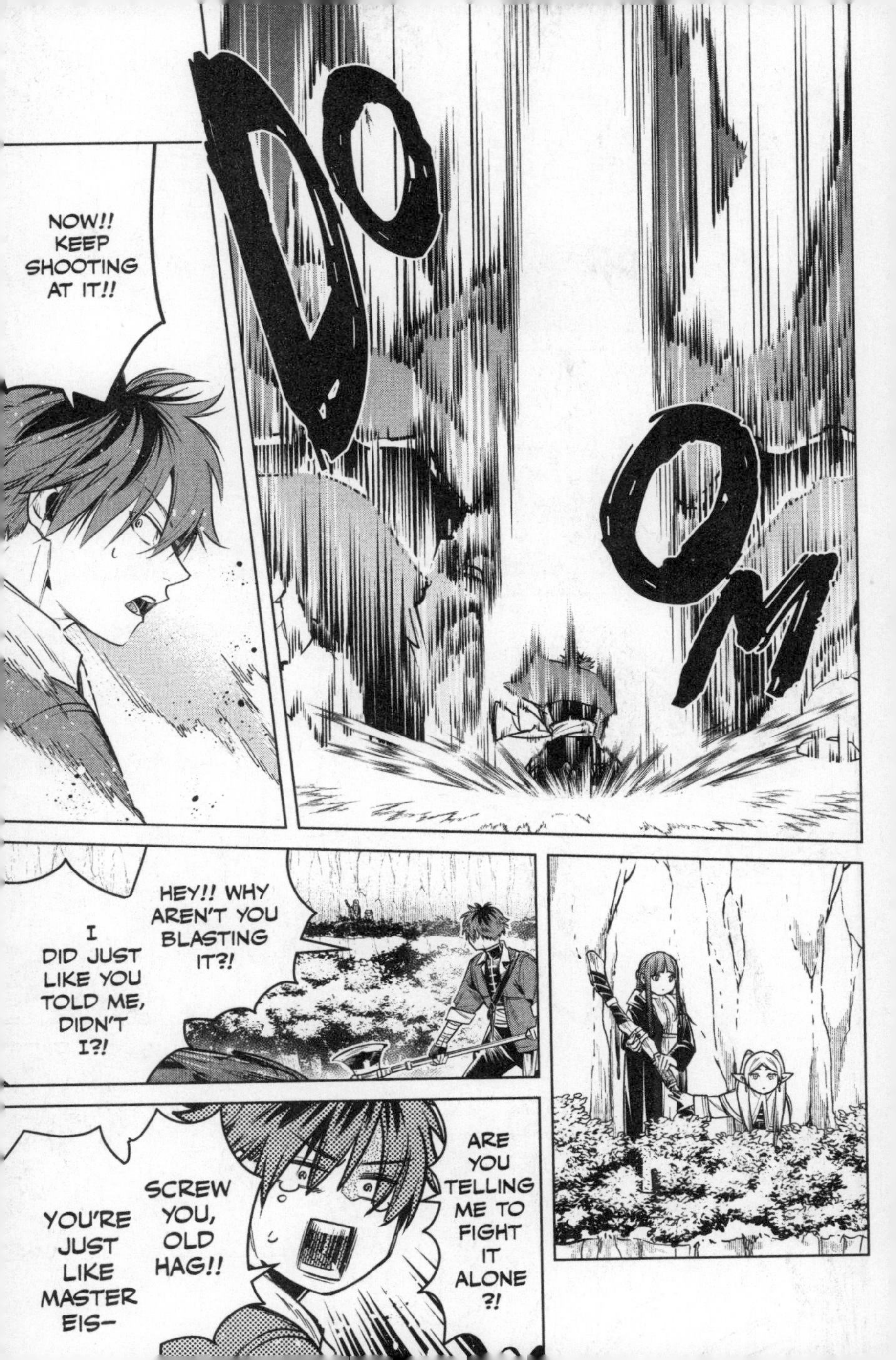
DOOM
NOW!! KEEP SHOOTING AT IT!!
HEY!! WHY AREN'T YOU BLASTING IT?!
I DID JUST LIKE YOU TOLD ME, DIDN'T I?!
ARE YOU TELLING ME TO FIGHT IT ALONE?!
SCREW YOU, OLD HAG!!
YOU'RE JUST LIKE MASTER EIS-

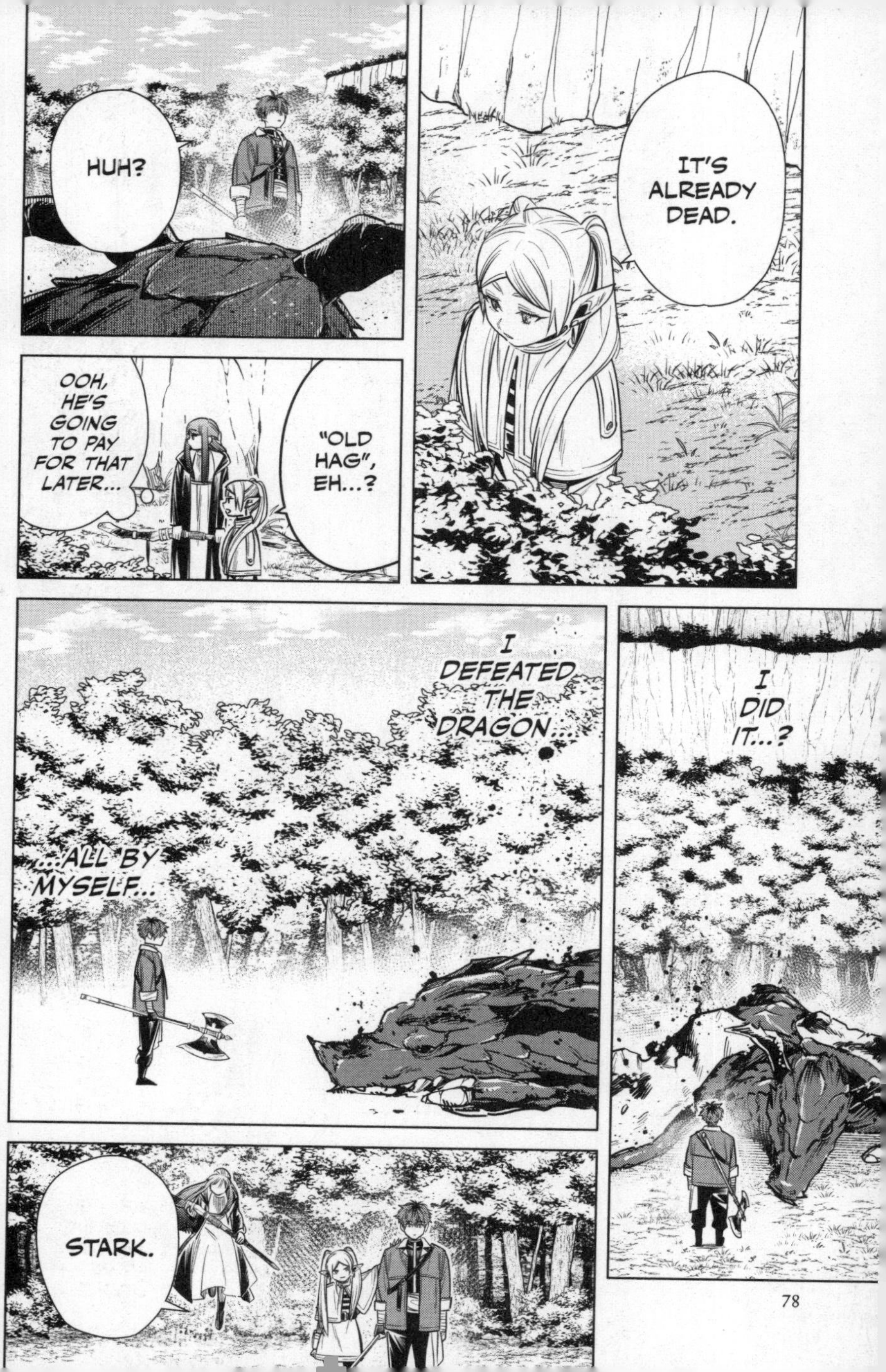
IT'S ALREADY DEAD.
HUH?
"OLD HAG", EH...?
OOH, HE'S GOING TO PAY FOR THAT LATER...
I DID IT...?
I DEFEATED THE DRAGON...
...ALL BY MYSELF...
STARK.

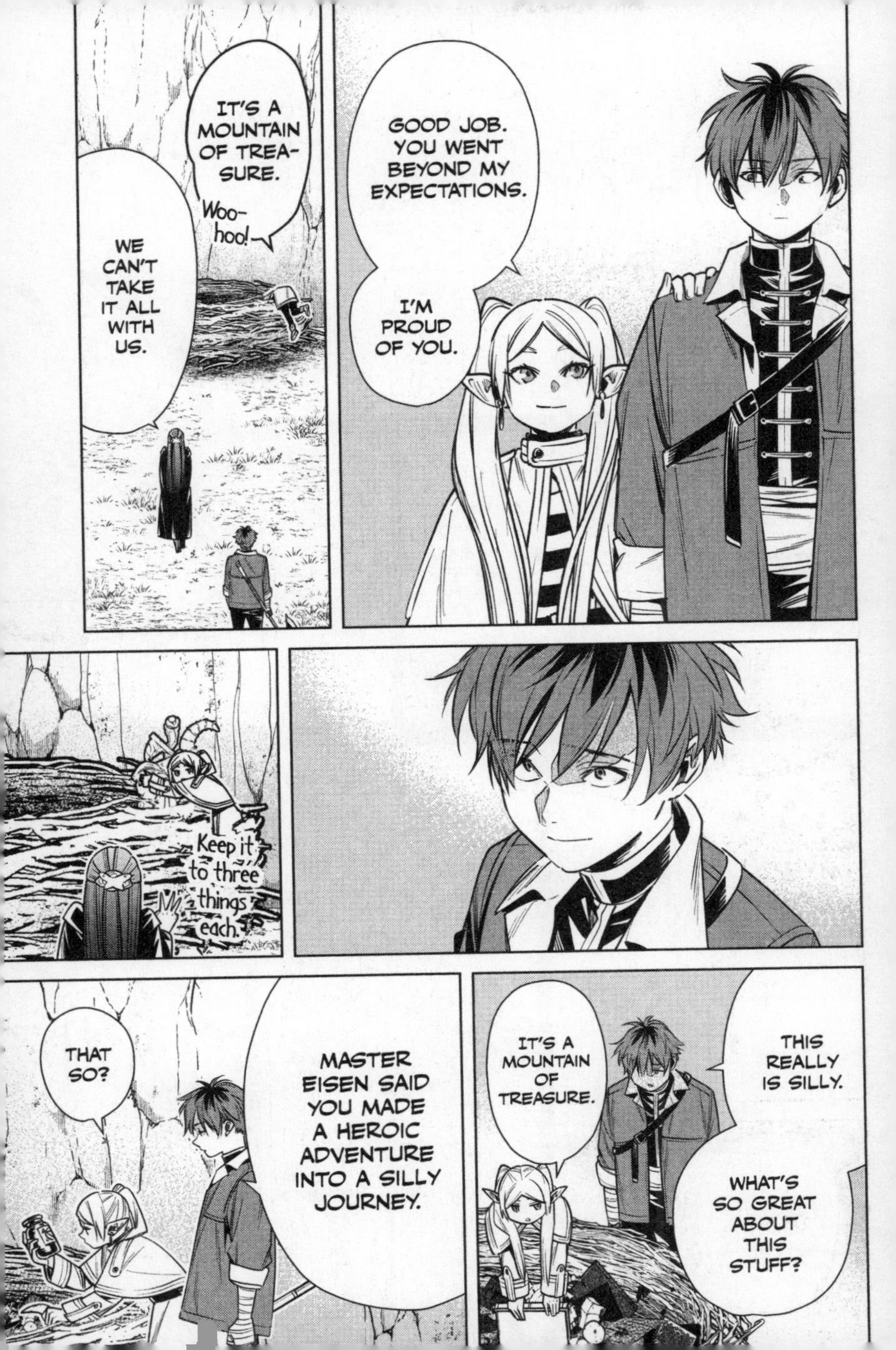
GOOD JOB. YOU WENT BEYOND MY EXPECTATIONS.
I'M PROUD OF YOU.
IT'S A MOUNTAIN OF TREA-SURE.
Woo-hoo!
WE CAN'T TAKE IT ALL WITH US.
Keep it to three things each.
THIS REALLY IS SILLY.
IT'S A MOUNTAIN OF TREASURE.
WHAT'S SO GREAT ABOUT THIS STUFF?
MASTER EISEN SAID YOU MADE A HEROIC ADVENTURE INTO A SILLY JOURNEY.
THAT SO?

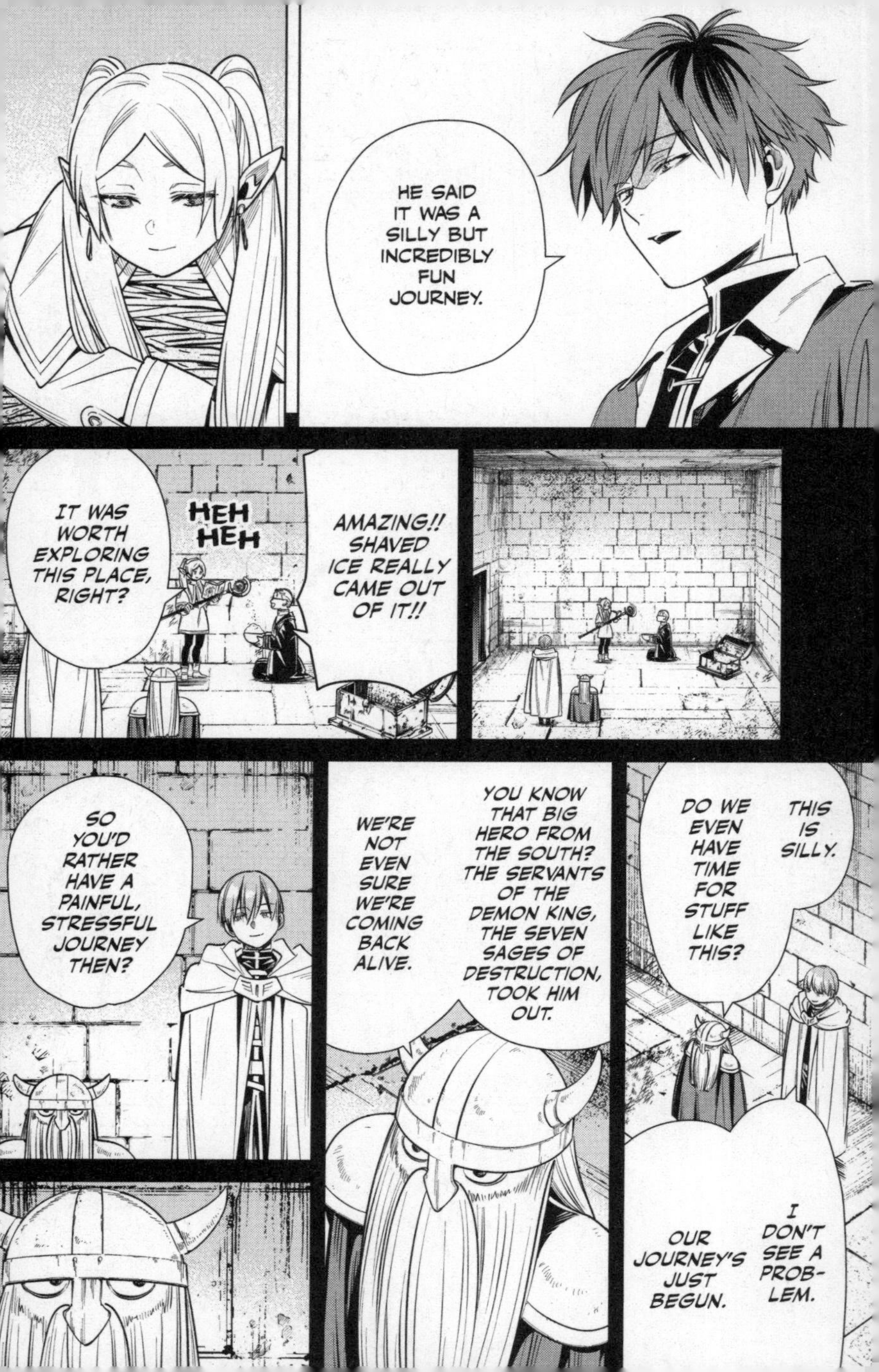
HE SAID IT WAS A SILLY BUT INCREDIBLY FUN JOURNEY.
AMAZING!! SHAVED ICE REALLY CAME OUT OF IT!!
HEH HEH
IT WAS WORTH EXPLORING THIS PLACE, RIGHT?
THIS IS SILLY.
DO WE EVEN HAVE TIME FOR STUFF LIKE THIS?
YOU KNOW THAT BIG HERO FROM THE SOUTH? THE SERVANTS OF THE DEMON KING, THE SEVEN SAGES OF DESTRUCTION, TOOK HIM OUT.
WE'RE NOT EVEN SURE WE'RE COMING BACK ALIVE.
SO YOU'D RATHER HAVE A PAINFUL, STRESSFUL JOURNEY THEN?
I DON'T SEE A PROBLEM.
OUR JOURNEY'S JUST BEGUN.

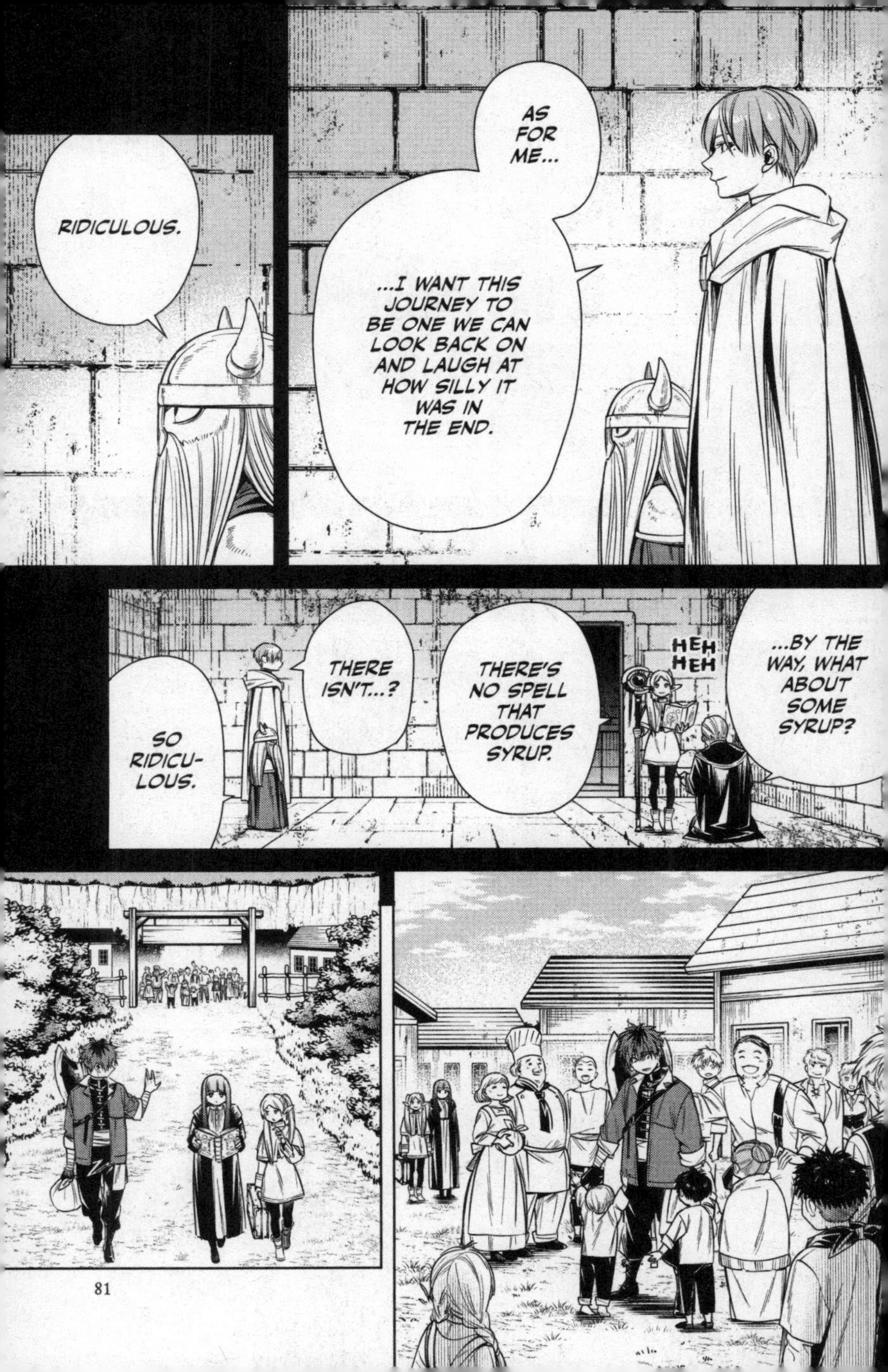
AS FOR ME...
...I WANT THIS JOURNEY TO BE ONE WE CAN LOOK BACK ON AND LAUGH AT HOW SILLY IT WAS IN THE END.
RIDICULOUS.
...BY THE WAY, WHAT ABOUT SOME SYRUP?
HEH HEH
THERE'S NO SPELL THAT PRODUCES SYRUP.
THERE ISN'T...?
SO RIDICU-LOUS.

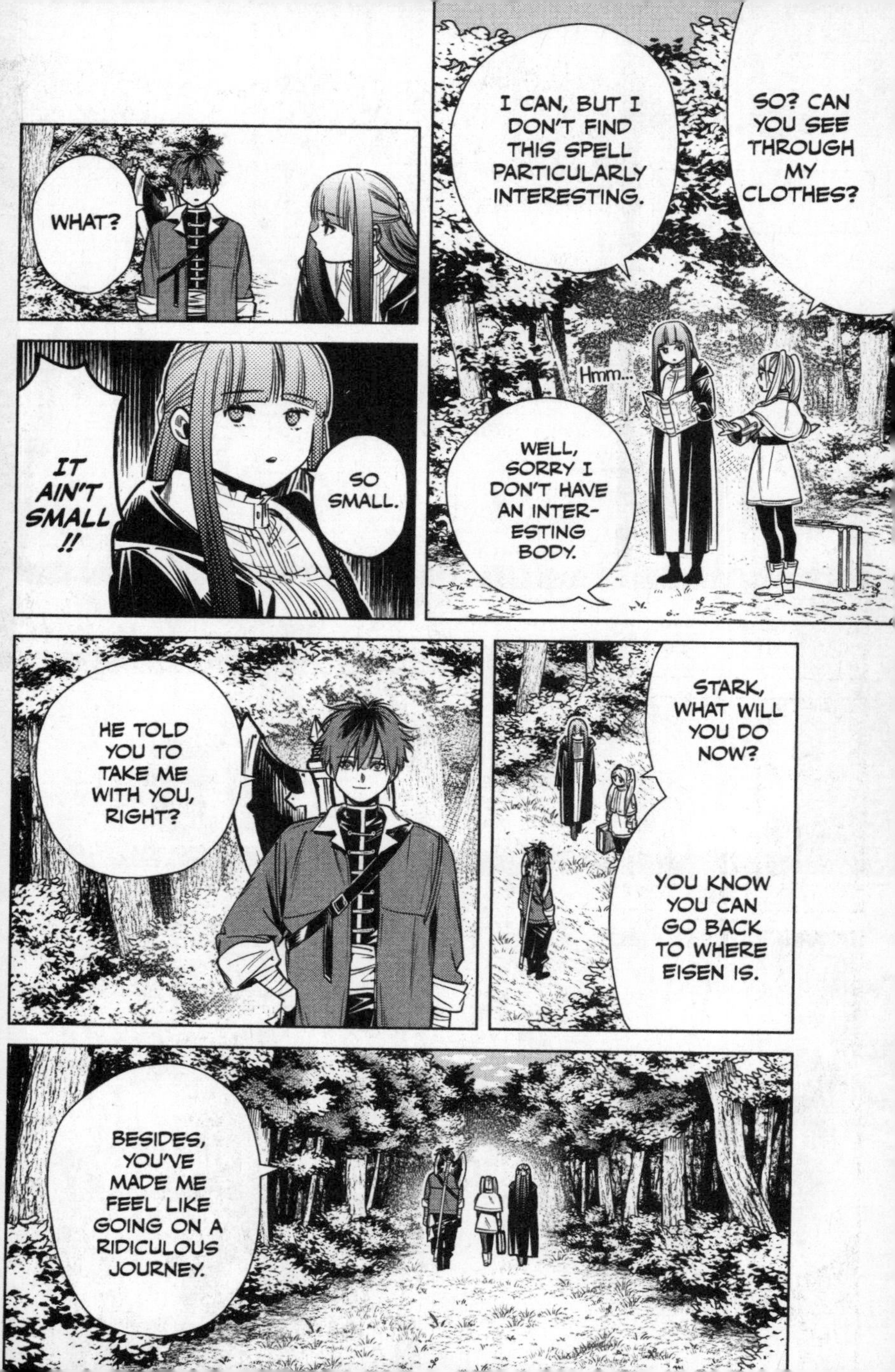
SO? CAN YOU SEE THROUGH MY CLOTHES?
I CAN, BUT I DON'T FIND THIS SPELL PARTICULARLY INTERESTING.
Hmm...
WELL, SORRY I DON'T HAVE AN INTER-ESTING BODY.
WHAT?
SO SMALL.
IT AIN'T SMALL!!
STARK, WHAT WILL YOU DO NOW?
YOU KNOW YOU CAN GO BACK TO WHERE EISEN IS.
HE TOLD YOU TO TAKE ME WITH YOU, RIGHT?
BESIDES, YOU'VE MADE ME FEEL LIKE GOING ON A RIDICULOUS JOURNEY.

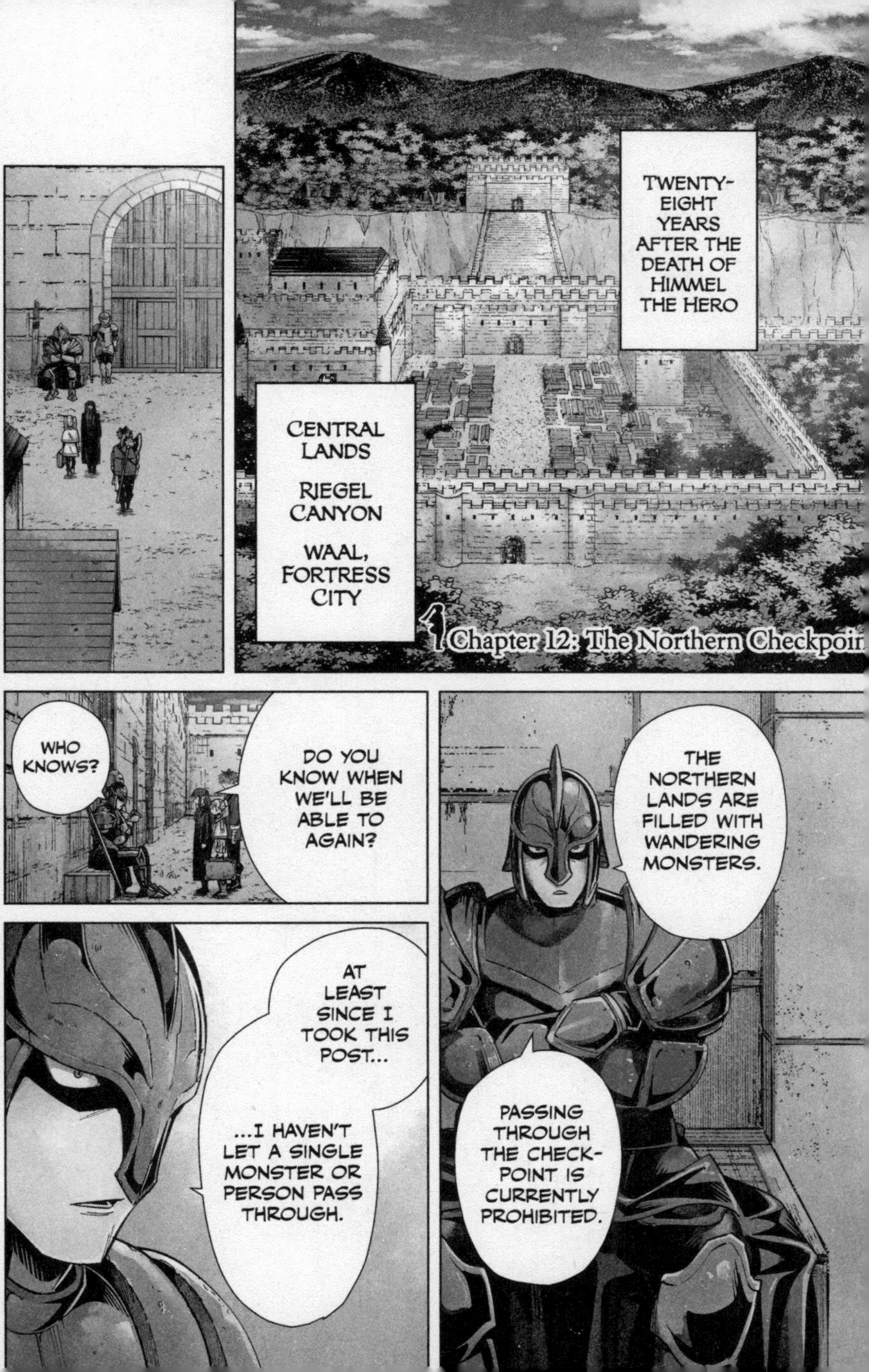
TWENTY-EIGHT YEARS AFTER THE DEATH OF HIMMEL THE HERO
CENTRAL LANDS
RIEGEL CANYON
WAAL, FORTRESS CITY
Chapter 12: The Northern Checkpoin
THE NORTHERN LANDS ARE FILLED WITH WANDERING MONSTERS.
PASSING THROUGH THE CHECK-POINT IS CURRENTLY PROHIBITED.
DO YOU KNOW WHEN WE'LL BE ABLE TO AGAIN?
WHO KNOWS?
AT LEAST SINCE I TOOK THIS POST...
...I HAVEN'T LET A SINGLE MONSTER OR PERSON PASS THROUGH.

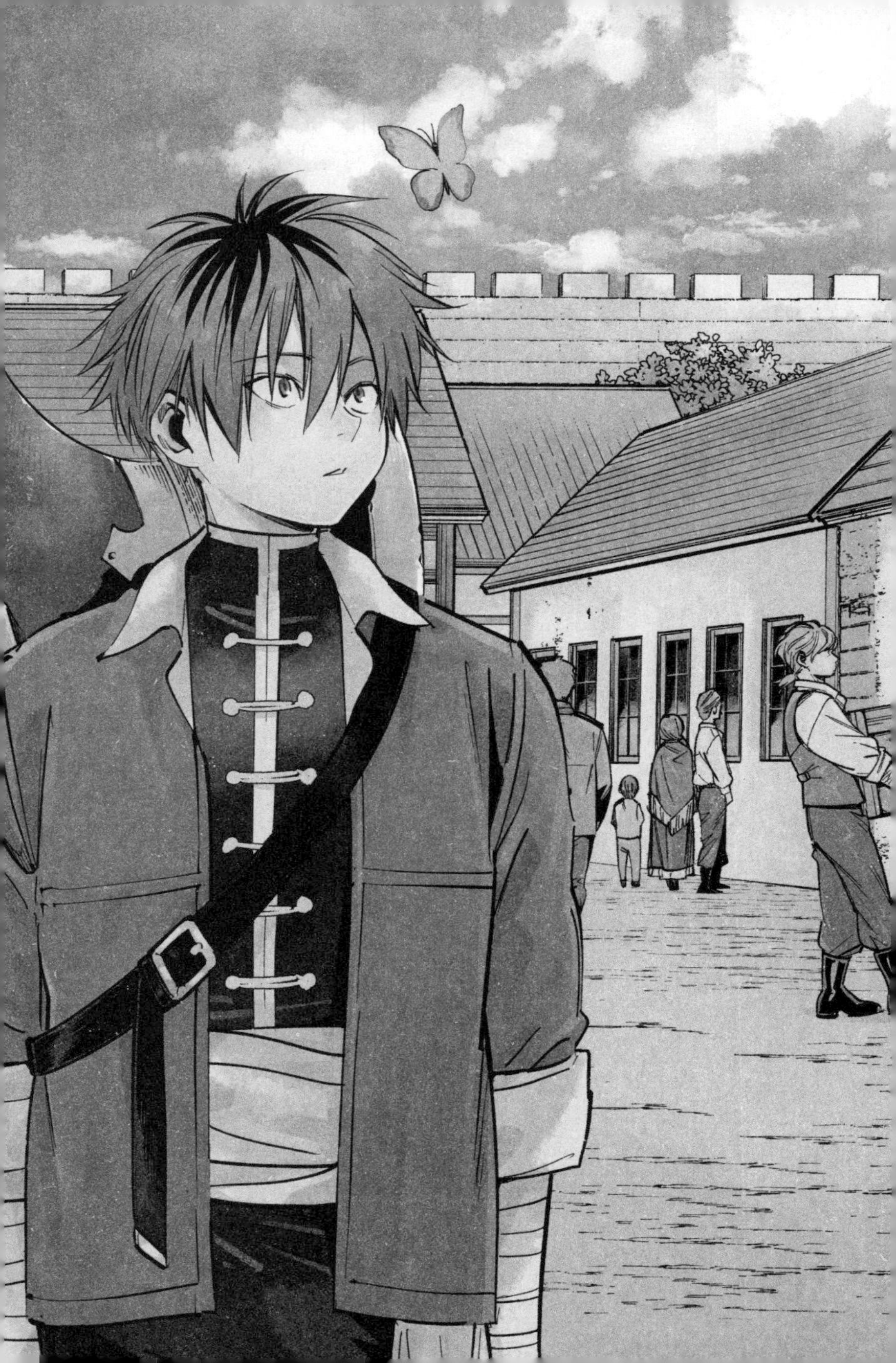

Chapter 12: The Northern Checkpoint

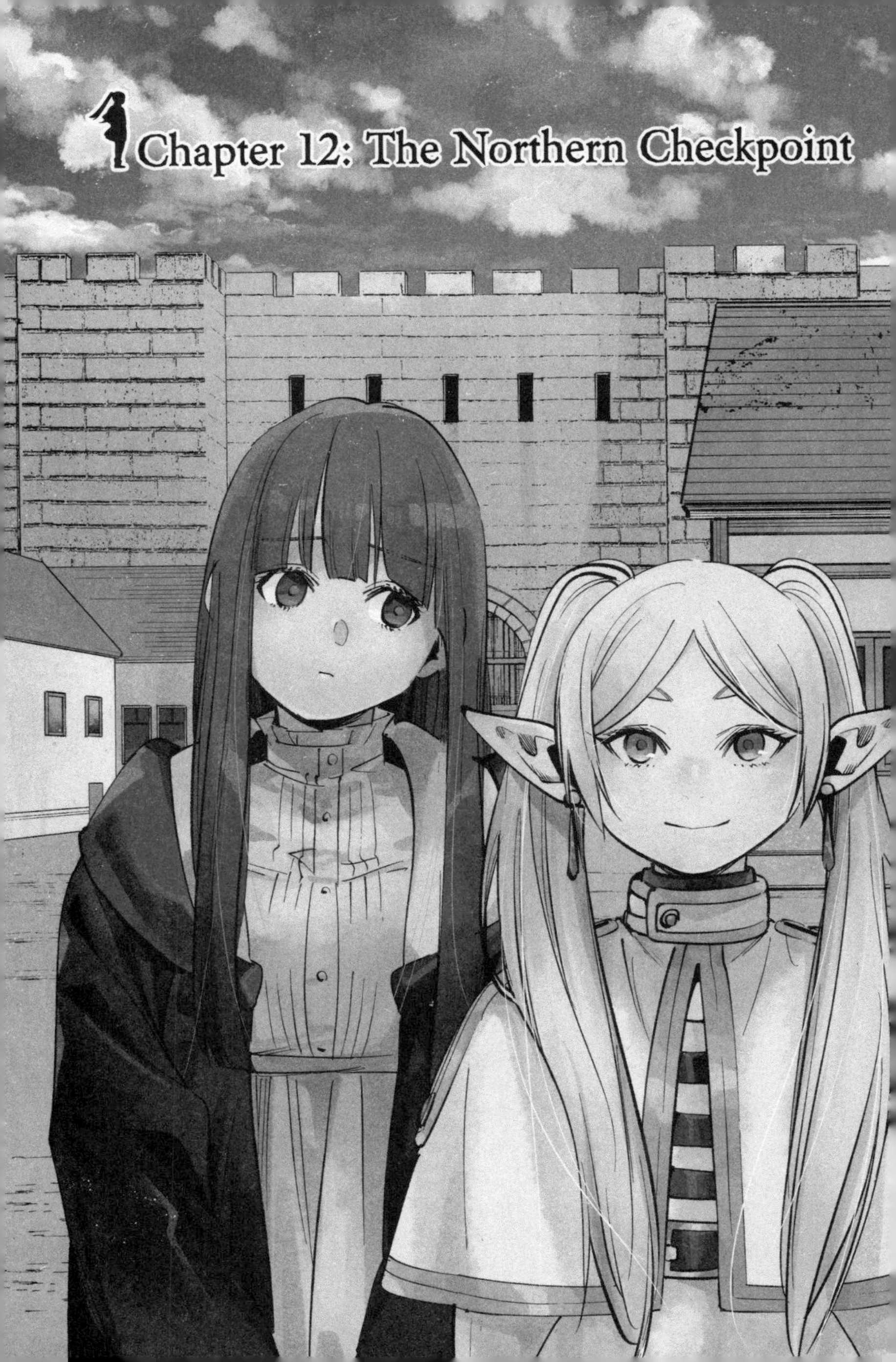

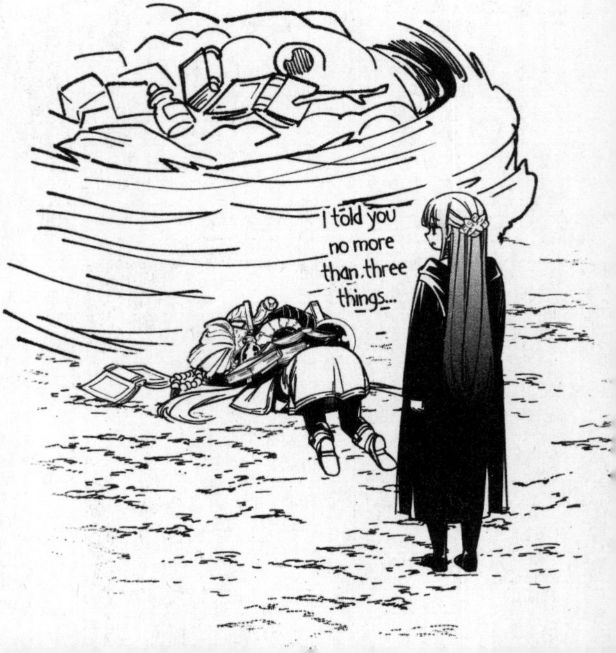
I told you no more than three things...

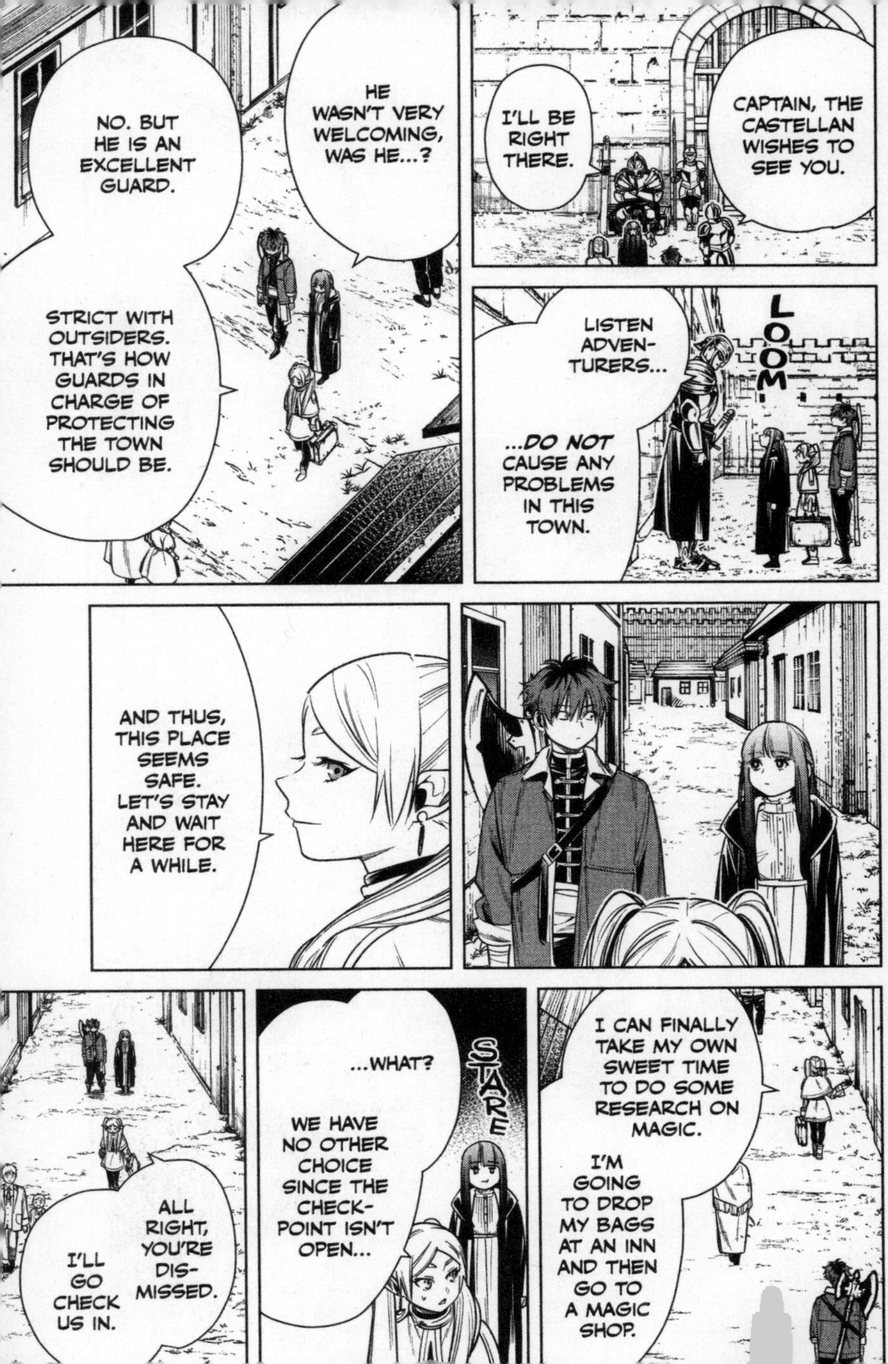

CAPTAIN, THE CASTELLAN WISHES TO SEE YOU.
I'LL BE RIGHT THERE.
LOOM
LISTEN ADVENTURERS...
...DO NOT CAUSE ANY PROBLEMS IN THIS TOWN.
HE WASN'T VERY WELCOMING, WAS HE...?
NO. BUT HE IS AN EXCELLENT GUARD.
STRICT WITH OUTSIDERS. THAT'S HOW GUARDS IN CHARGE OF PROTECTING THE TOWN SHOULD BE.
AND THUS, THIS PLACE SEEMS SAFE. LET'S STAY AND WAIT HERE FOR A WHILE.
I CAN FINALLY TAKE MY OWN SWEET TIME TO DO SOME RESEARCH ON MAGIC.
I'M GOING TO DROP MY BAGS AT AN INN AND THEN GO TO A MAGIC SHOP.
STARE
...WHAT?
WE HAVE NO OTHER CHOICE SINCE THE CHECKPOINT ISN'T OPEN...
ALL RIGHT, YOU'RE DISMISSED.
I'LL GO CHECK US IN.

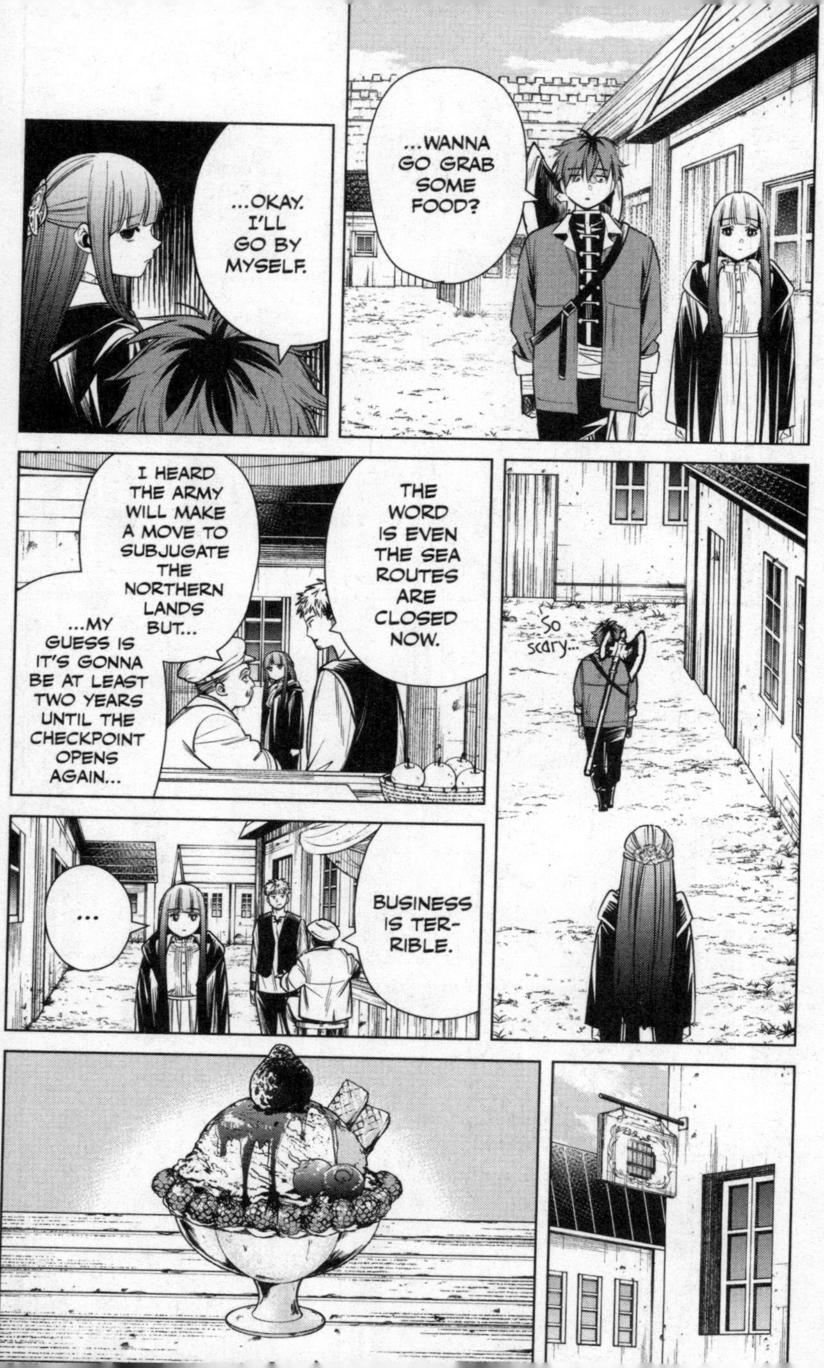
...WANNA GO GRAB SOME FOOD?
...OKAY. I'LL GO BY MYSELF.
So scary...
THE WORD IS EVEN THE SEA ROUTES ARE CLOSED NOW.
I HEARD THE ARMY WILL MAKE A MOVE TO SUBJUGATE THE NORTHERN LANDS BUT...
...MY GUESS IS IT'S GONNA BE AT LEAST TWO YEARS UNTIL THE CHECKPOINT OPENS AGAIN...
BUSINESS IS TER-RIBLE.
...

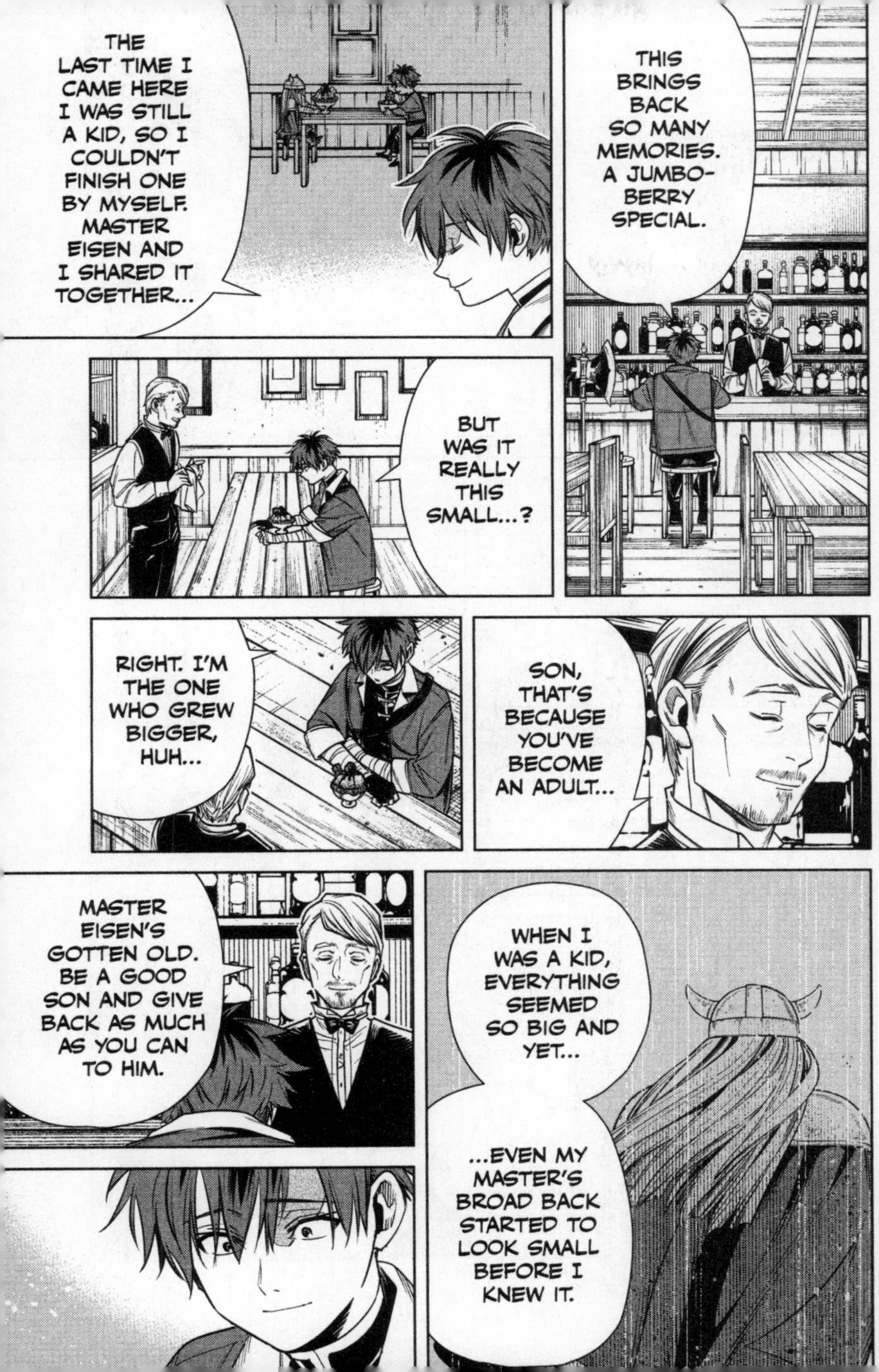
THIS BRINGS BACK SO MANY MEMORIES. A JUMBO-BERRY SPECIAL.
THE LAST TIME I CAME HERE I WAS STILL A KID, SO I COULDN'T FINISH ONE BY MYSELF. MASTER EISEN AND I SHARED IT TOGETHER...
BUT WAS IT REALLY THIS SMALL...?
SON, THAT'S BECAUSE YOU'VE BECOME AN ADULT...
RIGHT. I'M THE ONE WHO GREW BIGGER, HUH...
WHEN I WAS A KID, EVERYTHING SEEMED SO BIG AND YET...
...EVEN MY MASTER'S BROAD BACK STARTED TO LOOK SMALL BEFORE I KNEW IT.
MASTER EISEN'S GOTTEN OLD. BE A GOOD SON AND GIVE BACK AS MUCH AS YOU CAN TO HIM.

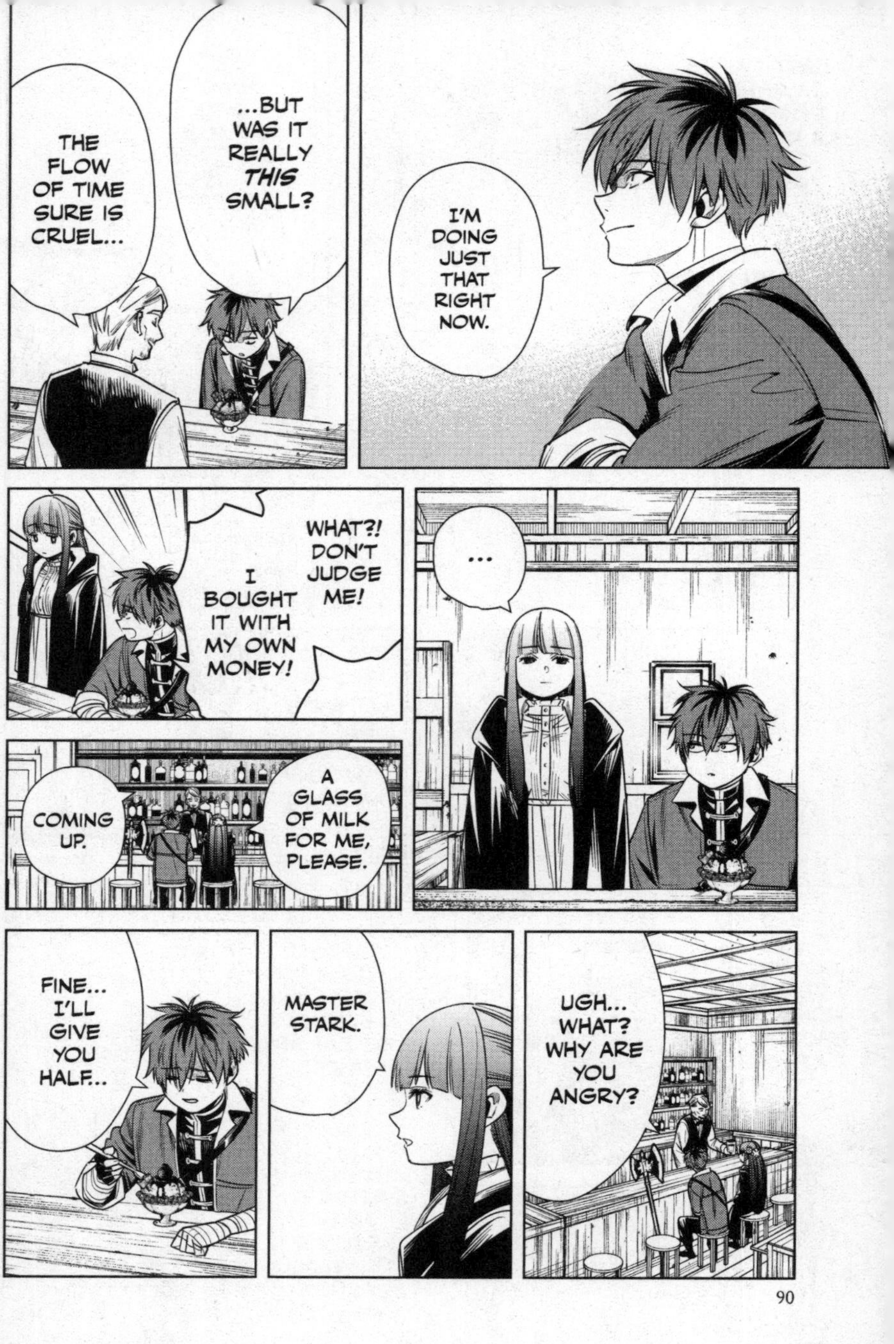
I'M DOING JUST THAT RIGHT NOW.
...BUT WAS IT REALLY *THIS* SMALL?
THE FLOW OF TIME SURE IS CRUEL...
...
WHAT?! DON'T JUDGE ME!
I BOUGHT IT WITH MY OWN MONEY!
A GLASS OF MILK FOR ME, PLEASE.
COMING UP.
UGH... WHAT? WHY ARE YOU ANGRY?
MASTER STARK.
FINE... I'LL GIVE YOU HALF...

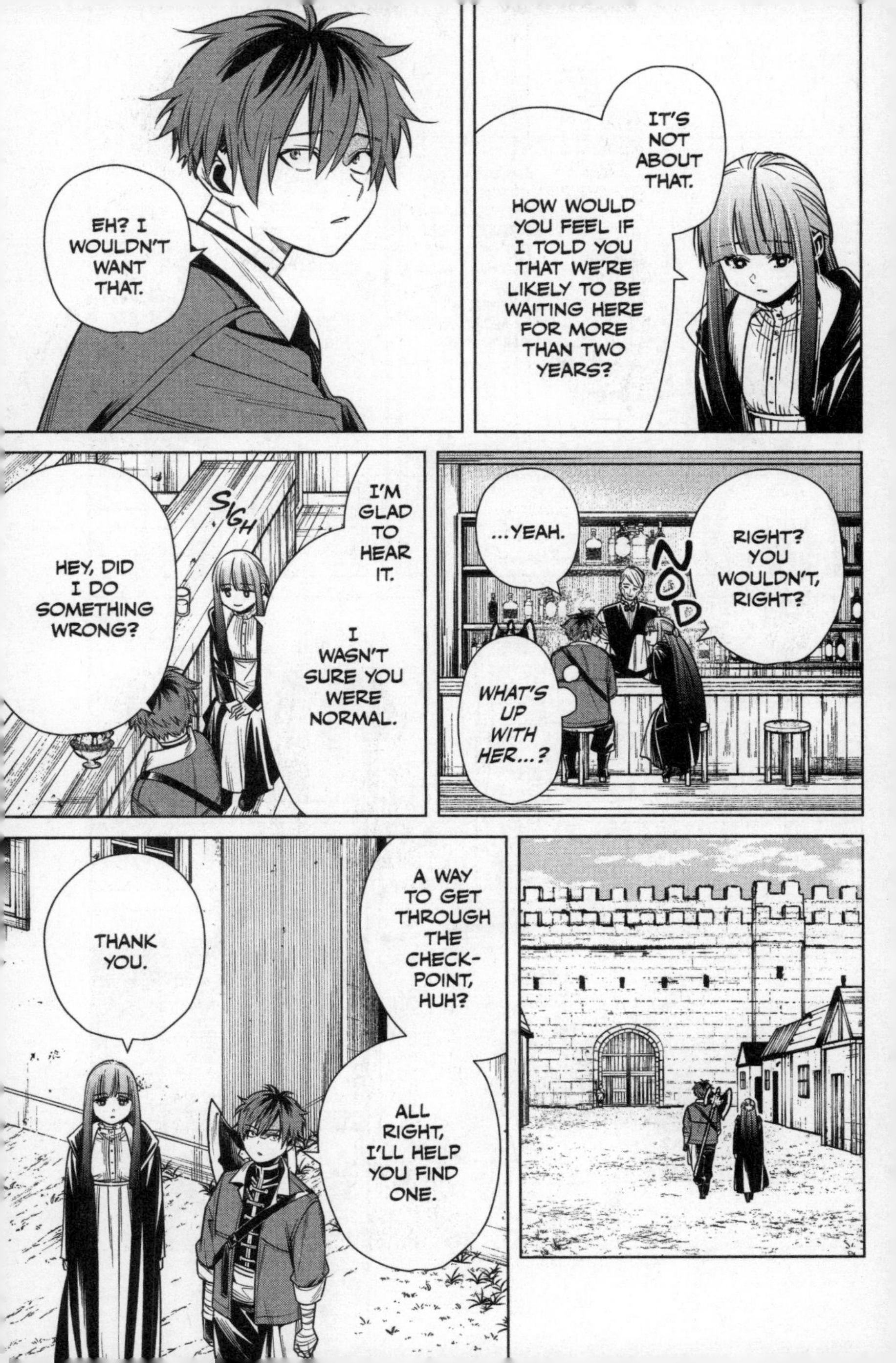
IT'S NOT ABOUT THAT.
HOW WOULD YOU FEEL IF I TOLD YOU THAT WE'RE LIKELY TO BE WAITING HERE FOR MORE THAN TWO YEARS?
EH? I WOULDN'T WANT THAT.
RIGHT? YOU WOULDN'T, RIGHT?
NOD
...YEAH.
WHAT'S UP WITH HER...?
I'M GLAD TO HEAR IT.
I WASN'T SURE YOU WERE NORMAL.
SIGH
HEY, DID I DO SOMETHING WRONG?
A WAY TO GET THROUGH THE CHECK-POINT, HUH?
ALL RIGHT, I'LL HELP YOU FIND ONE.
THANK YOU.

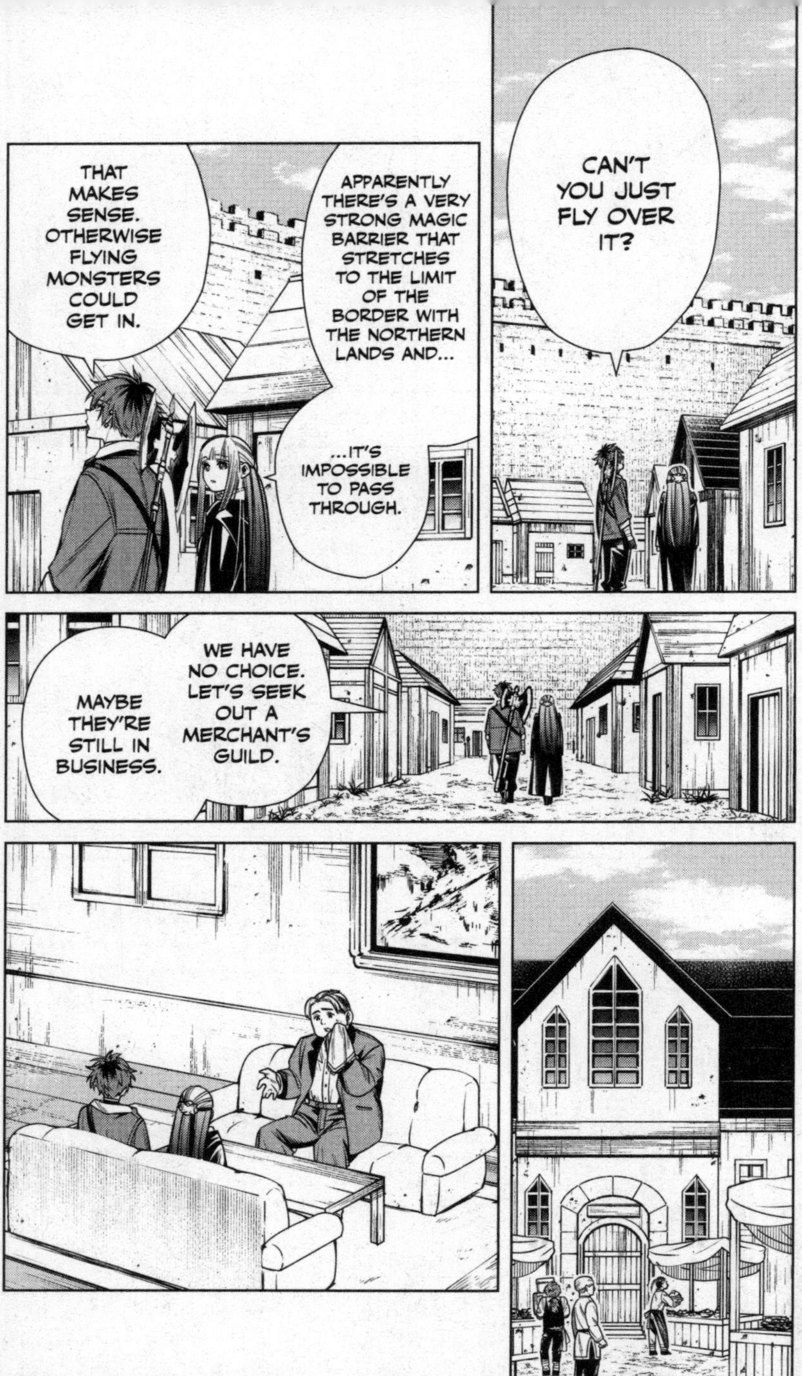
CAN'T YOU JUST FLY OVER IT?
APPARENTLY THERE'S A VERY STRONG MAGIC BARRIER THAT STRETCHES TO THE LIMIT OF THE BORDER WITH THE NORTHERN LANDS AND...
...IT'S IMPOSSIBLE TO PASS THROUGH.
THAT MAKES SENSE. OTHERWISE FLYING MONSTERS COULD GET IN.
WE HAVE NO CHOICE. LET'S SEEK OUT A MERCHANT'S GUILD.
MAYBE THEY'RE STILL IN BUSINESS.

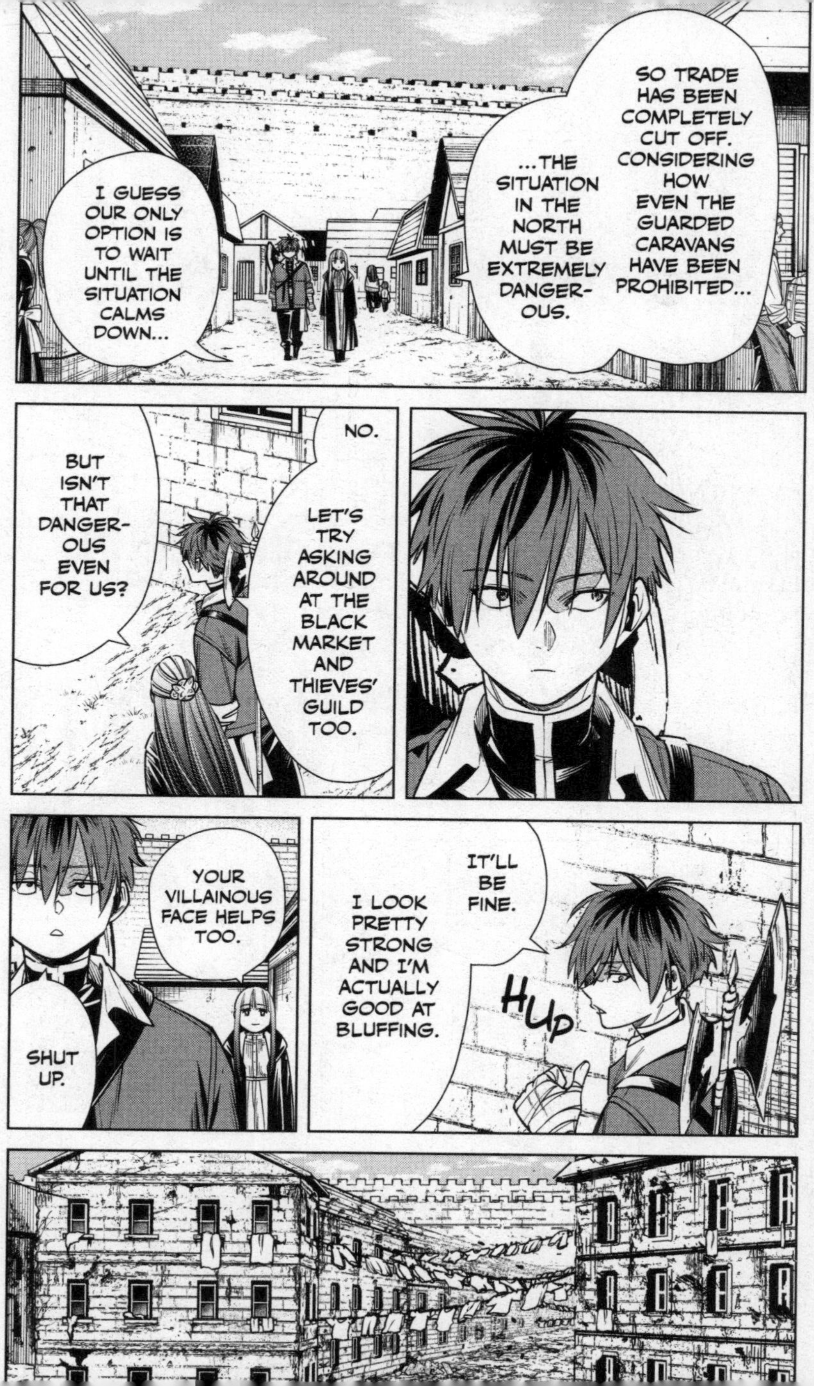
SO TRADE HAS BEEN COMPLETELY CUT OFF. CONSIDERING HOW EVEN THE GUARDED CARAVANS HAVE BEEN PROHIBITED...
...THE SITUATION IN THE NORTH MUST BE EXTREMELY DANGEROUS.
I GUESS OUR ONLY OPTION IS TO WAIT UNTIL THE SITUATION CALMS DOWN...
NO.
LET'S TRY ASKING AROUND AT THE BLACK MARKET AND THIEVES' GUILD TOO.
BUT ISN'T THAT DANGEROUS EVEN FOR US?
IT'LL BE FINE.
I LOOK PRETTY STRONG AND I'M ACTUALLY GOOD AT BLUFFING.
HUP
YOUR VILLAINOUS FACE HELPS TOO.
SHUT UP.

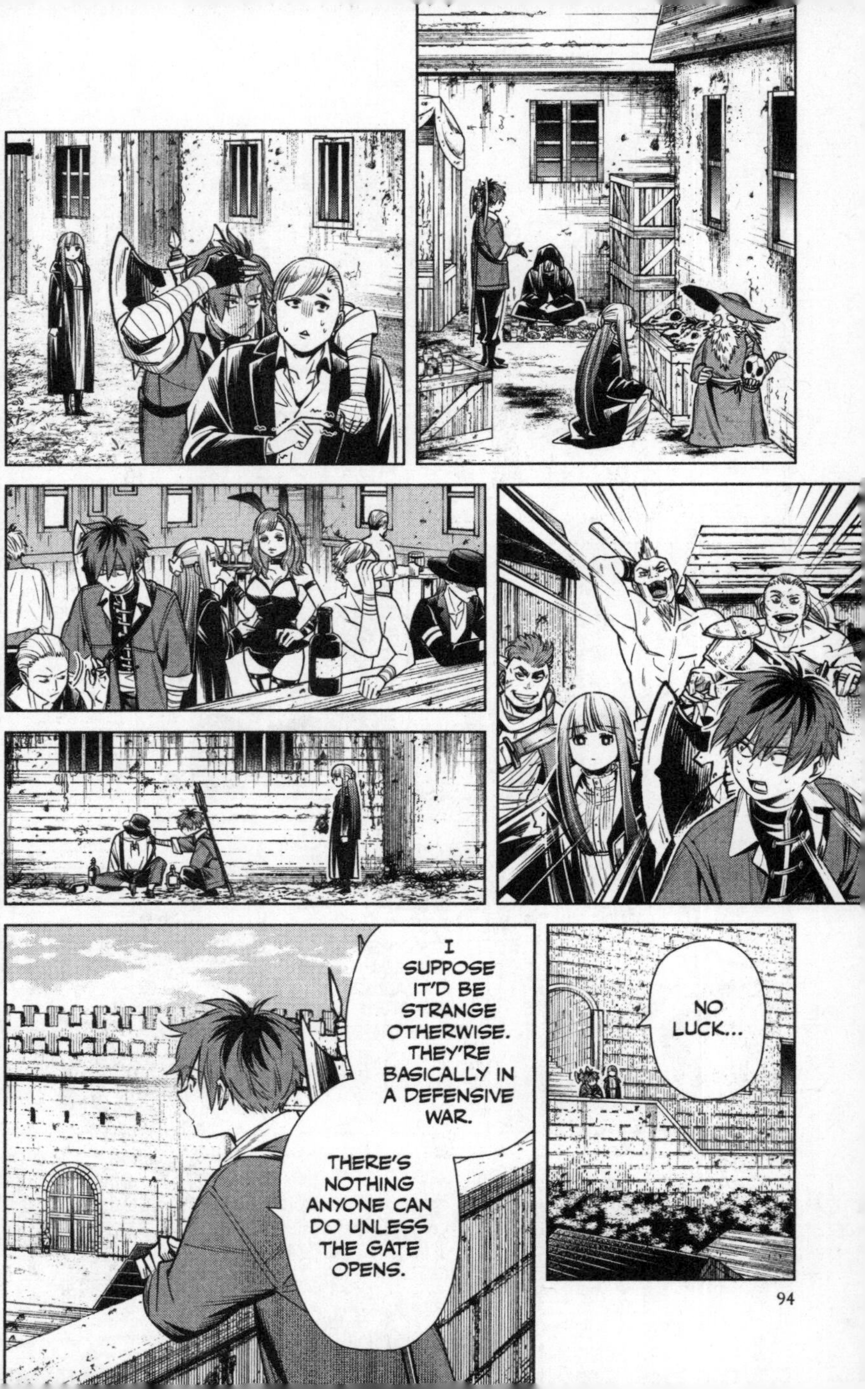
NO LUCK...
I SUPPOSE IT'D BE STRANGE OTHERWISE. THEY'RE BASICALLY IN A DEFENSIVE WAR.
THERE'S NOTHING ANYONE CAN DO UNLESS THE GATE OPENS.

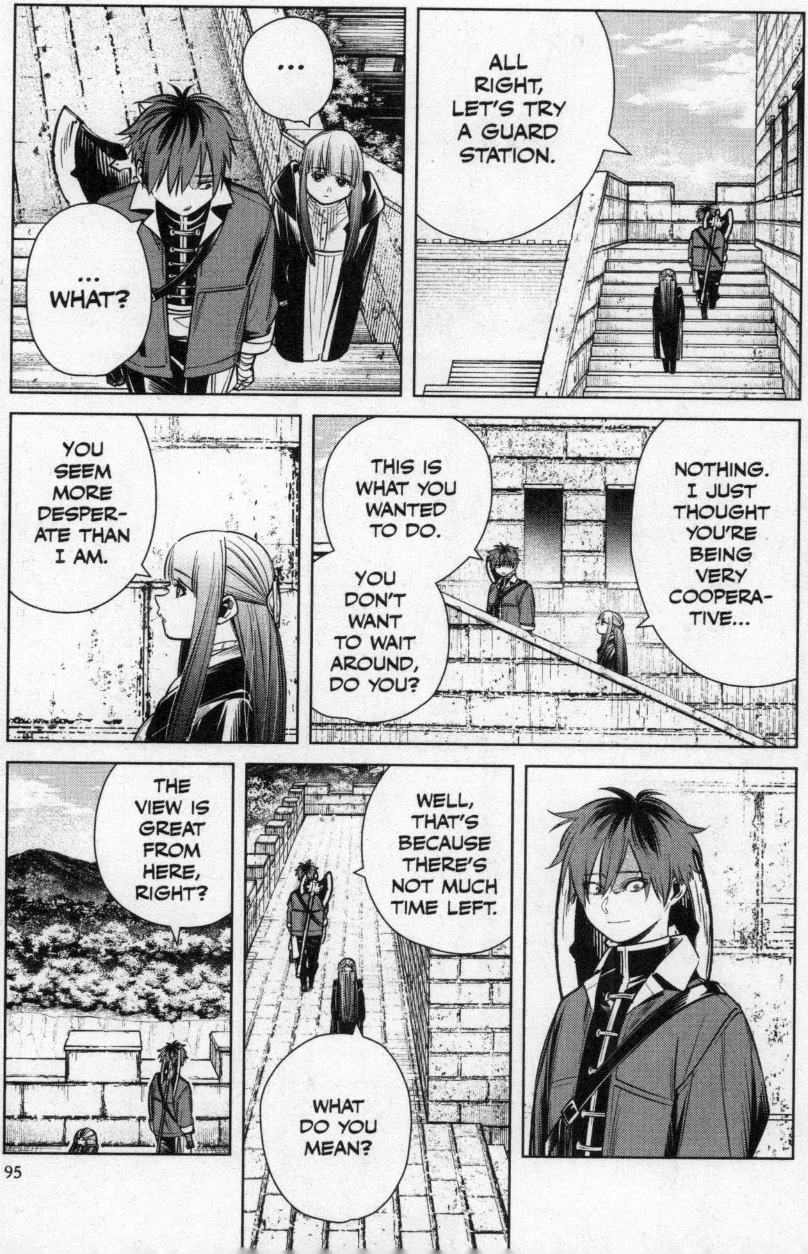
ALL RIGHT, LET'S TRY A GUARD STATION.
...
... WHAT?
NOTHING. I JUST THOUGHT YOU'RE BEING VERY COOPERATIVE...
THIS IS WHAT YOU WANTED TO DO.
YOU DON'T WANT TO WAIT AROUND, DO YOU?
YOU SEEM MORE DESPERATE THAN I AM.
WELL, THAT'S BECAUSE THERE'S NOT MUCH TIME LEFT.
WHAT DO YOU MEAN?
THE VIEW IS GREAT FROM HERE, RIGHT?

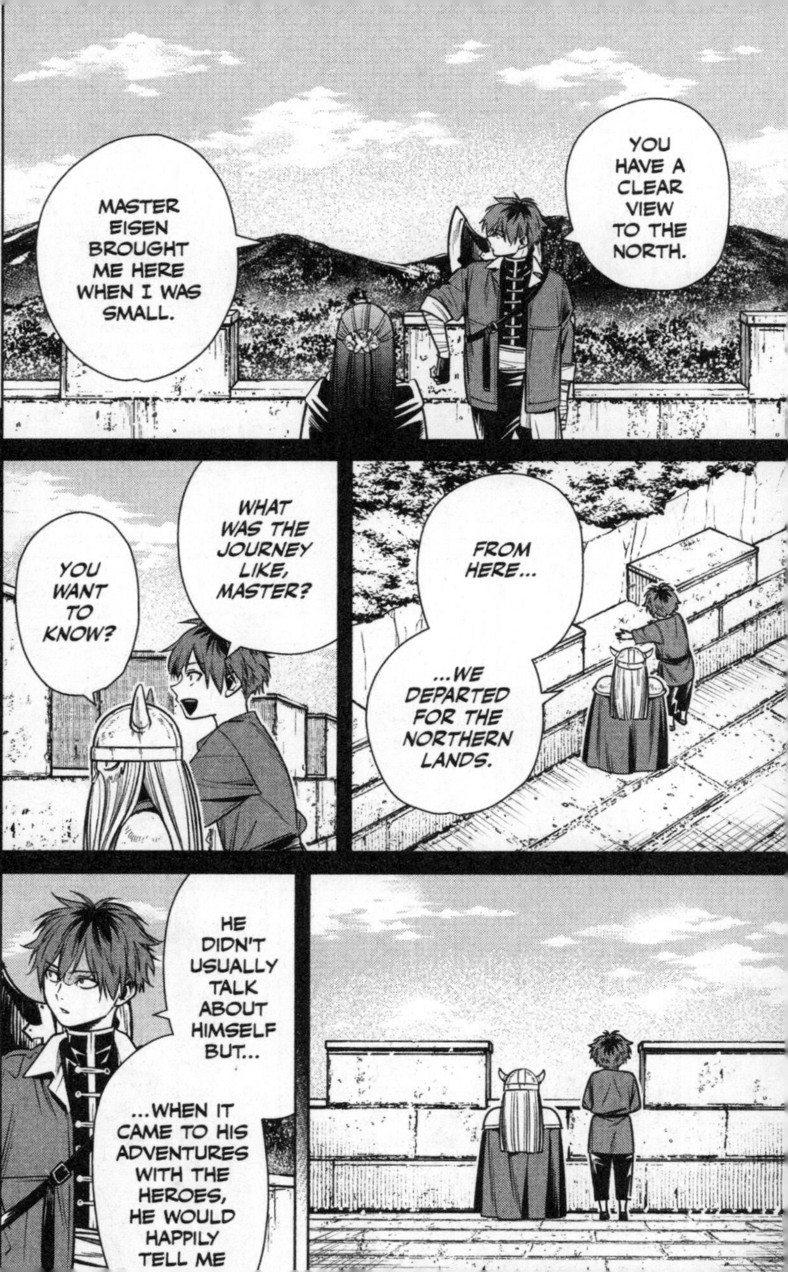
YOU HAVE A CLEAR VIEW TO THE NORTH.
MASTER EISEN BROUGHT ME HERE WHEN I WAS SMALL.
FROM HERE...
...WE DEPARTED FOR THE NORTHERN LANDS.
WHAT WAS THE JOURNEY LIKE, MASTER?
YOU WANT TO KNOW?
HE DIDN'T USUALLY TALK ABOUT HIMSELF BUT...
...WHEN IT CAME TO HIS ADVENTURES WITH THE HEROES, HE WOULD HAPPILY TELL ME

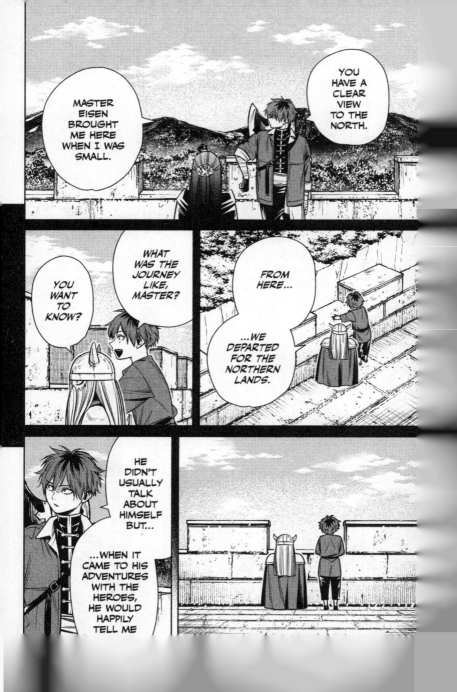

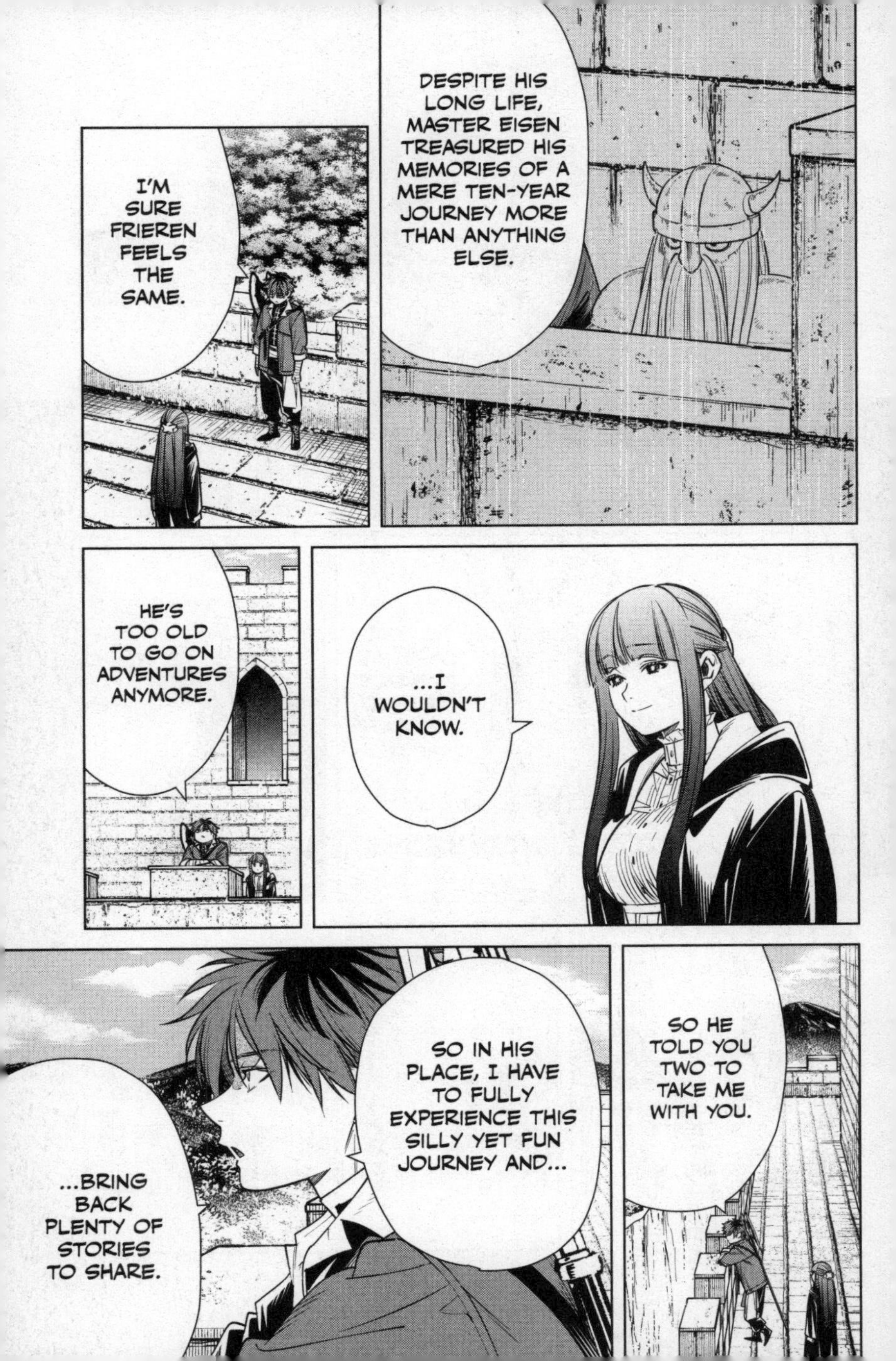
DESPITE HIS LONG LIFE, MASTER EISEN TREASURED HIS MEMORIES OF A MERE TEN-YEAR JOURNEY MORE THAN ANYTHING ELSE.
I'M SURE FRIEREN FEELS THE SAME.
...I WOULDN'T KNOW.
HE'S TOO OLD TO GO ON ADVENTURES ANYMORE.
SO HE TOLD YOU TWO TO TAKE ME WITH YOU.
SO IN HIS PLACE, I HAVE TO FULLY EXPERIENCE THIS SILLY YET FUN JOURNEY AND...
...BRING BACK PLENTY OF STORIES TO SHARE.

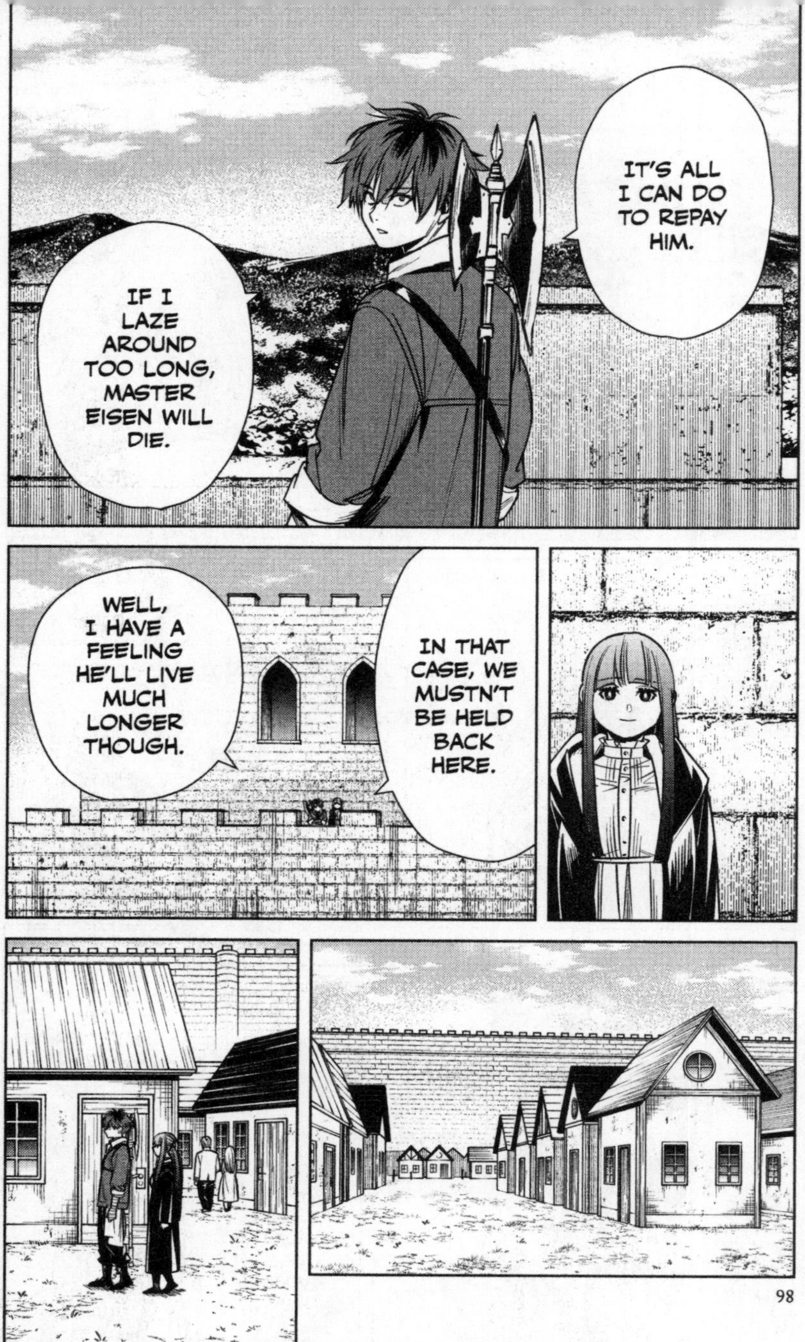
IT'S ALL I CAN DO TO REPAY HIM.
IF I LAZE AROUND TOO LONG, MASTER EISEN WILL DIE.
IN THAT CASE, WE MUSTN'T BE HELD BACK HERE.
WELL, I HAVE A FEELING HE'LL LIVE MUCH LONGER THOUGH.

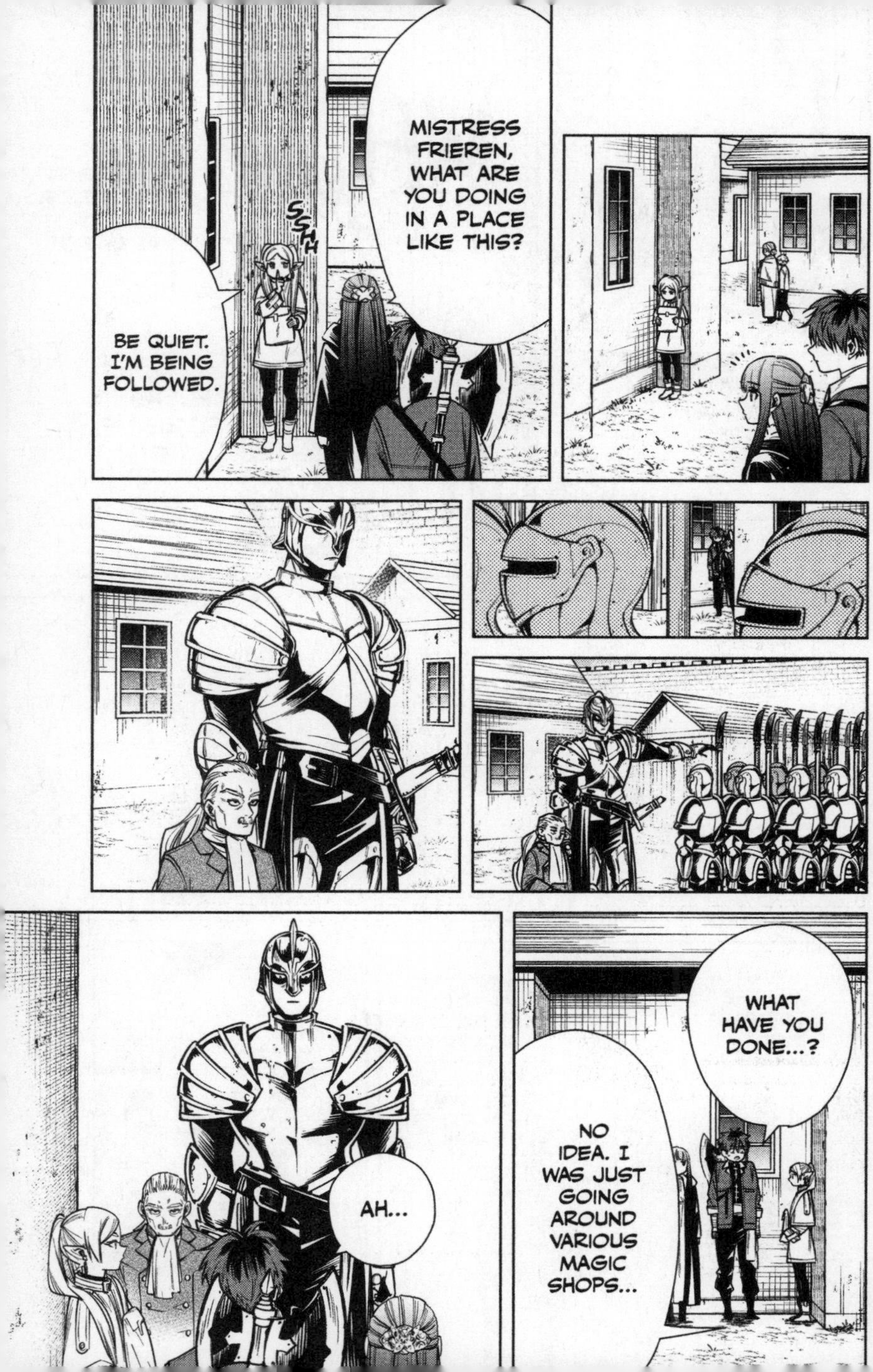
MISTRESS FRIEREN, WHAT ARE YOU DOING IN A PLACE LIKE THIS?
SSHH
BE QUIET. I'M BEING FOLLOWED.
WHAT HAVE YOU DONE...?
NO IDEA. I WAS JUST GOING AROUND VARIOUS MAGIC SHOPS...
AH...

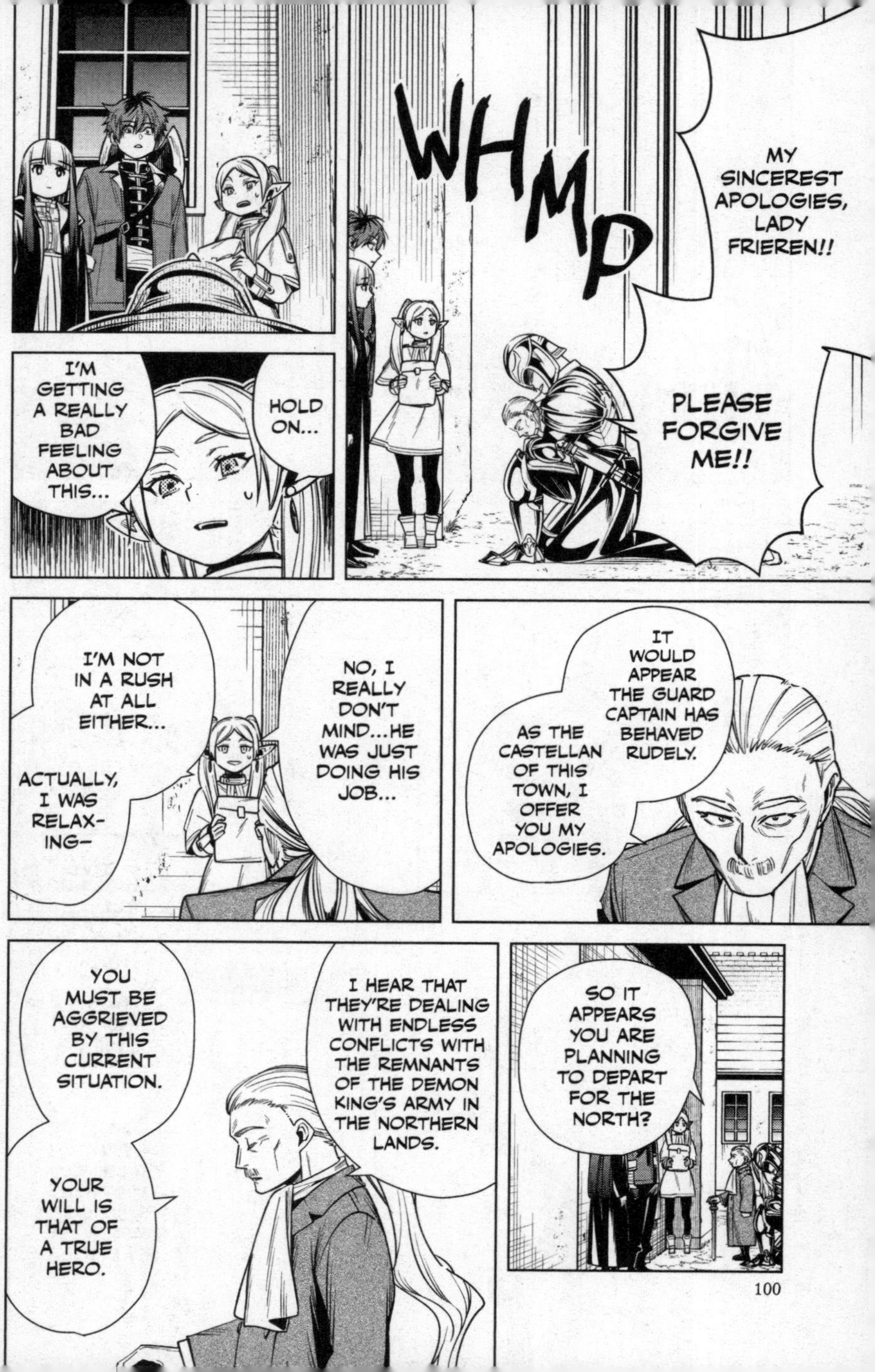
WHMP
MY SINCEREST APOLOGIES, LADY FRIEREN!!
PLEASE FORGIVE ME!!
HOLD ON...
I'M GETTING A REALLY BAD FEELING ABOUT THIS...
IT WOULD APPEAR THE GUARD CAPTAIN HAS BEHAVED RUDELY.
AS THE CASTELLAN OF THIS TOWN, I OFFER YOU MY APOLOGIES.
NO, I REALLY DON'T MIND...HE WAS JUST DOING HIS JOB...
I'M NOT IN A RUSH AT ALL EITHER...
ACTUALLY, I WAS RELAXING—
SO IT APPEARS YOU ARE PLANNING TO DEPART FOR THE NORTH?
I HEAR THAT THEY'RE DEALING WITH ENDLESS CONFLICTS WITH THE REMNANTS OF THE DEMON KING'S ARMY IN THE NORTHERN LANDS.
YOU MUST BE AGGRIEVED BY THIS CURRENT SITUATION.
YOUR WILL IS THAT OF A TRUE HERO.

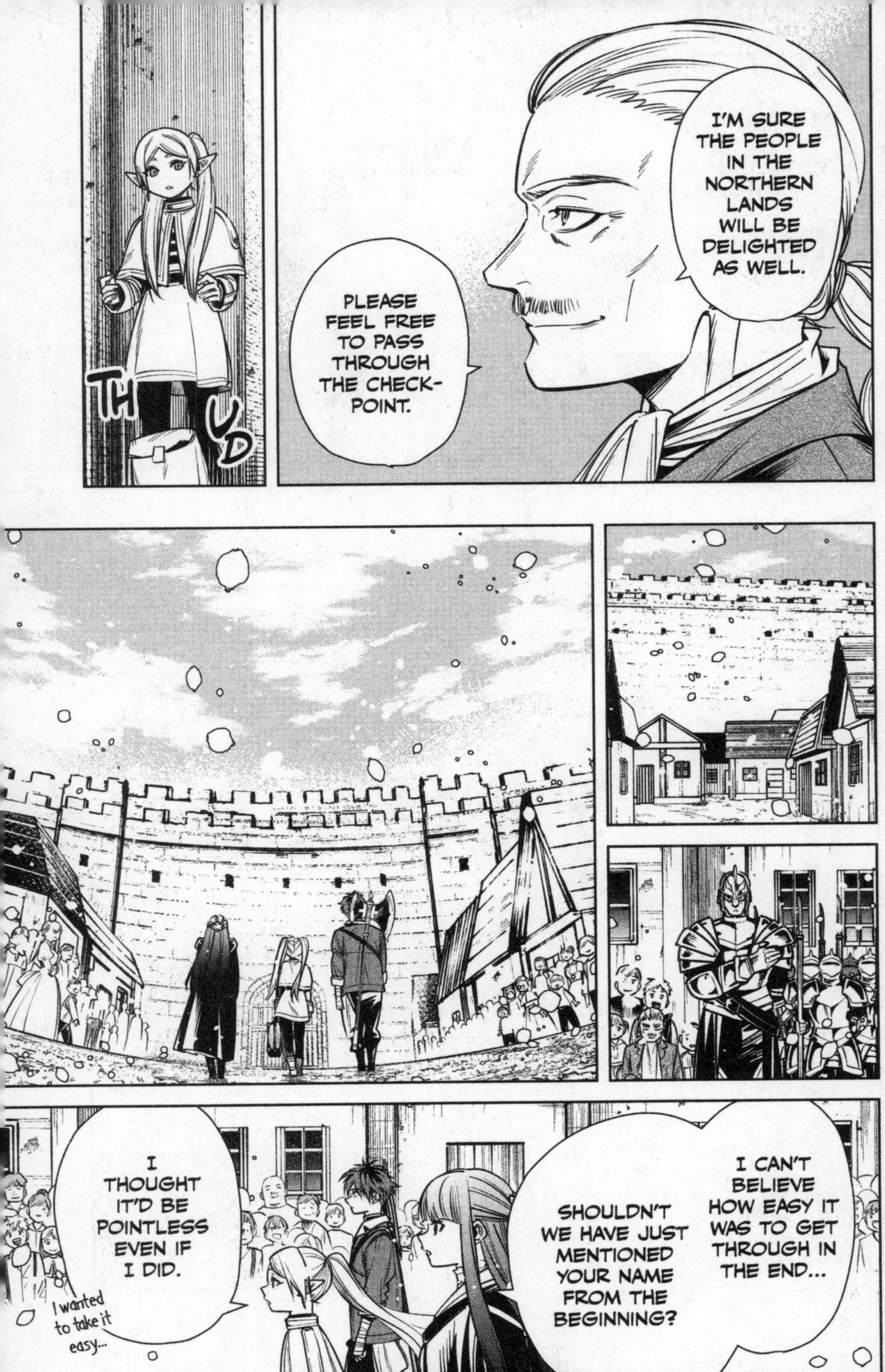
I'M SURE THE PEOPLE IN THE NORTHERN LANDS WILL BE DELIGHTED AS WELL.
PLEASE FEEL FREE TO PASS THROUGH THE CHECK-POINT.
THUD
I CAN'T BELIEVE HOW EASY IT WAS TO GET THROUGH IN THE END...
SHOULDN'T WE HAVE JUST MENTIONED YOUR NAME FROM THE BEGINNING?
I THOUGHT IT'D BE POINTLESS EVEN IF I DID.
I wanted to take it easy...

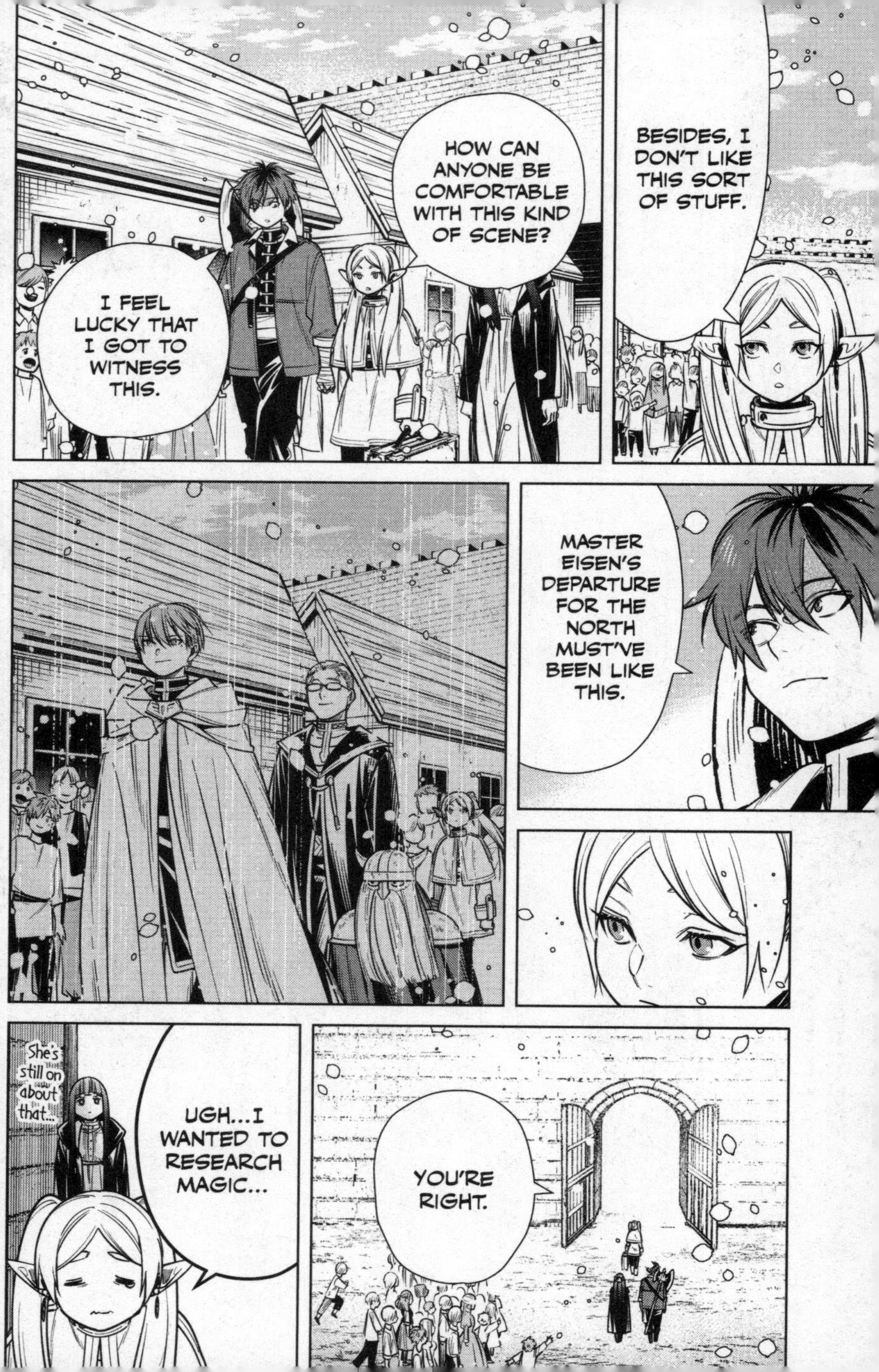
BESIDES, I DON'T LIKE THIS SORT OF STUFF.
HOW CAN ANYONE BE COMFORTABLE WITH THIS KIND OF SCENE?
I FEEL LUCKY THAT I GOT TO WITNESS THIS.
MASTER EISEN'S DEPARTURE FOR THE NORTH MUST'VE BEEN LIKE THIS.
YOU'RE RIGHT.
UGH...I WANTED TO RESEARCH MAGIC...
She's still on about that...

Chapter 13: Liberation Festival

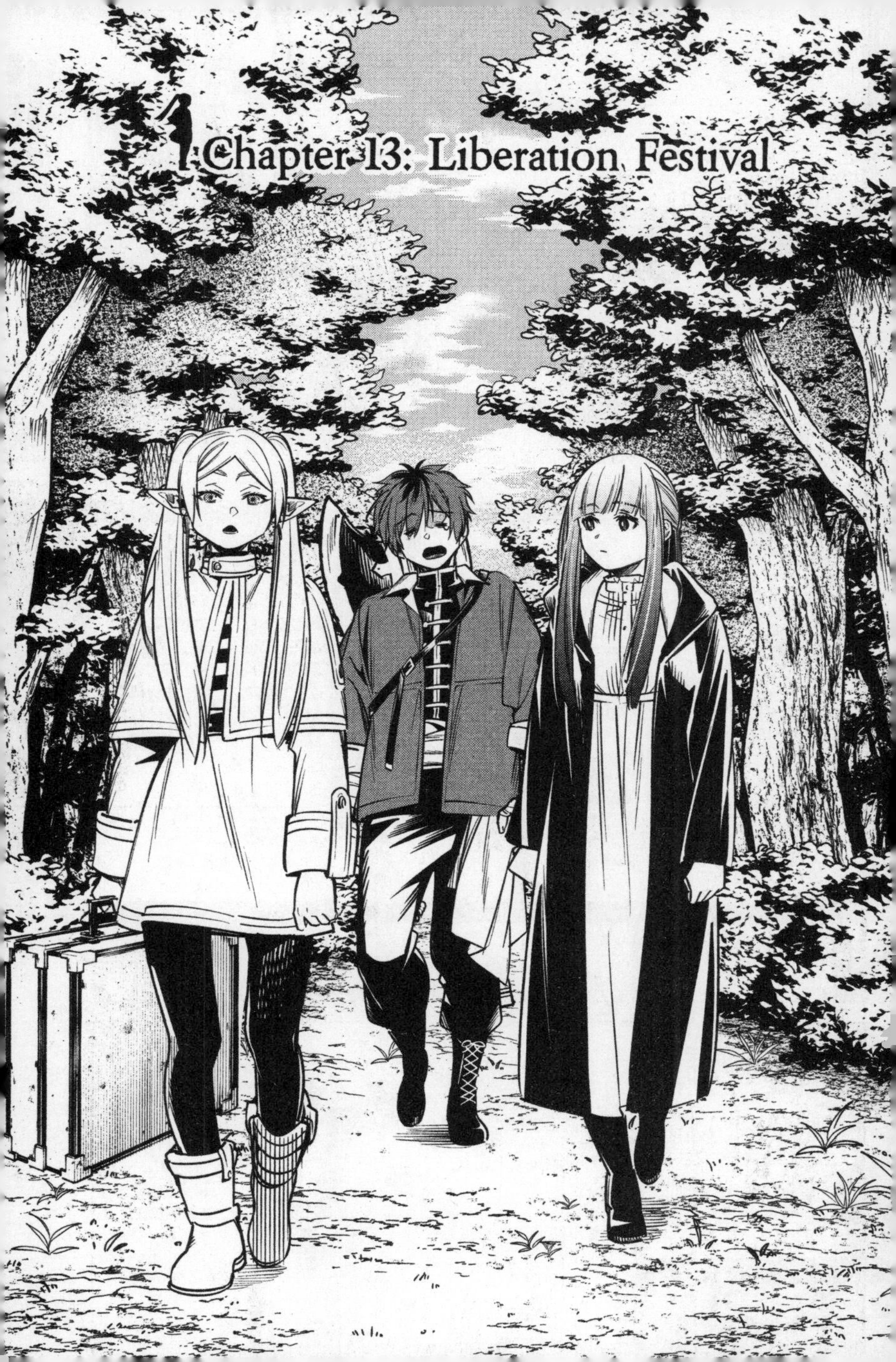

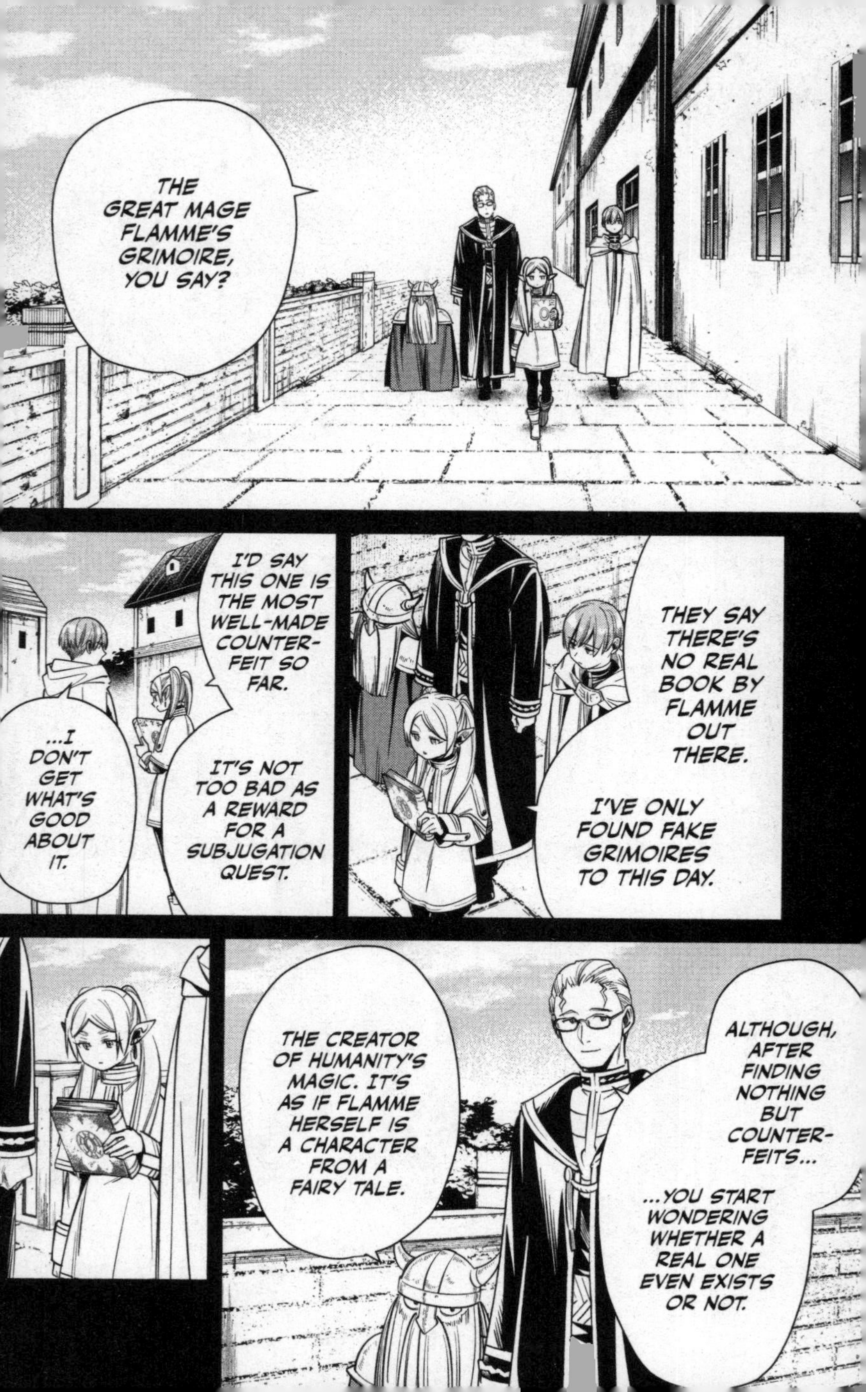
THE GREAT MAGE FLAMME'S GRIMOIRE, YOU SAY?
THEY SAY THERE'S NO REAL BOOK BY FLAMME OUT THERE.
I'VE ONLY FOUND FAKE GRIMOIRES TO THIS DAY.
I'D SAY THIS ONE IS THE MOST WELL-MADE COUNTER-FEIT SO FAR.
IT'S NOT TOO BAD AS A REWARD FOR A SUBJUGATION QUEST.
...I DON'T GET WHAT'S GOOD ABOUT IT.
ALTHOUGH, AFTER FINDING NOTHING BUT COUNTER-FEITS...
...YOU START WONDERING WHETHER A REAL ONE EVEN EXISTS OR NOT.
THE CREATOR OF HUMANITY'S MAGIC. IT'S AS IF FLAMME HERSELF IS A CHARACTER FROM A FAIRY TALE.

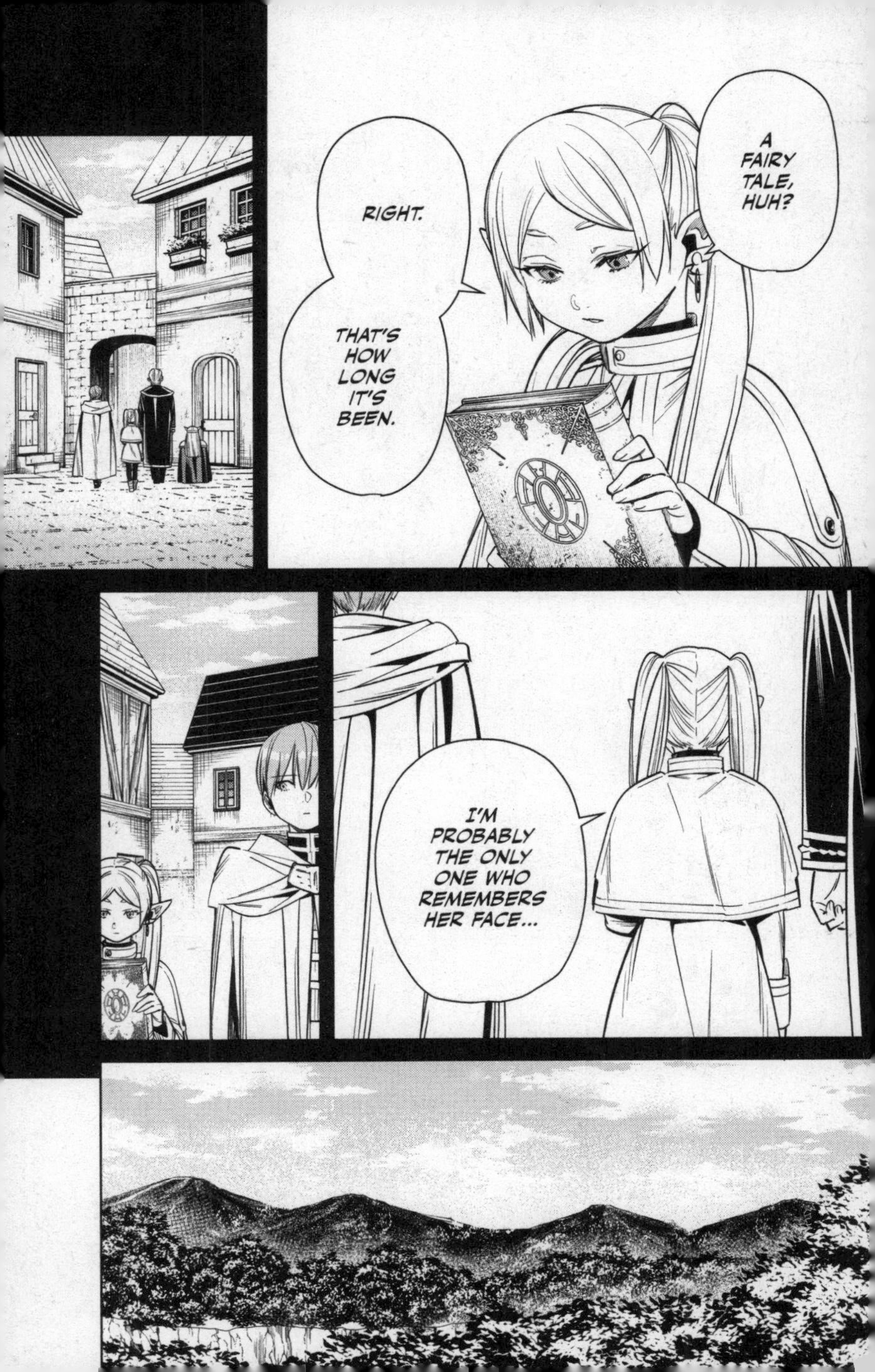
A FAIRY TALE, HUH?
RIGHT.
THAT'S HOW LONG IT'S BEEN.
I'M PROBABLY THE ONLY ONE WHO REMEMBERS HER FACE...

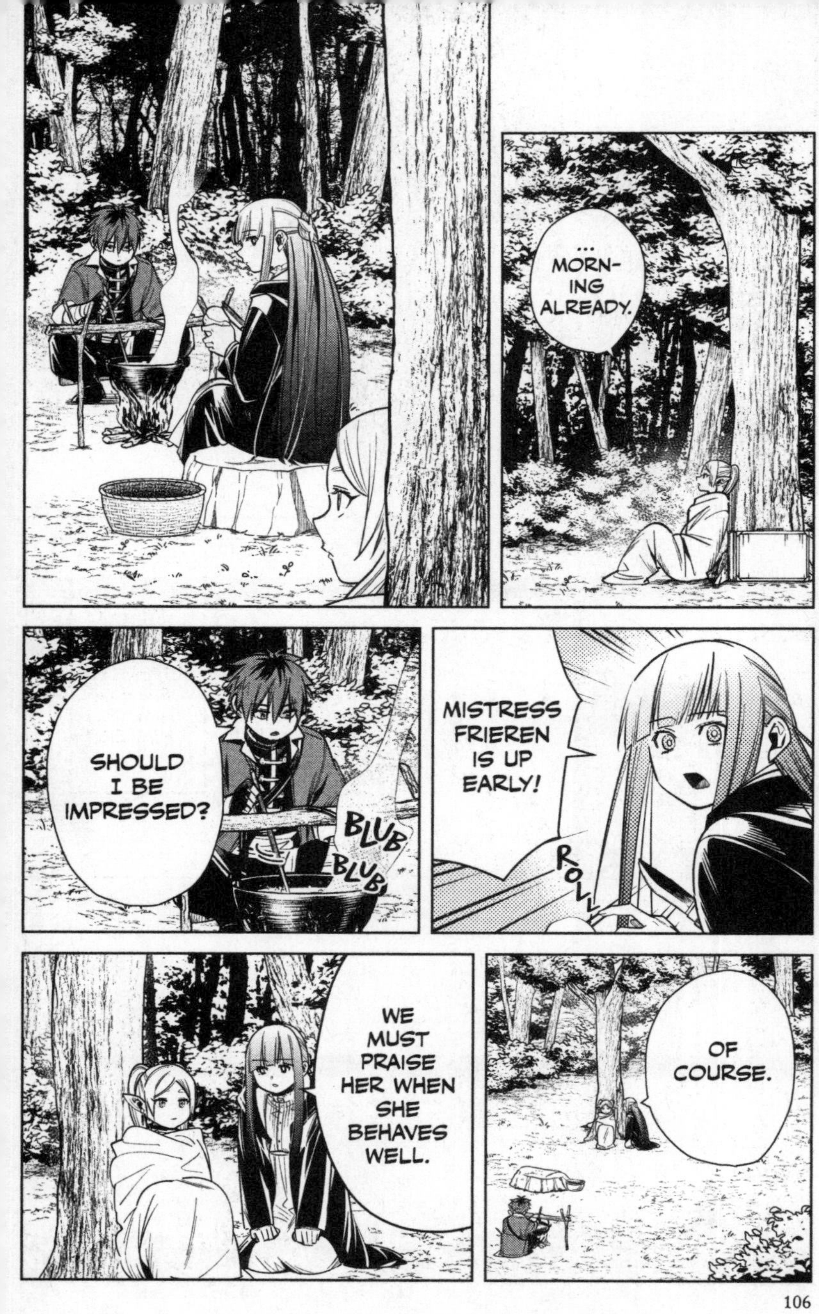
... MORNING ALREADY.
MISTRESS FRIEREN IS UP EARLY!
ROLL
SHOULD I BE IMPRESSED?
BLUB BLUB
OF COURSE.
WE MUST PRAISE HER WHEN SHE BEHAVES WELL.

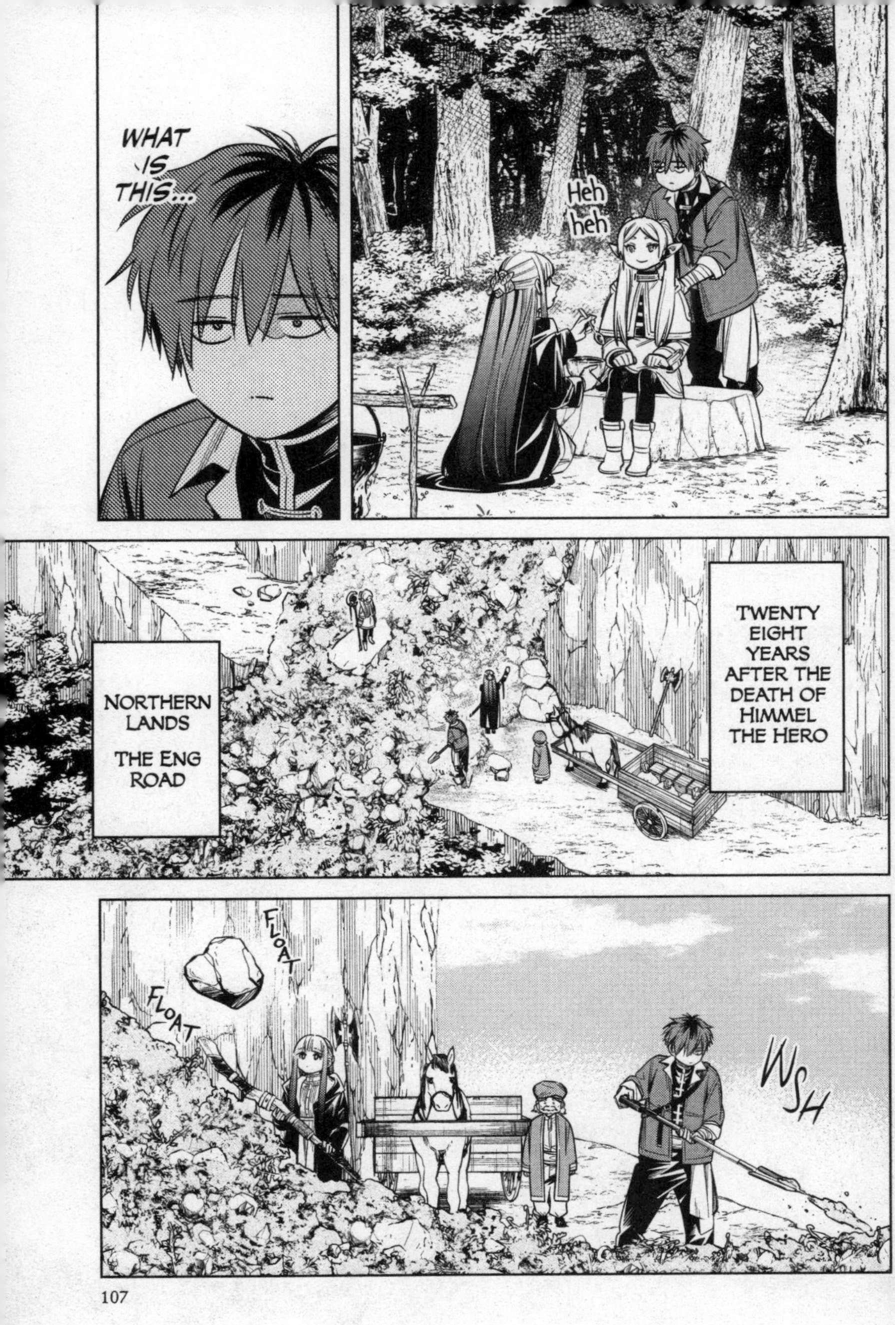
Heh heh
WHAT IS THIS...
TWENTY EIGHT YEARS AFTER THE DEATH OF HIMMEL THE HERO
NORTHERN LANDS
THE ENG ROAD
WSH
FLOAT
FLOAT

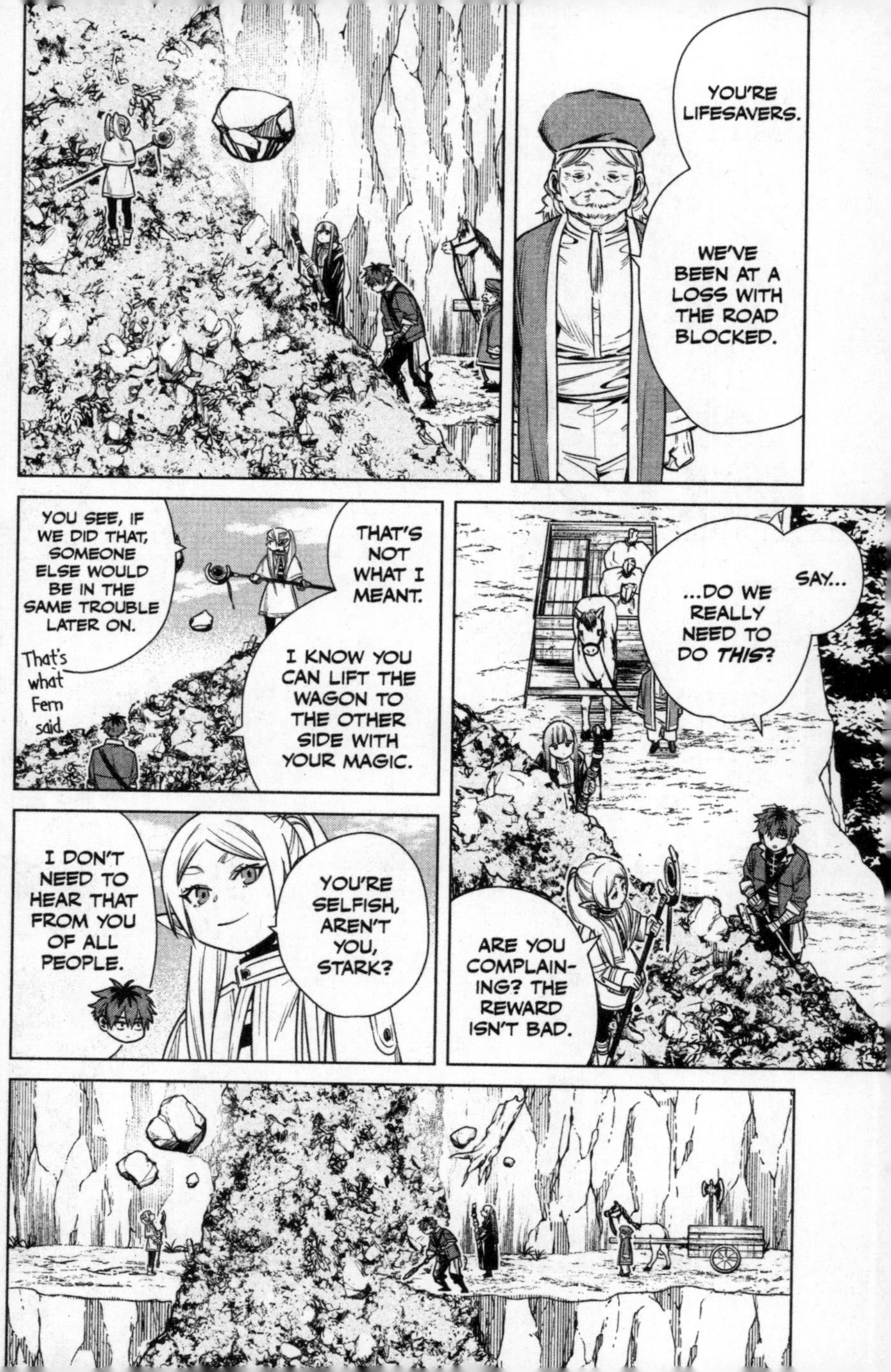
YOU'RE LIFESAVERS.
WE'VE BEEN AT A LOSS WITH THE ROAD BLOCKED.
SAY...
...DO WE REALLY NEED TO DO *THIS*?
ARE YOU COMPLAINING? THE REWARD ISN'T BAD.
THAT'S NOT WHAT I MEANT.
I KNOW YOU CAN LIFT THE WAGON TO THE OTHER SIDE WITH YOUR MAGIC.
YOU SEE, IF WE DID THAT, SOMEONE ELSE WOULD BE IN THE SAME TROUBLE LATER ON.
That's what Fern said.
YOU'RE SELFISH, AREN'T YOU, STARK?
I DON'T NEED TO HEAR THAT FROM YOU OF ALL PEOPLE.

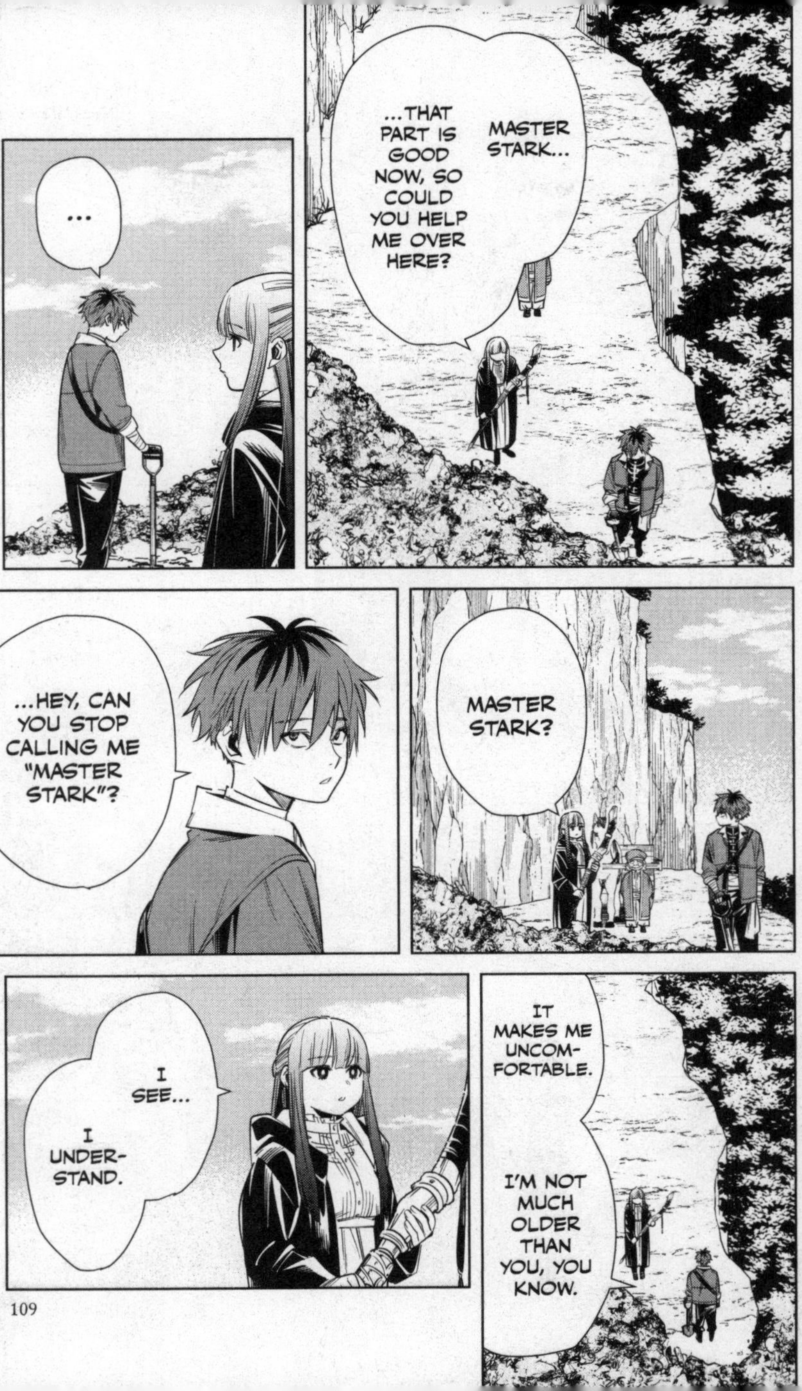
MASTER STARK...
...THAT PART IS GOOD NOW, SO COULD YOU HELP ME OVER HERE?
...
MASTER STARK?
...HEY, CAN YOU STOP CALLING ME "MASTER STARK"?
IT MAKES ME UNCOMFORTABLE.
I'M NOT MUCH OLDER THAN YOU, YOU KNOW.
I SEE...
I UNDERSTAND.

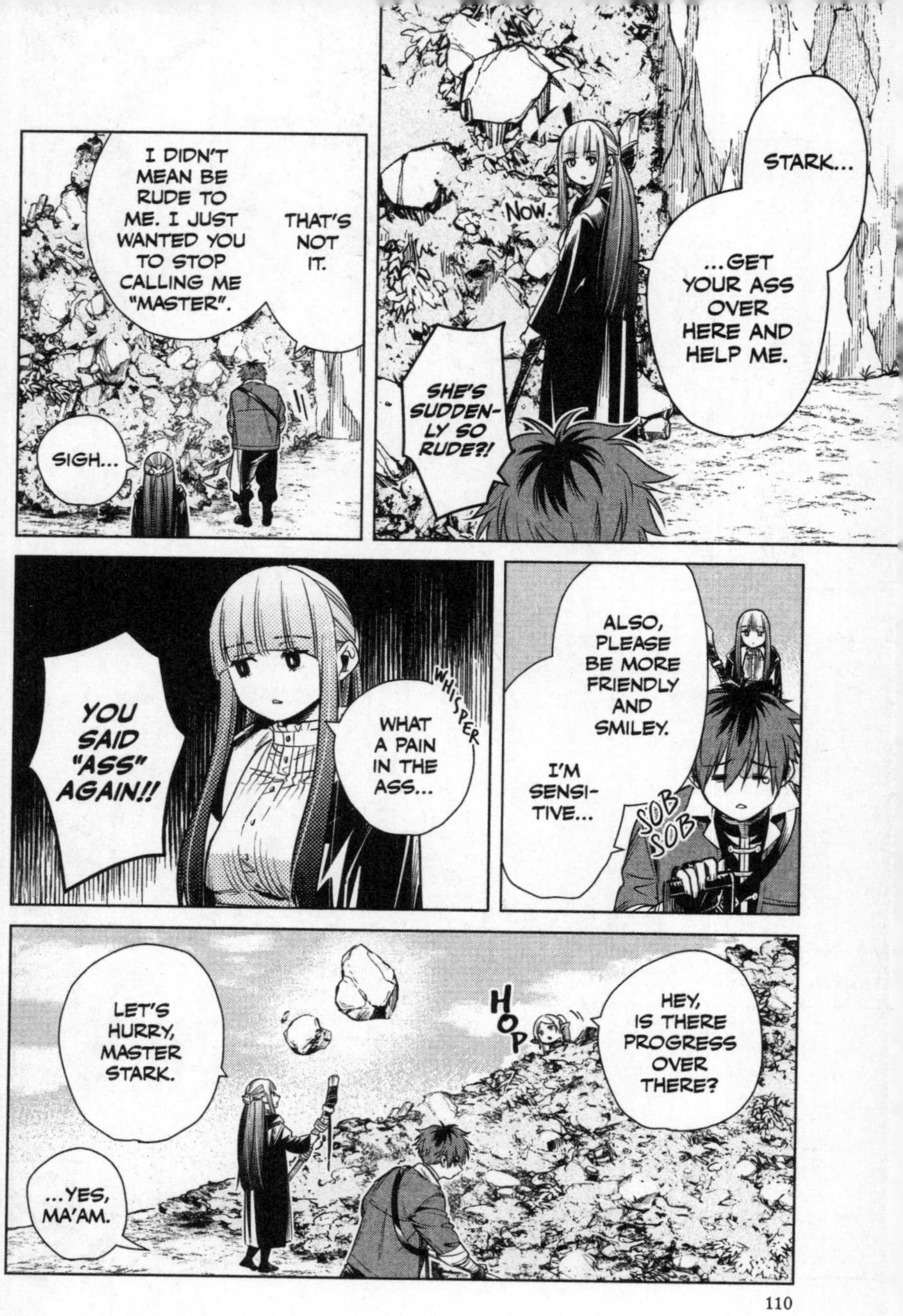
STARK...
...GET YOUR ASS OVER HERE AND HELP ME.
NOW.
SHE'S SUDDEN-LY SO RUDE?!
THAT'S NOT IT.
I DIDN'T MEAN BE RUDE TO ME. I JUST WANTED YOU TO STOP CALLING ME "MASTER".
SIGH...
ALSO, PLEASE BE MORE FRIENDLY AND SMILEY.
I'M SENSI-TIVE...
SOB SOB
WHISPER
WHAT A PAIN IN THE ASS...
YOU SAID "ASS" AGAIN!!
HEY, IS THERE PROGRESS OVER THERE?
HOP
LET'S HURRY, MASTER STARK.
...YES, MA'AM.

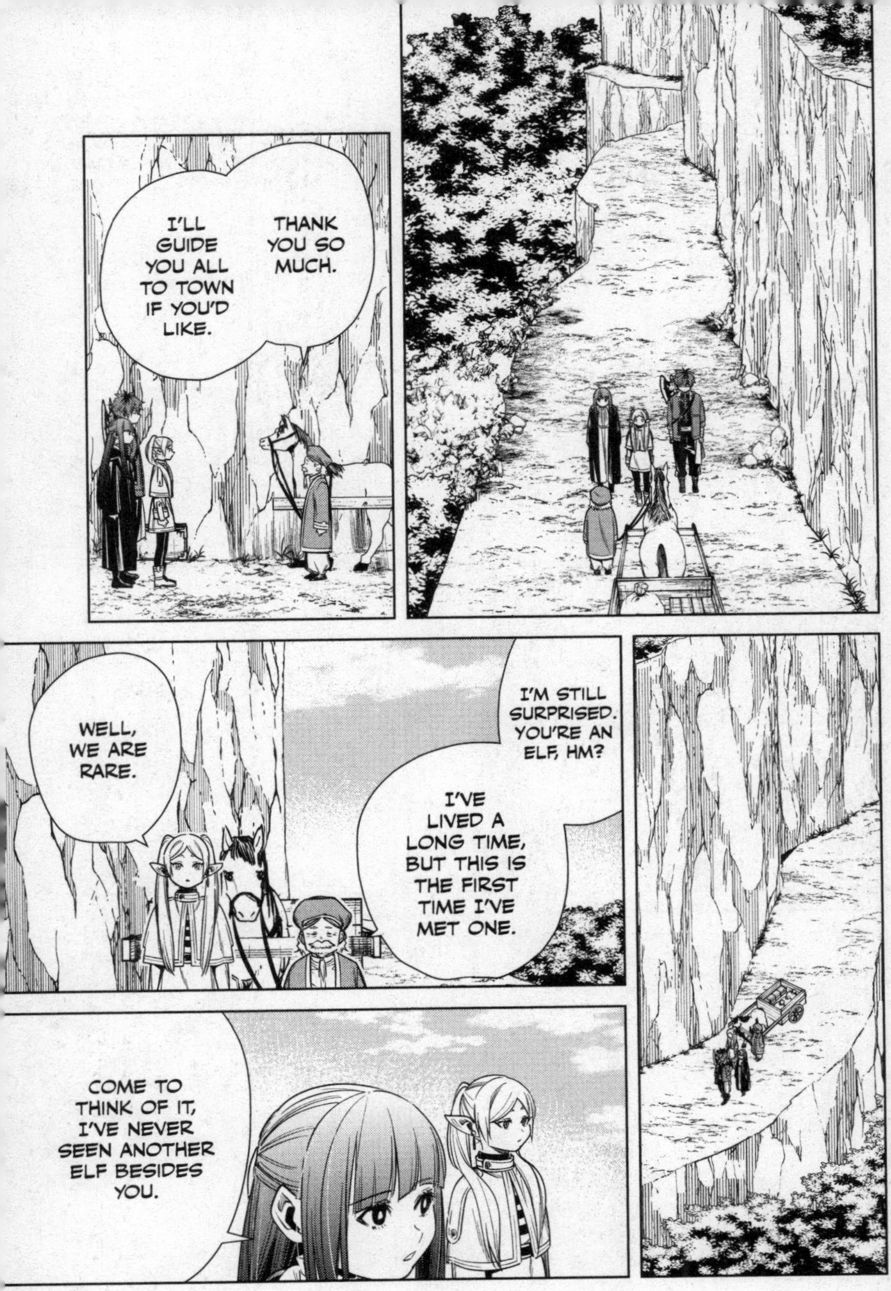
THANK YOU SO MUCH.
I'LL GUIDE YOU ALL TO TOWN IF YOU'D LIKE.
I'M STILL SURPRISED. YOU'RE AN ELF, HM?
I'VE LIVED A LONG TIME, BUT THIS IS THE FIRST TIME I'VE MET ONE.
WELL, WE ARE RARE.
COME TO THINK OF IT, I'VE NEVER SEEN ANOTHER ELF BESIDES YOU.

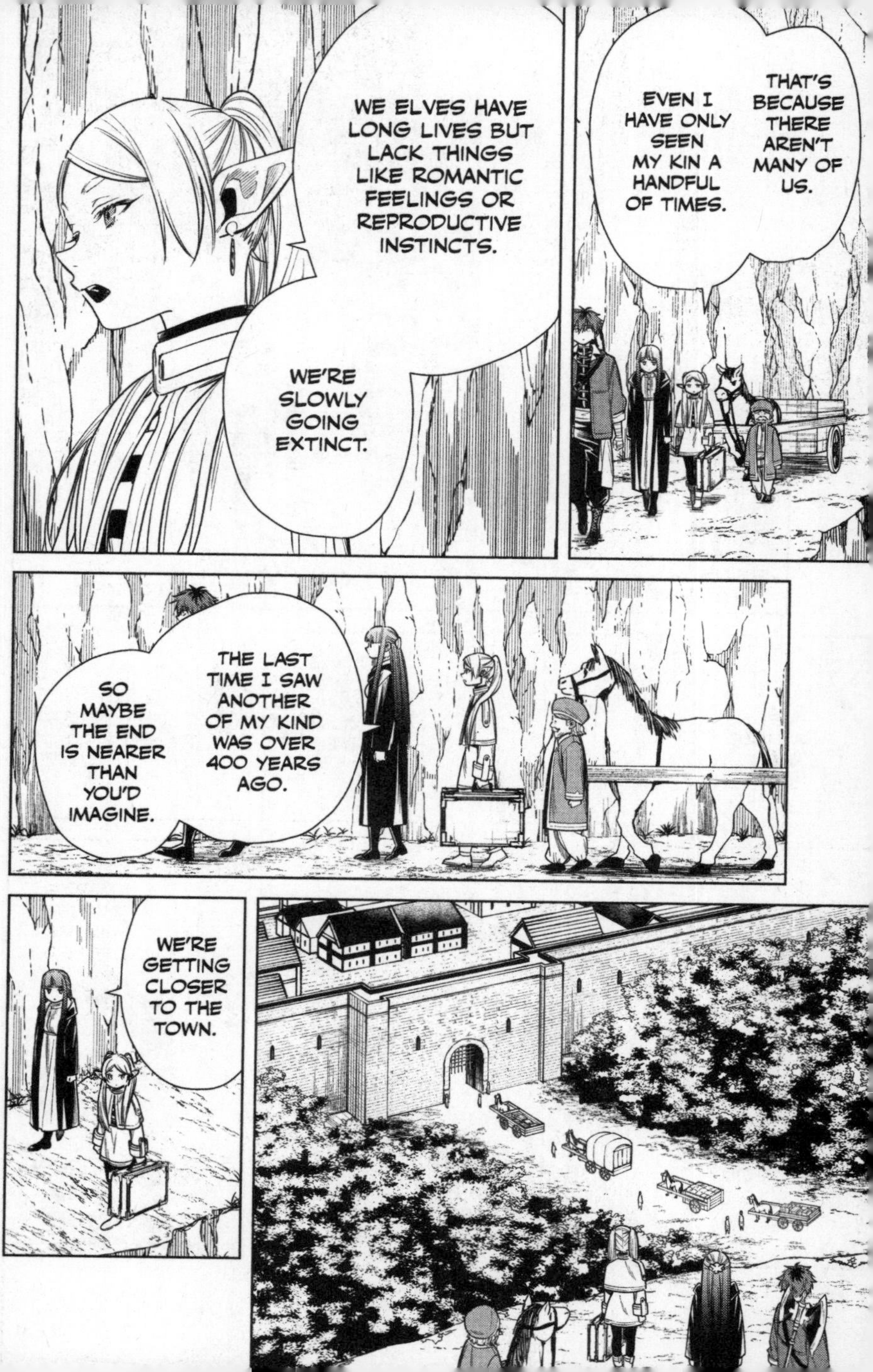
THAT'S BECAUSE THERE AREN'T MANY OF US.
EVEN I HAVE ONLY SEEN MY KIN A HANDFUL OF TIMES.
WE ELVES HAVE LONG LIVES BUT LACK THINGS LIKE ROMANTIC FEELINGS OR REPRODUCTIVE INSTINCTS.
WE'RE SLOWLY GOING EXTINCT.
THE LAST TIME I SAW ANOTHER OF MY KIND WAS OVER 400 YEARS AGO.
SO MAYBE THE END IS NEARER THAN YOU'D IMAGINE.
WE'RE GETTING CLOSER TO THE TOWN.

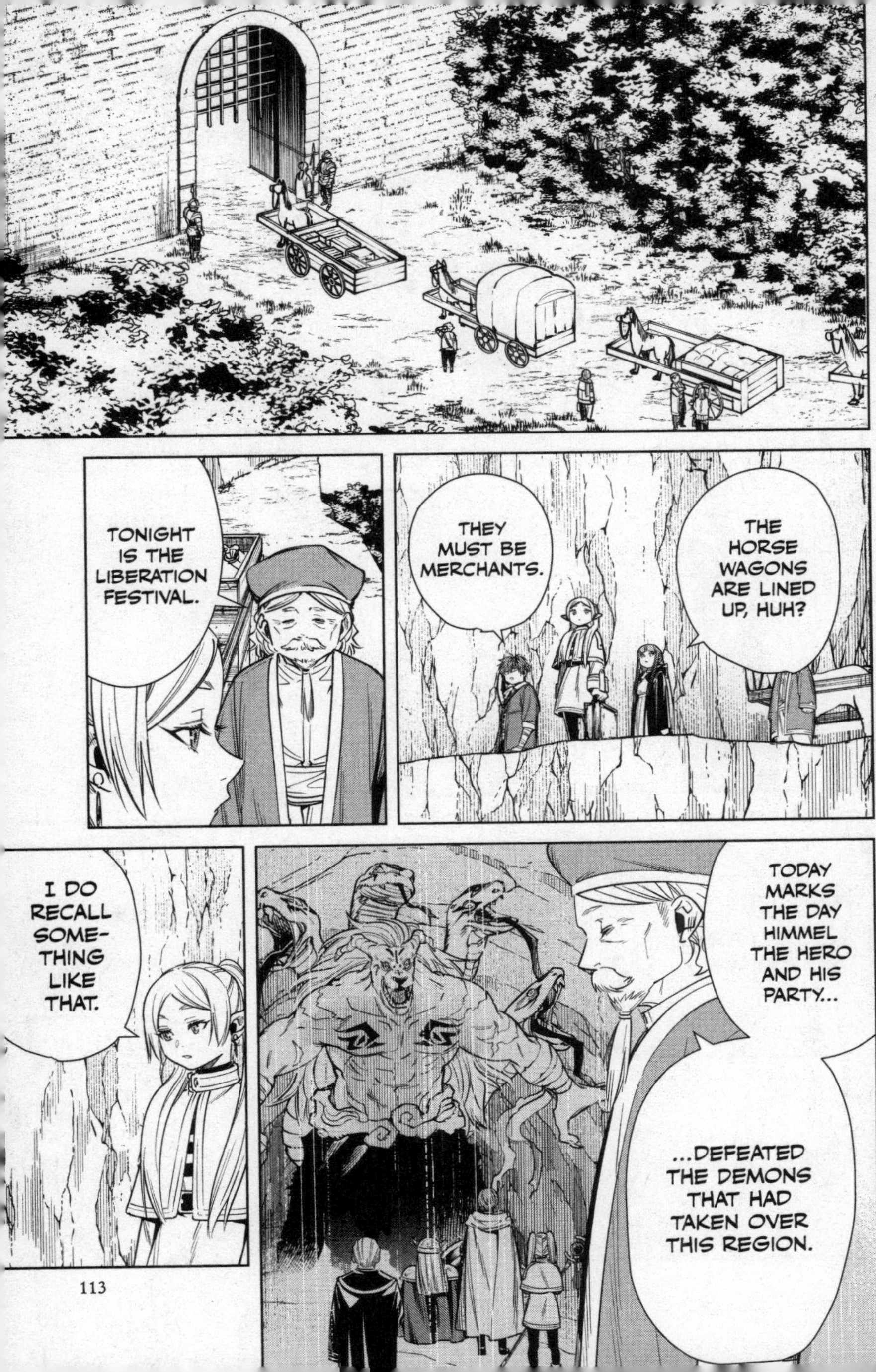
THE HORSE WAGONS ARE LINED UP, HUH?
THEY MUST BE MERCHANTS.
TONIGHT IS THE LIBERATION FESTIVAL.
TODAY MARKS THE DAY HIMMEL THE HERO AND HIS PARTY...
...DEFEATED THE DEMONS THAT HAD TAKEN OVER THIS REGION.
I DO RECALL SOME-THING LIKE THAT.

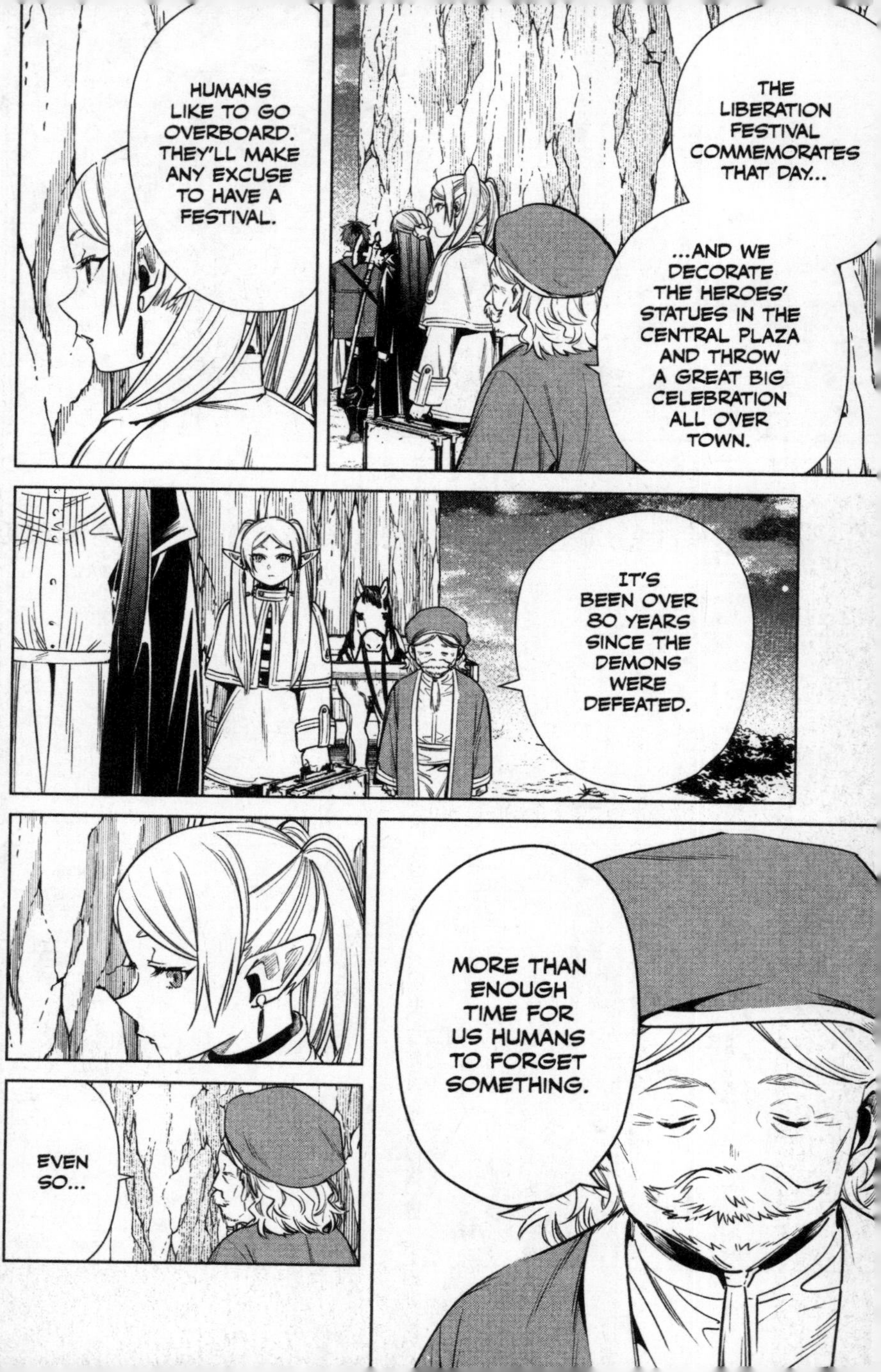
THE LIBERATION FESTIVAL COMMEMORATES THAT DAY...
...AND WE DECORATE THE HEROES' STATUES IN THE CENTRAL PLAZA AND THROW A GREAT BIG CELEBRATION ALL OVER TOWN.
HUMANS LIKE TO GO OVERBOARD. THEY'LL MAKE ANY EXCUSE TO HAVE A FESTIVAL.
IT'S BEEN OVER 80 YEARS SINCE THE DEMONS WERE DEFEATED.
MORE THAN ENOUGH TIME FOR US HUMANS TO FORGET SOMETHING.
EVEN SO...

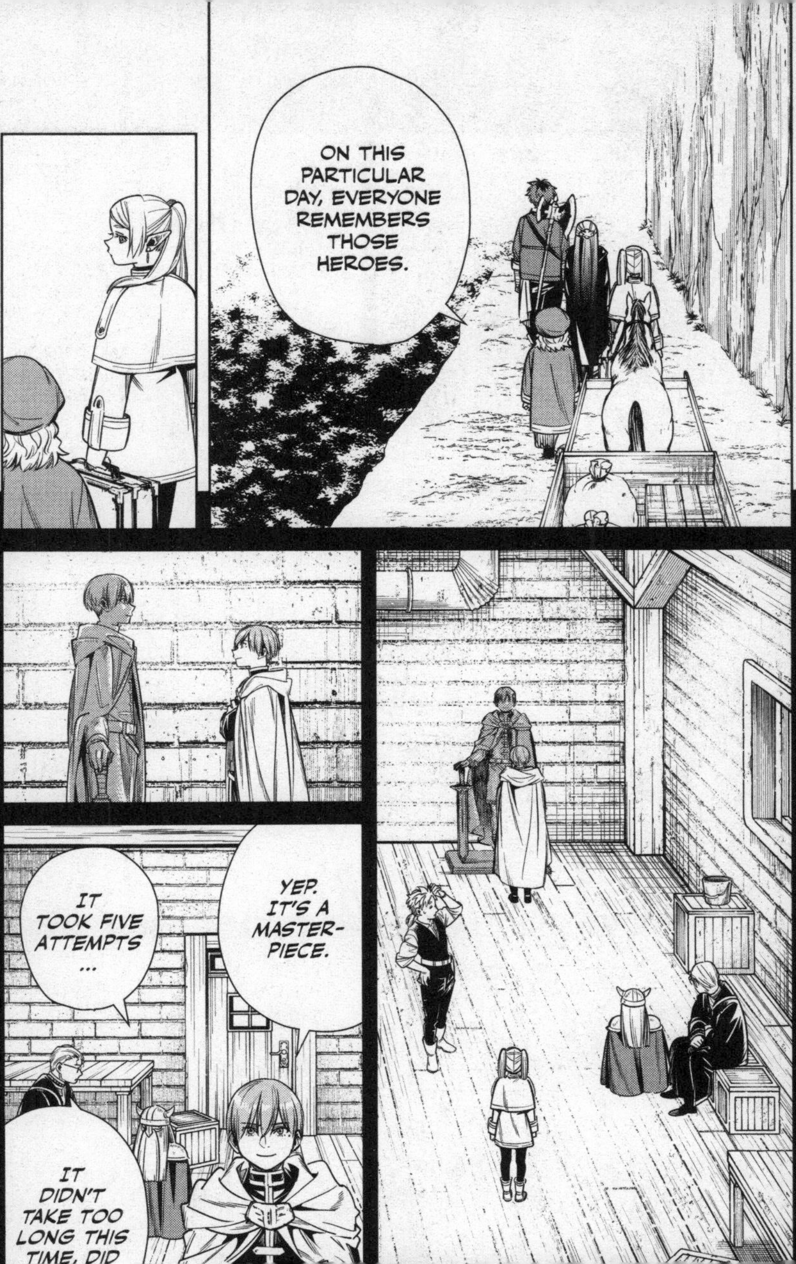
ON THIS PARTICULAR DAY, EVERYONE REMEMBERS THOSE HEROES.
YEP. IT'S A MASTER-PIECE.
IT TOOK FIVE ATTEMPTS ...
IT DIDN'T TAKE TOO LONG THIS TIME, DID

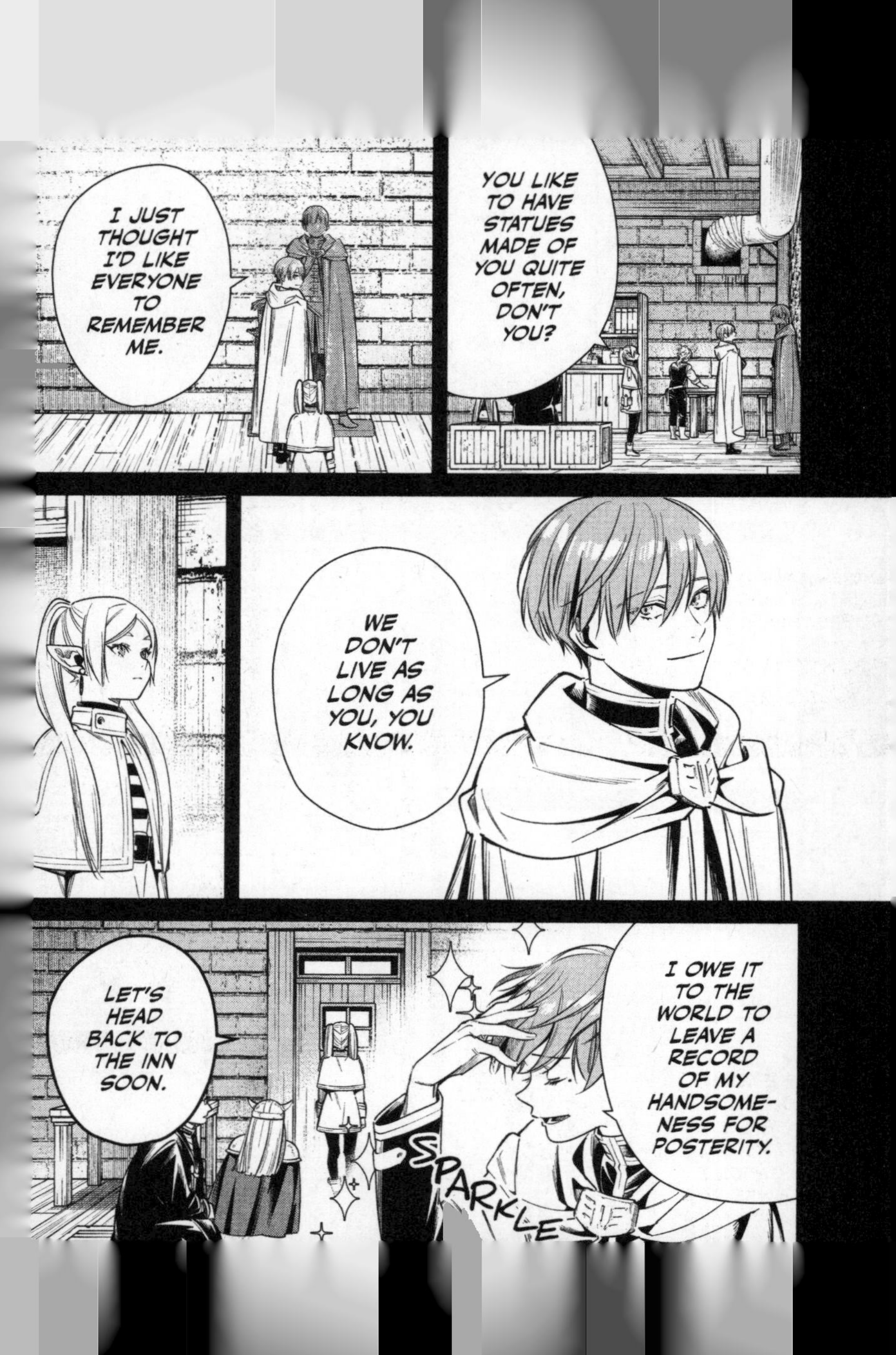
YOU LIKE TO HAVE STATUES MADE OF YOU QUITE OFTEN, DON'T YOU?
I JUST THOUGHT I'D LIKE EVERYONE TO REMEMBER ME.
WE DON'T LIVE AS LONG AS YOU, YOU KNOW.
I OWE IT TO THE WORLD TO LEAVE A RECORD OF MY HANDSOME-NESS FOR POSTERITY.
SPARKLE
LET'S HEAD BACK TO THE INN SOON.

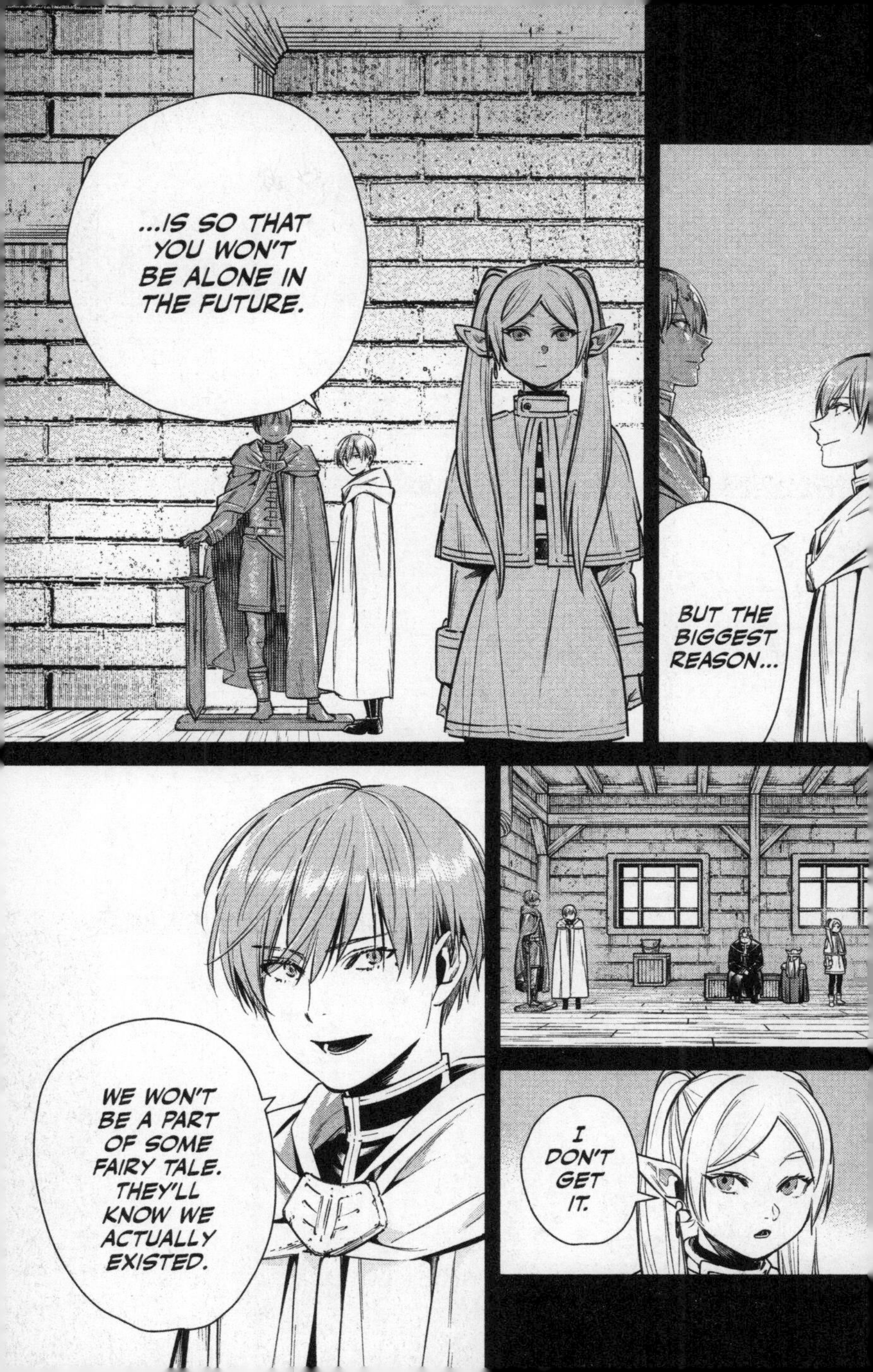
BUT THE BIGGEST REASON...
...IS SO THAT YOU WON'T BE ALONE IN THE FUTURE.
I DON'T GET IT.
WE WON'T BE A PART OF SOME FAIRY TALE. THEY'LL KNOW WE ACTUALLY EXISTED.

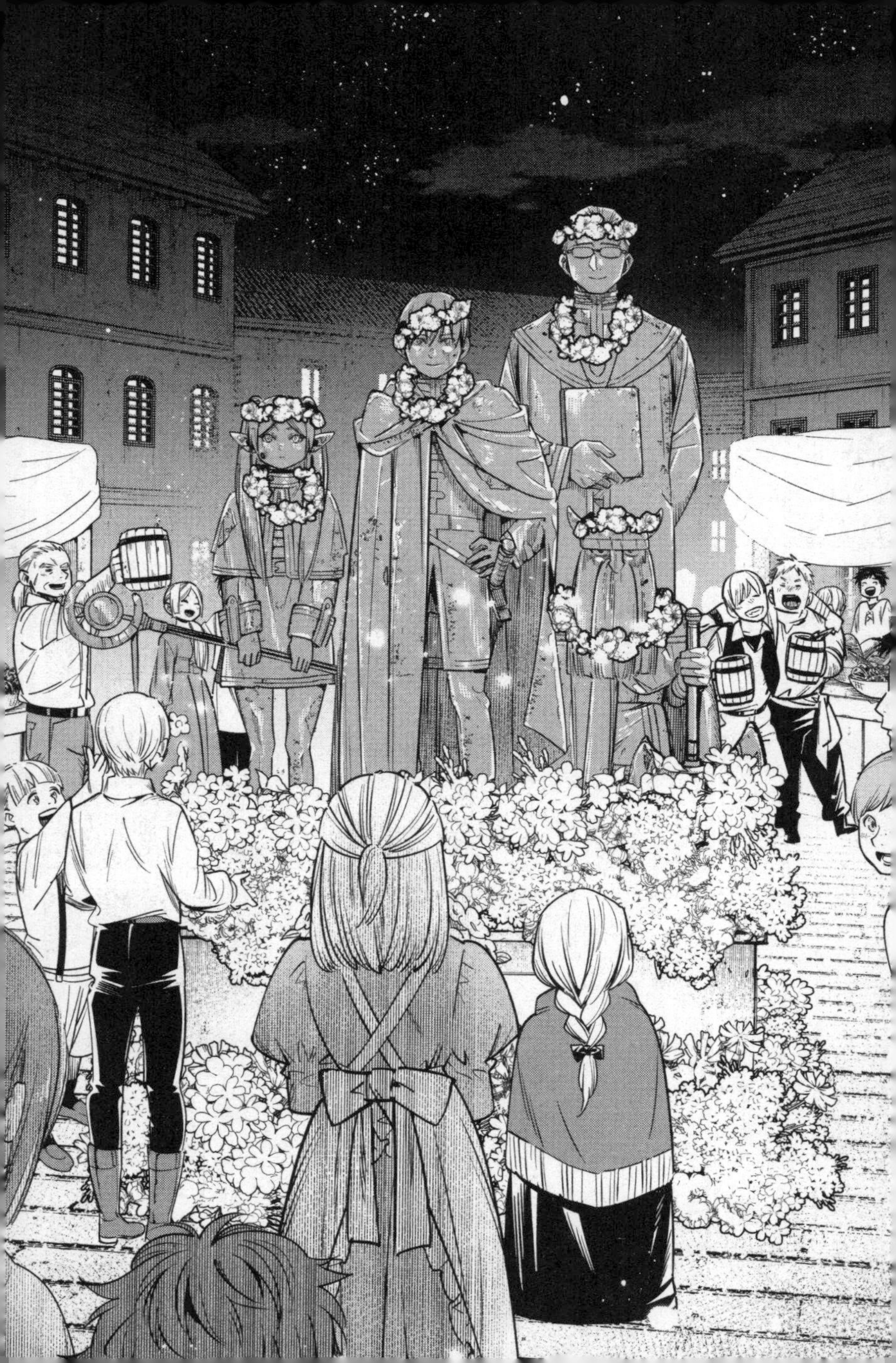

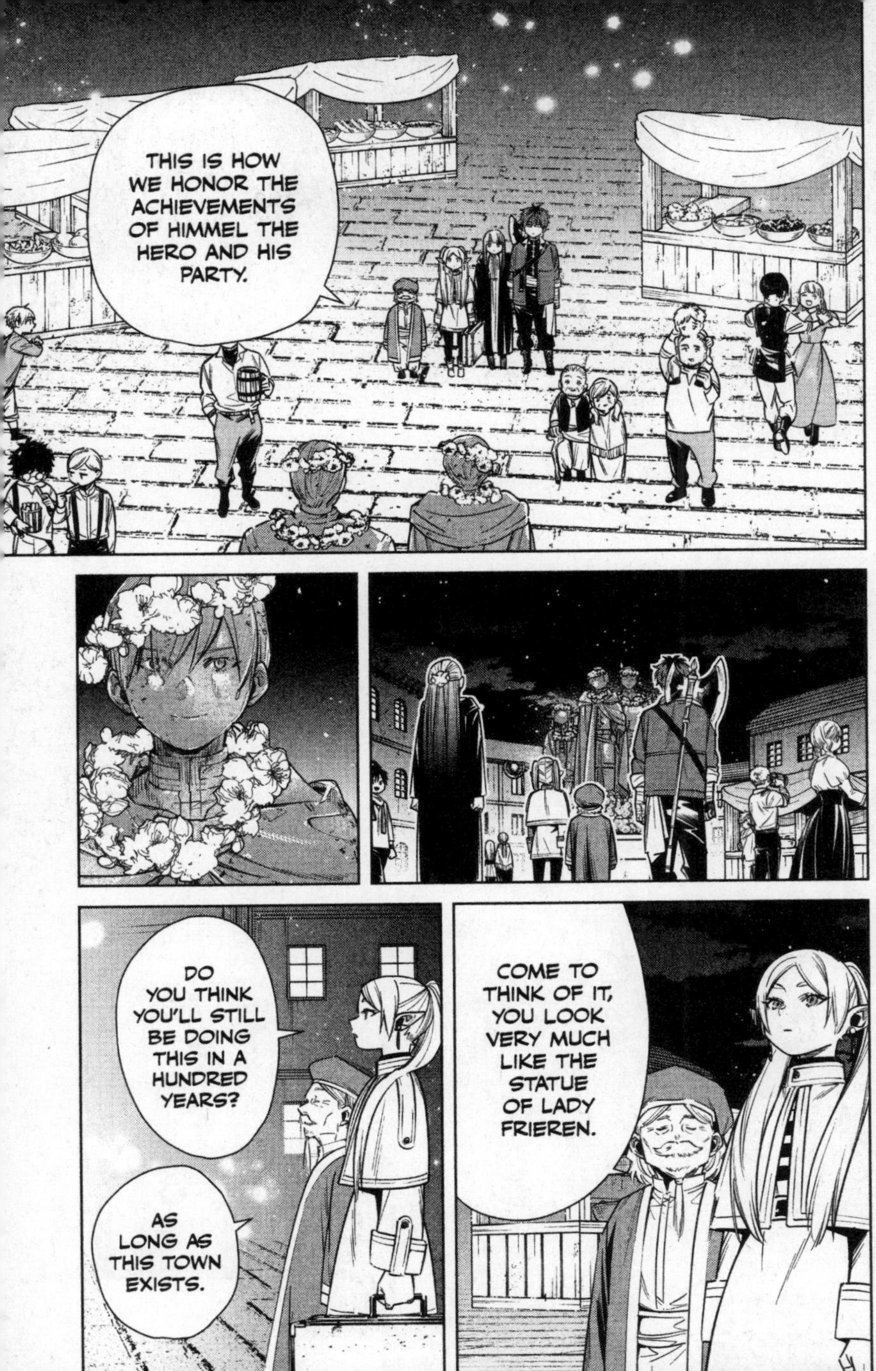
THIS IS HOW WE HONOR THE ACHIEVEMENTS OF HIMMEL THE HERO AND HIS PARTY.
COME TO THINK OF IT, YOU LOOK VERY MUCH LIKE THE STATUE OF LADY FRIEREN.
DO YOU THINK YOU'LL STILL BE DOING THIS IN A HUNDRED YEARS?
AS LONG AS THIS TOWN EXISTS.

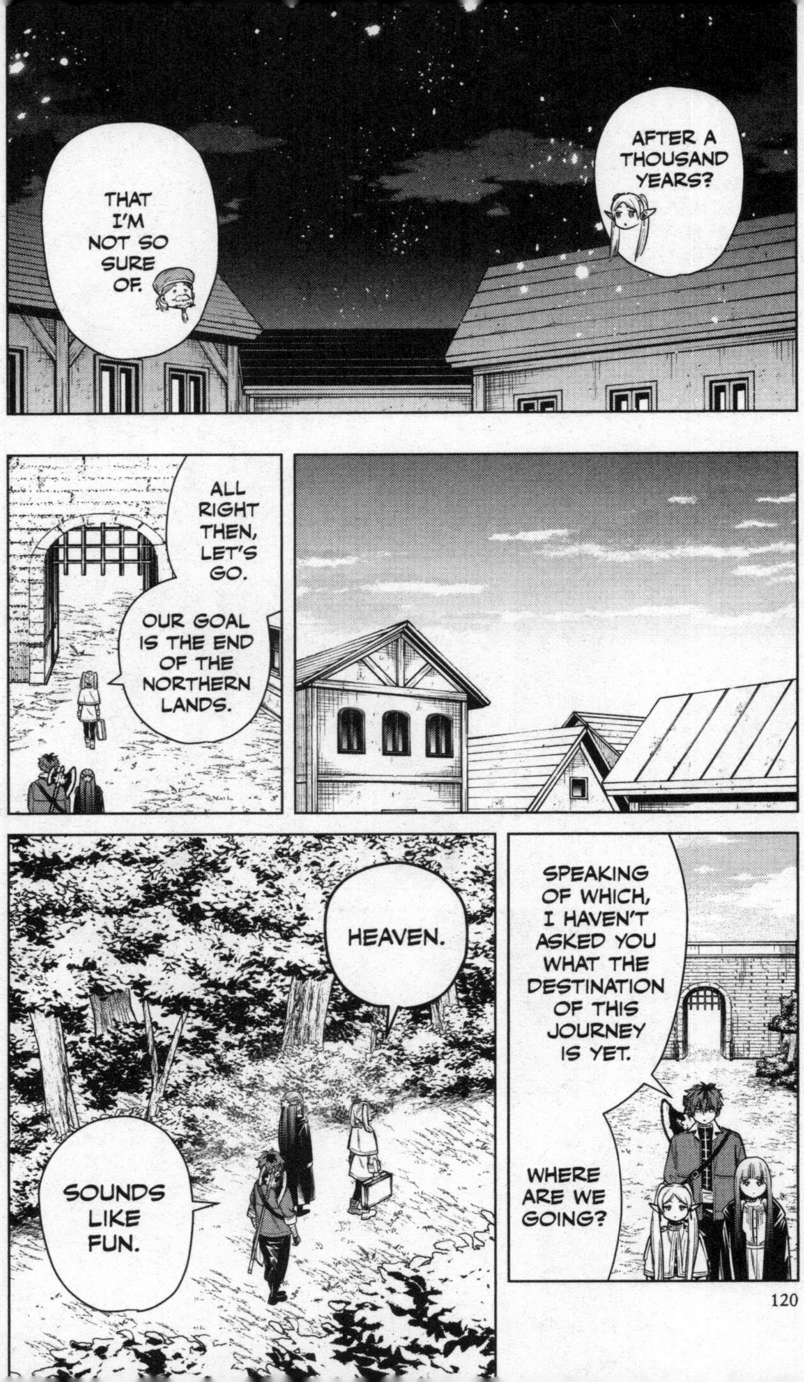
AFTER A THOUSAND YEARS?
THAT I'M NOT SO SURE OF.
ALL RIGHT THEN, LET'S GO.
OUR GOAL IS THE END OF THE NORTHERN LANDS.
SPEAKING OF WHICH, I HAVEN'T ASKED YOU WHAT THE DESTINATION OF THIS JOURNEY IS YET.
WHERE ARE WE GOING?
HEAVEN.
SOUNDS LIKE FUN.

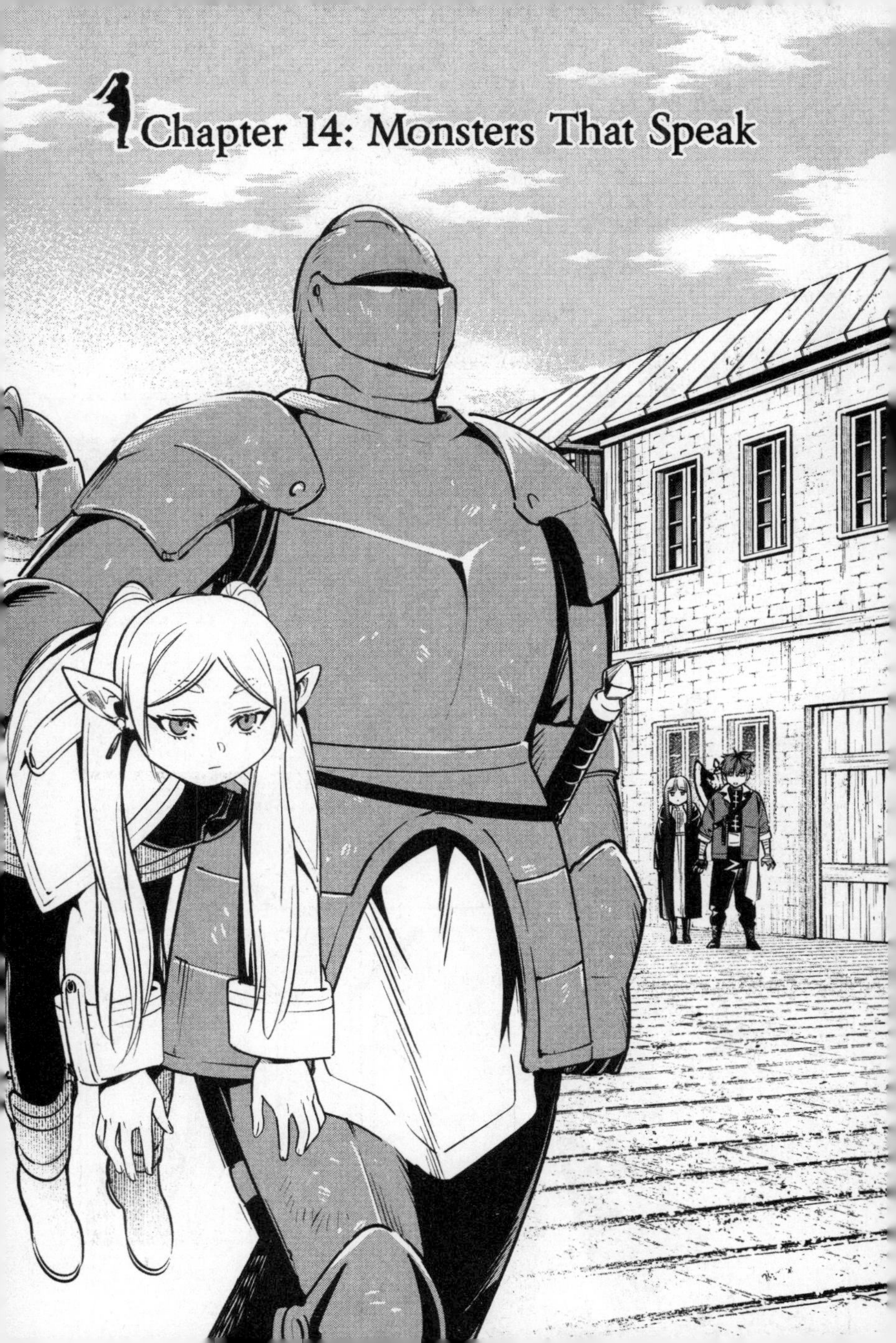
Chapter 14: Monsters That Speak

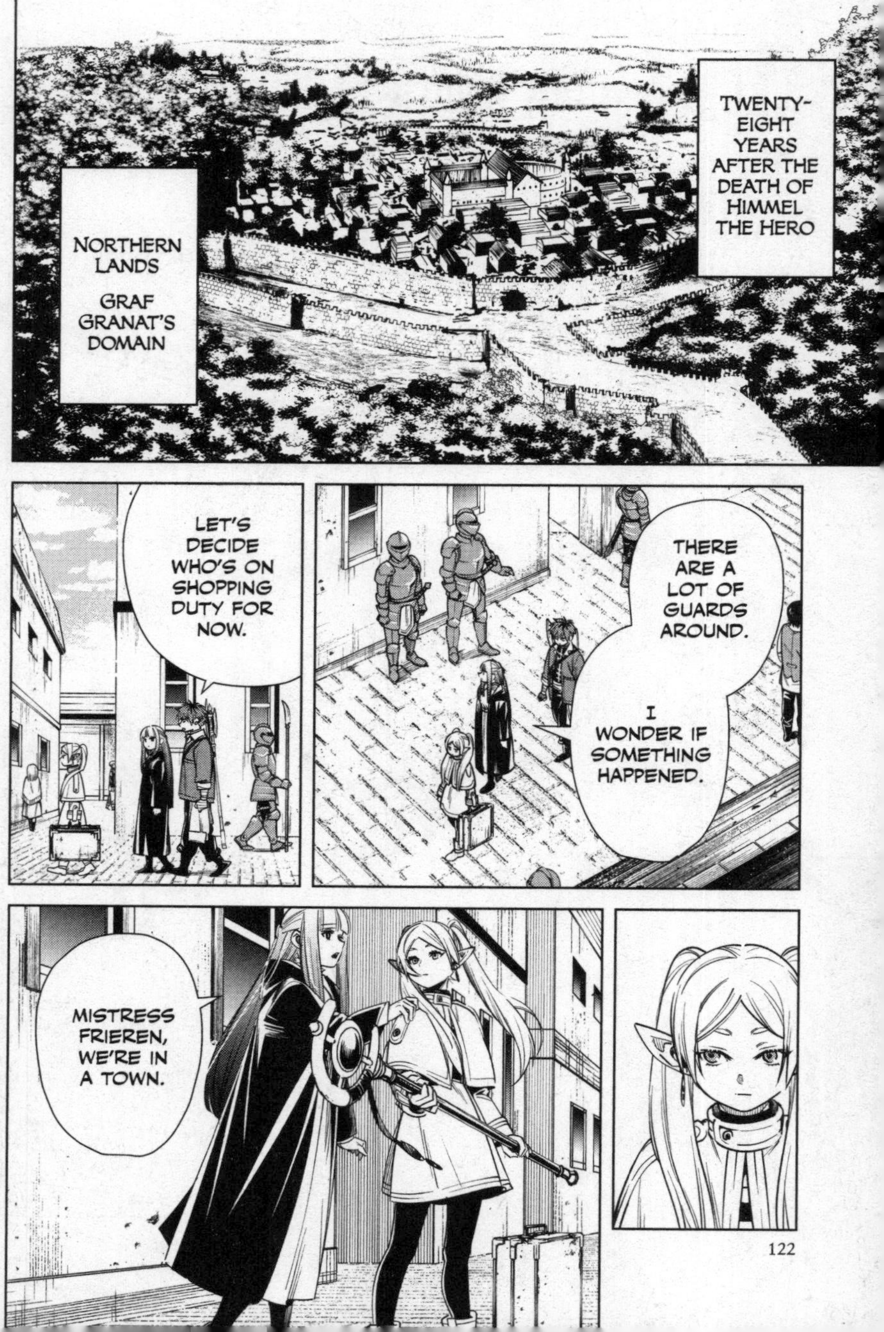
TWENTY-EIGHT YEARS AFTER THE DEATH OF HIMMEL THE HERO
NORTHERN LANDS
GRAF GRANAT'S DOMAIN
THERE ARE A LOT OF GUARDS AROUND.
I WONDER IF SOMETHING HAPPENED.
LET'S DECIDE WHO'S ON SHOPPING DUTY FOR NOW.
MISTRESS FRIEREN, WE'RE IN A TOWN.

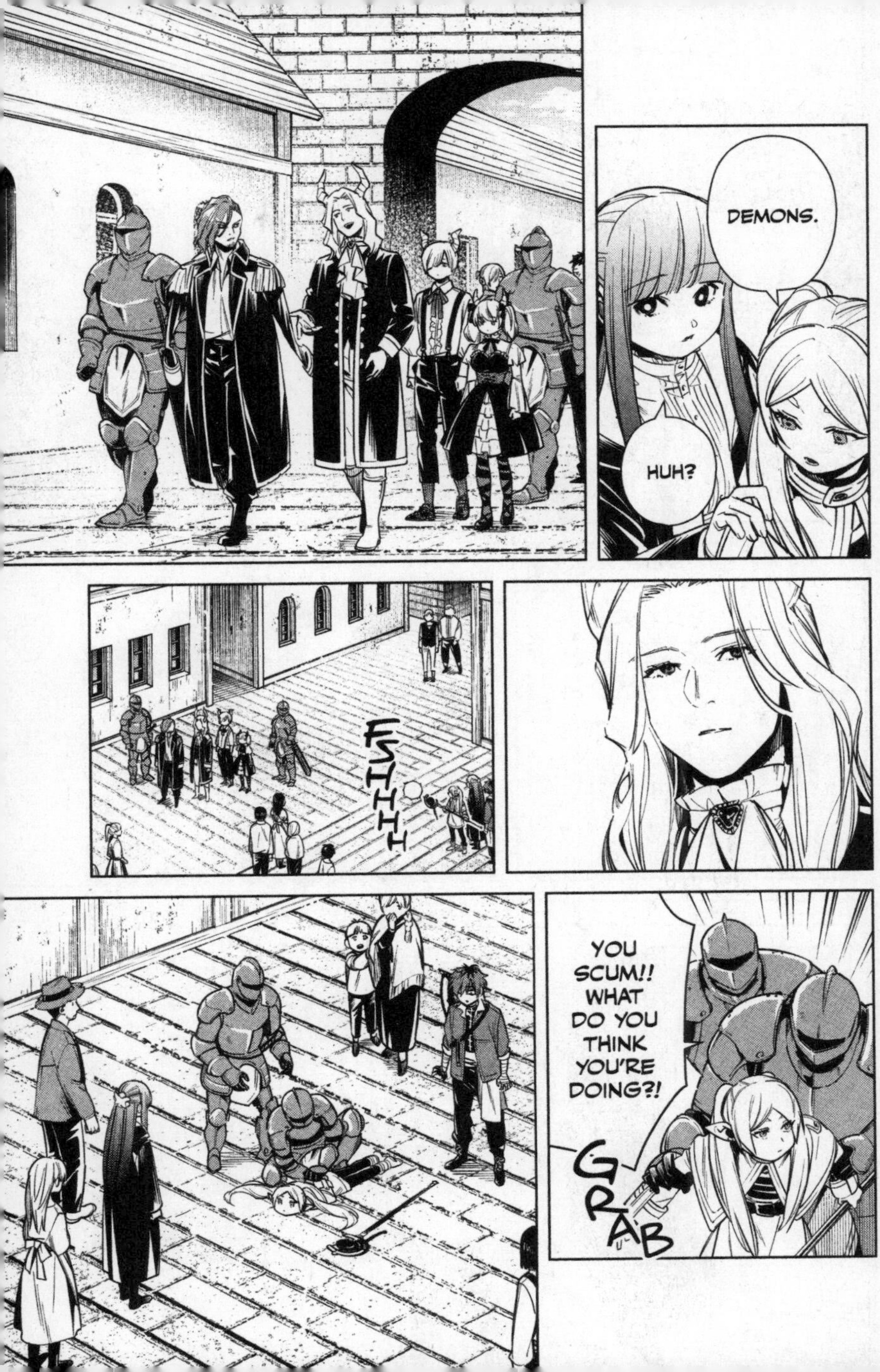
DEMONS.
HUH?
FSHHHH
YOU SCUM!! WHAT DO YOU THINK YOU'RE DOING?!
GRAB

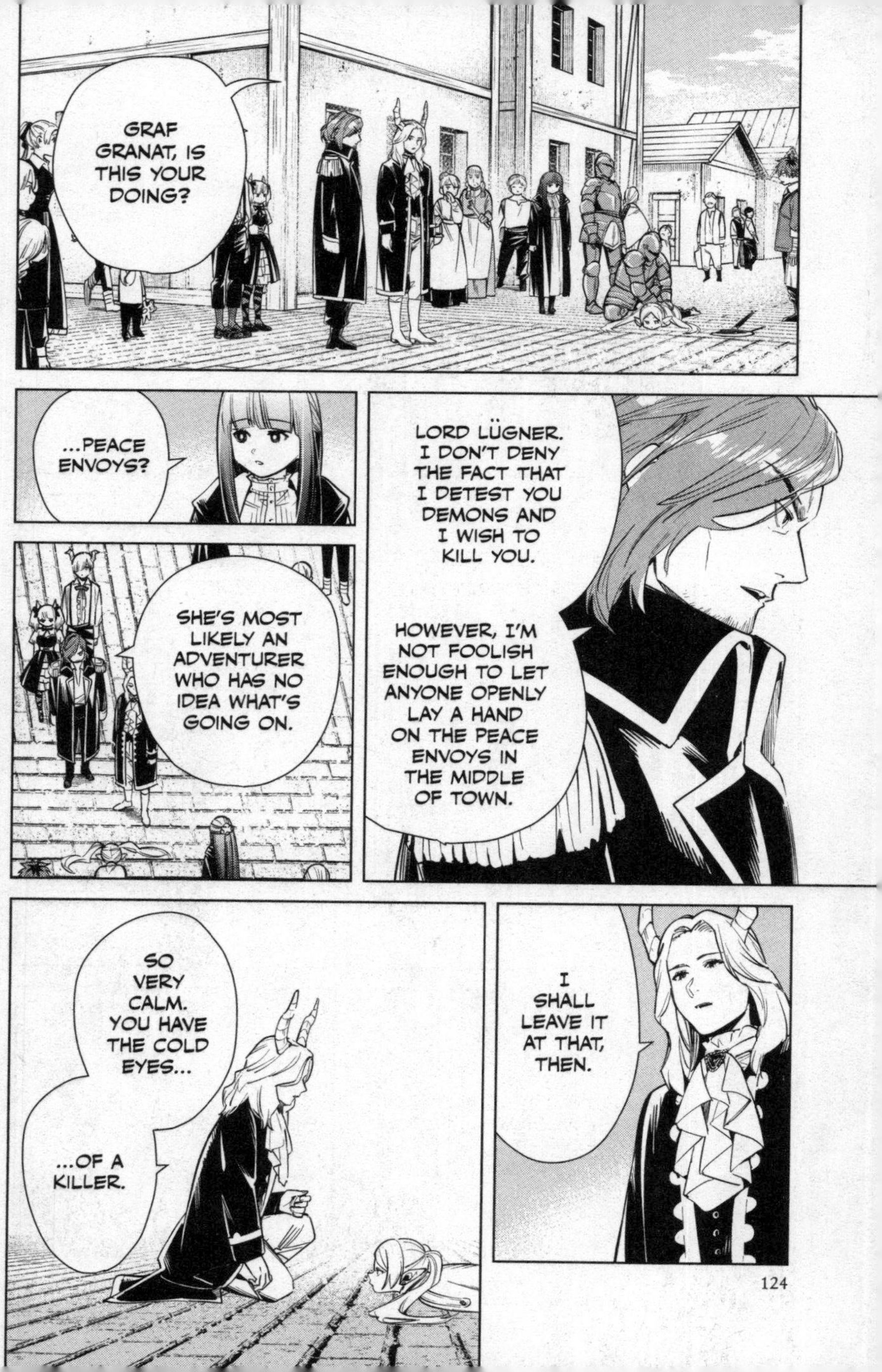
GRAF GRANAT, IS THIS YOUR DOING?
LORD LÜGNER. I DON'T DENY THE FACT THAT I DETEST YOU DEMONS AND I WISH TO KILL YOU.
HOWEVER, I'M NOT FOOLISH ENOUGH TO LET ANYONE OPENLY LAY A HAND ON THE PEACE ENVOYS IN THE MIDDLE OF TOWN.
...PEACE ENVOYS?
SHE'S MOST LIKELY AN ADVENTURER WHO HAS NO IDEA WHAT'S GOING ON.
I SHALL LEAVE IT AT THAT, THEN.
SO VERY CALM. YOU HAVE THE COLD EYES...
...OF A KILLER.

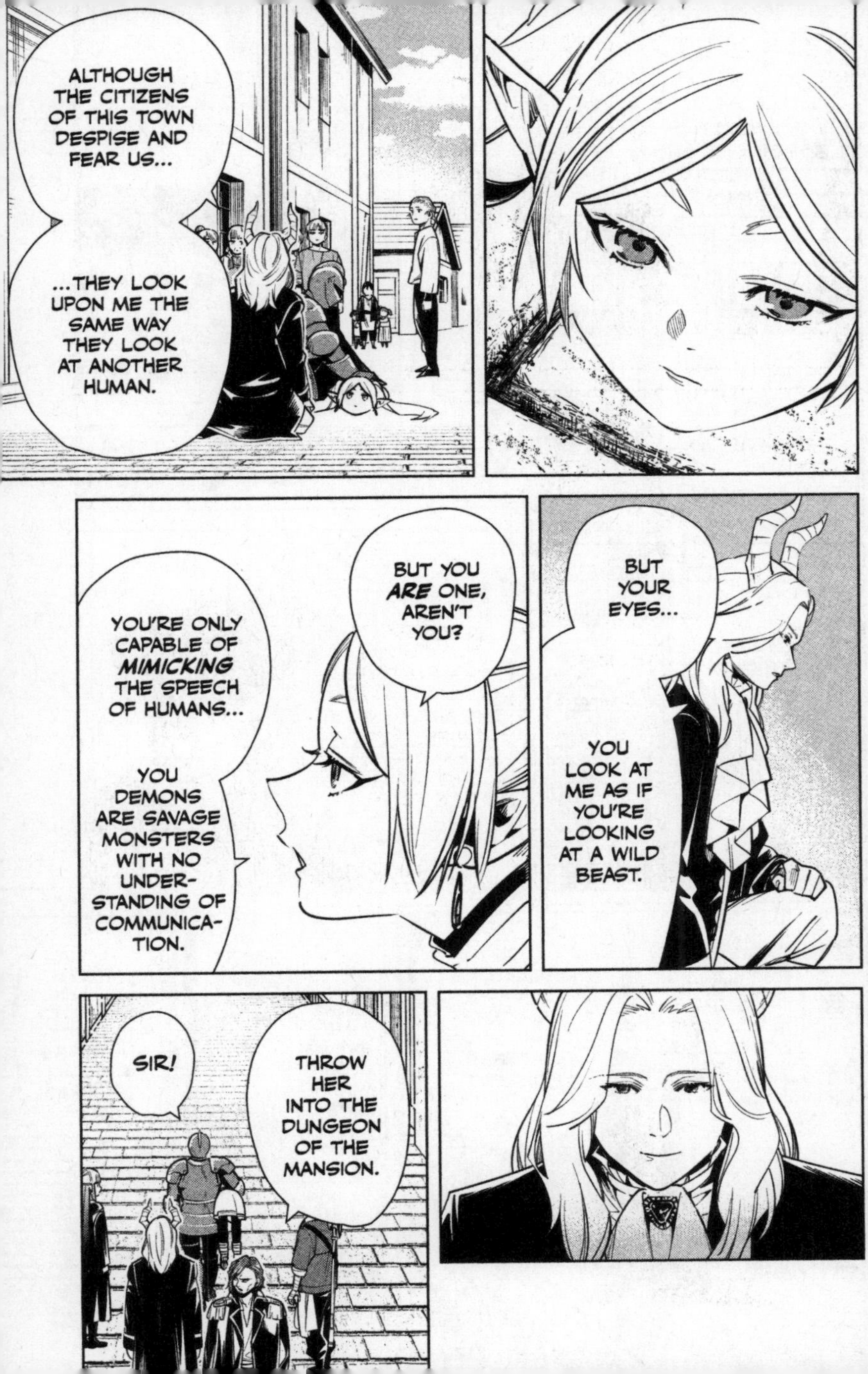
ALTHOUGH THE CITIZENS OF THIS TOWN DESPISE AND FEAR US...
...THEY LOOK UPON ME THE SAME WAY THEY LOOK AT ANOTHER HUMAN.
BUT YOUR EYES...
YOU LOOK AT ME AS IF YOU'RE LOOKING AT A WILD BEAST.
BUT YOU *ARE* ONE, AREN'T YOU?
YOU'RE ONLY CAPABLE OF *MIMICKING* THE SPEECH OF HUMANS...
YOU DEMONS ARE SAVAGE MONSTERS WITH NO UNDER-STANDING OF COMMUNICA-TION.
THROW HER INTO THE DUNGEON OF THE MANSION.
SIR!

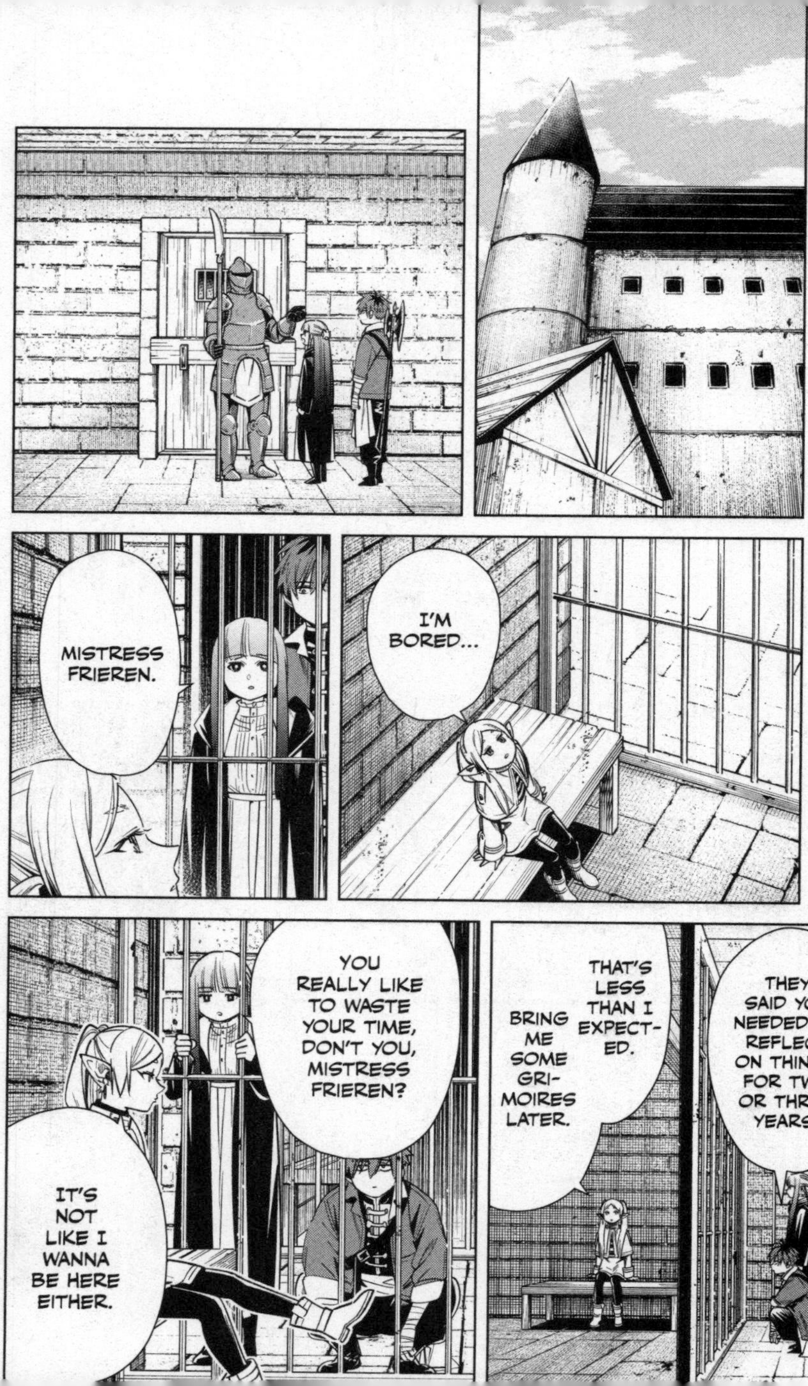
I'M BORED...
MISTRESS FRIEREN.
THEY SAID YOU NEEDED TO REFLECT ON THINGS FOR TWO OR THREE YEARS.
THAT'S LESS THAN I EXPECTED.
BRING ME SOME GRIMOIRES LATER.
YOU REALLY LIKE TO WASTE YOUR TIME, DON'T YOU, MISTRESS FRIEREN?
IT'S NOT LIKE I WANNA BE HERE EITHER.

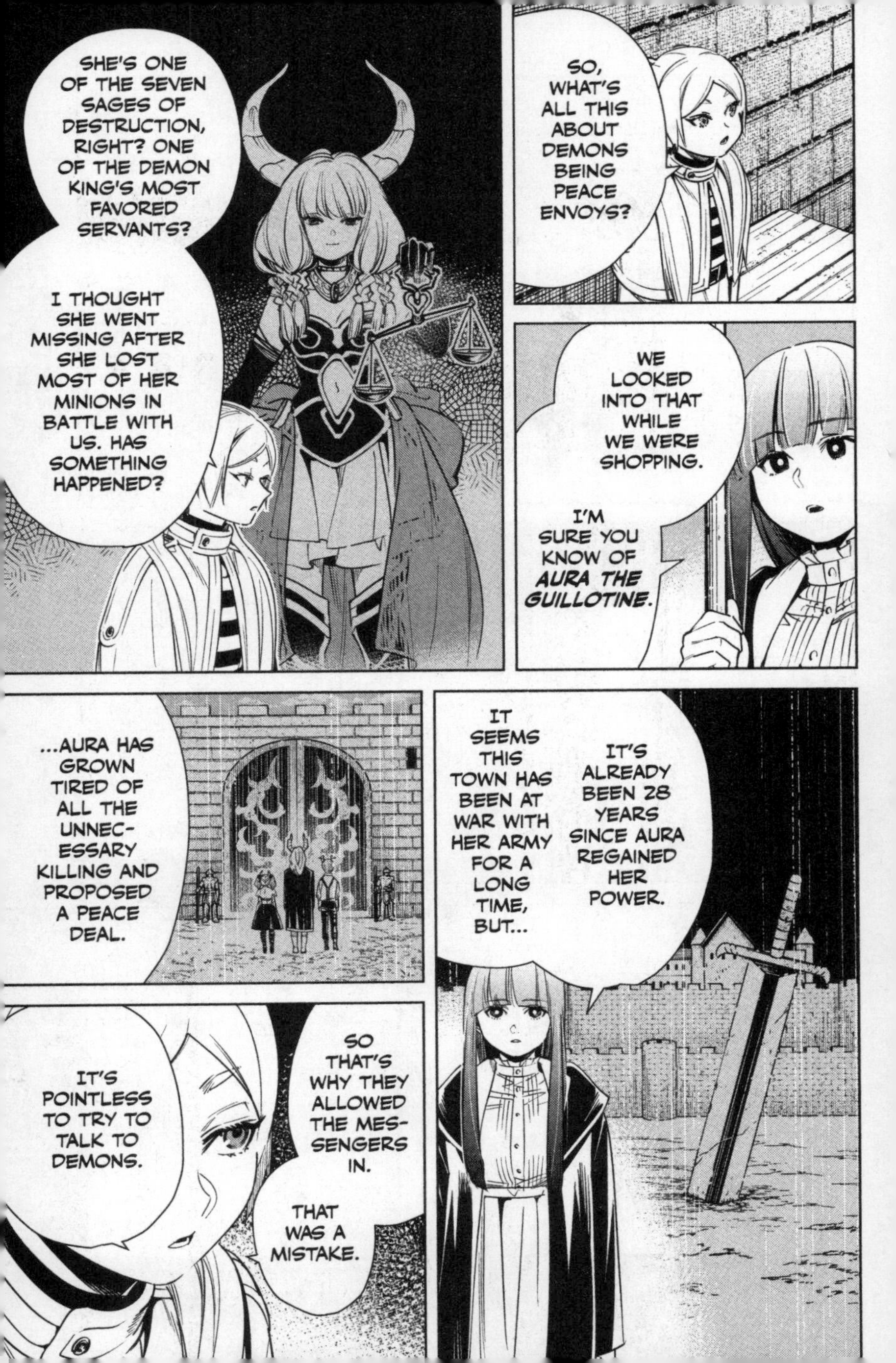
SO, WHAT'S ALL THIS ABOUT DEMONS BEING PEACE ENVOYS?
WE LOOKED INTO THAT WHILE WE WERE SHOPPING.
I'M SURE YOU KNOW OF *AURA THE GUILLOTINE*.
SHE'S ONE OF THE SEVEN SAGES OF DESTRUCTION, RIGHT? ONE OF THE DEMON KING'S MOST FAVORED SERVANTS?
I THOUGHT SHE WENT MISSING AFTER SHE LOST MOST OF HER MINIONS IN BATTLE WITH US. HAS SOMETHING HAPPENED?
IT'S ALREADY BEEN 28 YEARS SINCE AURA REGAINED HER POWER.
IT SEEMS THIS TOWN HAS BEEN AT WAR WITH HER ARMY FOR A LONG TIME, BUT...
...AURA HAS GROWN TIRED OF ALL THE UNNEC-ESSARY KILLING AND PROPOSED A PEACE DEAL.
SO THAT'S WHY THEY ALLOWED THE MES-SENGERS IN.
THAT WAS A MISTAKE.
IT'S POINTLESS TO TRY TO TALK TO DEMONS.

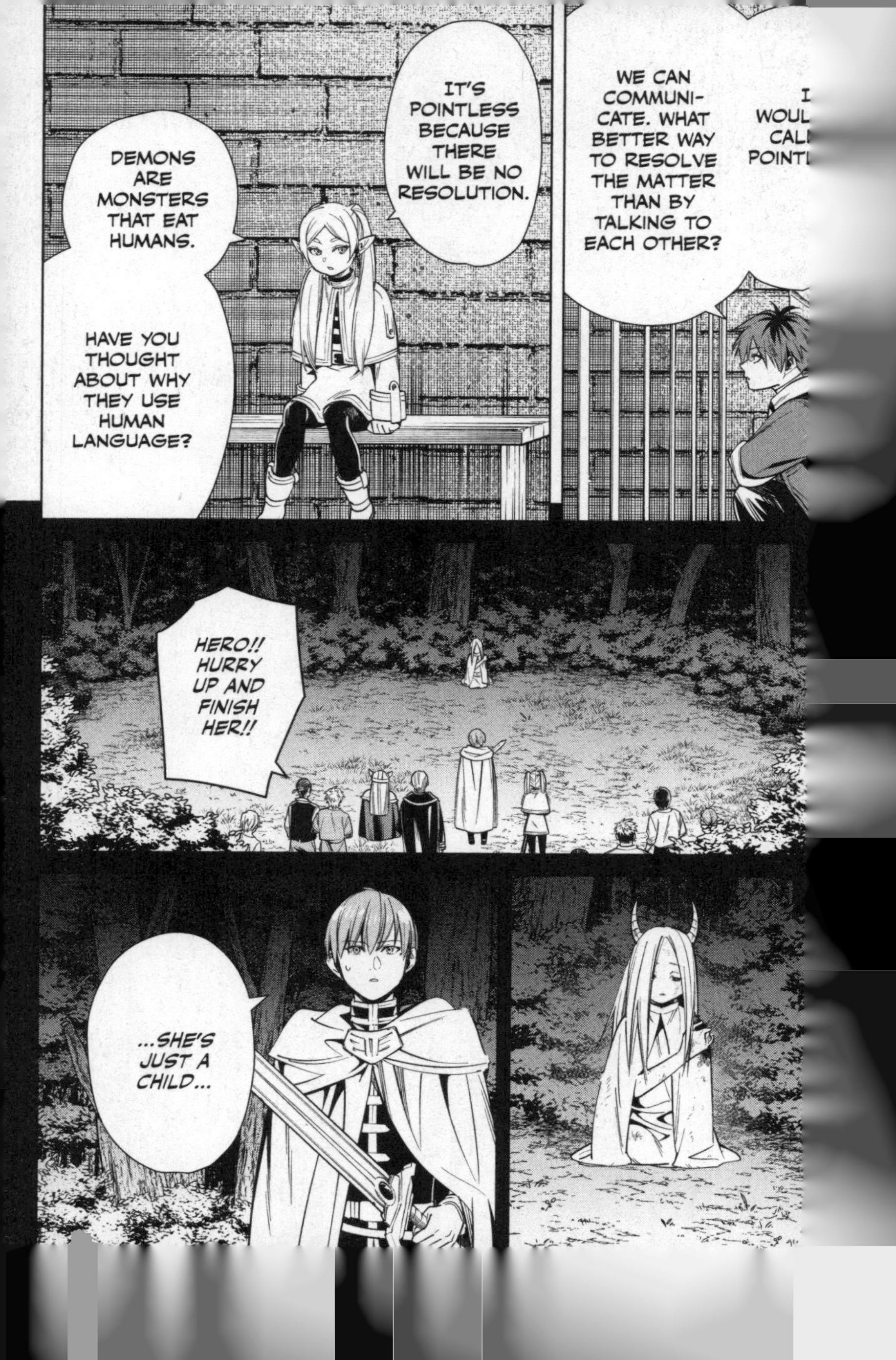
WE CAN COMMUNICATE. WHAT BETTER WAY TO RESOLVE THE MATTER THAN BY TALKING TO EACH OTHER?
IT'S POINTLESS BECAUSE THERE WILL BE NO RESOLUTION.
DEMONS ARE MONSTERS THAT EAT HUMANS.
HAVE YOU THOUGHT ABOUT WHY THEY USE HUMAN LANGUAGE?
HERO!! HURRY UP AND FINISH HER!!
...SHE'S JUST A CHILD...

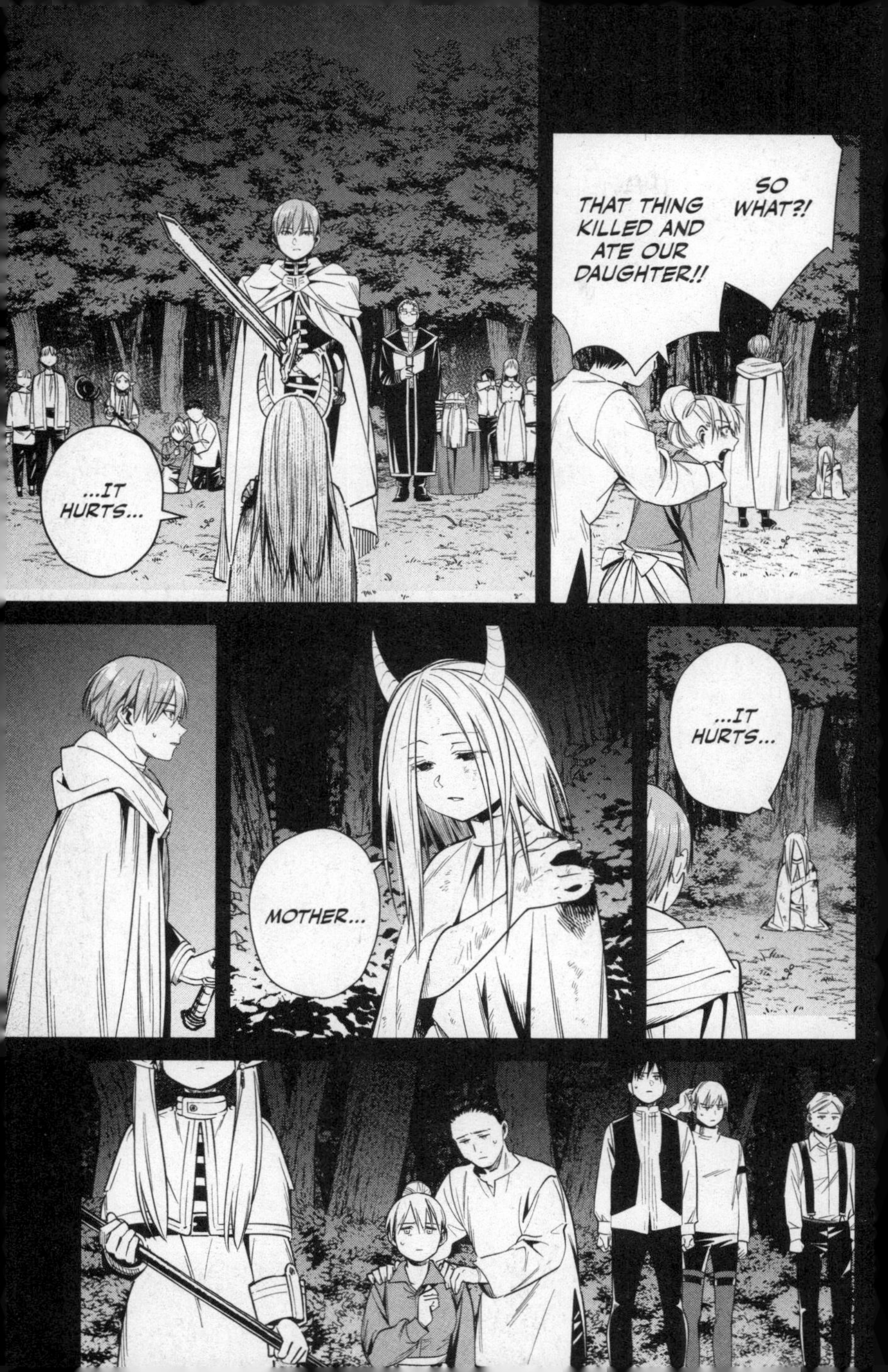
SO WHAT?!
THAT THING KILLED AND ATE OUR DAUGHTER!!
...IT HURTS...
...IT HURTS...
MOTHER...

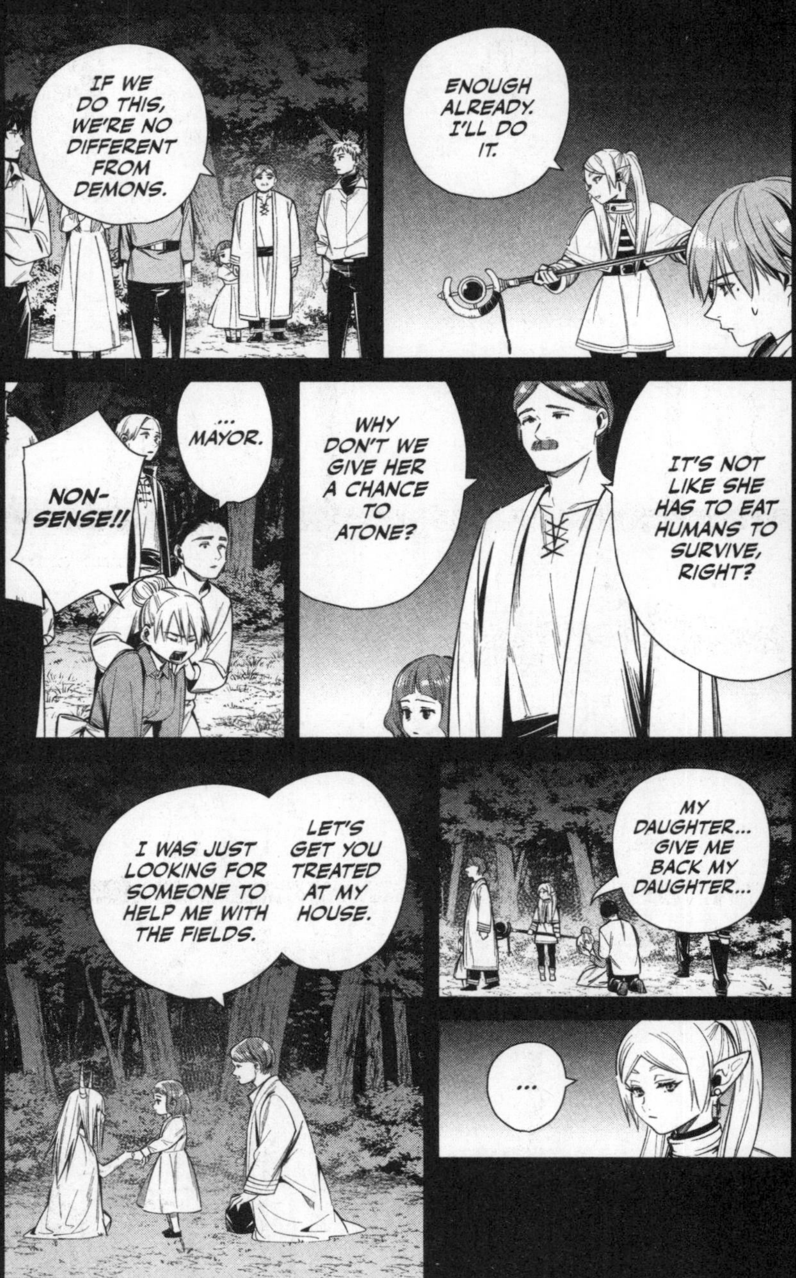
ENOUGH ALREADY. I'LL DO IT.
IF WE DO THIS, WE'RE NO DIFFERENT FROM DEMONS.
IT'S NOT LIKE SHE HAS TO EAT HUMANS TO SURVIVE, RIGHT?
WHY DON'T WE GIVE HER A CHANCE TO ATONE?
... MAYOR.
NON-SENSE!!
MY DAUGHTER... GIVE ME BACK MY DAUGHTER...
...
LET'S GET YOU TREATED AT MY HOUSE.
I WAS JUST LOOKING FOR SOMEONE TO HELP ME WITH THE FIELDS.

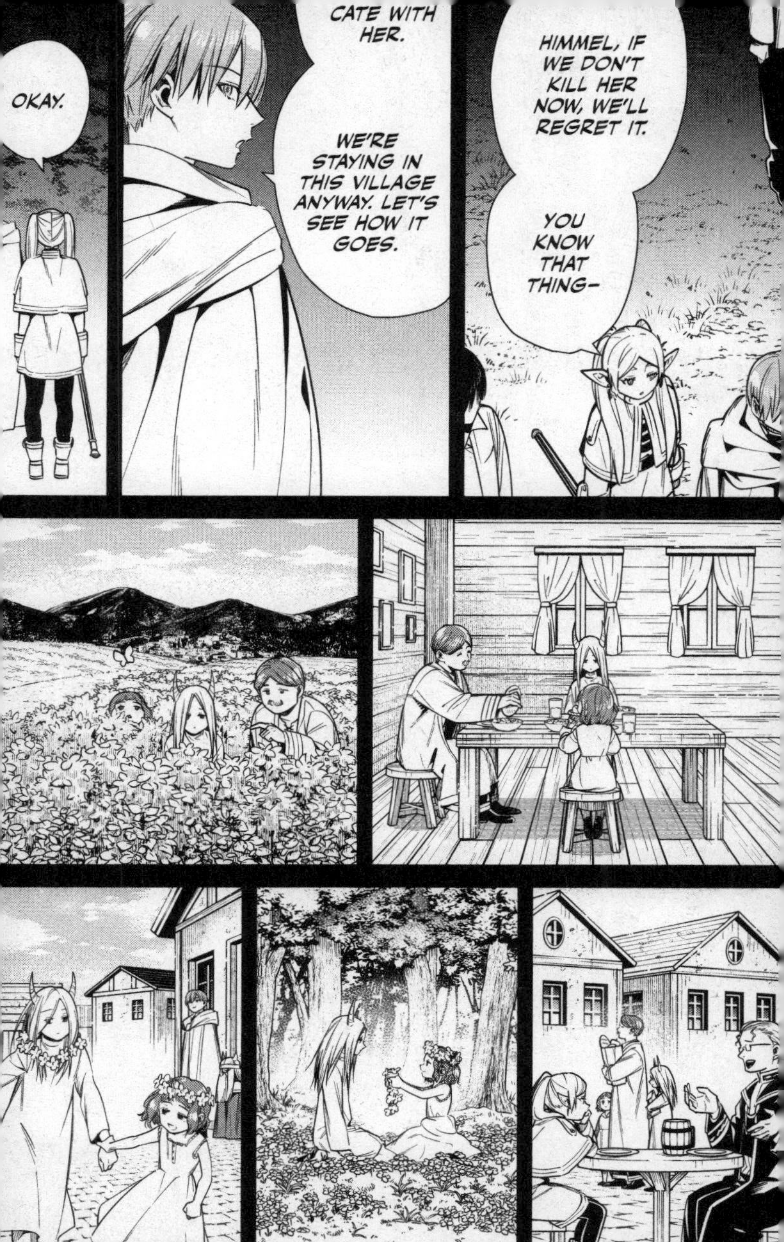
HIMMEL, IF WE DON'T KILL HER NOW, WE'LL REGRET IT.
YOU KNOW THAT THING–
CATE WITH HER.
WE'RE STAYING IN THIS VILLAGE ANYWAY. LET'S SEE HOW IT GOES.
OKAY.

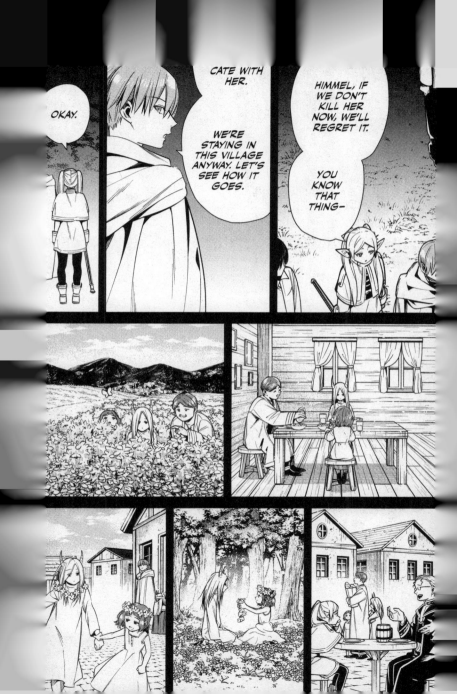

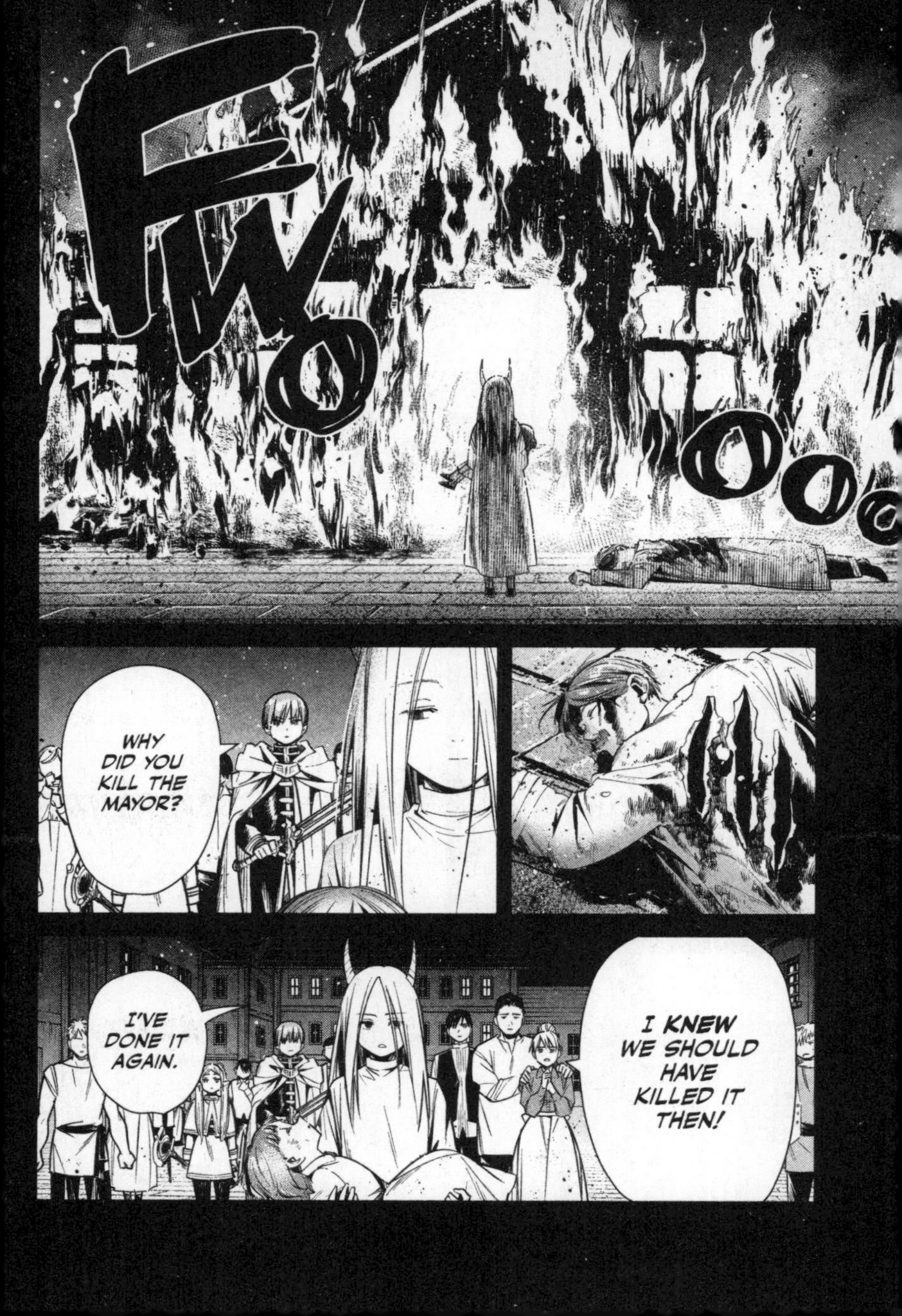
FWOOOOO
WHY DID YOU KILL THE MAYOR?
I KNEW WE SHOULD HAVE KILLED IT THEN!
I'VE DONE IT AGAIN.

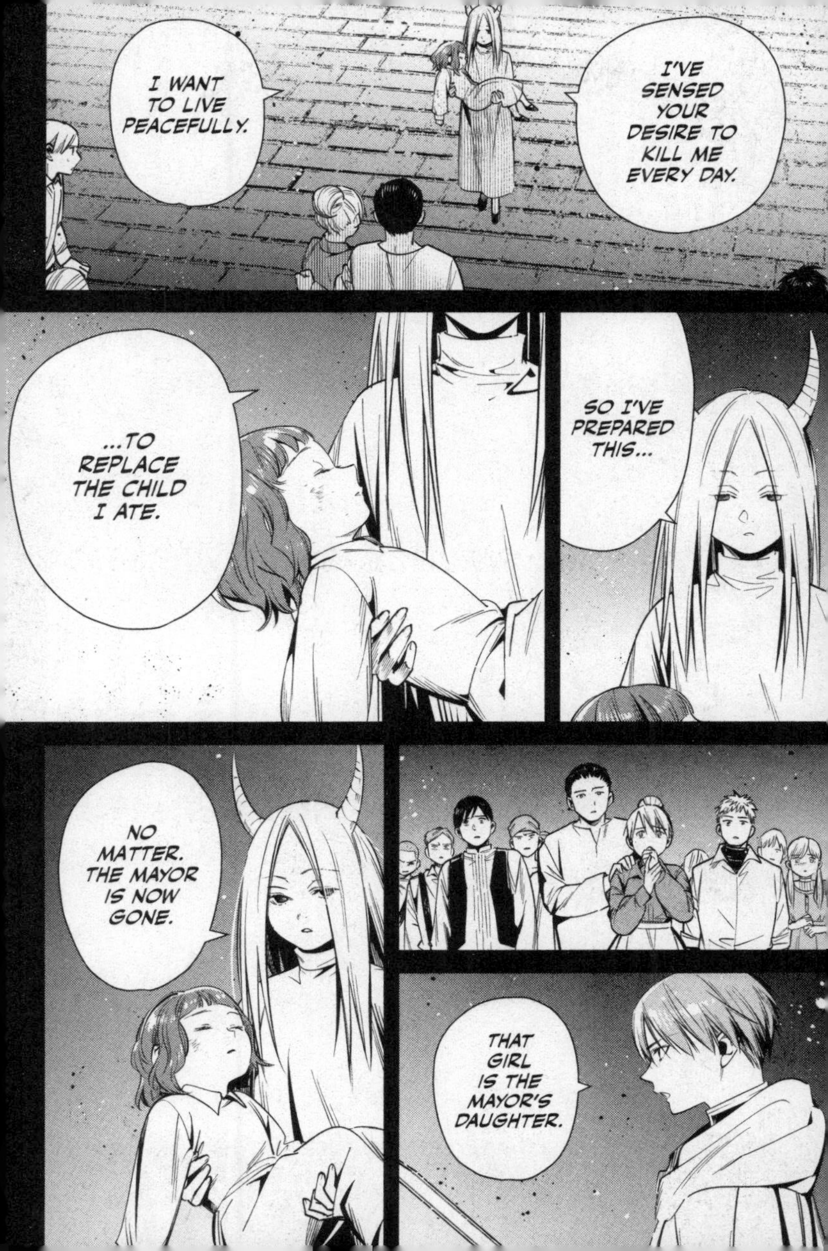
I'VE SENSED YOUR DESIRE TO KILL ME EVERY DAY.
I WANT TO LIVE PEACEFULLY.
SO I'VE PREPARED THIS...
...TO REPLACE THE CHILD I ATE.
THAT GIRL IS THE MAYOR'S DAUGHTER.
NO MATTER. THE MAYOR IS NOW GONE.

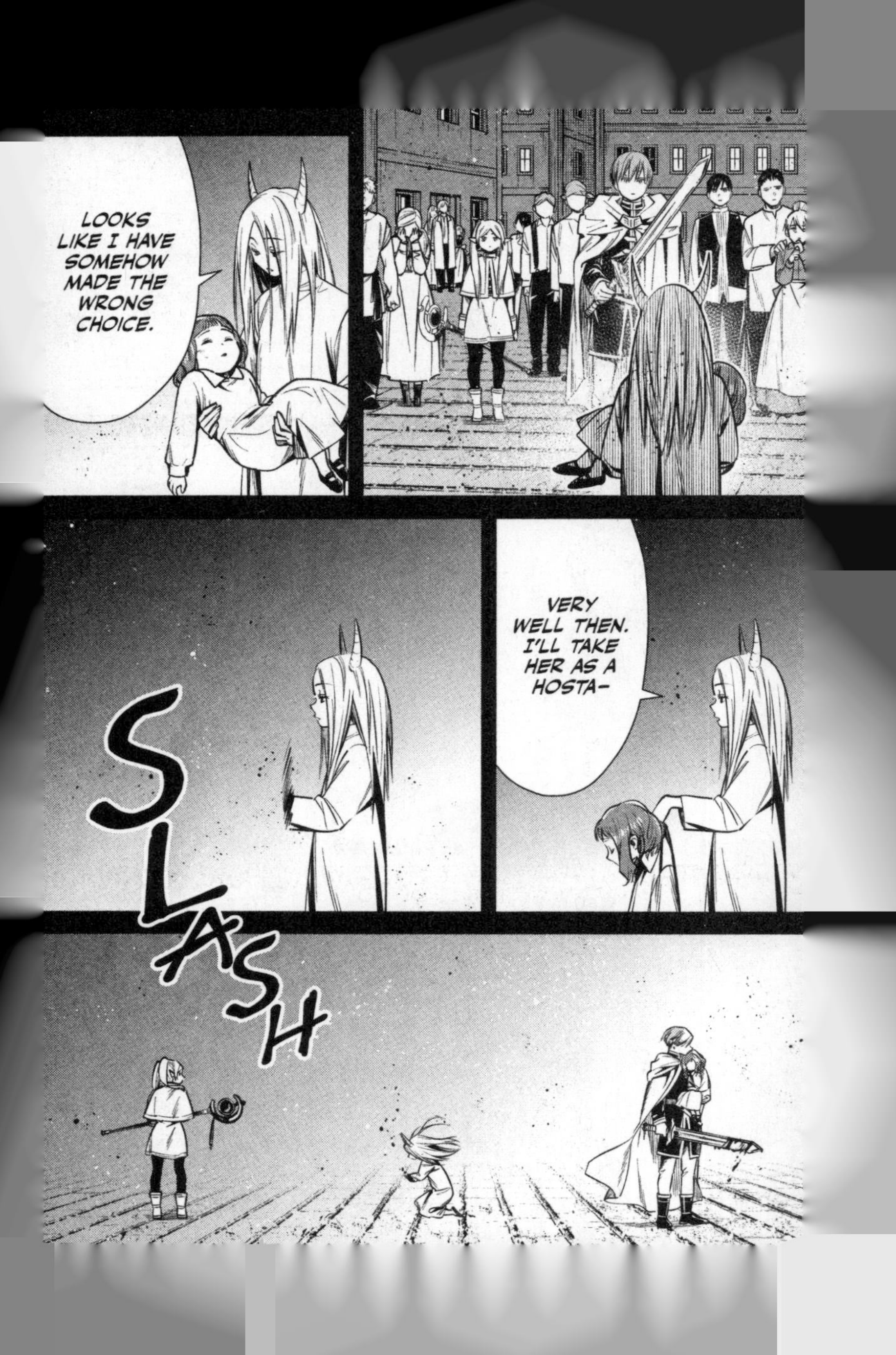
LOOKS LIKE I HAVE SOMEHOW MADE THE WRONG CHOICE.
VERY WELL THEN. I'LL TAKE HER AS A HOSTA-
SLASH

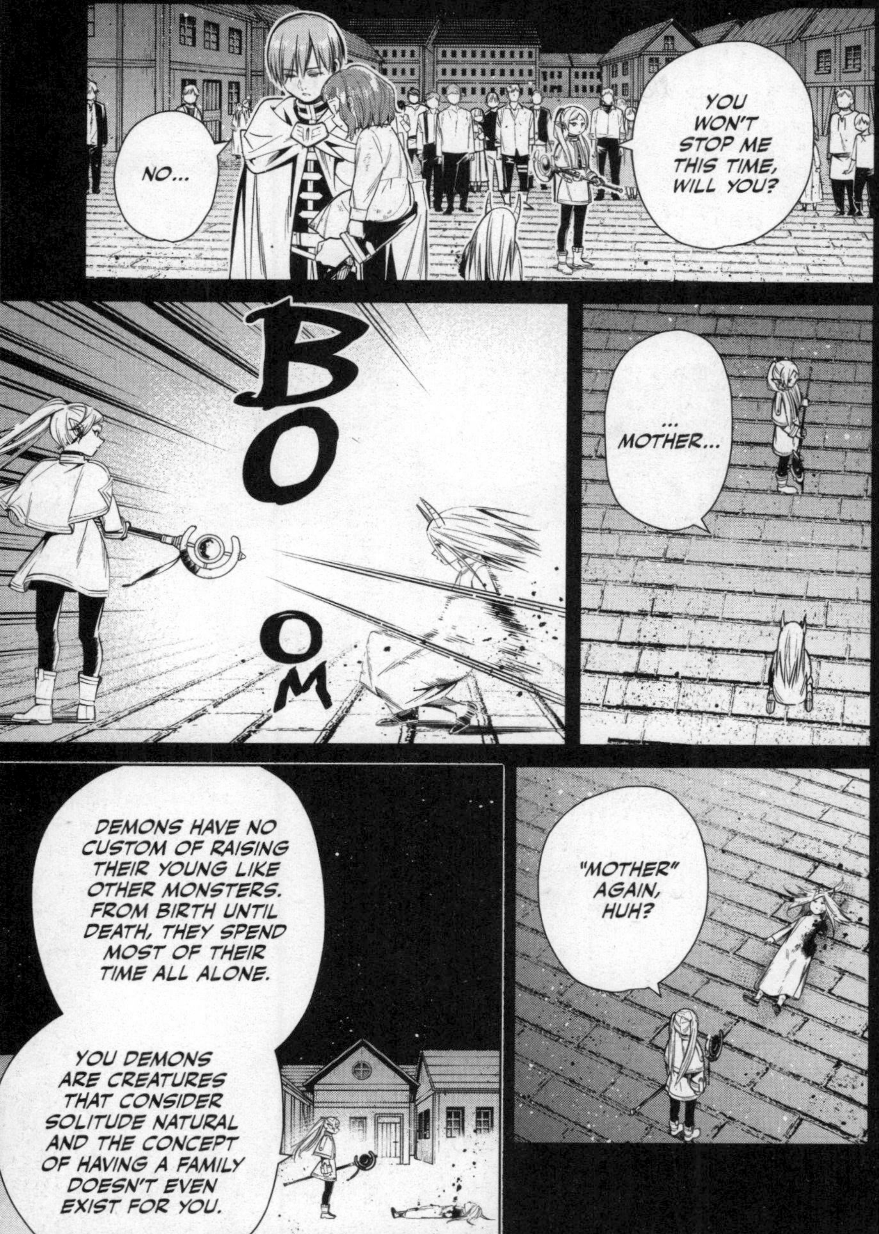
YOU WON'T STOP ME THIS TIME, WILL YOU?
NO...
... MOTHER...
BOOM
"MOTHER" AGAIN, HUH?
DEMONS HAVE NO CUSTOM OF RAISING THEIR YOUNG LIKE OTHER MONSTERS. FROM BIRTH UNTIL DEATH, THEY SPEND MOST OF THEIR TIME ALL ALONE.
YOU DEMONS ARE CREATURES THAT CONSIDER SOLITUDE NATURAL AND THE CONCEPT OF HAVING A FAMILY DOESN'T EVEN EXIST FOR YOU.

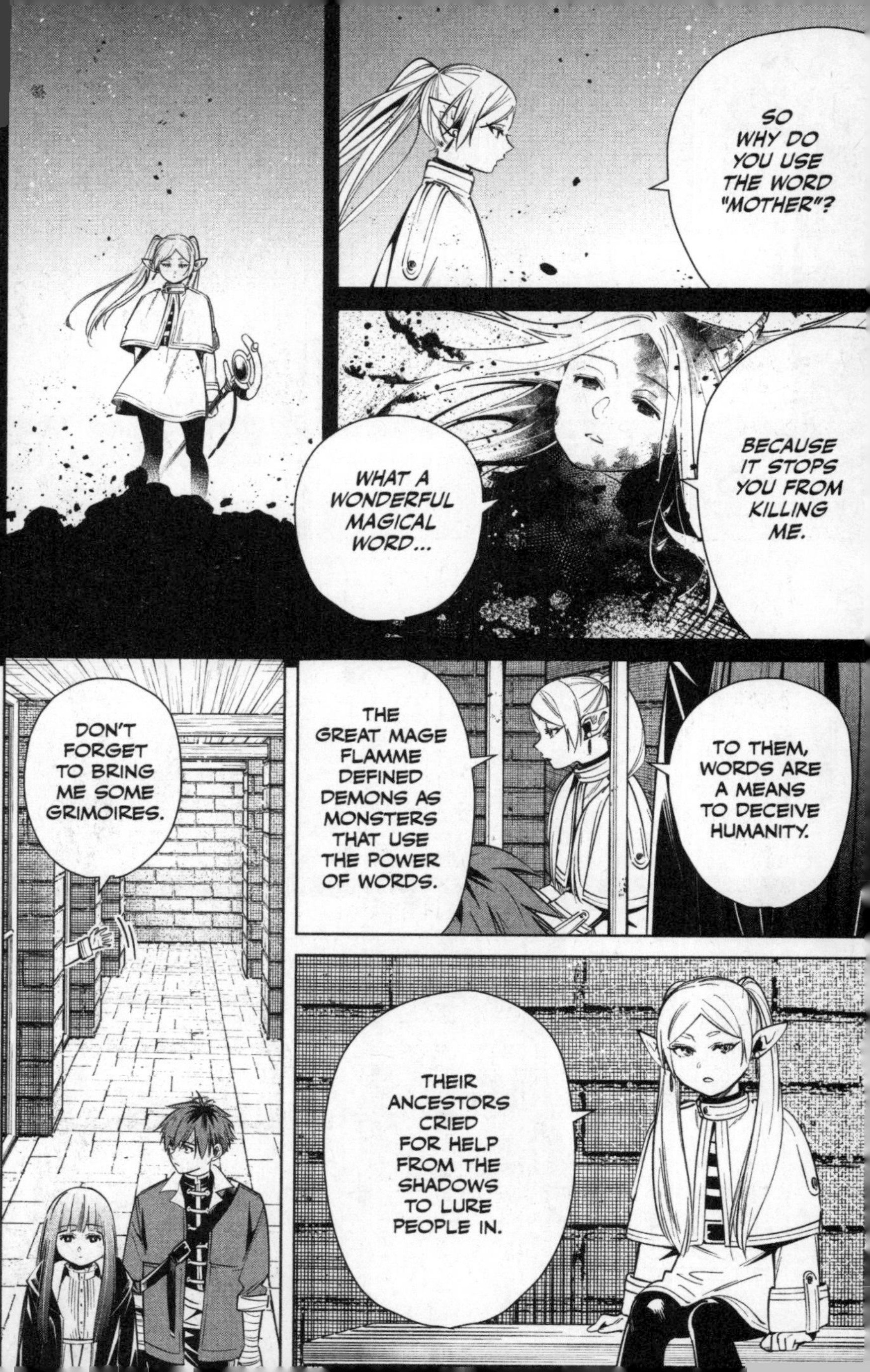
SO WHY DO YOU USE THE WORD "MOTHER"?
BECAUSE IT STOPS YOU FROM KILLING ME.
WHAT A WONDERFUL MAGICAL WORD...
THE GREAT MAGE FLAMME DEFINED DEMONS AS MONSTERS THAT USE THE POWER OF WORDS.
TO THEM, WORDS ARE A MEANS TO DECEIVE HUMANITY.
THEIR ANCESTORS CRIED FOR HELP FROM THE SHADOWS TO LURE PEOPLE IN.
DON'T FORGET TO BRING ME SOME GRIMOIRES.

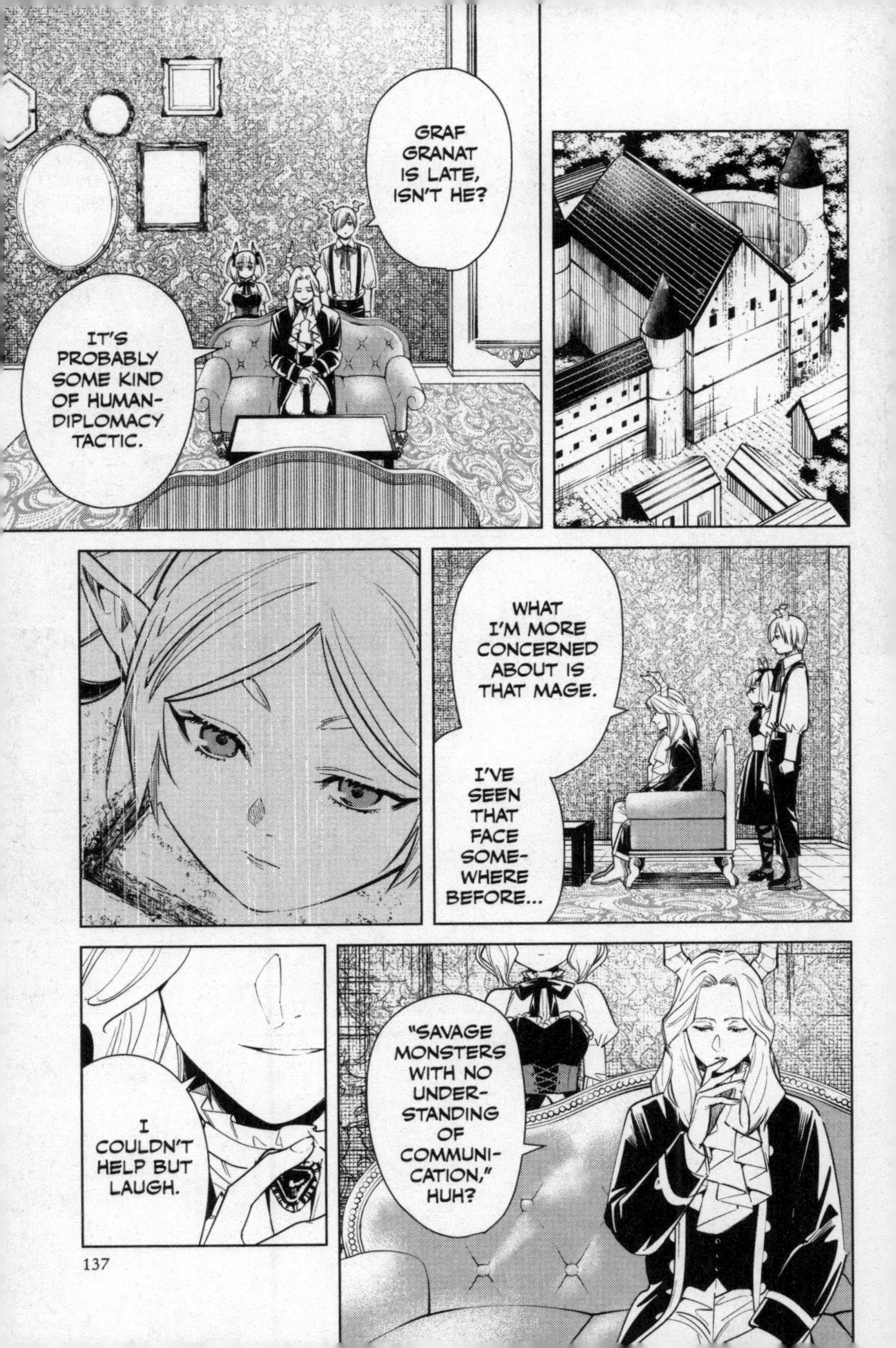
GRAF GRANAT IS LATE, ISN'T HE?
IT'S PROBABLY SOME KIND OF HUMAN-DIPLOMACY TACTIC.
WHAT I'M MORE CONCERNED ABOUT IS THAT MAGE.
I'VE SEEN THAT FACE SOME-WHERE BEFORE...
"SAVAGE MONSTERS WITH NO UNDER-STANDING OF COMMUNI-CATION," HUH?
I COULDN'T HELP BUT LAUGH.

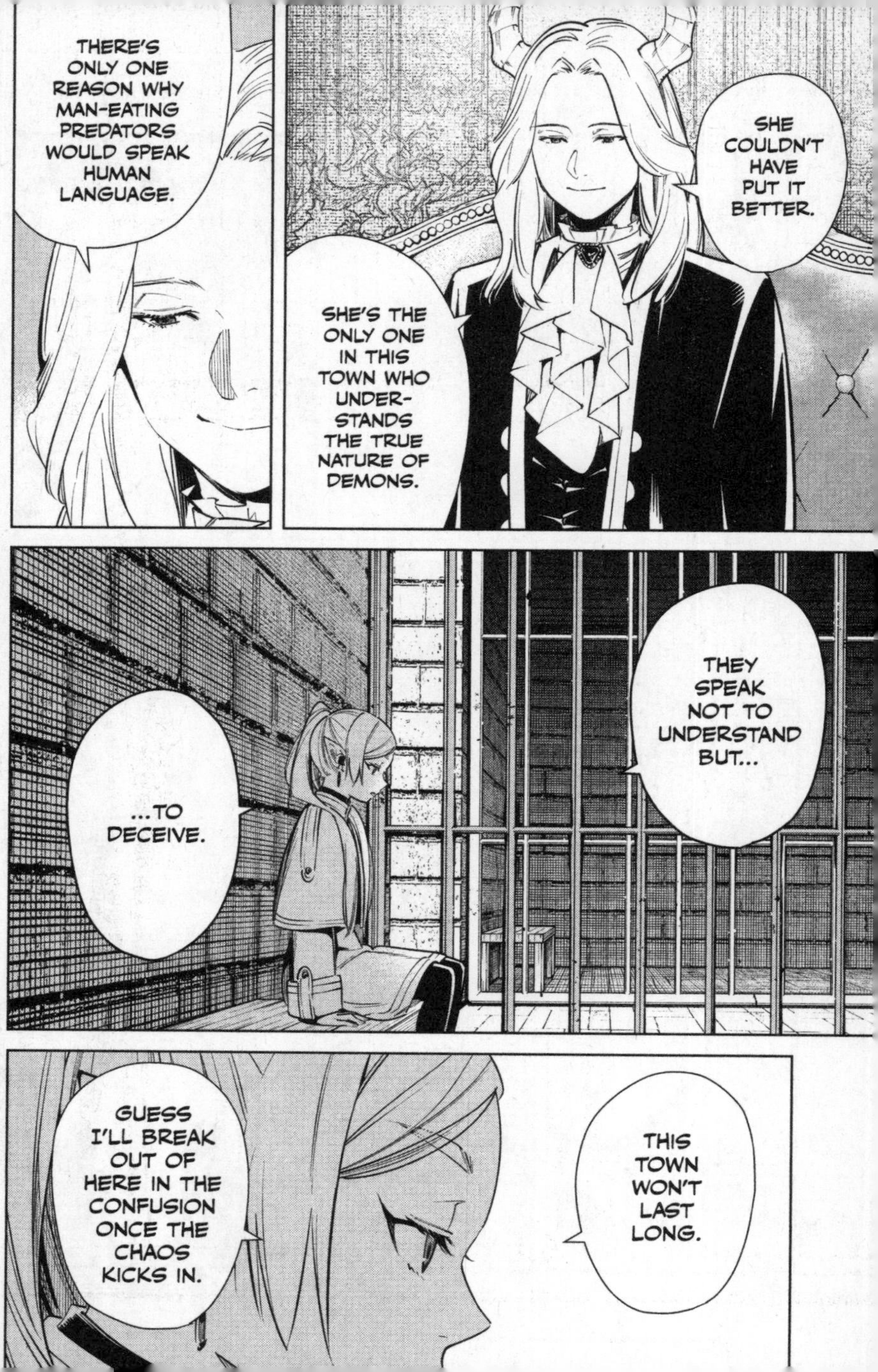
SHE COULDN'T HAVE PUT IT BETTER.
SHE'S THE ONLY ONE IN THIS TOWN WHO UNDER-STANDS THE TRUE NATURE OF DEMONS.
THERE'S ONLY ONE REASON WHY MAN-EATING PREDATORS WOULD SPEAK HUMAN LANGUAGE.
THEY SPEAK NOT TO UNDERSTAND BUT...
...TO DECEIVE.
THIS TOWN WON'T LAST LONG.
GUESS I'LL BREAK OUT OF HERE IN THE CONFUSION ONCE THE CHAOS KICKS IN.

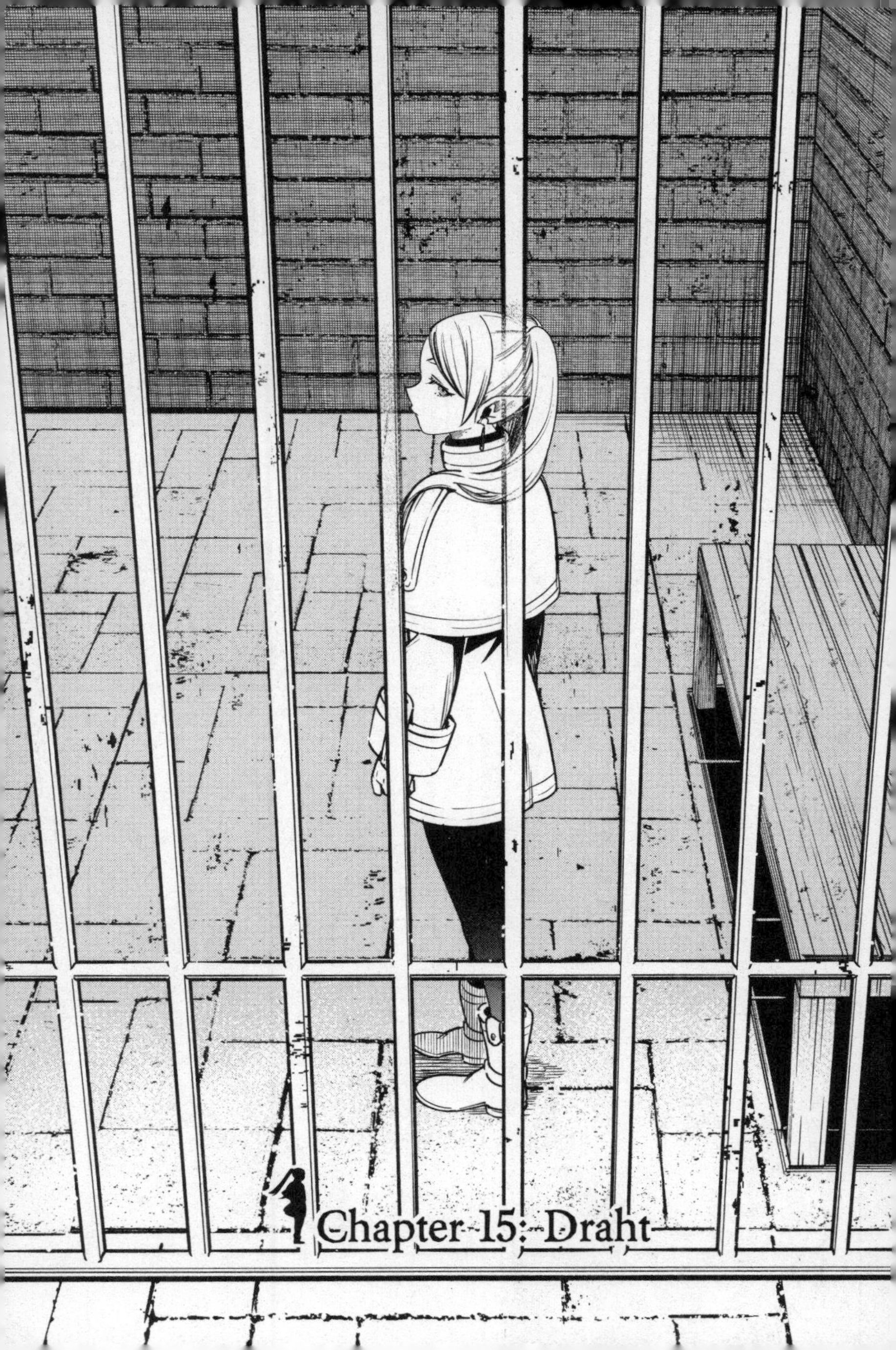

Chapter 15: Draht

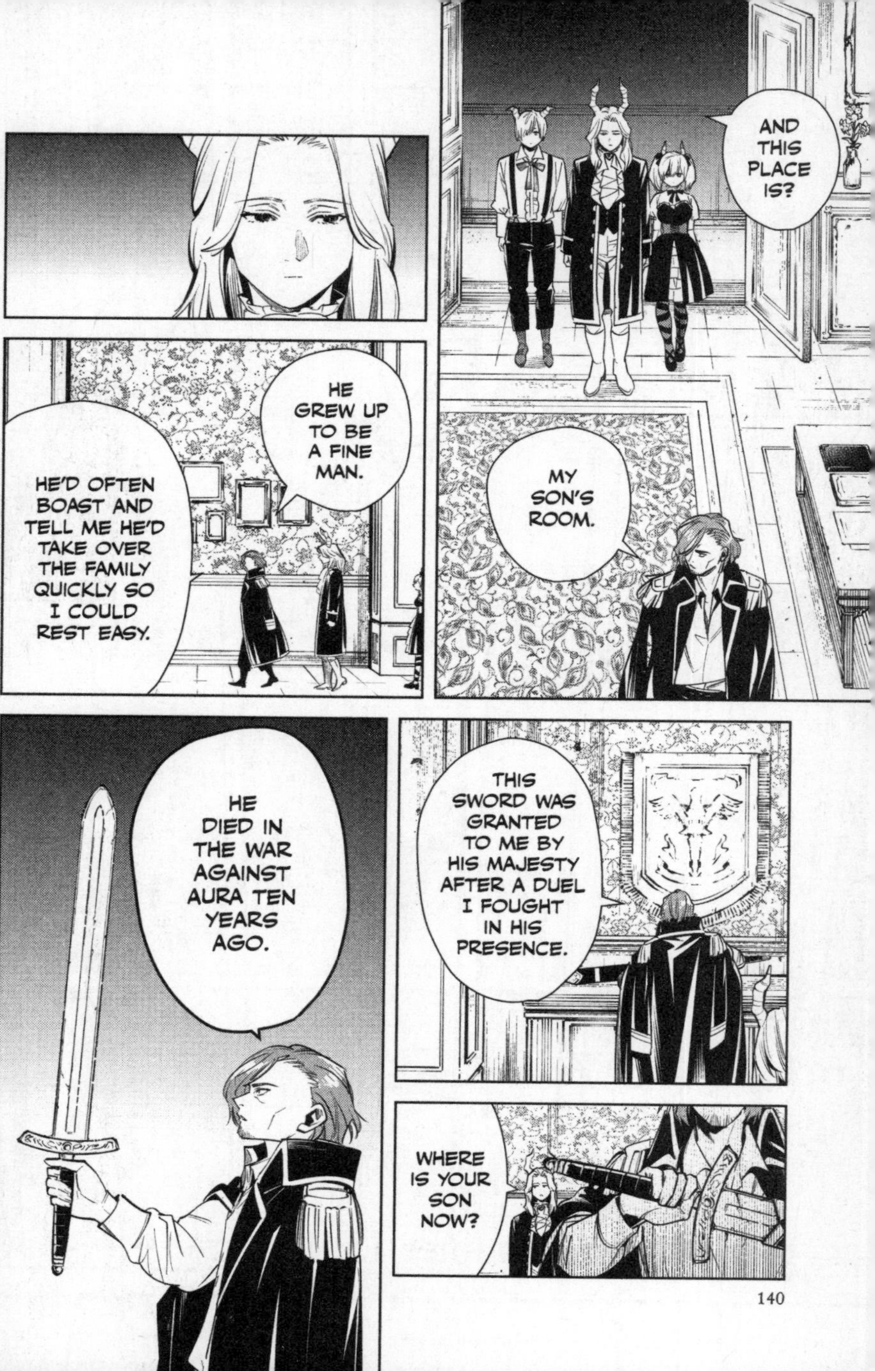
AND THIS PLACE IS?
MY SON'S ROOM.
HE GREW UP TO BE A FINE MAN.
HE'D OFTEN BOAST AND TELL ME HE'D TAKE OVER THE FAMILY QUICKLY SO I COULD REST EASY.
THIS SWORD WAS GRANTED TO ME BY HIS MAJESTY AFTER A DUEL I FOUGHT IN HIS PRESENCE.
WHERE IS YOUR SON NOW?
HE DIED IN THE WAR AGAINST AURA TEN YEARS AGO.

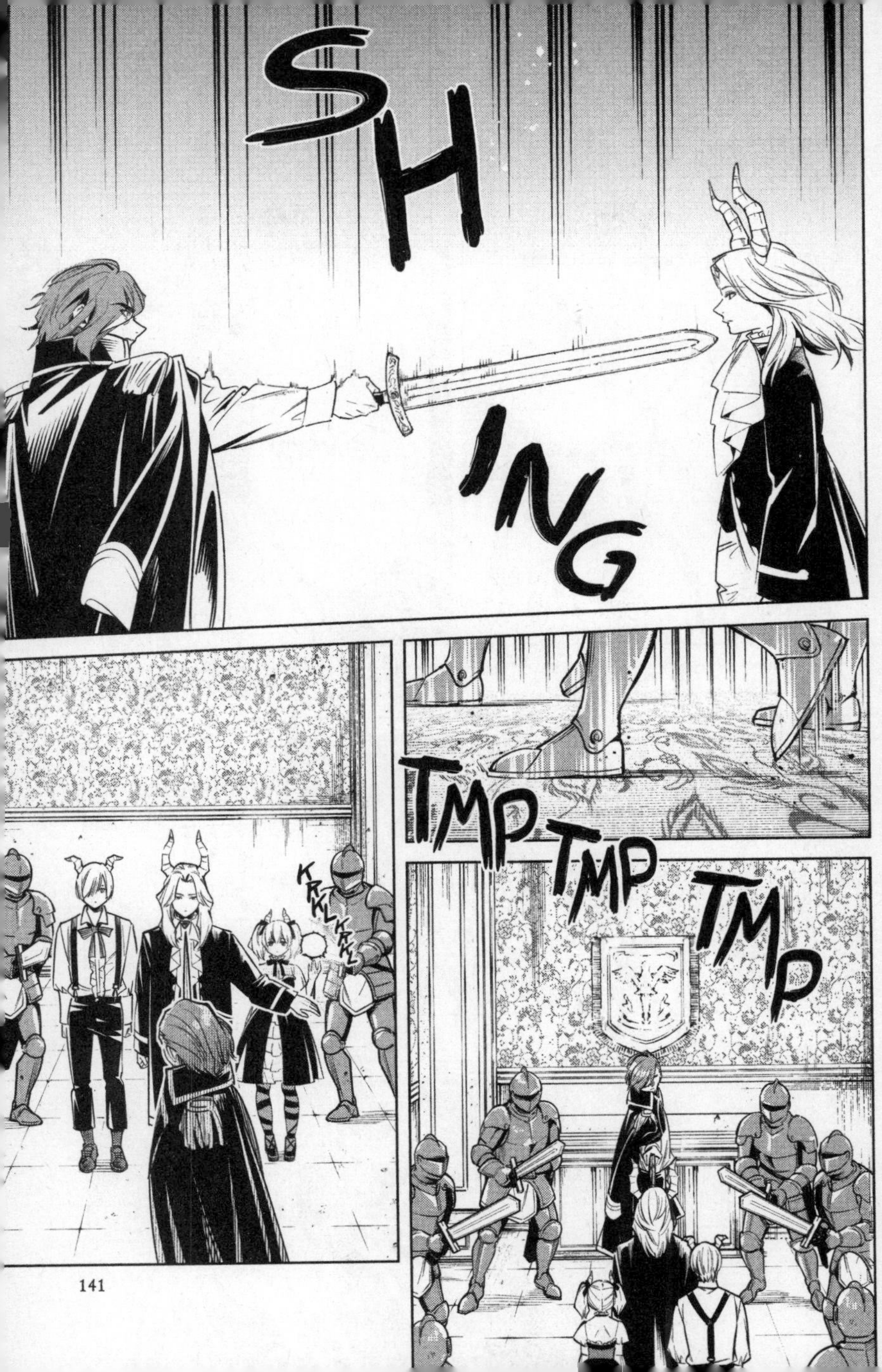
SHING
TMP TMP TMP TMP
KRKL KRKL

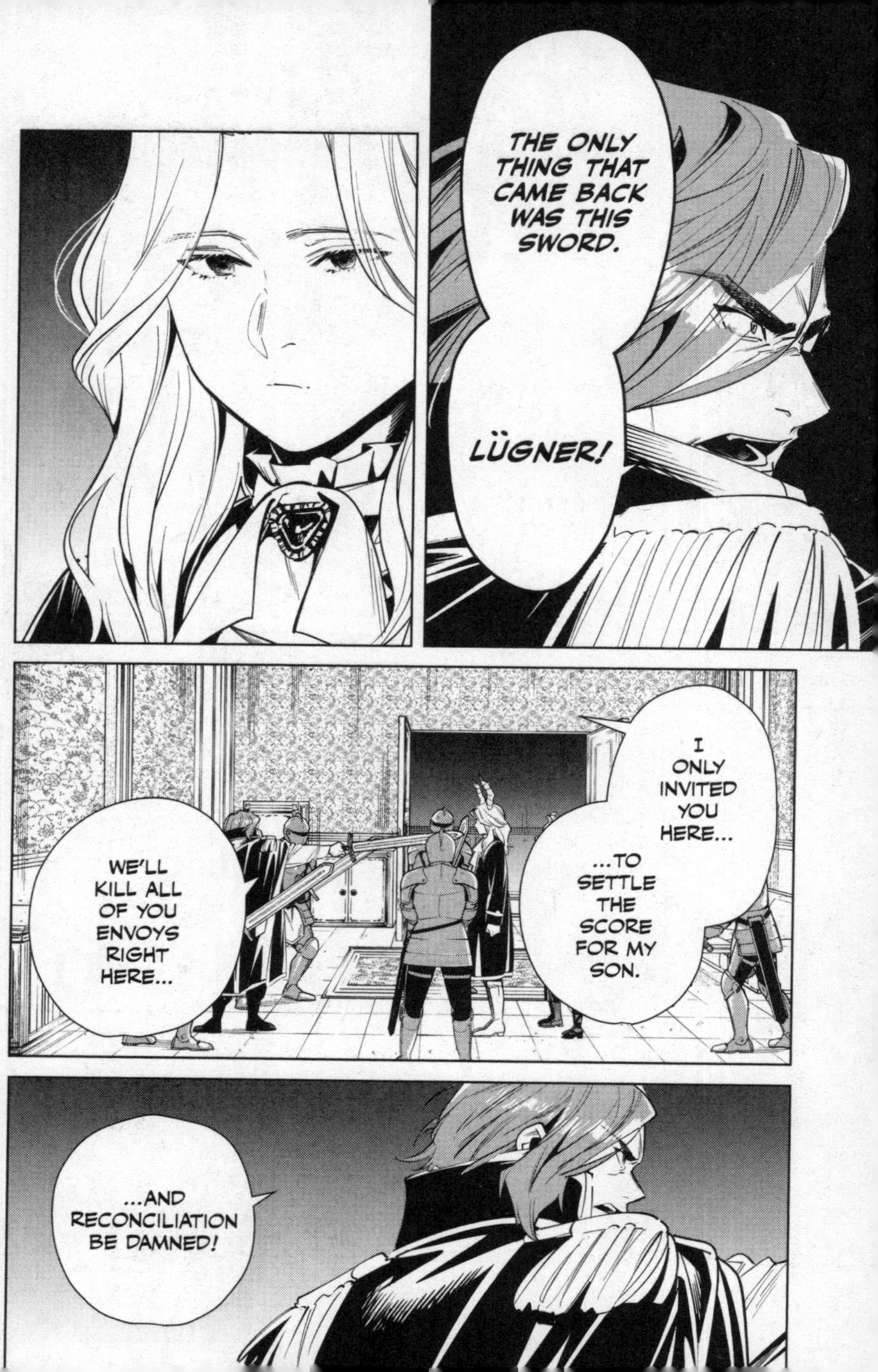
THE ONLY THING THAT CAME BACK WAS THIS SWORD.
LÜGNER!
I ONLY INVITED YOU HERE...
...TO SETTLE THE SCORE FOR MY SON.
WE'LL KILL ALL OF YOU ENVOYS RIGHT HERE...
...AND RECONCILIATION BE DAMNED!

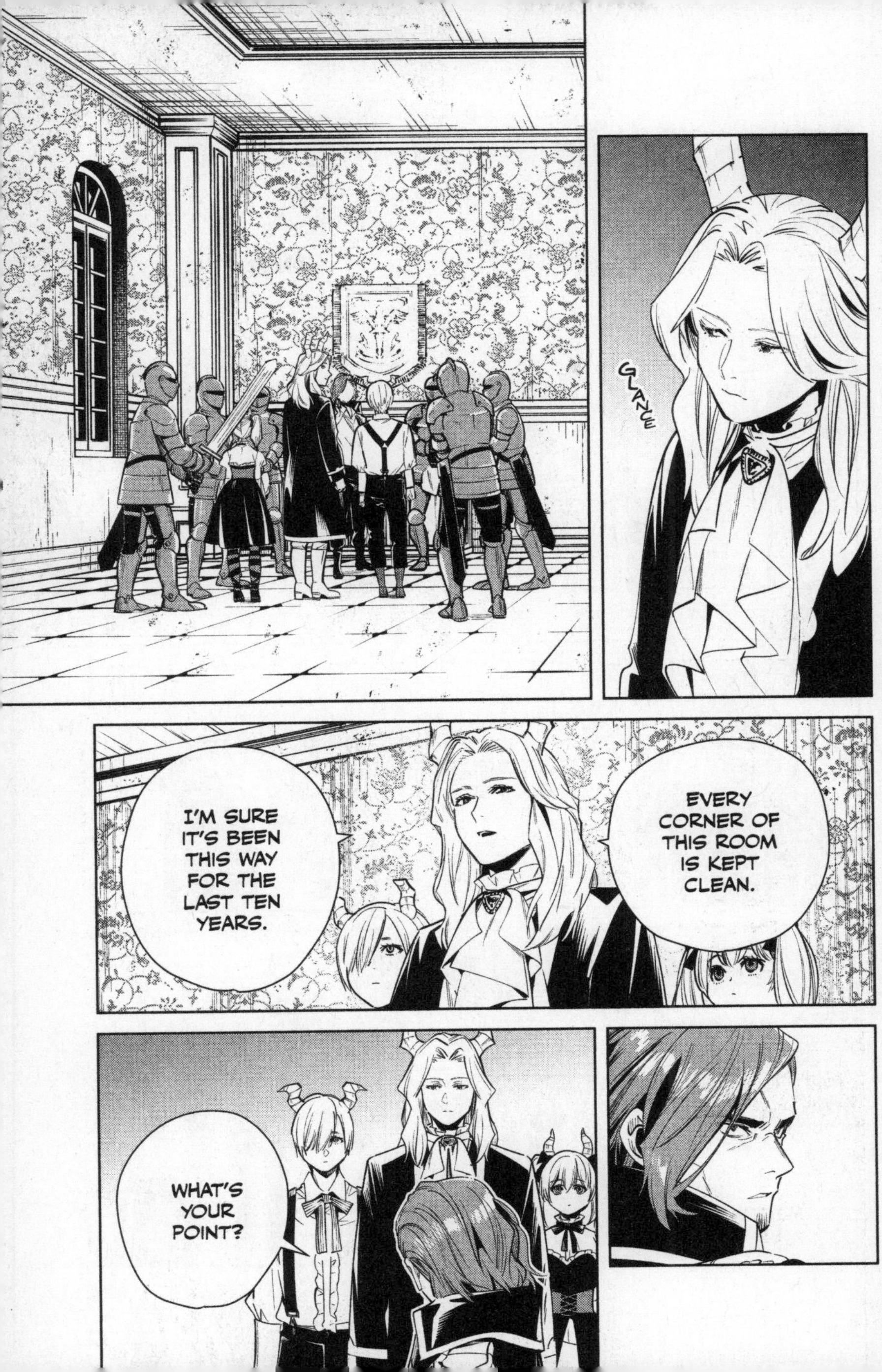
GLANCE
EVERY CORNER OF THIS ROOM IS KEPT CLEAN.
I'M SURE IT'S BEEN THIS WAY FOR THE LAST TEN YEARS.
WHAT'S YOUR POINT?

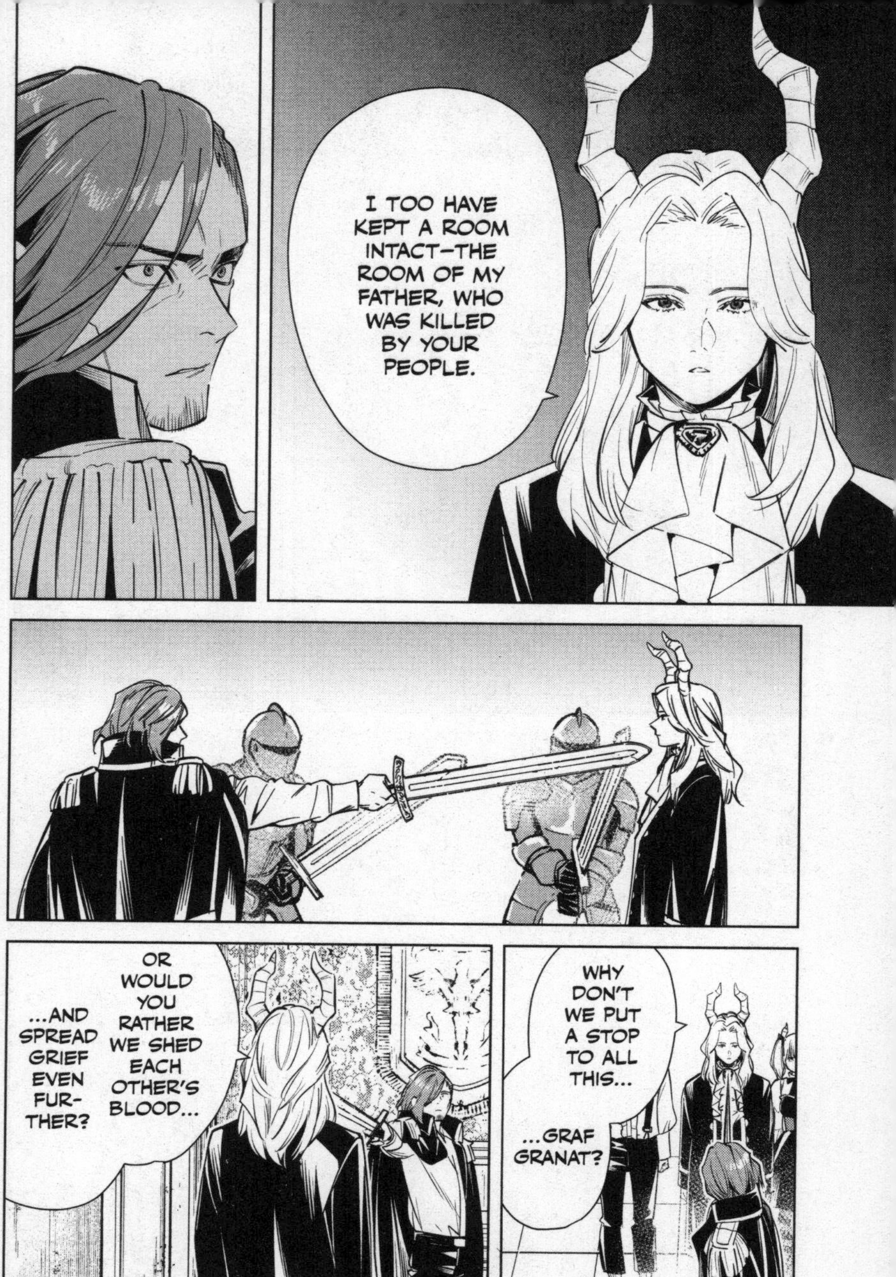
I TOO HAVE KEPT A ROOM INTACT—THE ROOM OF MY FATHER, WHO WAS KILLED BY YOUR PEOPLE.
WHY DON'T WE PUT A STOP TO ALL THIS...
...GRAF GRANAT?
OR WOULD YOU RATHER WE SHED EACH OTHER'S BLOOD...
...AND SPREAD GRIEF EVEN FUR-THER?

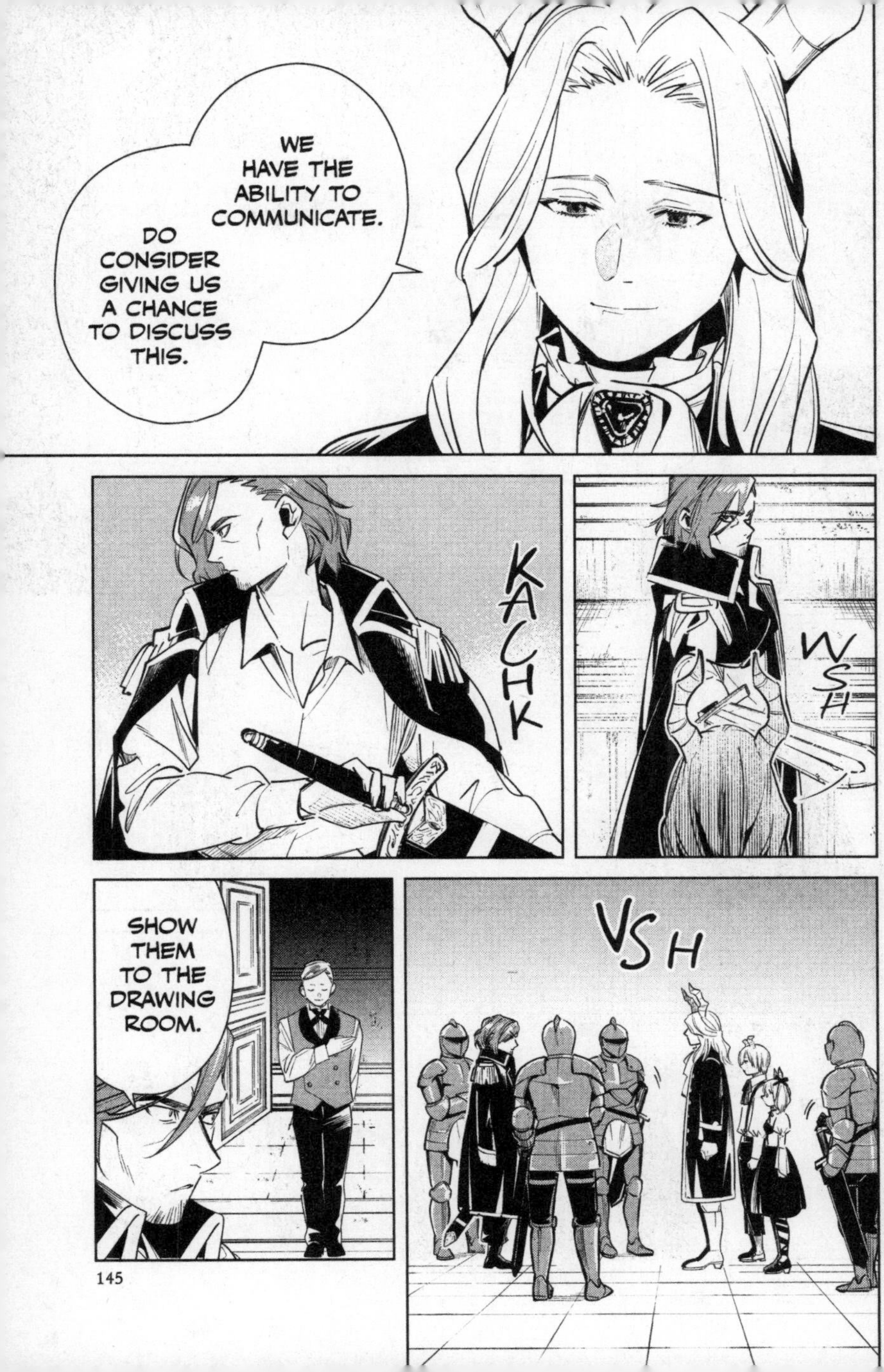
WE HAVE THE ABILITY TO COMMUNICATE.
DO CONSIDER GIVING US A CHANCE TO DISCUSS THIS.
WSH
KACHK
VSH
SHOW THEM TO THE DRAWING ROOM.

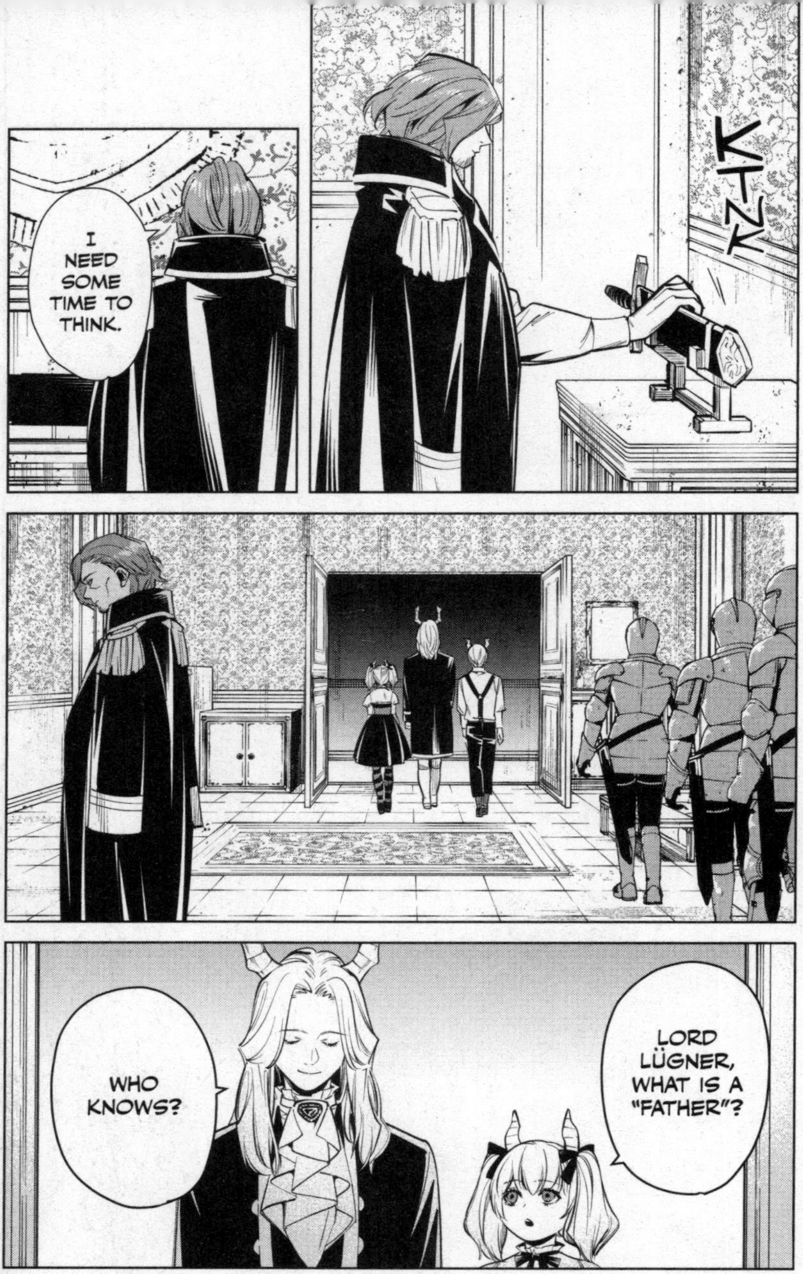
KTNK
I NEED SOME TIME TO THINK.
LORD LÜGNER, WHAT IS A "FATHER"?
WHO KNOWS?

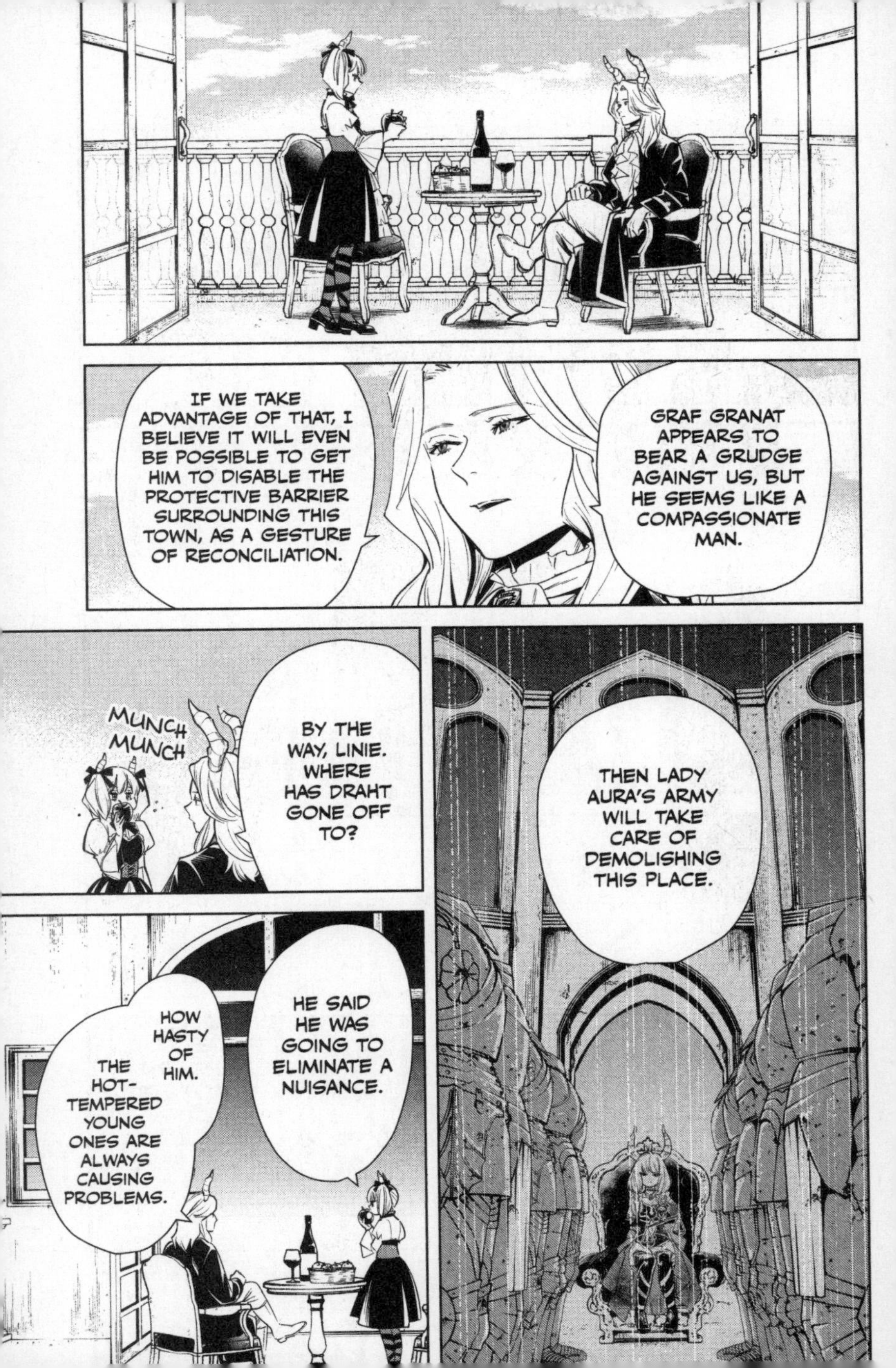
GRAF GRANAT APPEARS TO BEAR A GRUDGE AGAINST US, BUT HE SEEMS LIKE A COMPASSIONATE MAN.
IF WE TAKE ADVANTAGE OF THAT, I BELIEVE IT WILL EVEN BE POSSIBLE TO GET HIM TO DISABLE THE PROTECTIVE BARRIER SURROUNDING THIS TOWN, AS A GESTURE OF RECONCILIATION.
THEN LADY AURA'S ARMY WILL TAKE CARE OF DEMOLISHING THIS PLACE.
BY THE WAY, LINIE. WHERE HAS DRAHT GONE OFF TO?
MUNCH MUNCH
HE SAID HE WAS GOING TO ELIMINATE A NUISANCE.
HOW HASTY OF HIM.
THE HOT-TEMPERED YOUNG ONES ARE ALWAYS CAUSING PROBLEMS.

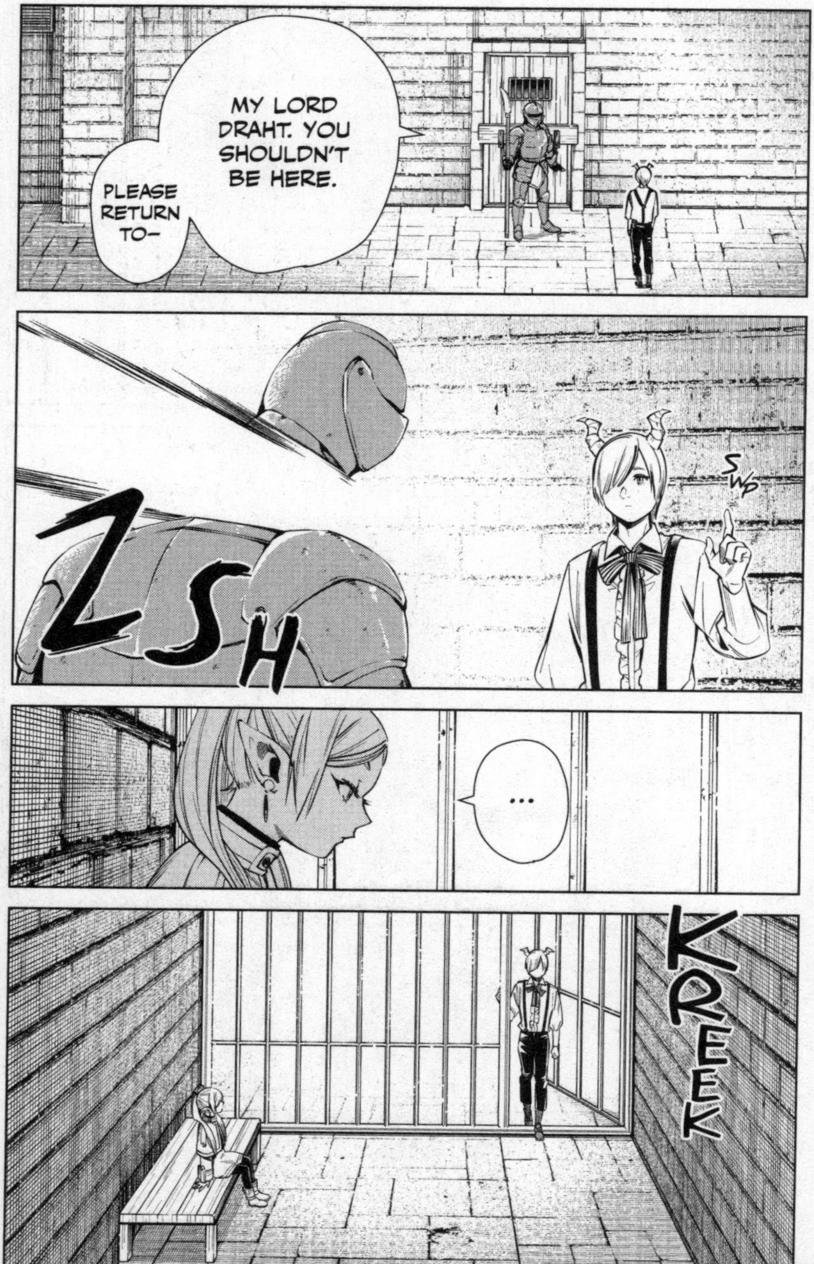
MY LORD DRAHT. YOU SHOULDN'T BE HERE.
PLEASE RETURN TO–
SWP
ZSH
...
KREEK

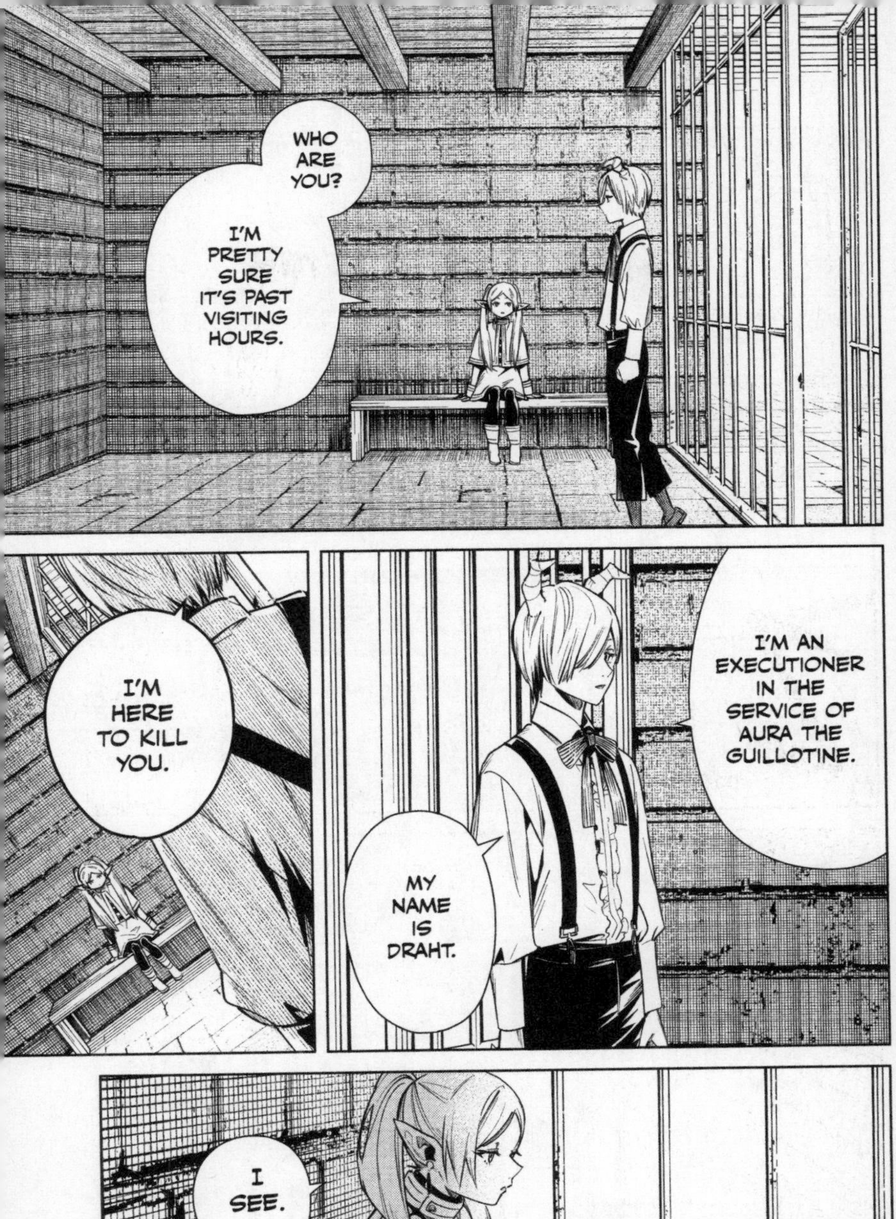
WHO ARE YOU?
I'M PRETTY SURE IT'S PAST VISITING HOURS.
I'M AN EXECUTIONER IN THE SERVICE OF AURA THE GUILLOTINE.
MY NAME IS DRAHT.
I'M HERE TO KILL YOU.
I SEE.

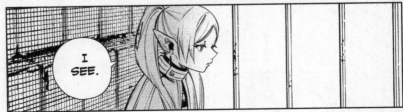

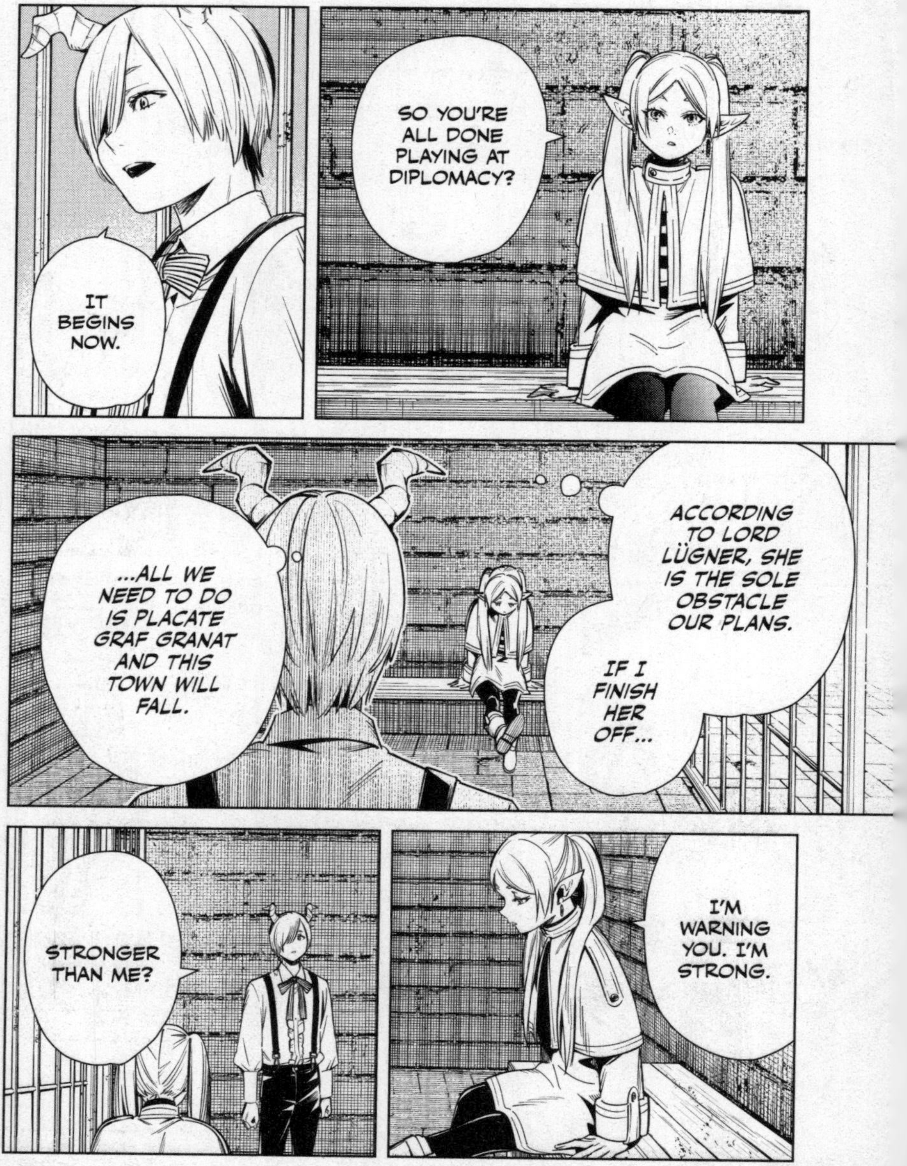
SO YOU'RE ALL DONE PLAYING AT DIPLOMACY?
IT BEGINS NOW.
ACCORDING TO LORD LÜGNER, SHE IS THE SOLE OBSTACLE OUR PLANS.
IF I FINISH HER OFF...
...ALL WE NEED TO DO IS PLACATE GRAF GRANAT AND THIS TOWN WILL FALL.
I'M WARNING YOU. I'M STRONG.
STRONGER THAN ME?

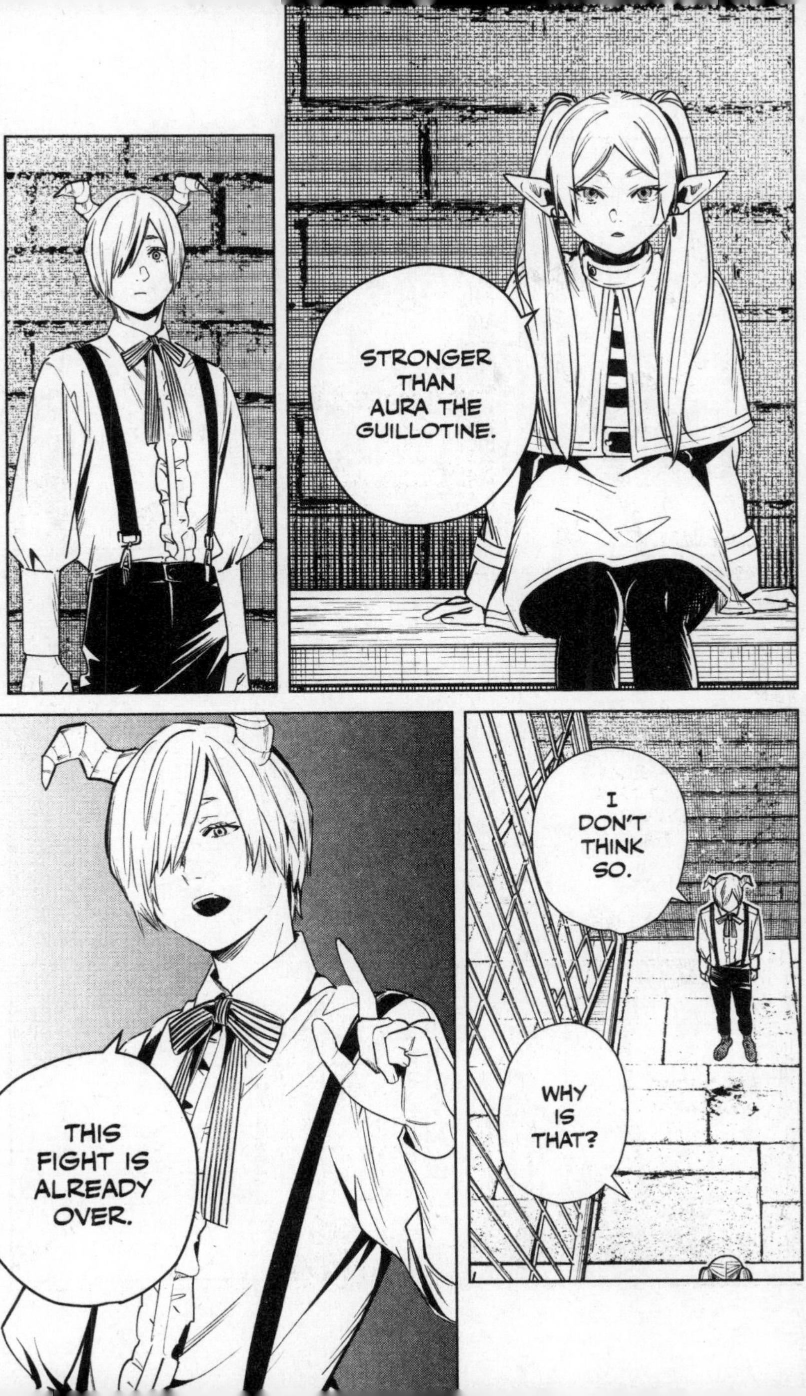
STRONGER THAN AURA THE GUILLOTINE.
I DON'T THINK SO.
WHY IS THAT?
THIS FIGHT IS ALREADY OVER.

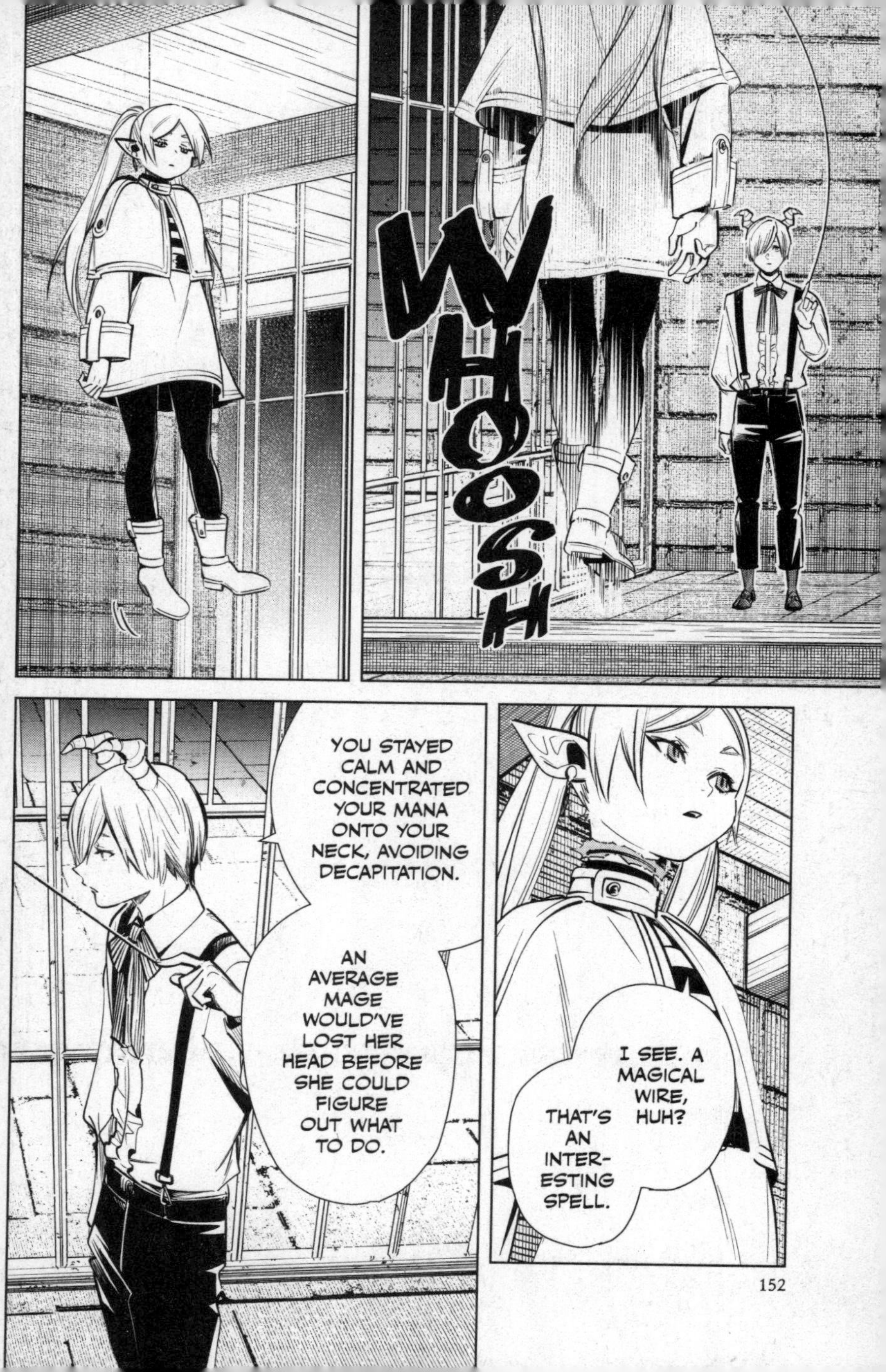
WHOOSH
I SEE. A MAGICAL WIRE, HUH?
THAT'S AN INTER-ESTING SPELL.
YOU STAYED CALM AND CONCENTRATED YOUR MANA ONTO YOUR NECK, AVOIDING DECAPITATION.
AN AVERAGE MAGE WOULD'VE LOST HER HEAD BEFORE SHE COULD FIGURE OUT WHAT TO DO.

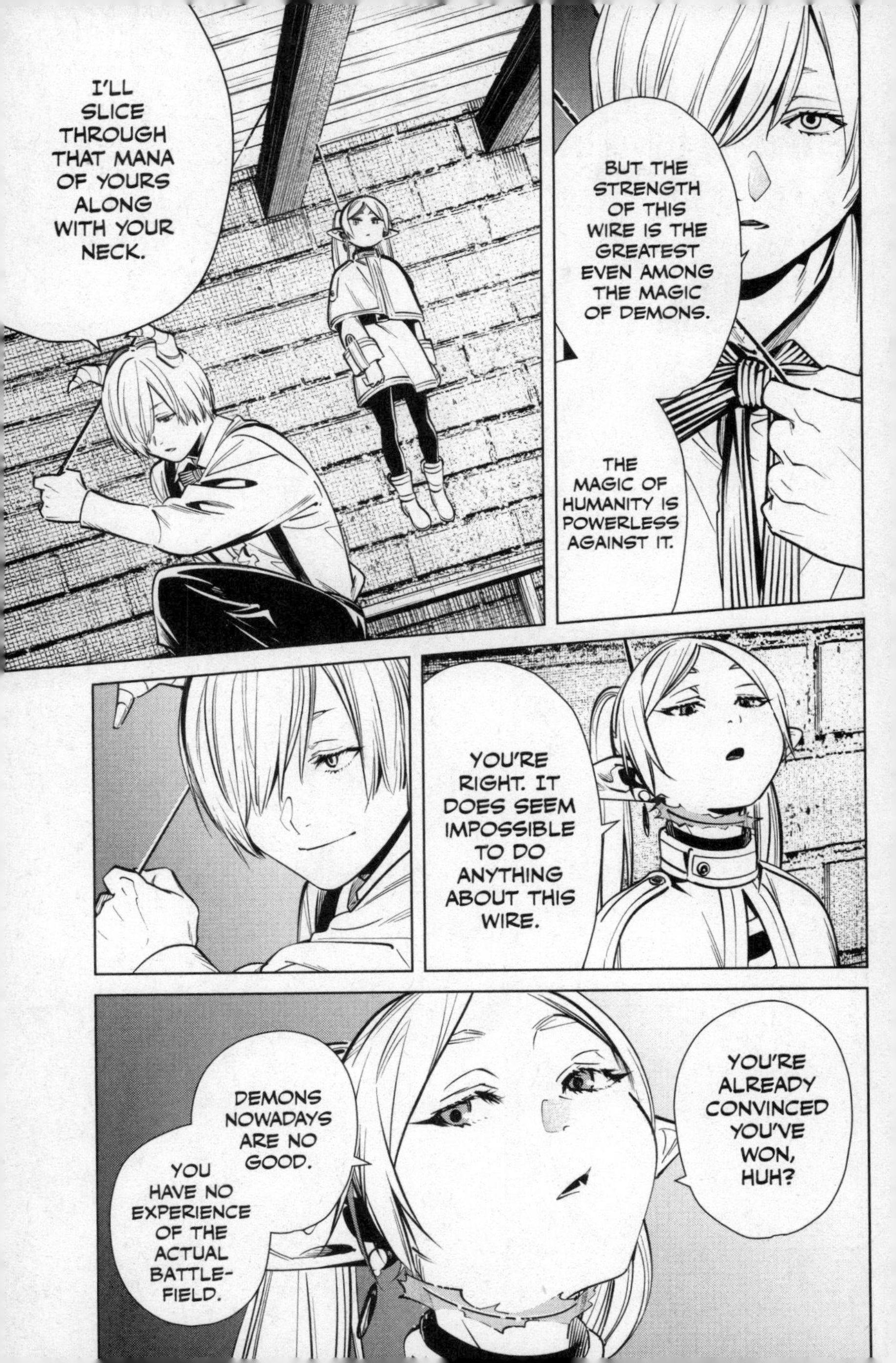
BUT THE STRENGTH OF THIS WIRE IS THE GREATEST EVEN AMONG THE MAGIC OF DEMONS.
THE MAGIC OF HUMANITY IS POWERLESS AGAINST IT.
I'LL SLICE THROUGH THAT MANA OF YOURS ALONG WITH YOUR NECK.
YOU'RE RIGHT. IT DOES SEEM IMPOSSIBLE TO DO ANYTHING ABOUT THIS WIRE.
YOU'RE ALREADY CONVINCED YOU'VE WON, HUH?
DEMONS NOWADAYS ARE NO GOOD.
YOU HAVE NO EXPERIENCE OF THE ACTUAL BATTLE-FIELD.

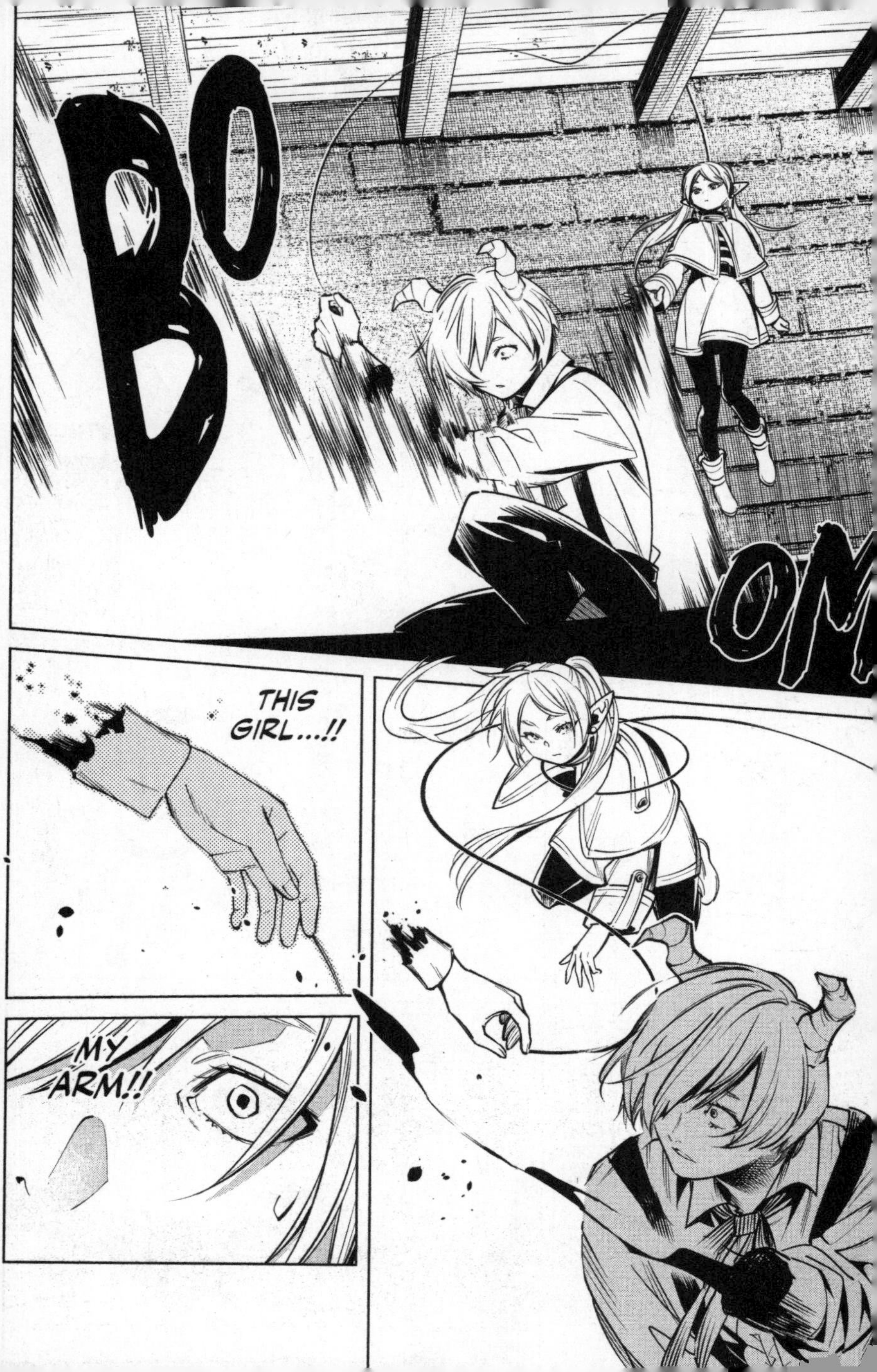
BOOM
THIS GIRL...!!
MY ARM!!

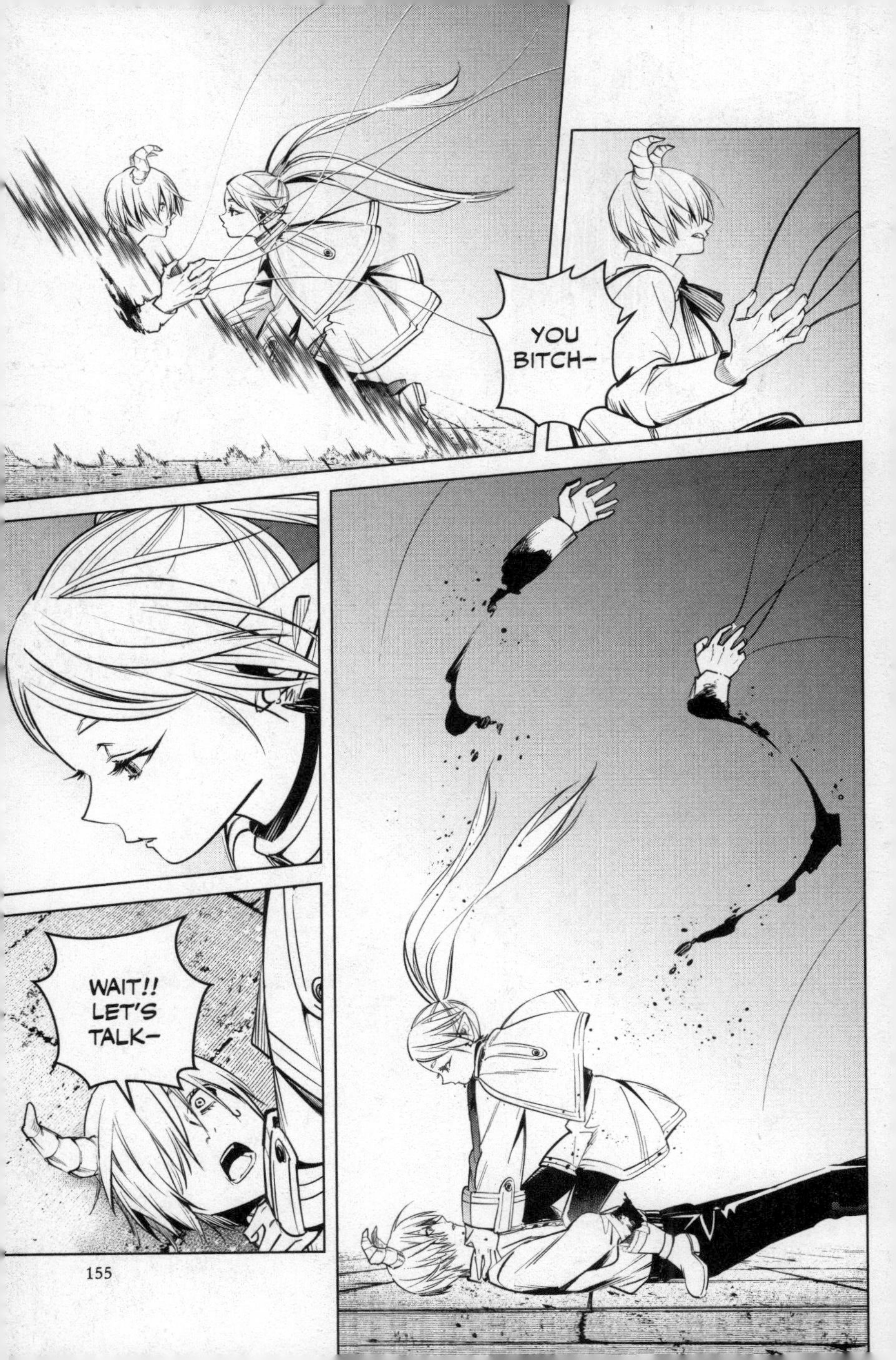
YOU BITCH—
WAIT!! LET'S TALK—

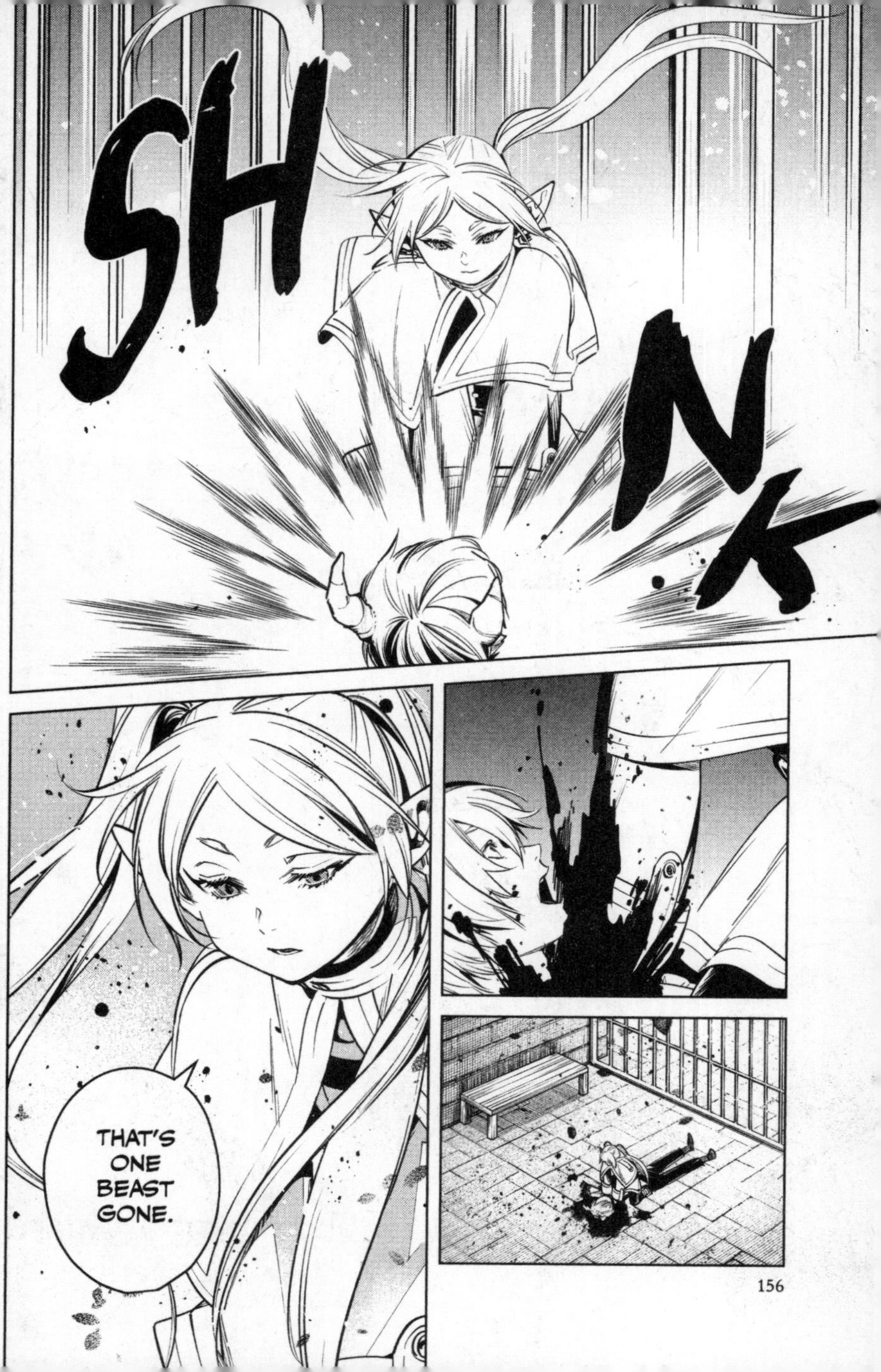
SHINK
THAT'S ONE BEAST GONE.

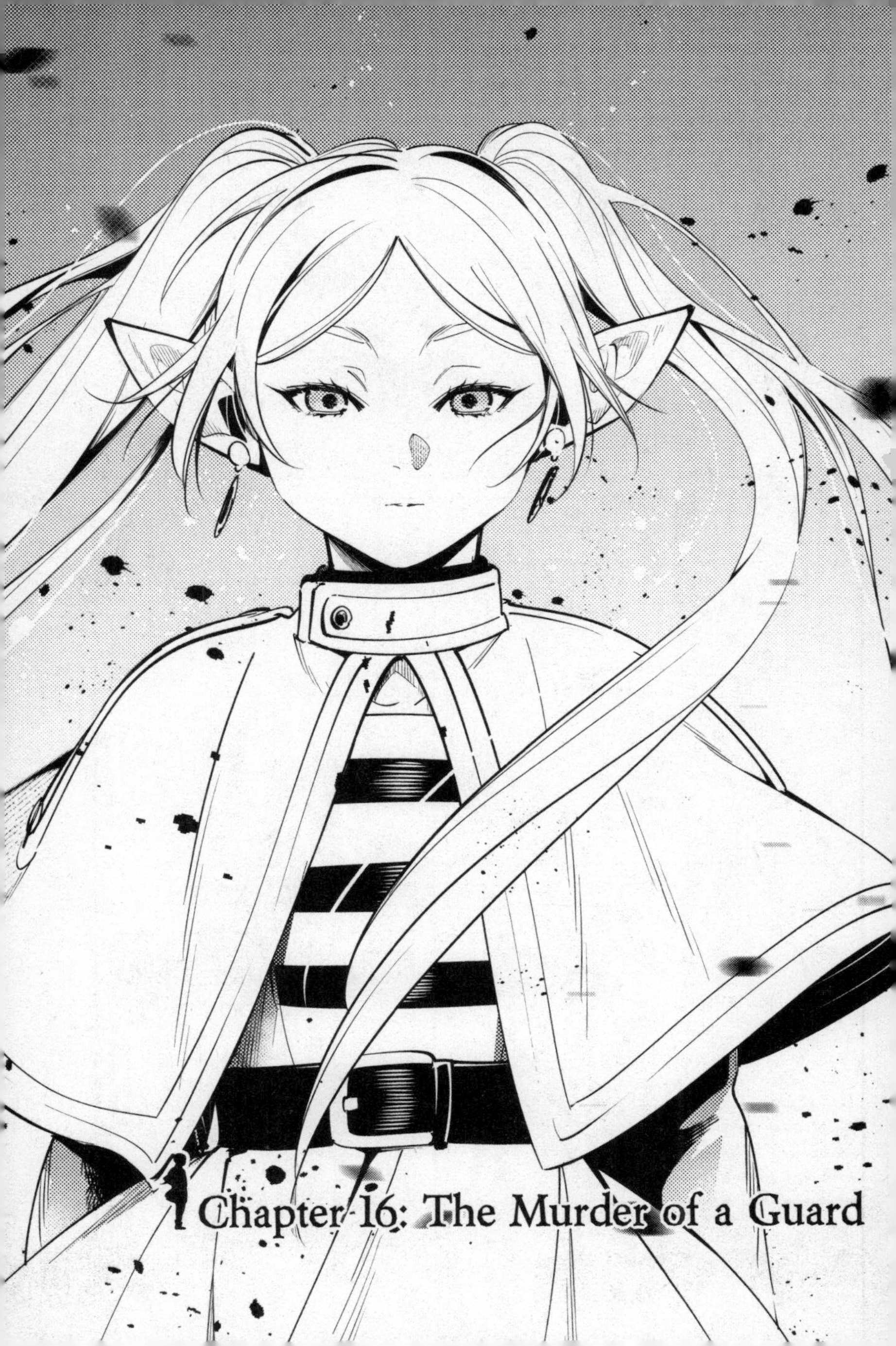
Chapter 16: The Murder of a Guard

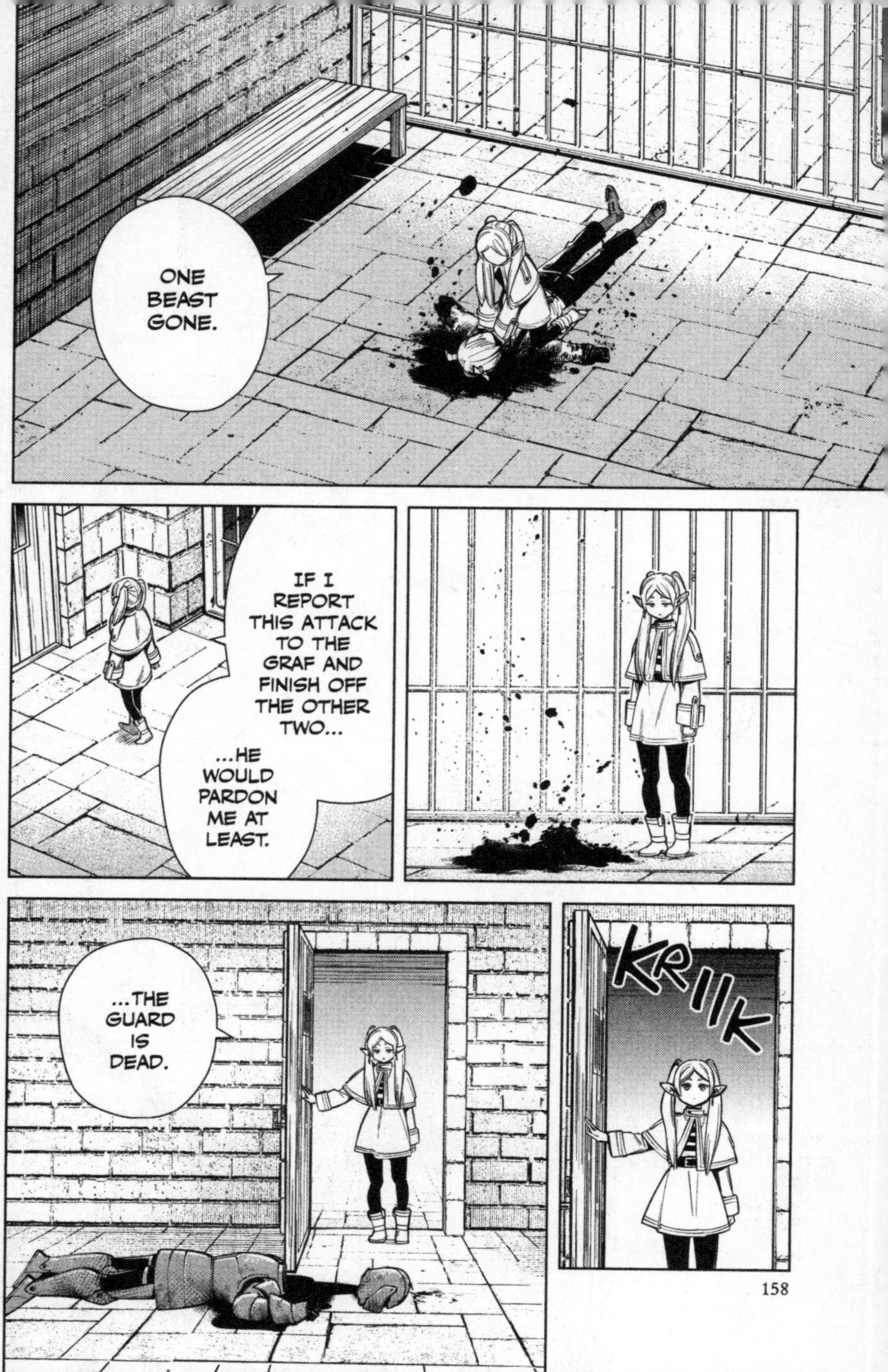
ONE BEAST GONE.
IF I REPORT THIS ATTACK TO THE GRAF AND FINISH OFF THE OTHER TWO...
...HE WOULD PARDON ME AT LEAST.
KRIIK
...THE GUARD IS DEAD.

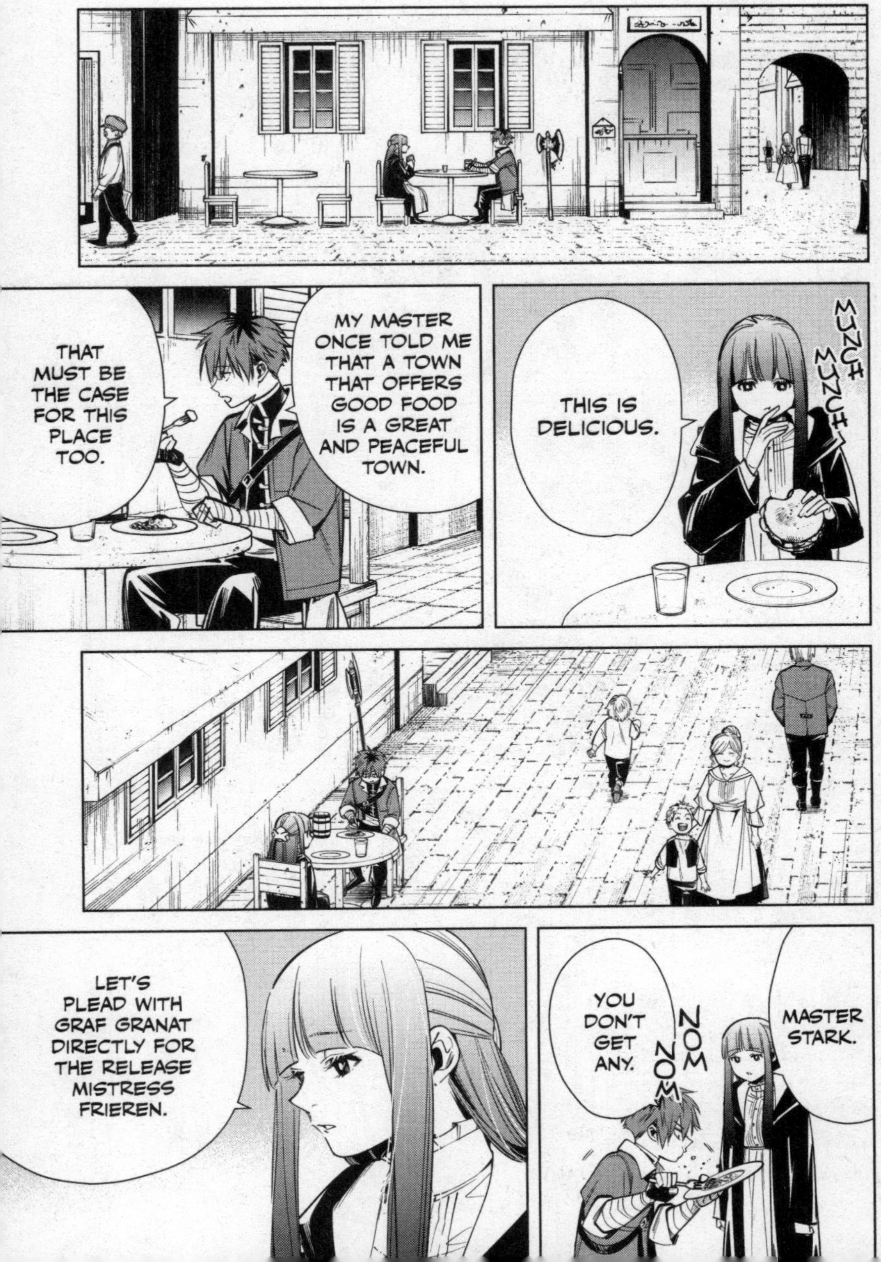
MUNCH MUNCH
THIS IS DELICIOUS.
MY MASTER ONCE TOLD ME THAT A TOWN THAT OFFERS GOOD FOOD IS A GREAT AND PEACEFUL TOWN.
THAT MUST BE THE CASE FOR THIS PLACE TOO.
MASTER STARK.
NOM NOM
YOU DON'T GET ANY.
LET'S PLEAD WITH GRAF GRANAT DIRECTLY FOR THE RELEASE MISTRESS FRIEREN.

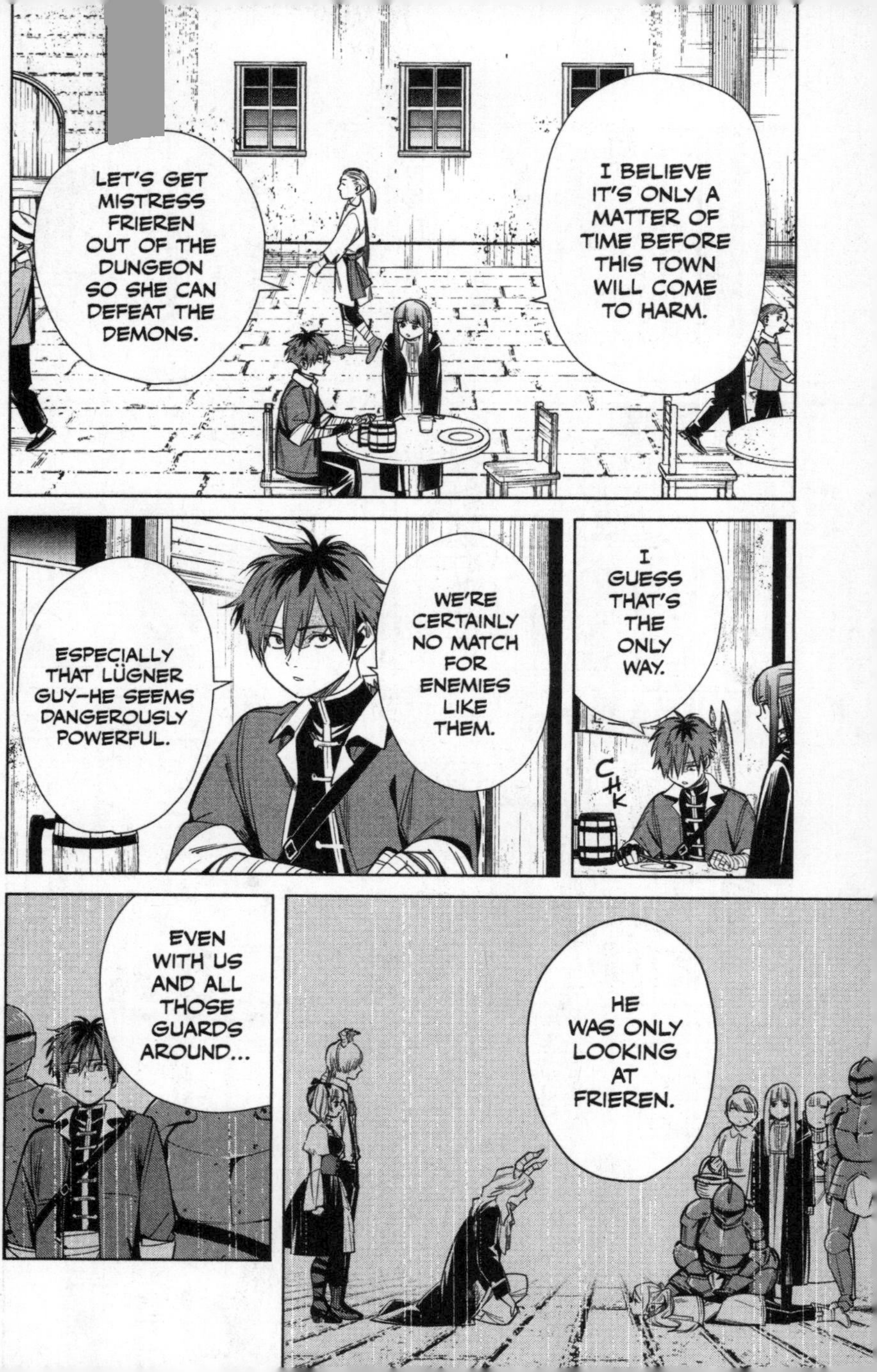
I BELIEVE IT'S ONLY A MATTER OF TIME BEFORE THIS TOWN WILL COME TO HARM.
LET'S GET MISTRESS FRIEREN OUT OF THE DUNGEON SO SHE CAN DEFEAT THE DEMONS.
I GUESS THAT'S THE ONLY WAY.
CHK
WE'RE CERTAINLY NO MATCH FOR ENEMIES LIKE THEM.
ESPECIALLY THAT LÜGNER GUY—HE SEEMS DANGEROUSLY POWERFUL.
HE WAS ONLY LOOKING AT FRIEREN.
EVEN WITH US AND ALL THOSE GUARDS AROUND...

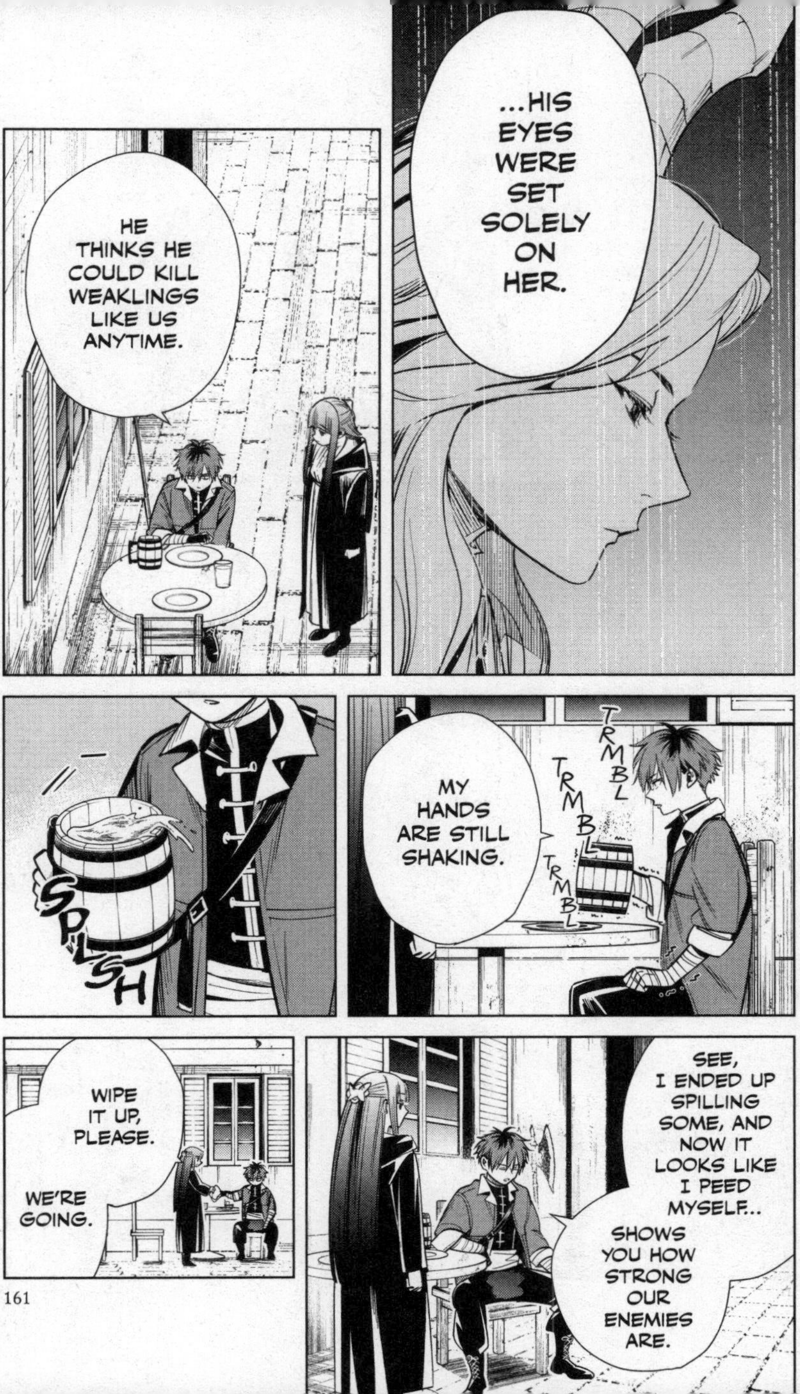
...HIS EYES WERE SET SOLELY ON HER.
HE THINKS HE COULD KILL WEAKLINGS LIKE US ANYTIME.
MY HANDS ARE STILL SHAKING.
TRMBL
TRMBL
TRMBL
SPLSH
SEE, I ENDED UP SPILLING SOME, AND NOW IT LOOKS LIKE I PEED MYSELF...
SHOWS YOU HOW STRONG OUR ENEMIES ARE.
WIPE IT UP, PLEASE.
WE'RE GOING.

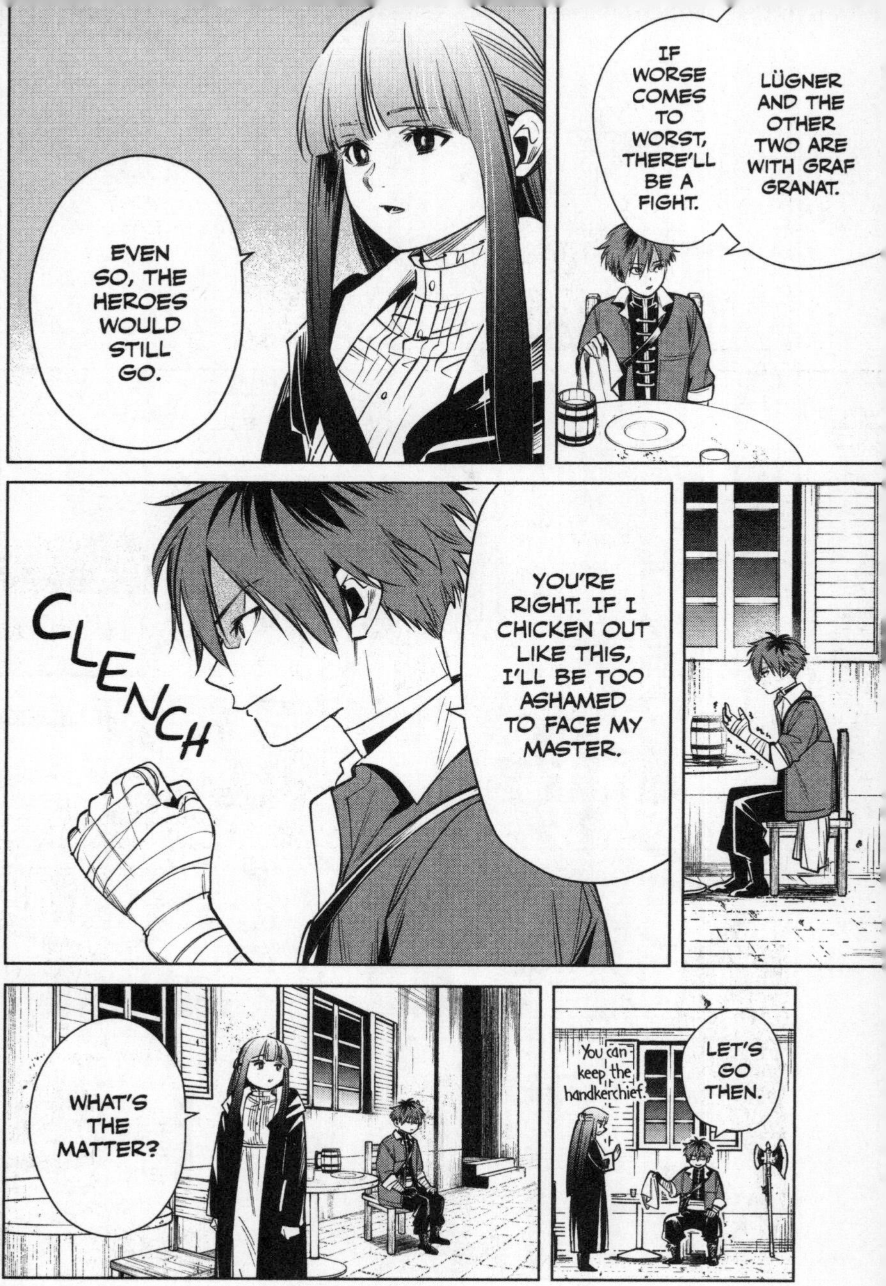
LÜGNER AND THE OTHER TWO ARE WITH GRAF GRANAT.
IF WORSE COMES TO WORST, THERE'LL BE A FIGHT.
EVEN SO, THE HEROES WOULD STILL GO.
YOU'RE RIGHT. IF I CHICKEN OUT LIKE THIS, I'LL BE TOO ASHAMED TO FACE MY MASTER.
CLENCH
LET'S GO THEN.
You can keep the handkerchief.
WHAT'S THE MATTER?

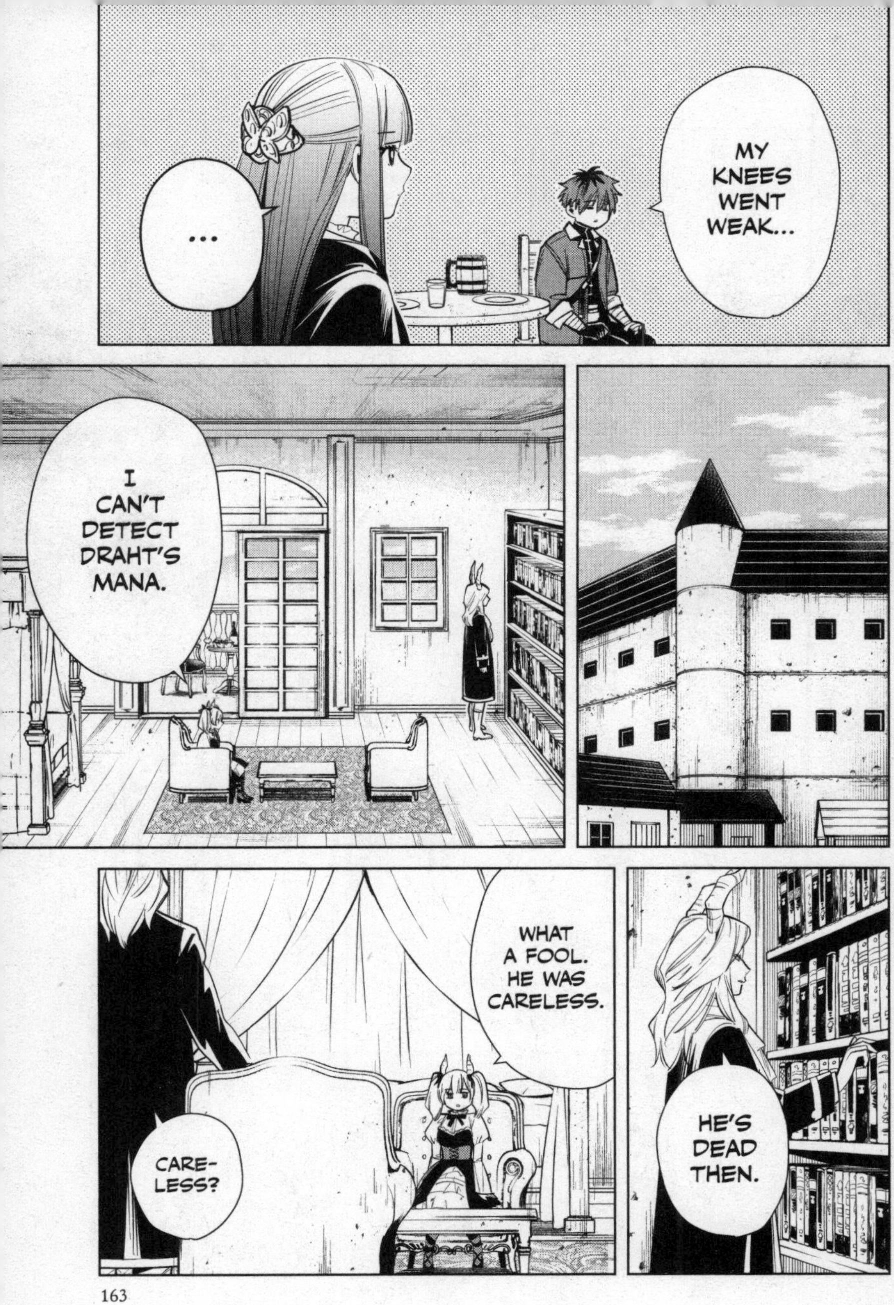
MY KNEES WENT WEAK...
...
I CAN'T DETECT DRAHT'S MANA.
HE'S DEAD THEN.
WHAT A FOOL. HE WAS CARELESS.
CARE-LESS?

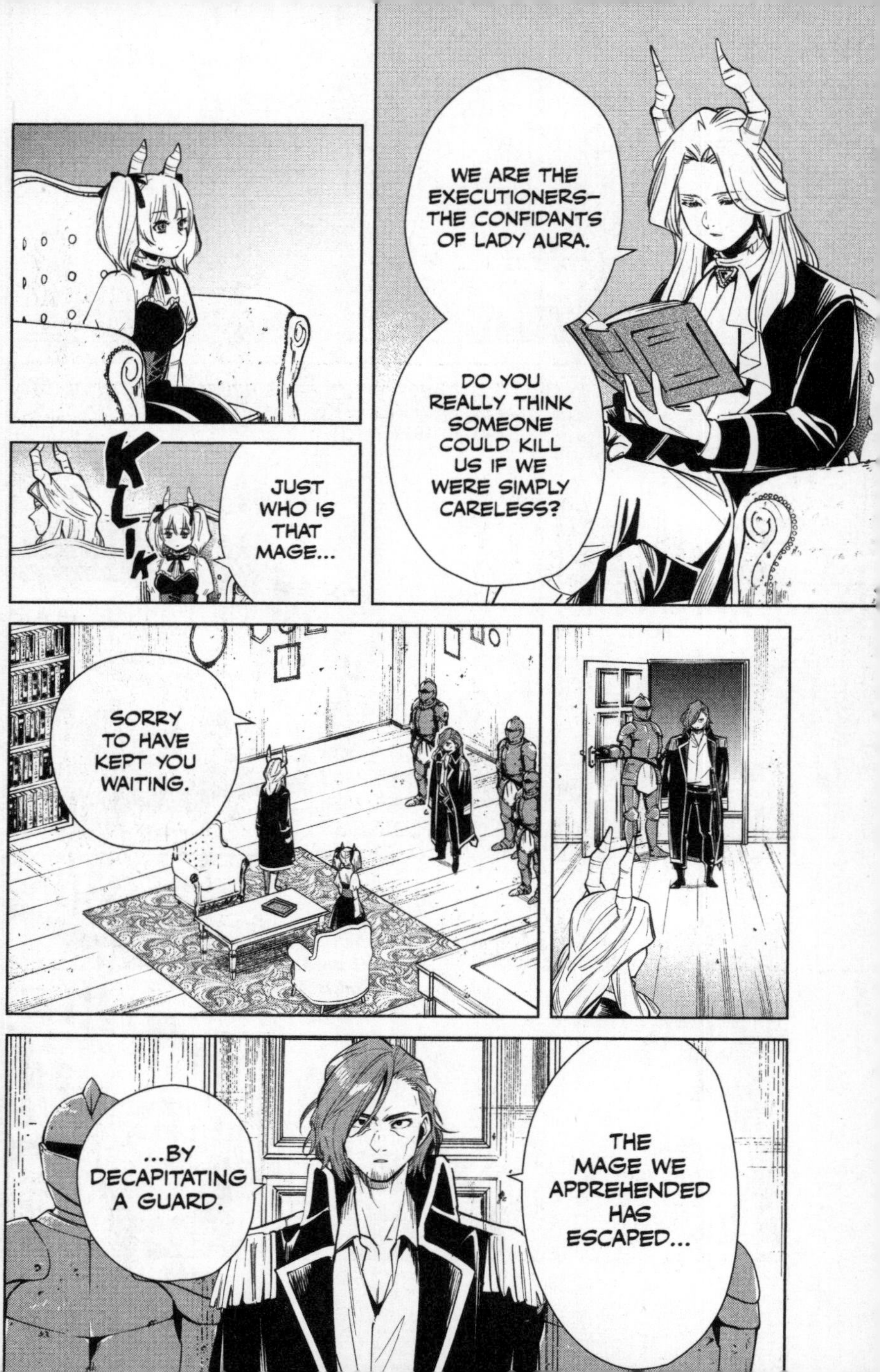
WE ARE THE EXECUTIONERS— THE CONFIDANTS OF LADY AURA.
DO YOU REALLY THINK SOMEONE COULD KILL US IF WE WERE SIMPLY CARELESS?
KLIK
JUST WHO IS THAT MAGE...
SORRY TO HAVE KEPT YOU WAITING.
THE MAGE WE APPREHENDED HAS ESCAPED...
...BY DECAPITATING A GUARD.

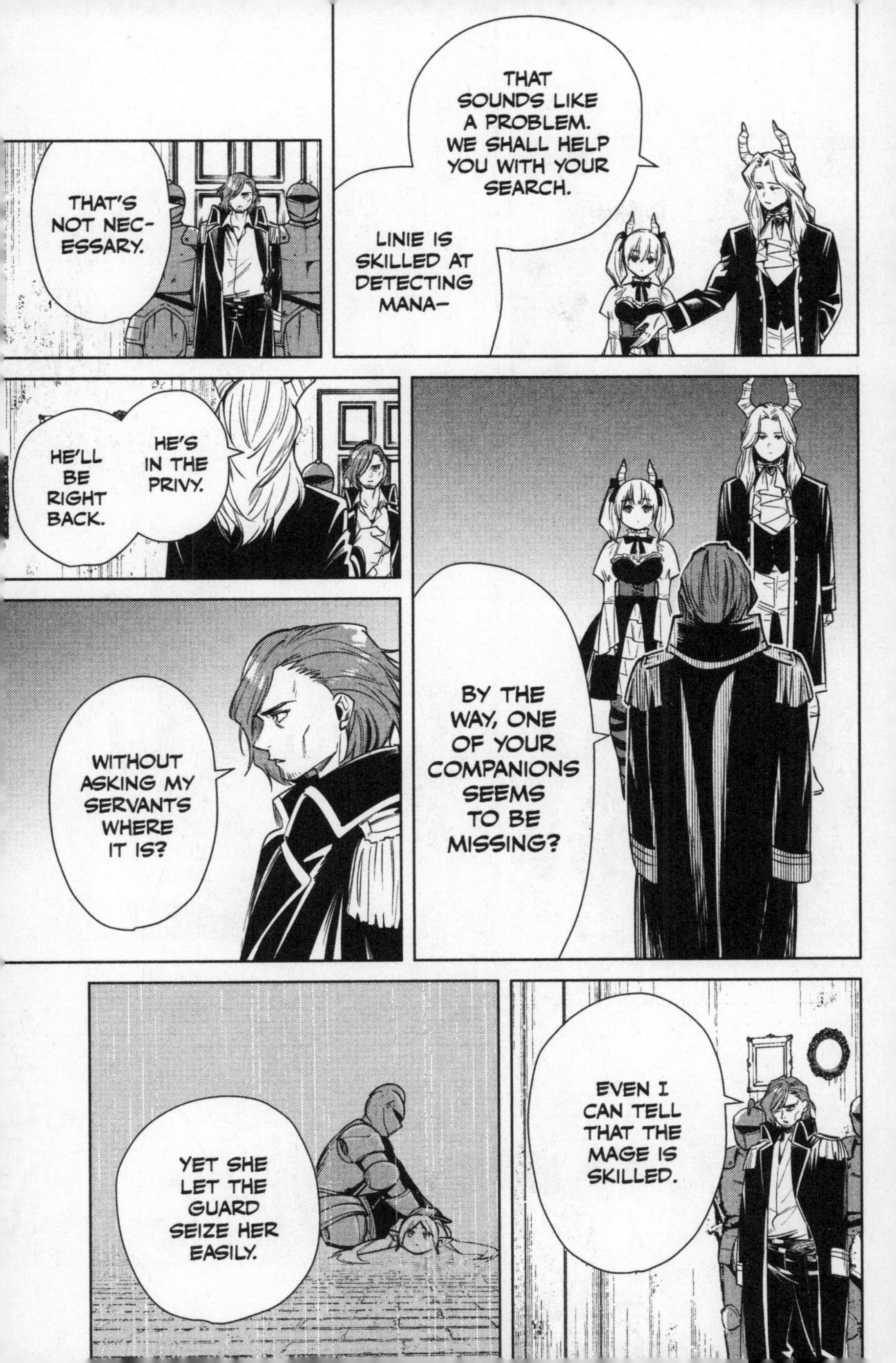
THAT SOUNDS LIKE A PROBLEM. WE SHALL HELP YOU WITH YOUR SEARCH.
LINIE IS SKILLED AT DETECTING MANA–
THAT'S NOT NECESSARY.
BY THE WAY, ONE OF YOUR COMPANIONS SEEMS TO BE MISSING?
HE'S IN THE PRIVY.
HE'LL BE RIGHT BACK.
WITHOUT ASKING MY SERVANTS WHERE IT IS?
EVEN I CAN TELL THAT THE MAGE IS SKILLED.
YET SHE LET THE GUARD SEIZE HER EASILY.

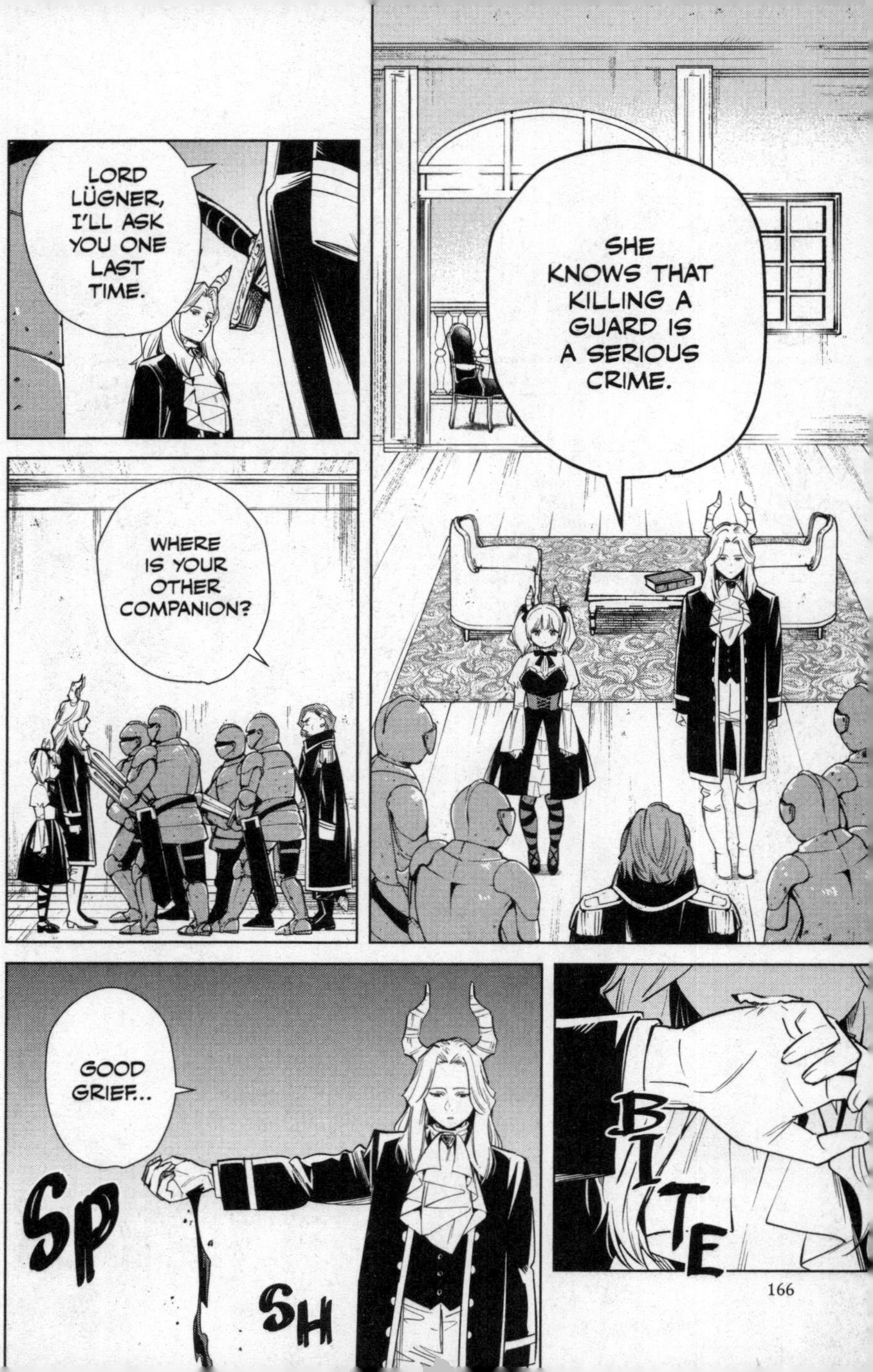
SHE KNOWS THAT KILLING A GUARD IS A SERIOUS CRIME.
LORD LÜGNER, I'LL ASK YOU ONE LAST TIME.
WHERE IS YOUR OTHER COMPANION?
BITE
GOOD GRIEF...
SP
SH

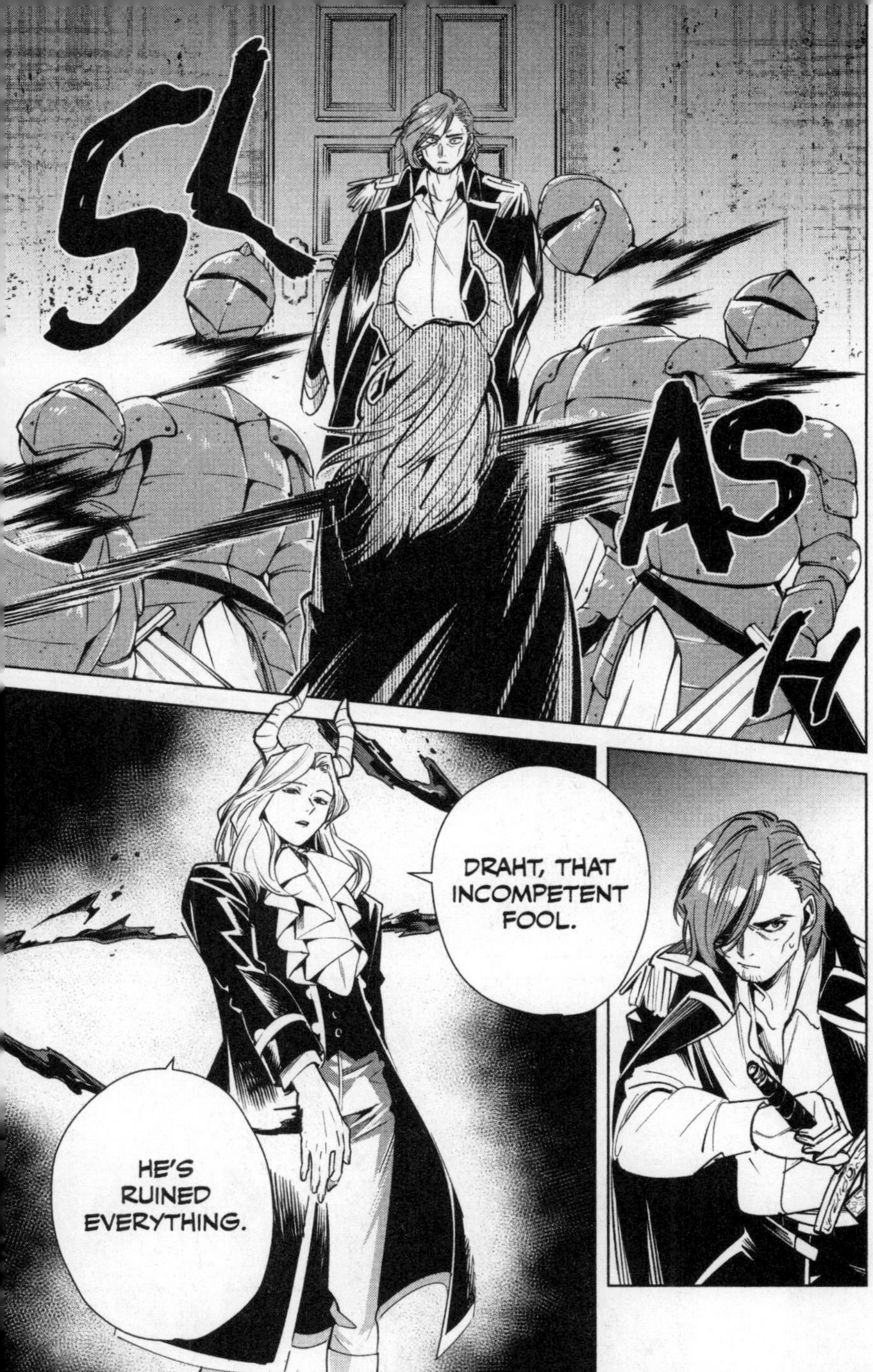
SLASH
DRAHT, THAT INCOMPETENT FOOL.
HE'S RUINED EVERYTHING.

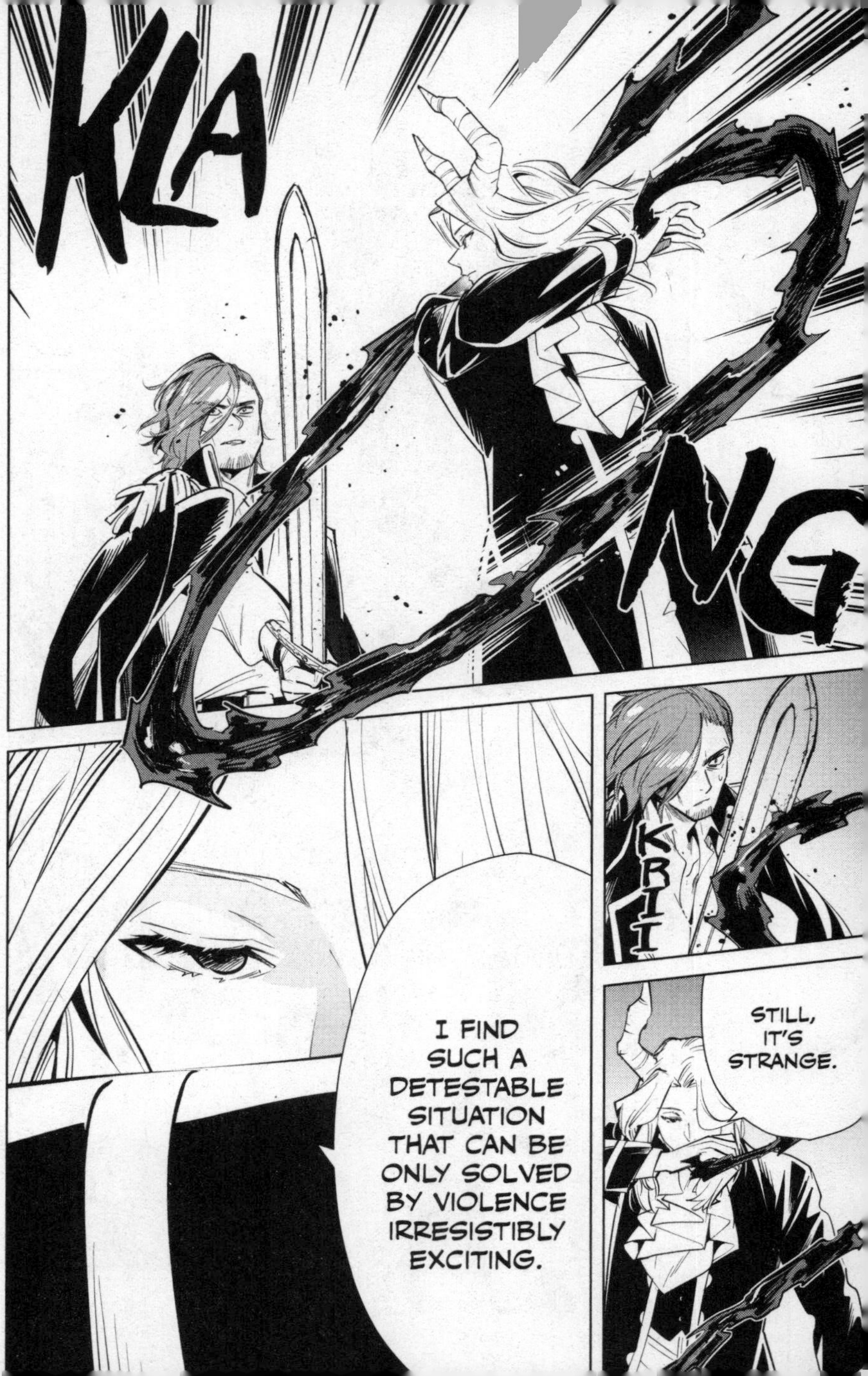
KLA
NG
KRII
STILL, IT'S STRANGE.
I FIND SUCH A DETESTABLE SITUATION THAT CAN BE ONLY SOLVED BY VIOLENCE IRRESISTIBLY EXCITING.

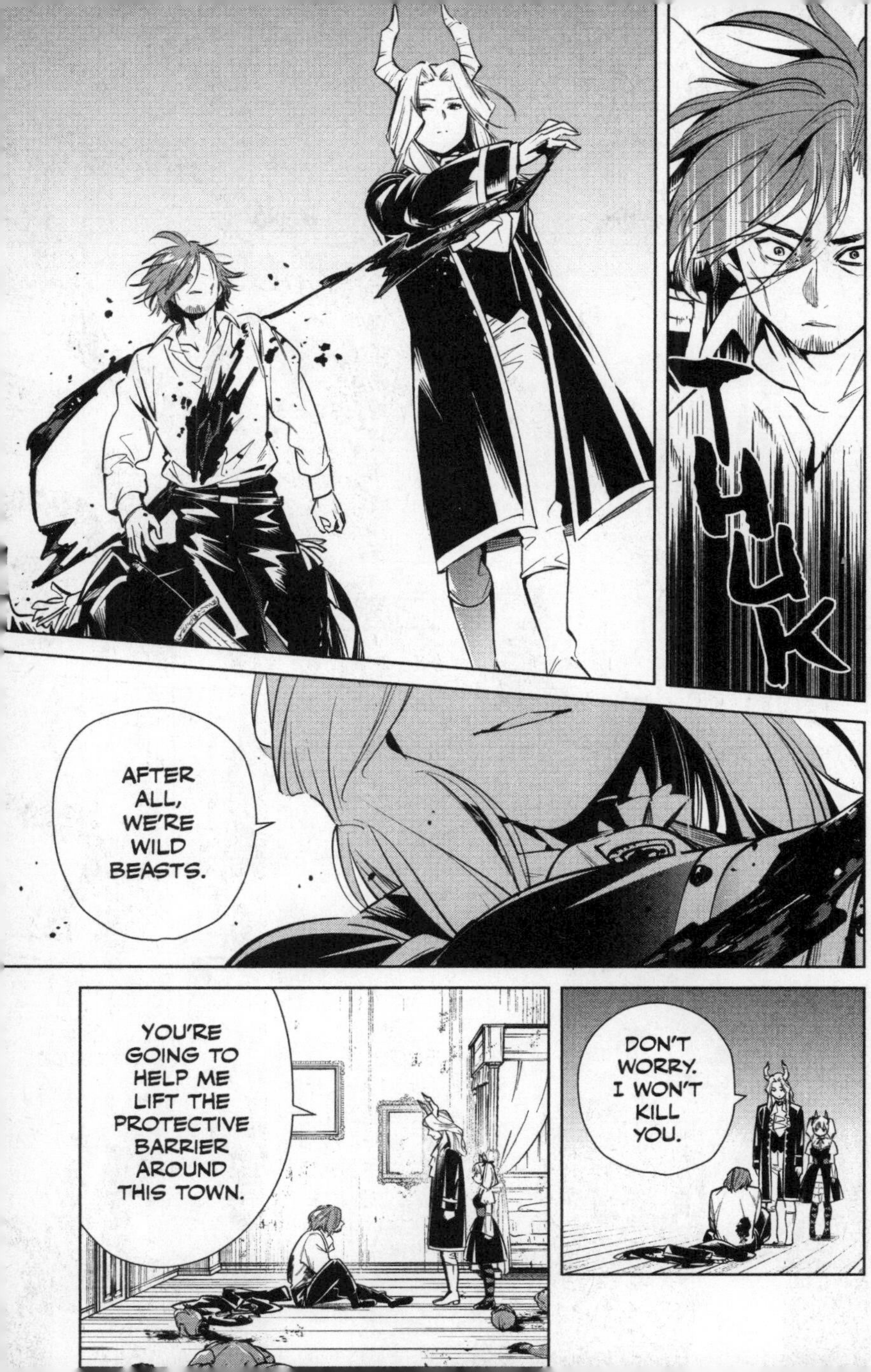
HUK
AFTER ALL, WE'RE WILD BEASTS.
DON'T WORRY. I WON'T KILL YOU.
YOU'RE GOING TO HELP ME LIFT THE PROTECTIVE BARRIER AROUND THIS TOWN.

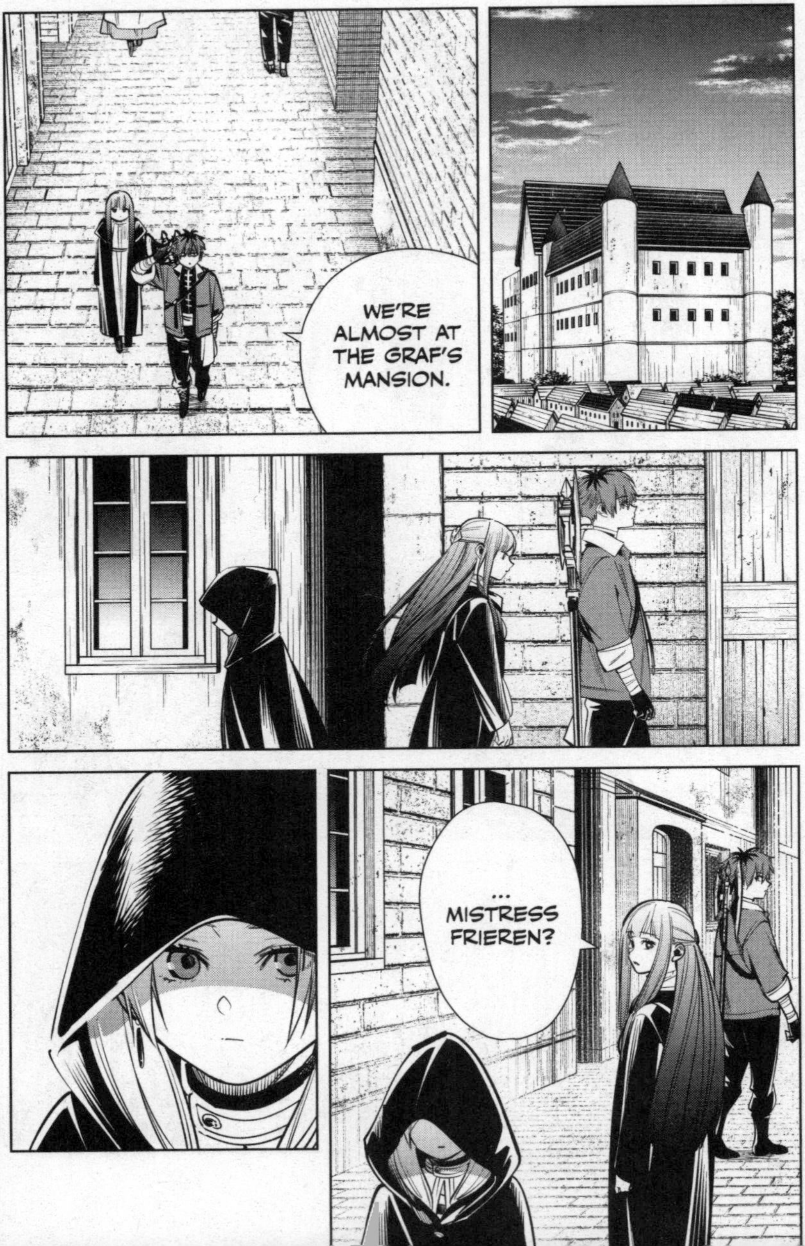
WE'RE ALMOST AT THE GRAF'S MANSION.
... MISTRESS FRIEREN?

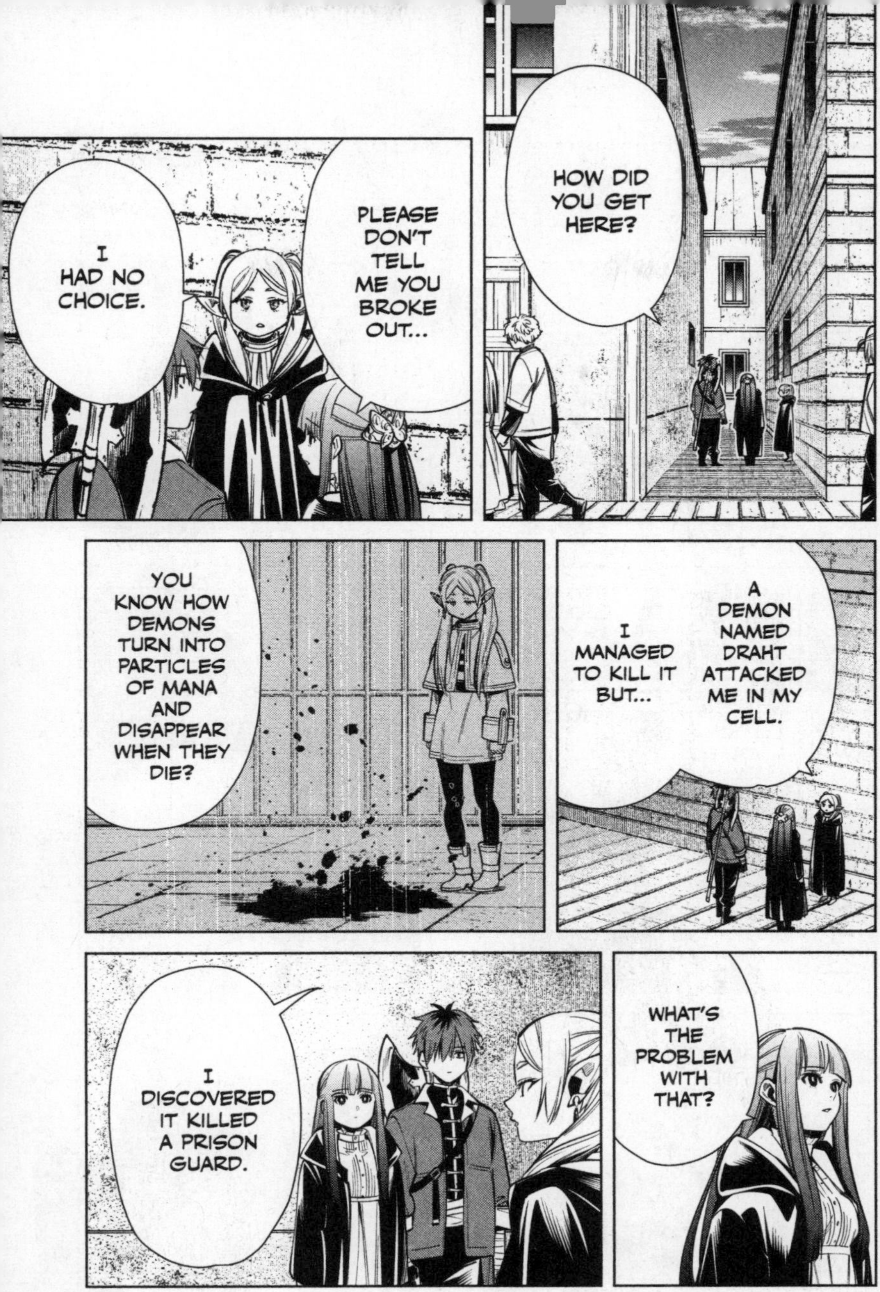
HOW DID YOU GET HERE?
PLEASE DON'T TELL ME YOU BROKE OUT...
I HAD NO CHOICE.
A DEMON NAMED DRAHT ATTACKED ME IN MY CELL.
I MANAGED TO KILL IT BUT...
YOU KNOW HOW DEMONS TURN INTO PARTICLES OF MANA AND DISAPPEAR WHEN THEY DIE?
WHAT'S THE PROBLEM WITH THAT?
I DISCOVERED IT KILLED A PRISON GUARD.

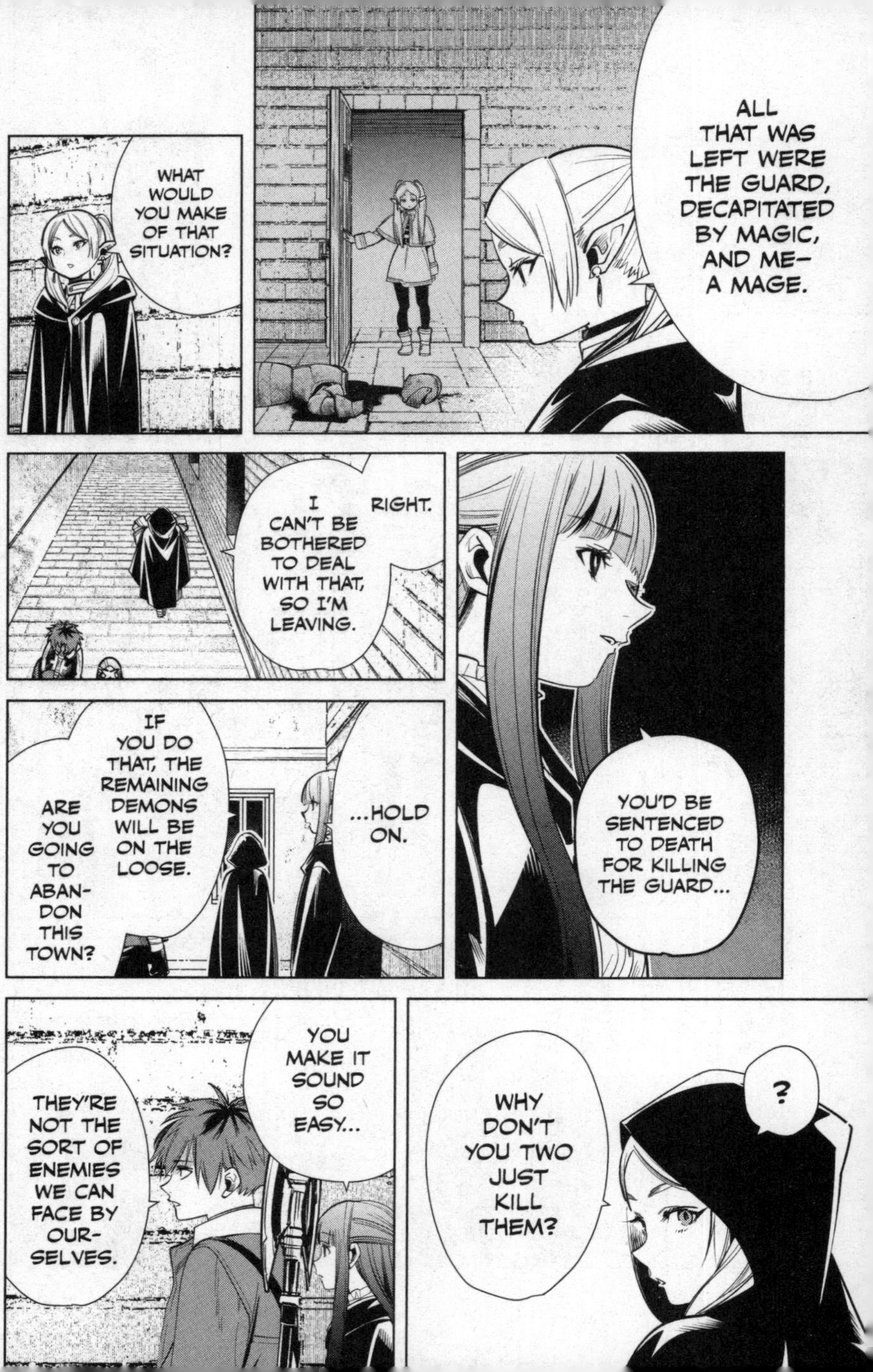
ALL THAT WAS LEFT WERE THE GUARD, DECAPITATED BY MAGIC, AND ME—A MAGE.
WHAT WOULD YOU MAKE OF THAT SITUATION?
YOU'D BE SENTENCED TO DEATH FOR KILLING THE GUARD...
RIGHT.
I CAN'T BE BOTHERED TO DEAL WITH THAT, SO I'M LEAVING.
...HOLD ON.
IF YOU DO THAT, THE REMAINING DEMONS WILL BE ON THE LOOSE.
ARE YOU GOING TO ABANDON THIS TOWN?
?
WHY DON'T YOU TWO JUST KILL THEM?
YOU MAKE IT SOUND SO EASY...
THEY'RE NOT THE SORT OF ENEMIES WE CAN FACE BY OURSELVES.

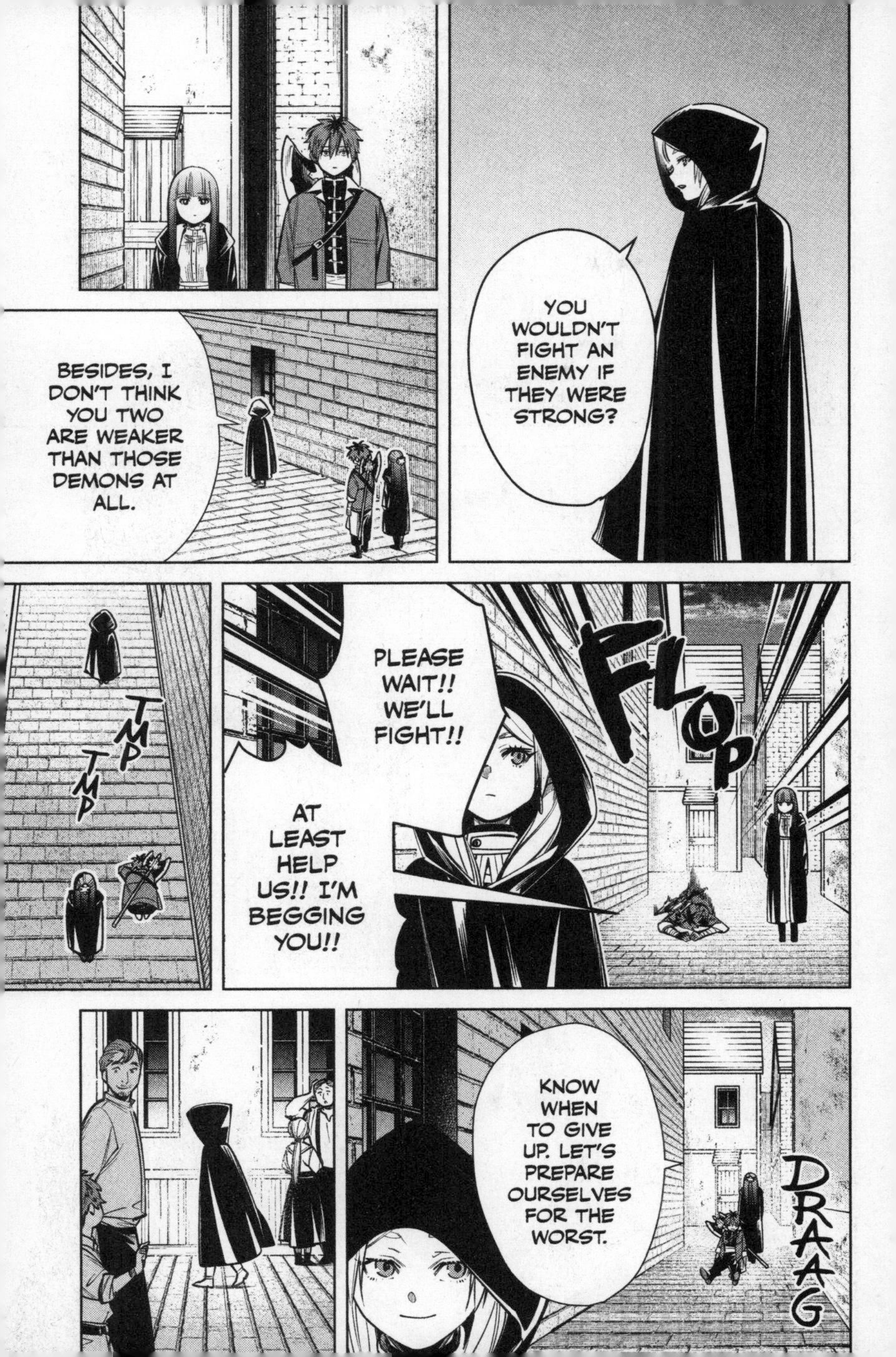
YOU WOULDN'T FIGHT AN ENEMY IF THEY WERE STRONG?
BESIDES, I DON'T THINK YOU TWO ARE WEAKER THAN THOSE DEMONS AT ALL.
FLOP
PLEASE WAIT!! WE'LL FIGHT!!
AT LEAST HELP US!! I'M BEGGING YOU!!
TMP TMP
KNOW WHEN TO GIVE UP. LET'S PREPARE OURSELVES FOR THE WORST.
DRAG

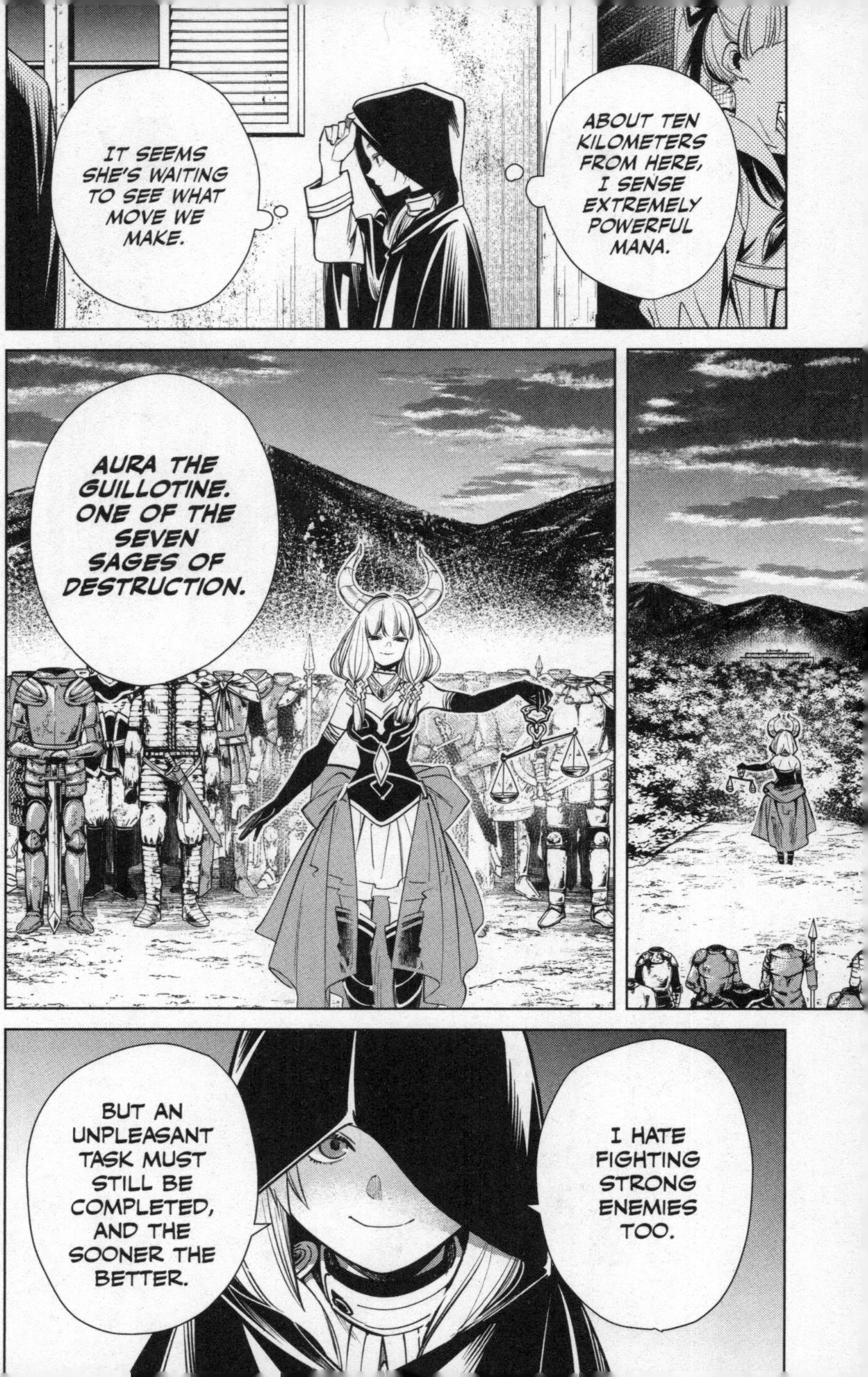
ABOUT TEN KILOMETERS FROM HERE, I SENSE EXTREMELY POWERFUL MANA.
IT SEEMS SHE'S WAITING TO SEE WHAT MOVE WE MAKE.
AURA THE GUILLOTINE. ONE OF THE SEVEN SAGES OF DESTRUCTION.
I HATE FIGHTING STRONG ENEMIES TOO.
BUT AN UNPLEASANT TASK MUST STILL BE COMPLETED, AND THE SOONER THE BETTER.

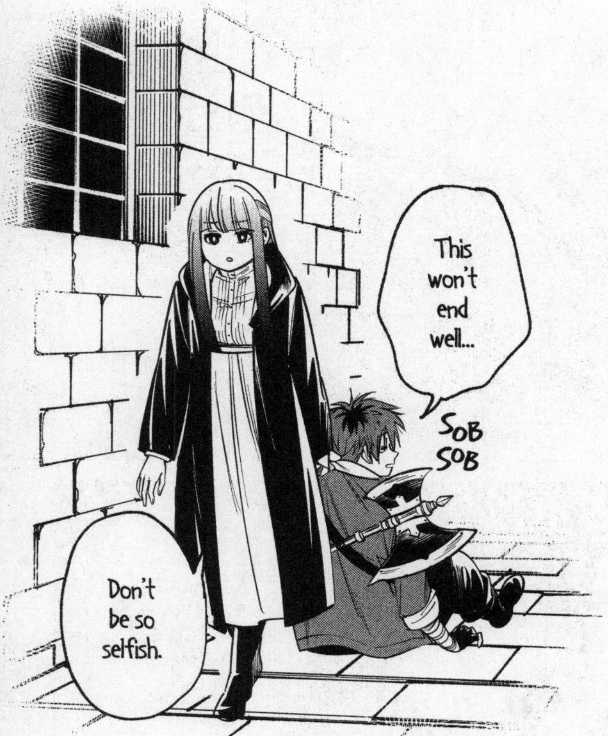
This won't end well...
SOB SOB
Don't be so selfish.

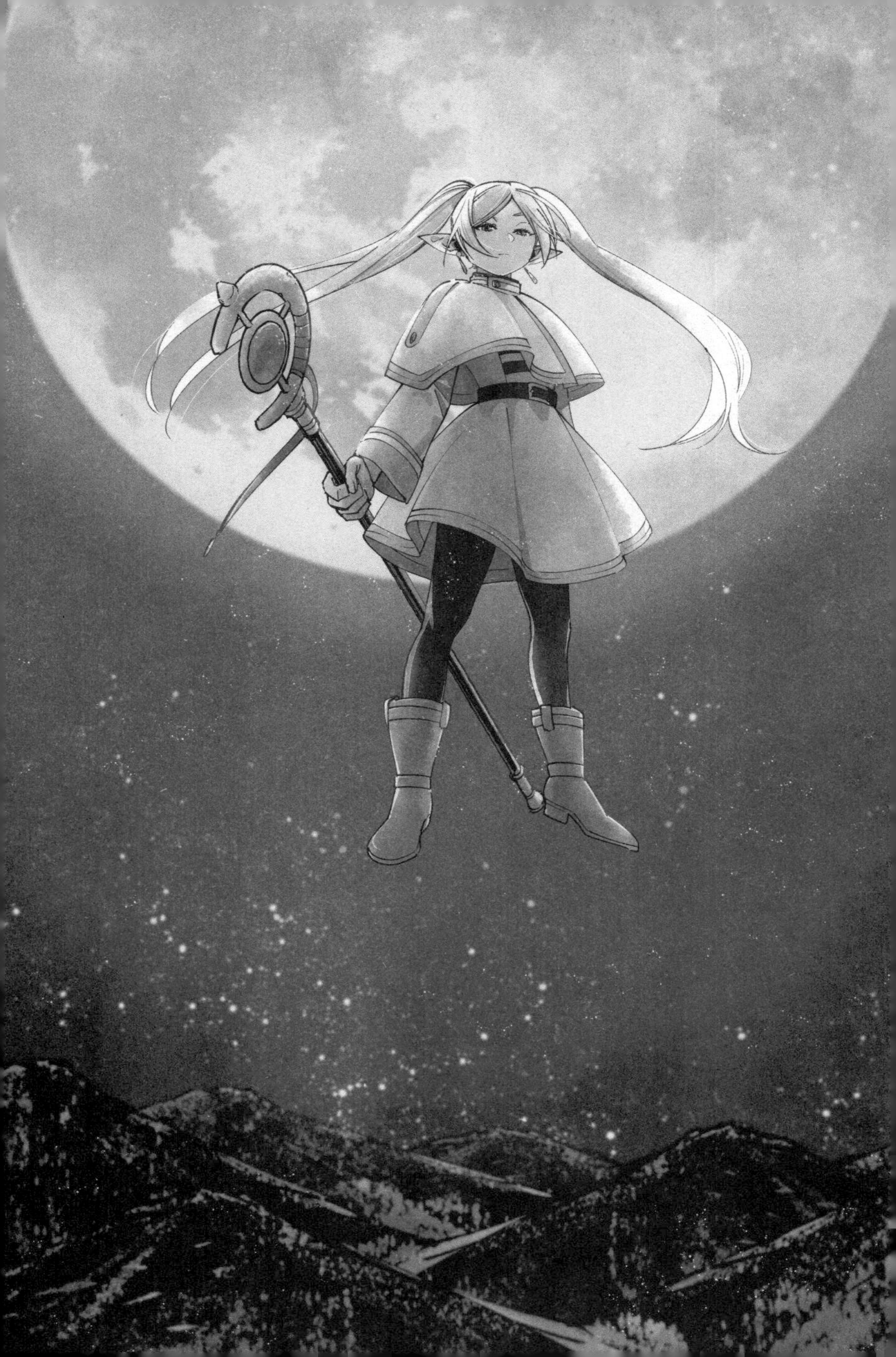

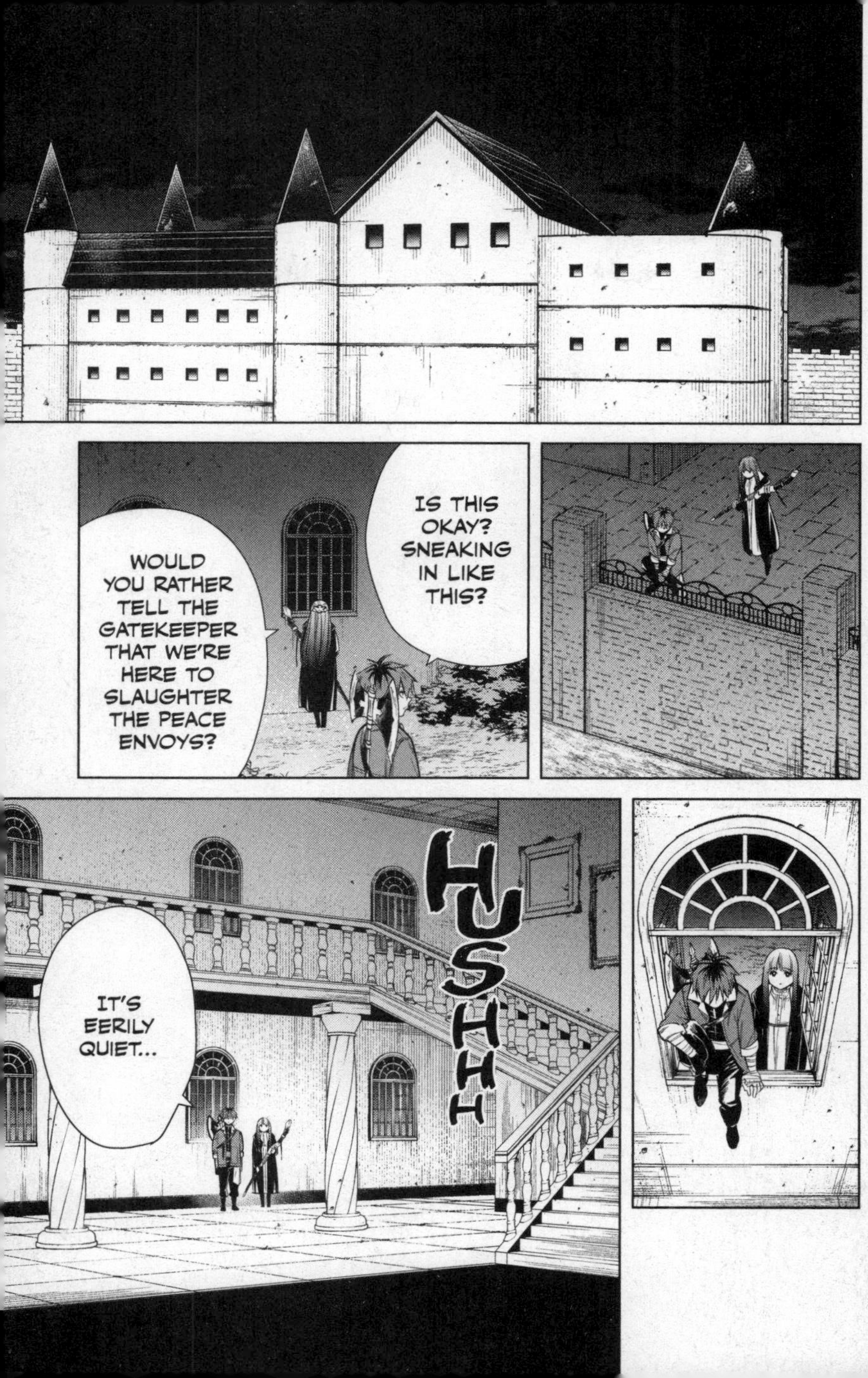
IS THIS OKAY? SNEAKING IN LIKE THIS?
WOULD YOU RATHER TELL THE GATEKEEPER THAT WE'RE HERE TO SLAUGHTER THE PEACE ENVOYS?
HUSHHH
IT'S EERILY QUIET...

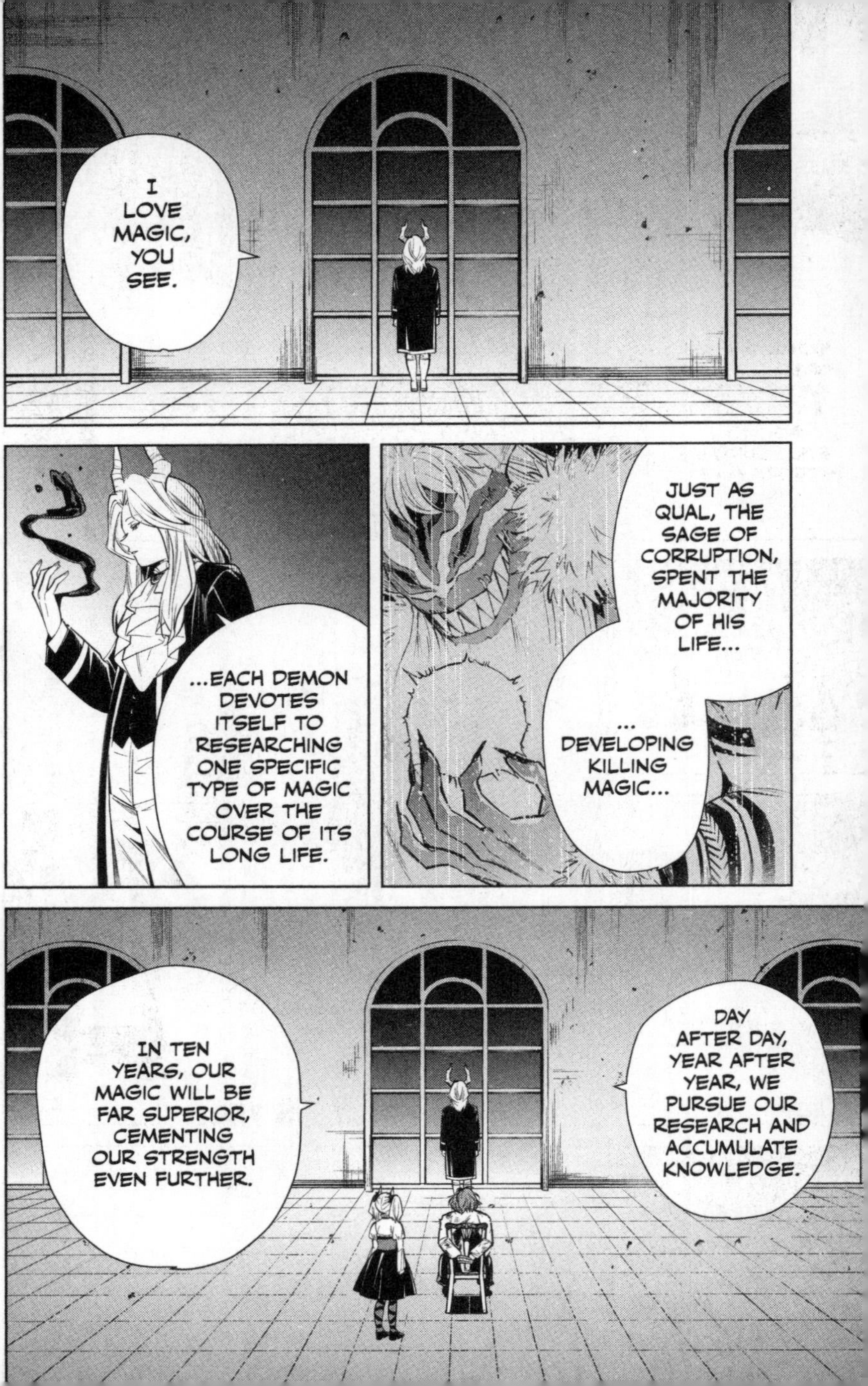
I LOVE MAGIC, YOU SEE.
JUST AS QUAL, THE SAGE OF CORRUPTION, SPENT THE MAJORITY OF HIS LIFE...
...DEVELOPING KILLING MAGIC...
...EACH DEMON DEVOTES ITSELF TO RESEARCHING ONE SPECIFIC TYPE OF MAGIC OVER THE COURSE OF ITS LONG LIFE.
DAY AFTER DAY, YEAR AFTER YEAR, WE PURSUE OUR RESEARCH AND ACCUMULATE KNOWLEDGE.
IN TEN YEARS, OUR MAGIC WILL BE FAR SUPERIOR, CEMENTING OUR STRENGTH EVEN FURTHER.

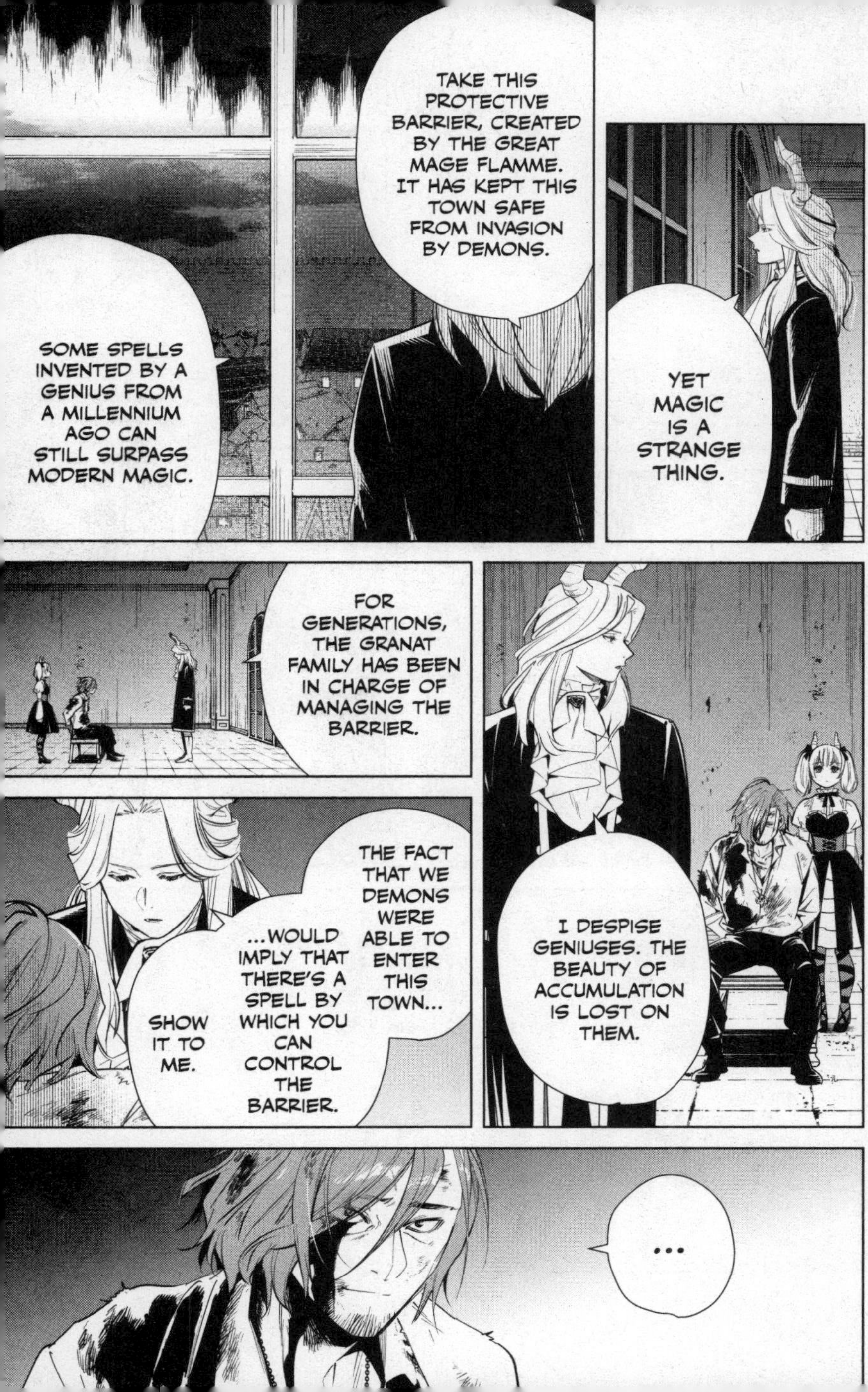
YET MAGIC IS A STRANGE THING.
TAKE THIS PROTECTIVE BARRIER, CREATED BY THE GREAT MAGE FLAMME. IT HAS KEPT THIS TOWN SAFE FROM INVASION BY DEMONS.
SOME SPELLS INVENTED BY A GENIUS FROM A MILLENNIUM AGO CAN STILL SURPASS MODERN MAGIC.
I DESPISE GENIUSES. THE BEAUTY OF ACCUMULATION IS LOST ON THEM.
FOR GENERATIONS, THE GRANAT FAMILY HAS BEEN IN CHARGE OF MANAGING THE BARRIER.
THE FACT THAT WE DEMONS WERE ABLE TO ENTER THIS TOWN...
...WOULD IMPLY THAT THERE'S A SPELL BY WHICH YOU CAN CONTROL THE BARRIER.
SHOW IT TO ME.
...

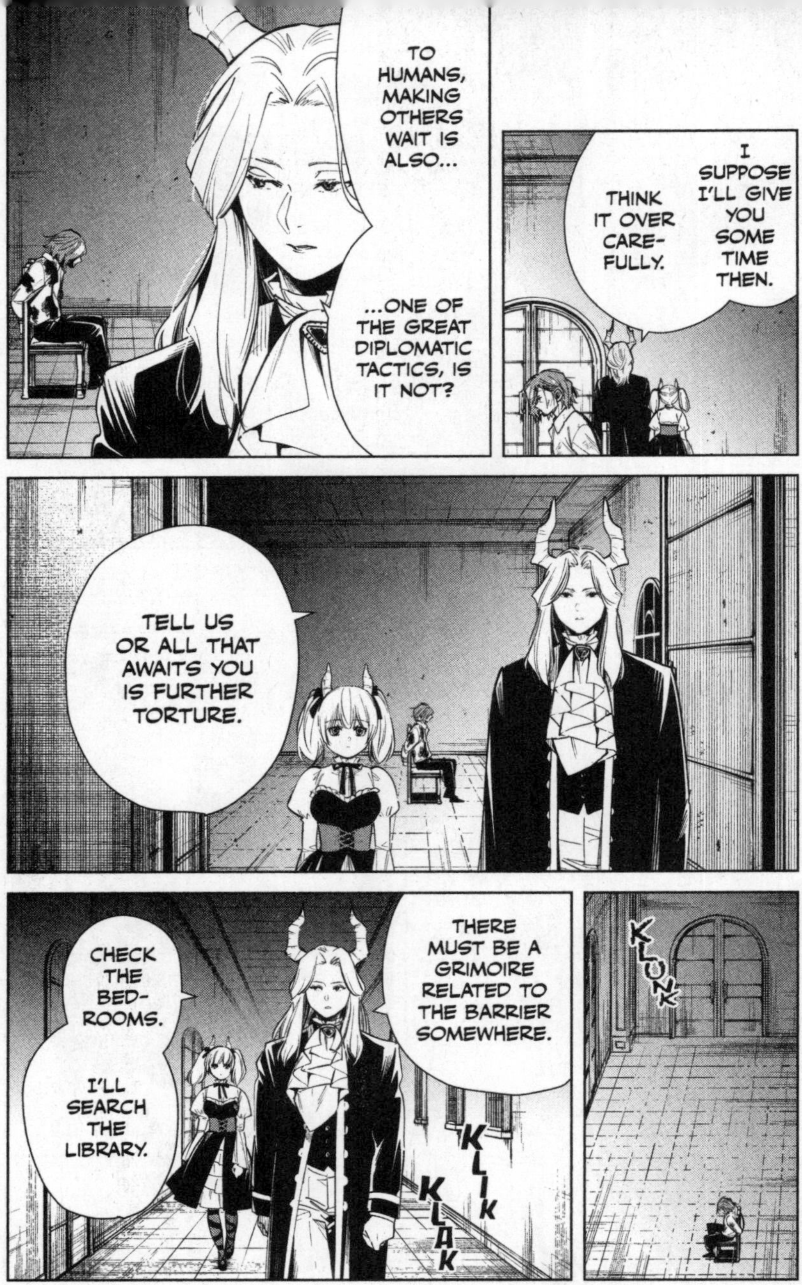
I SUPPOSE I'LL GIVE YOU SOME TIME THEN.
THINK IT OVER CARE-FULLY.
TO HUMANS, MAKING OTHERS WAIT IS ALSO...
...ONE OF THE GREAT DIPLOMATIC TACTICS, IS IT NOT?
TELL US OR ALL THAT AWAITS YOU IS FURTHER TORTURE.
KLUNK
THERE MUST BE A GRIMOIRE RELATED TO THE BARRIER SOMEWHERE.
CHECK THE BED-ROOMS.
I'LL SEARCH THE LIBRARY.
KLIK
KLAK

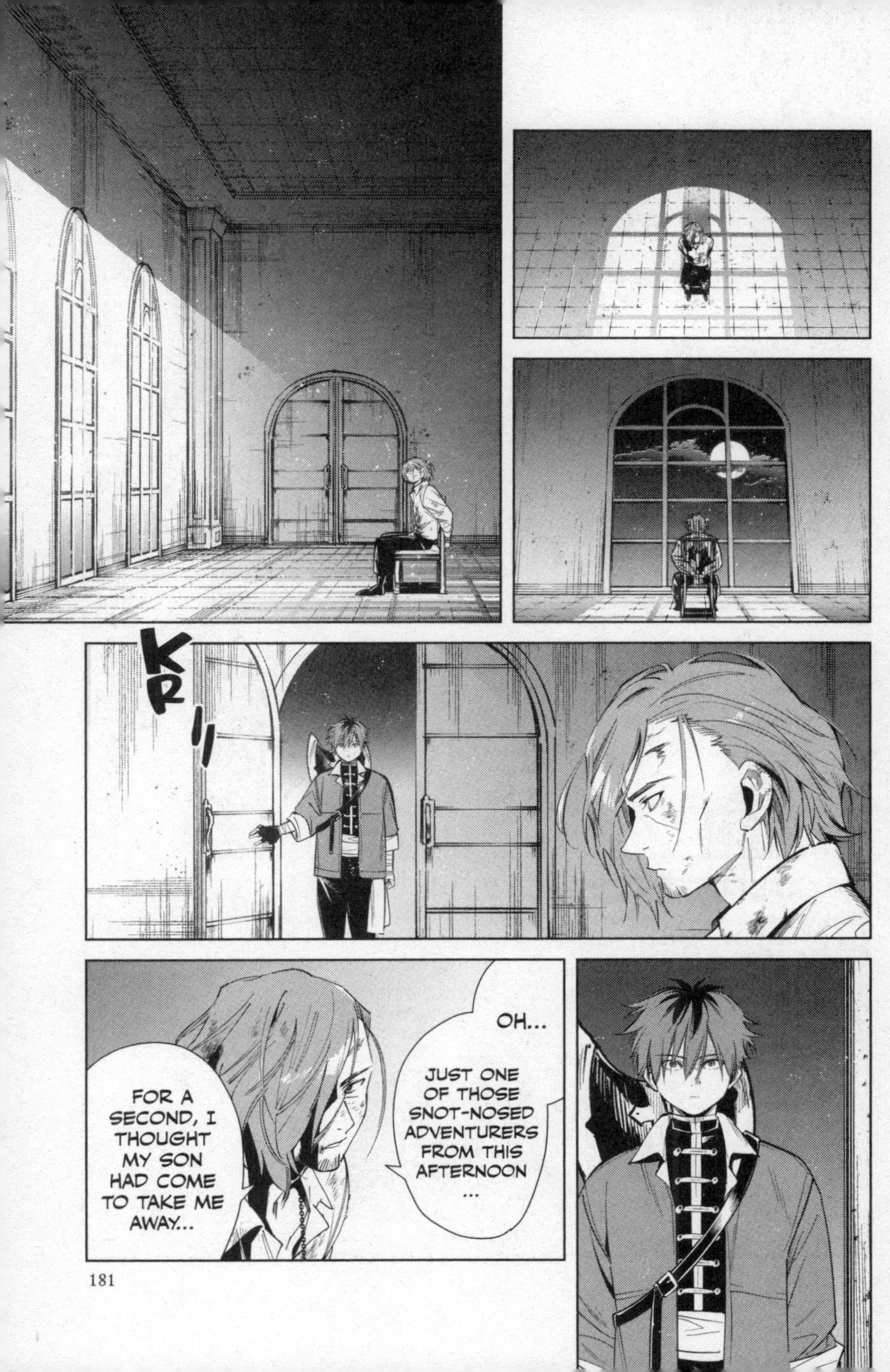
KRII
OH...
JUST ONE OF THOSE SNOT-NOSED ADVENTURERS FROM THIS AFTERNOON ...
FOR A SECOND, I THOUGHT MY SON HAD COME TO TAKE ME AWAY...

YOU LOOK TERRIBLE. WHAT'D THEY DO TO YOU?
LET ME HELP YOU.
YOU'RE SHAKING.
YOU HAVE A PROBLEM WITH THAT?

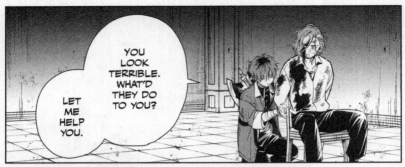

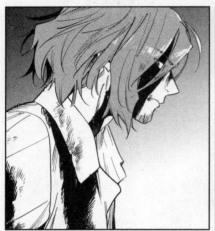

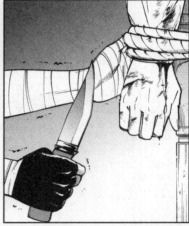

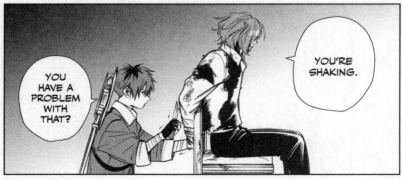

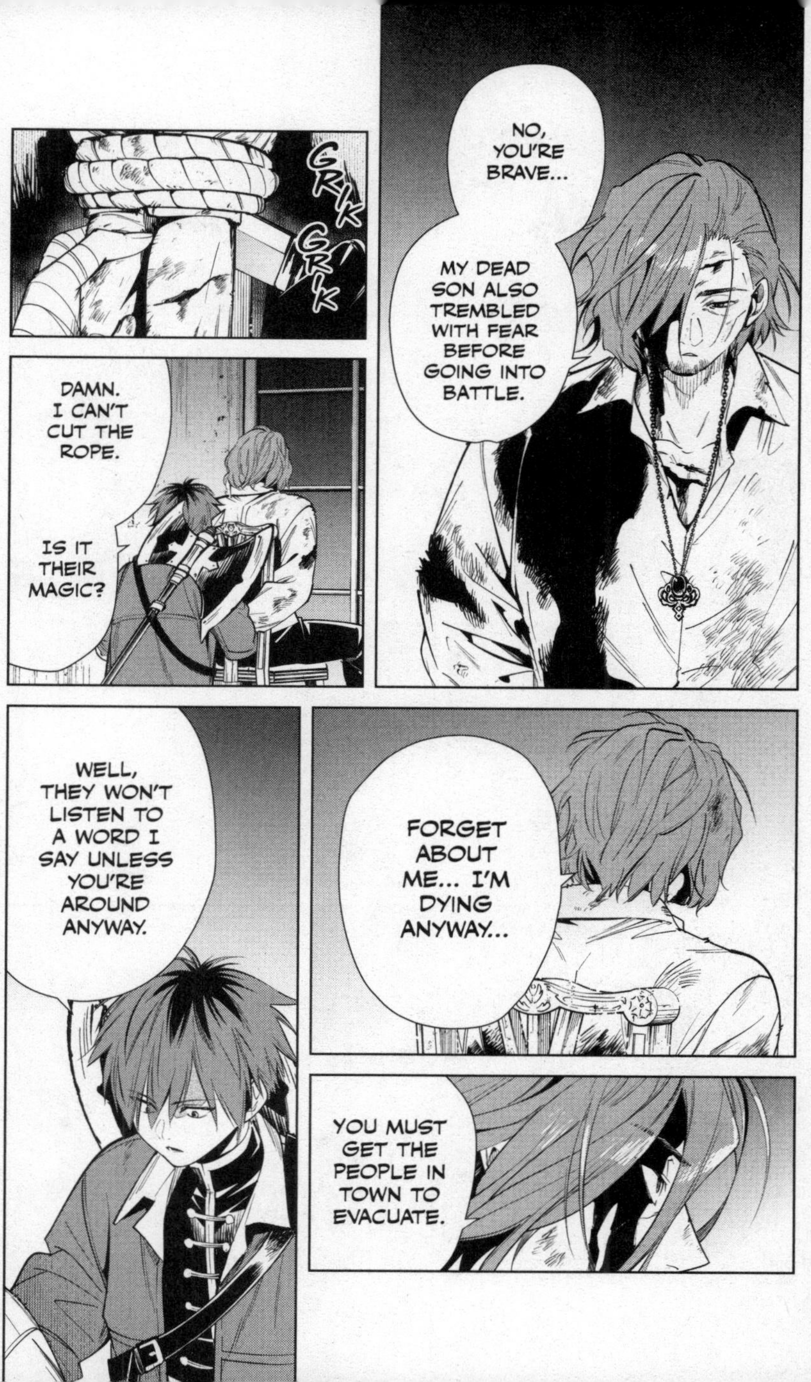
NO, YOU'RE BRAVE...
MY DEAD SON ALSO TREMBLED WITH FEAR BEFORE GOING INTO BATTLE.
GRIK GRIK
DAMN. I CAN'T CUT THE ROPE.
IS IT THEIR MAGIC?
FORGET ABOUT ME... I'M DYING ANYWAY...
YOU MUST GET THE PEOPLE IN TOWN TO EVACUATE.
WELL, THEY WON'T LISTEN TO A WORD I SAY UNLESS YOU'RE AROUND ANYWAY.

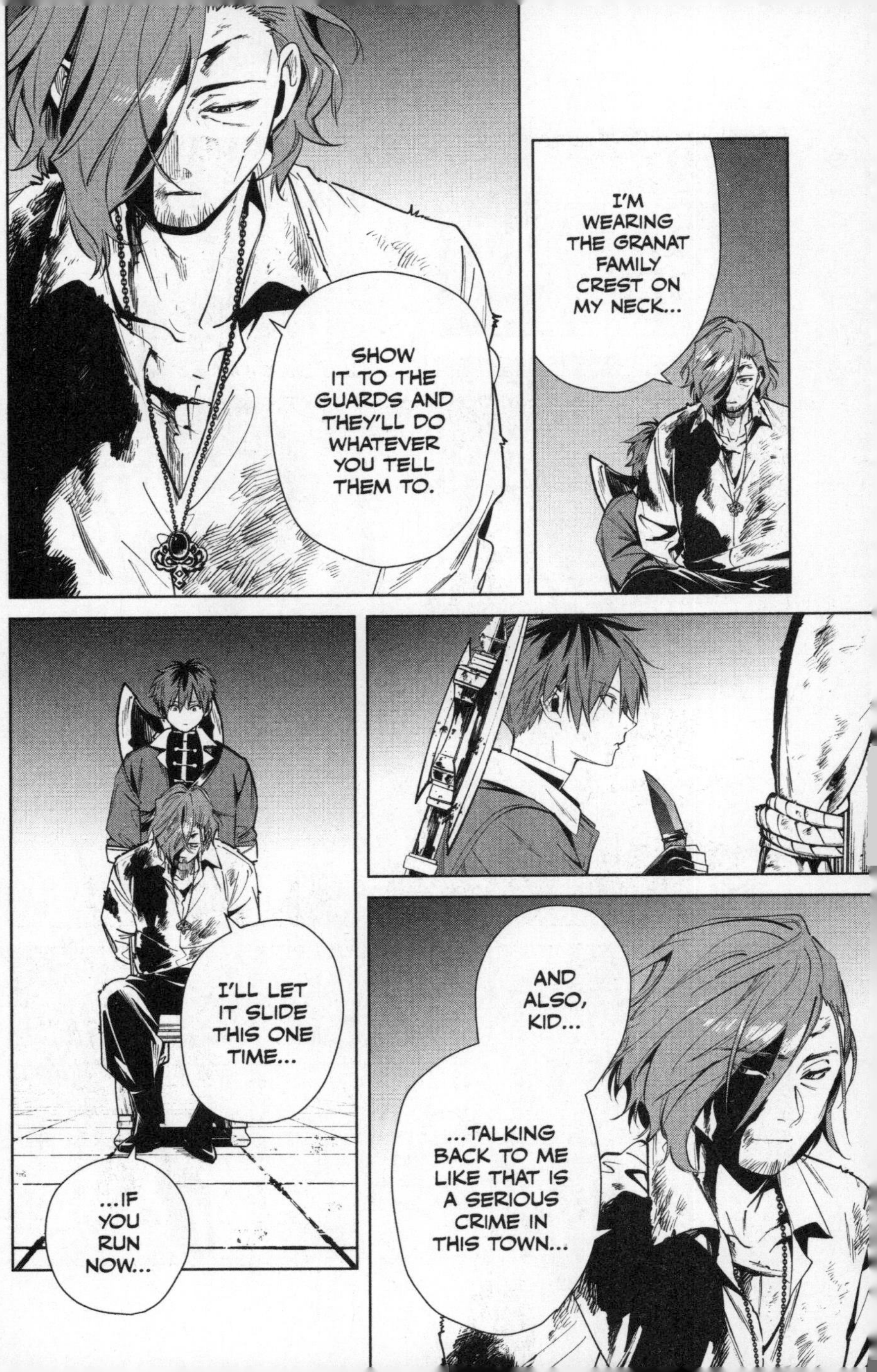
I'M WEARING THE GRANAT FAMILY CREST ON MY NECK...
SHOW IT TO THE GUARDS AND THEY'LL DO WHATEVER YOU TELL THEM TO.
AND ALSO, KID...
...TALKING BACK TO ME LIKE THAT IS A SERIOUS CRIME IN THIS TOWN...
I'LL LET IT SLIDE THIS ONE TIME...
...IF YOU RUN NOW...

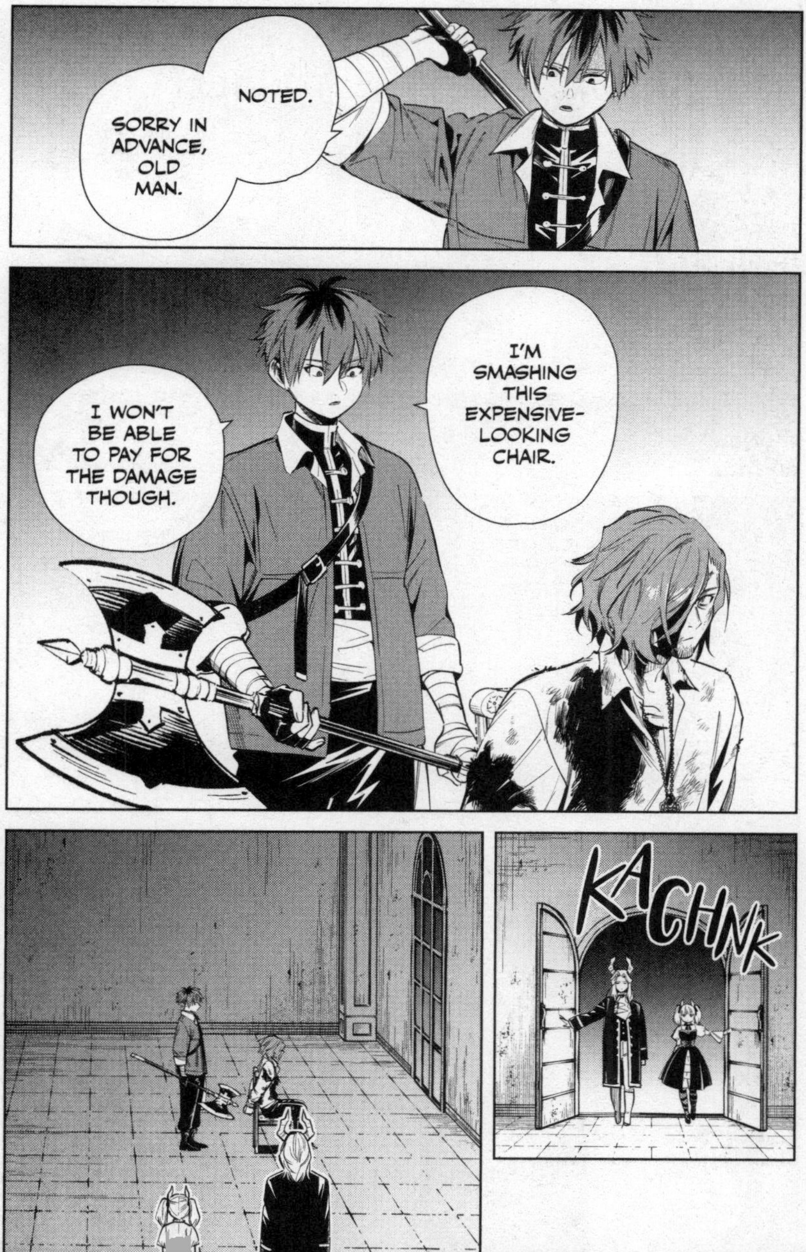
NOTED.
SORRY IN ADVANCE, OLD MAN.
I'M SMASHING THIS EXPENSIVE-LOOKING CHAIR.
I WON'T BE ABLE TO PAY FOR THE DAMAGE THOUGH.
KACHNK

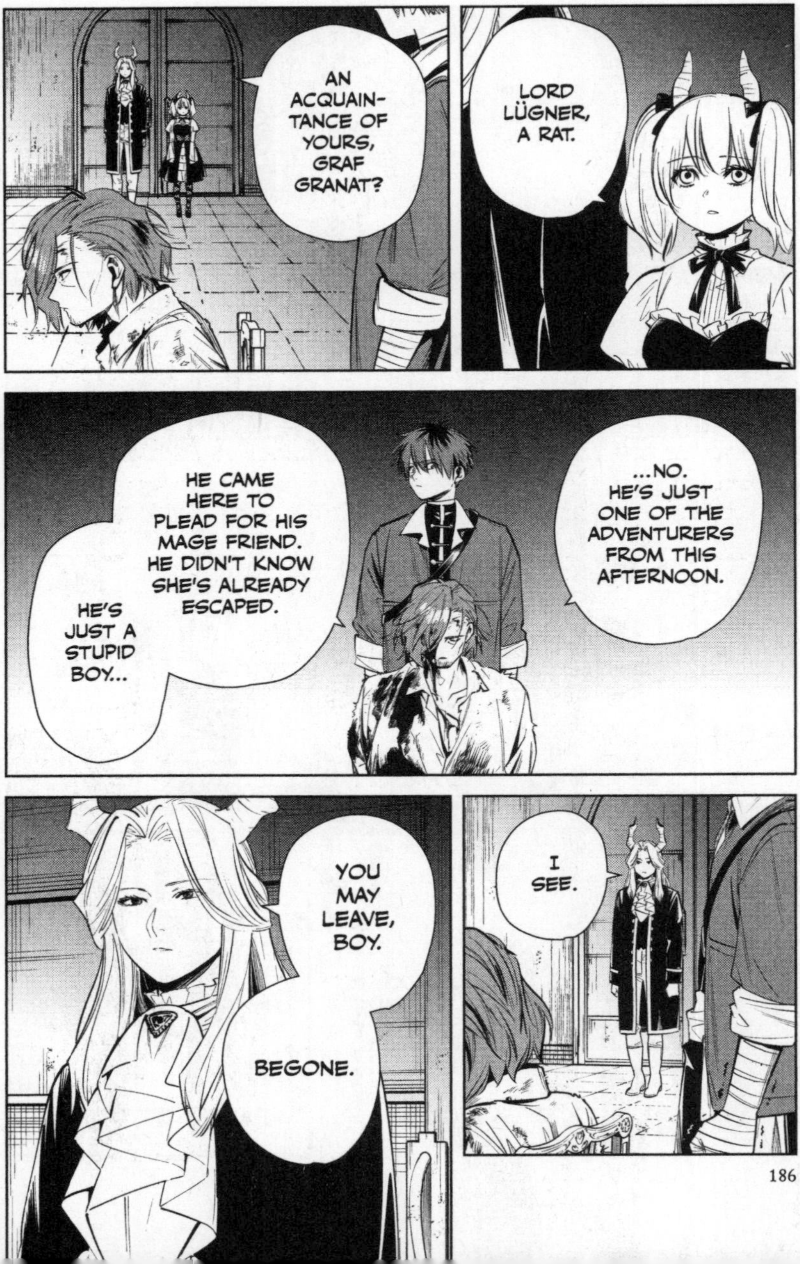
LORD LÜGNER, A RAT.
AN ACQUAINTANCE OF YOURS, GRAF GRANAT?
...NO. HE'S JUST ONE OF THE ADVENTURERS FROM THIS AFTERNOON.
HE CAME HERE TO PLEAD FOR HIS MAGE FRIEND. HE DIDN'T KNOW SHE'S ALREADY ESCAPED.
HE'S JUST A STUPID BOY...
I SEE.
YOU MAY LEAVE, BOY.
BEGONE.

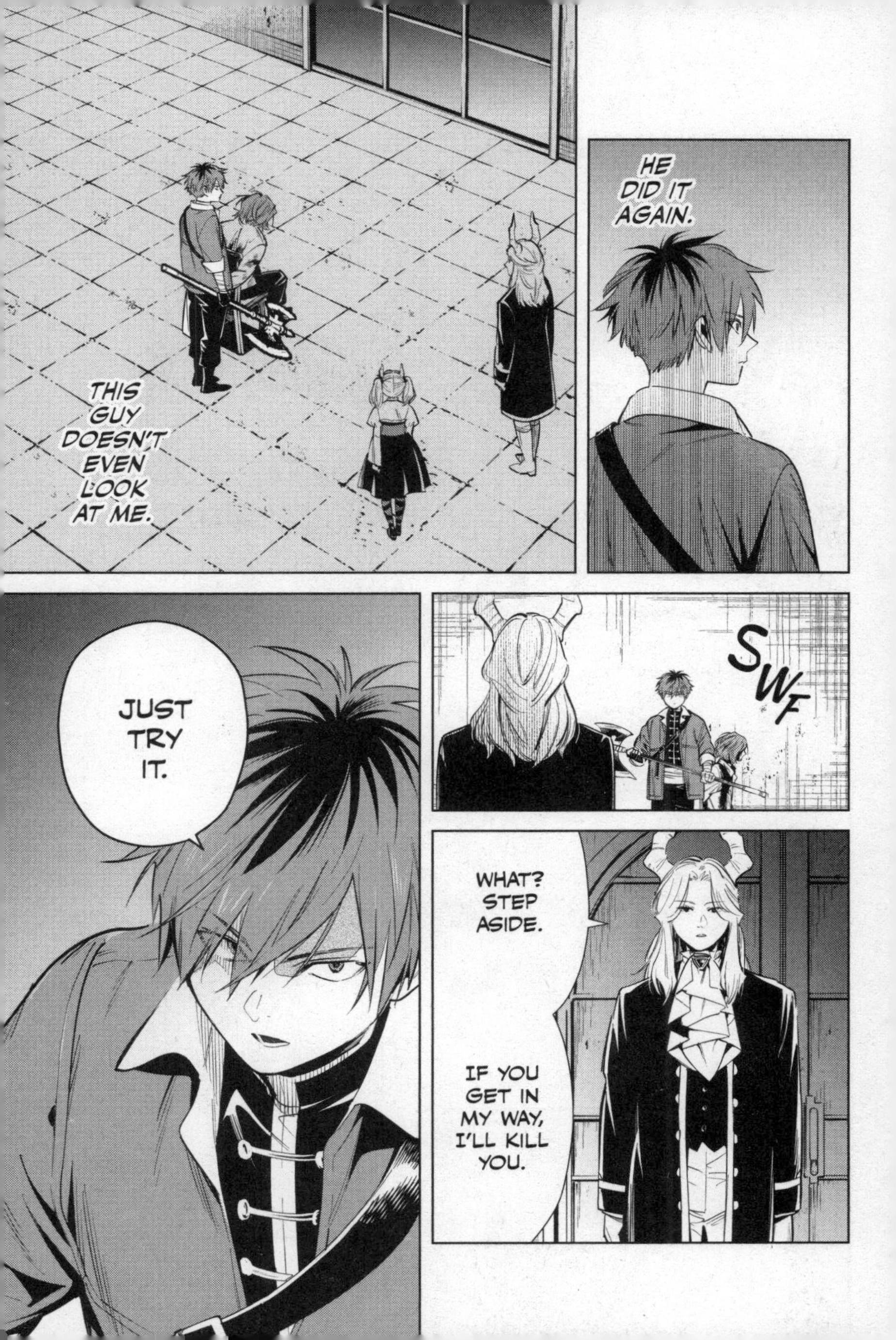
HE DID IT AGAIN.
THIS GUY DOESN'T EVEN LOOK AT ME.
SWF
WHAT? STEP ASIDE.
IF YOU GET IN MY WAY, I'LL KILL YOU.
JUST TRY IT.

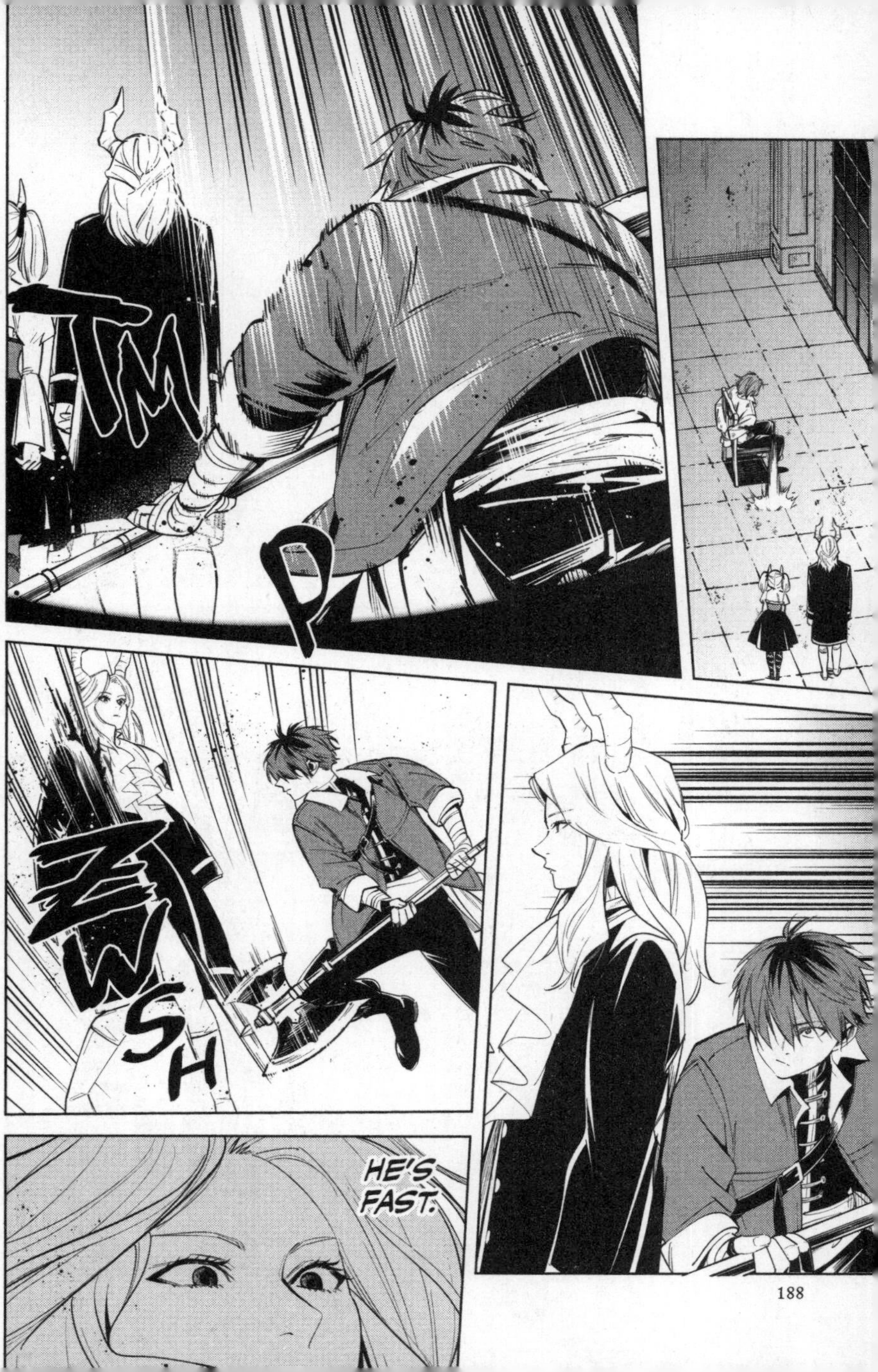
TMP
ZWSH
HE'S FAST.

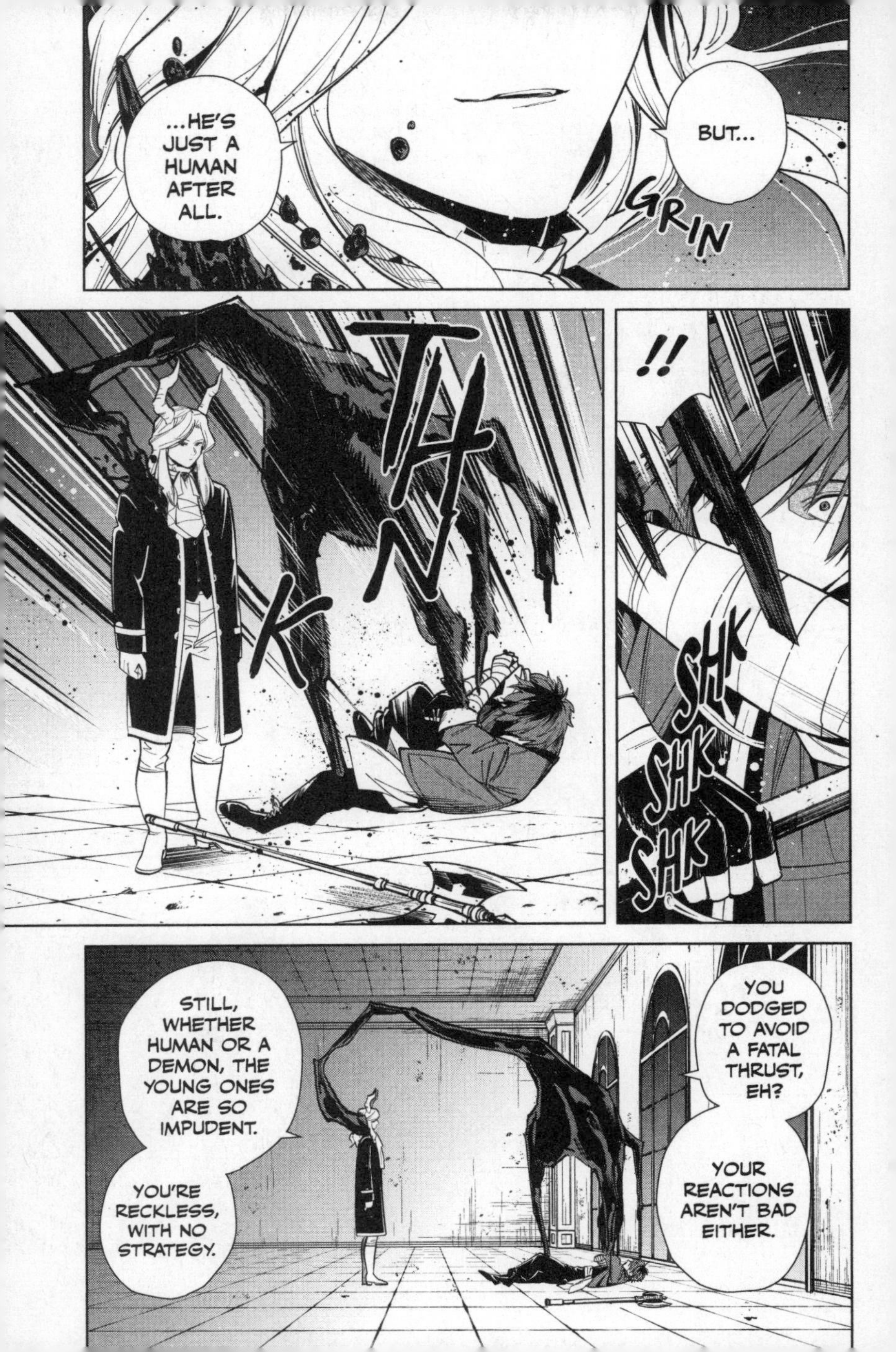

BUT...
GRIN
...HE'S JUST A HUMAN AFTER ALL.
!!
SHK SHK SHK
THUNK
YOU DODGED TO AVOID A FATAL THRUST, EH?
YOUR REACTIONS AREN'T BAD EITHER.
STILL, WHETHER HUMAN OR A DEMON, THE YOUNG ONES ARE SO IMPUDENT.
YOU'RE RECKLESS, WITH NO STRATEGY.

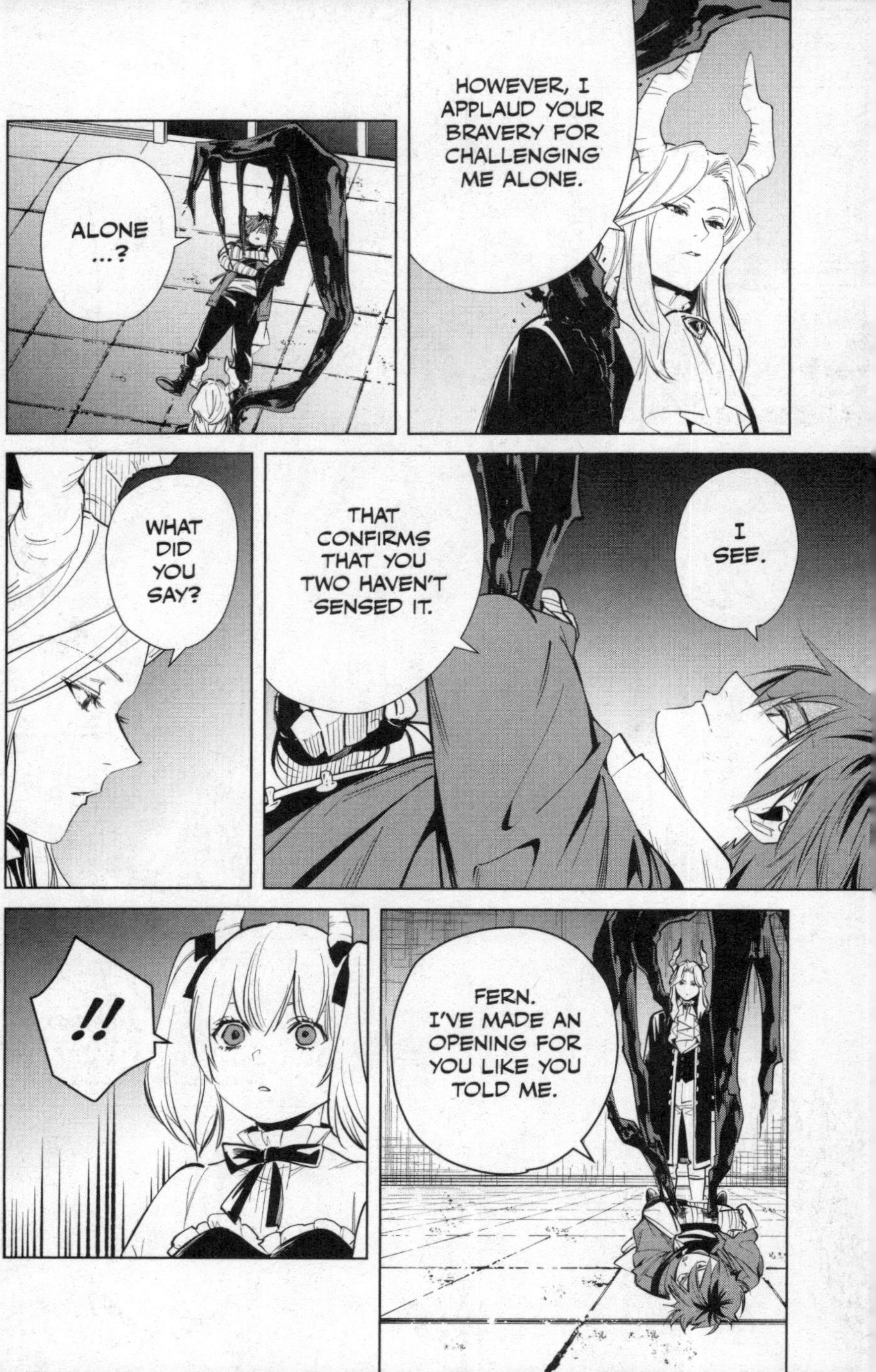
HOWEVER, I APPLAUD YOUR BRAVERY FOR CHALLENGING ME ALONE.
ALONE ...?
I SEE.
THAT CONFIRMS THAT YOU TWO HAVEN'T SENSED IT.
WHAT DID YOU SAY?
FERN. I'VE MADE AN OPENING FOR YOU LIKE YOU TOLD ME.
!!

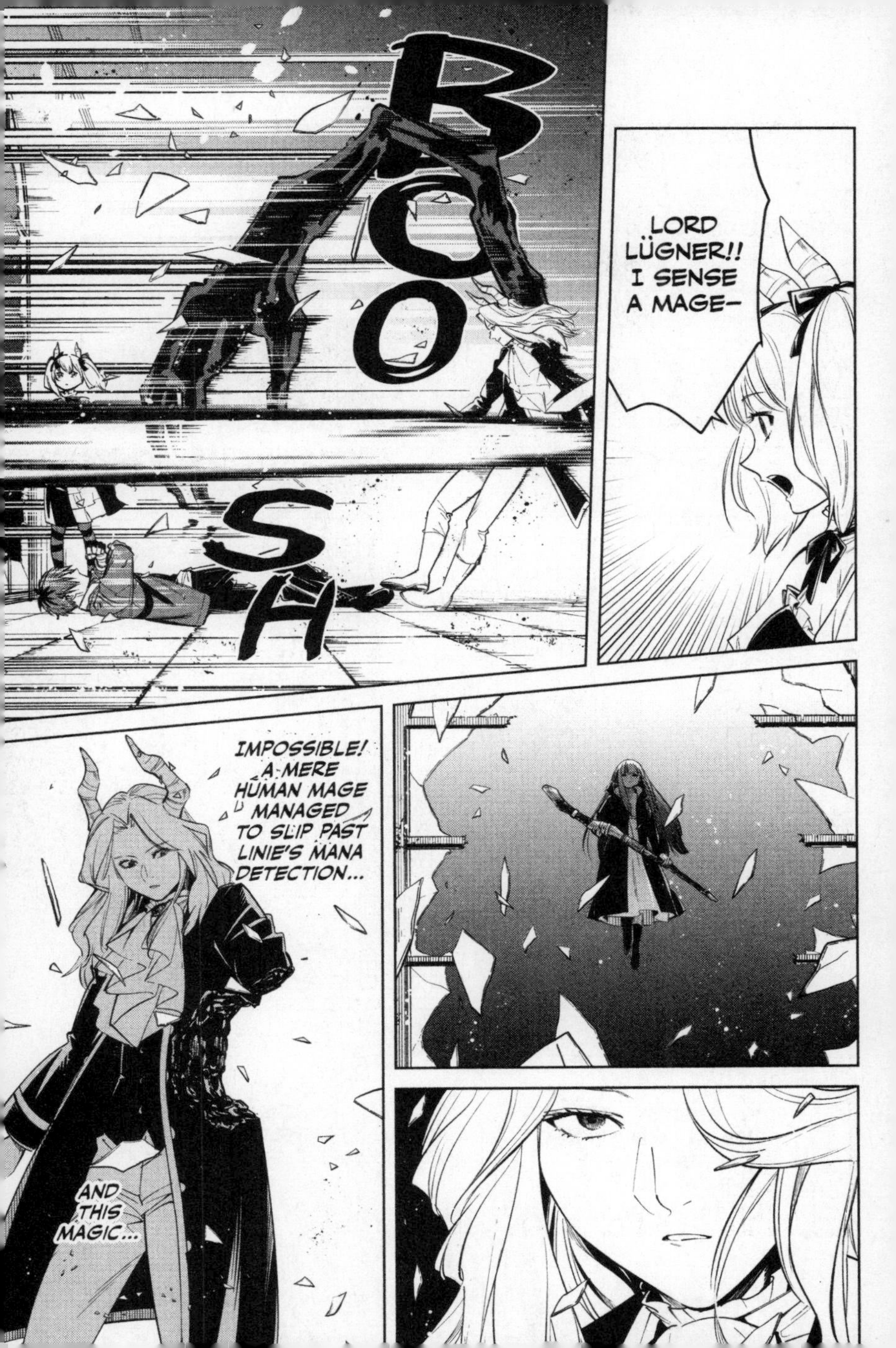
LORD LÜGNER!! I SENSE A MAGE–
BOOSH
IMPOSSIBLE! A MERE HUMAN MAGE MANAGED TO SLIP PAST LINIE'S MANA DETECTION...
AND THIS MAGIC...

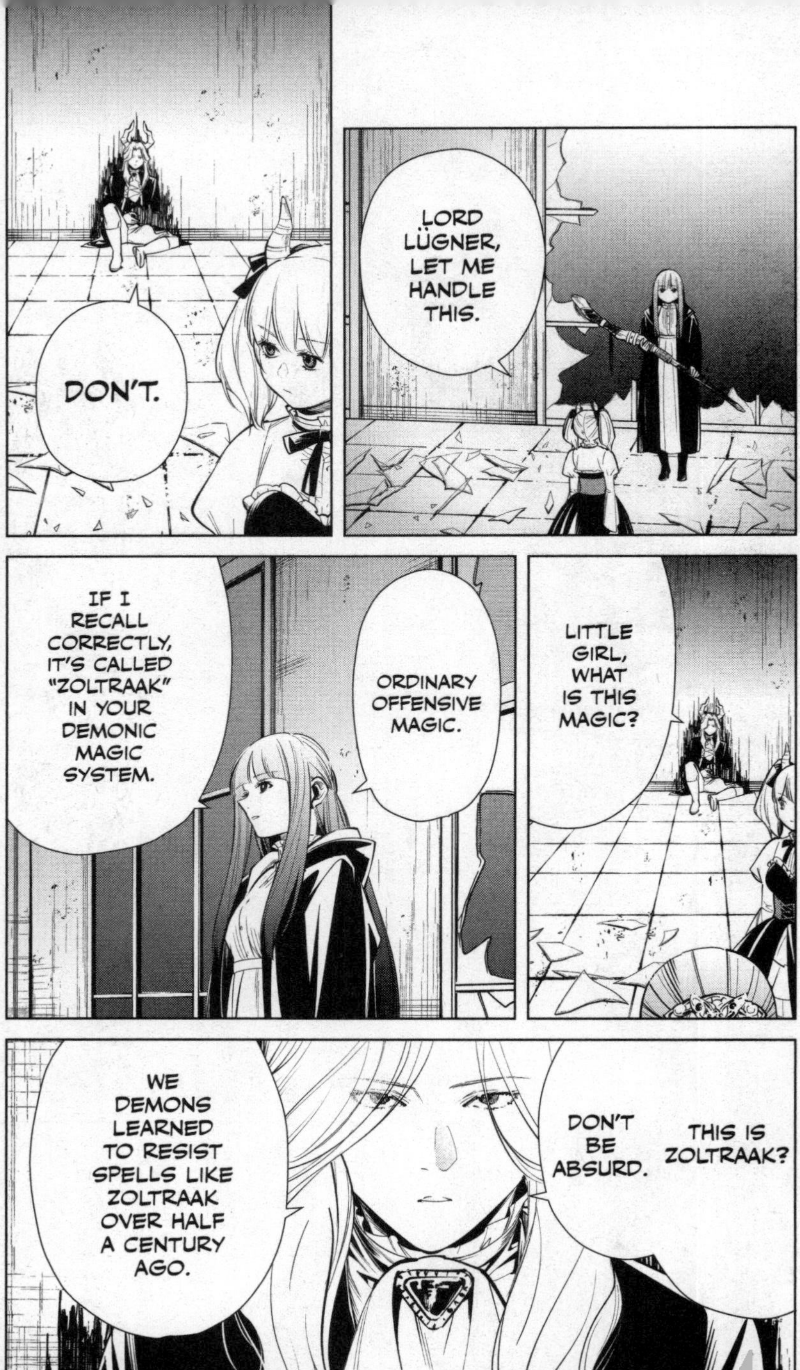
LORD LÜGNER, LET ME HANDLE THIS.
DON'T.
LITTLE GIRL, WHAT IS THIS MAGIC?
ORDINARY OFFENSIVE MAGIC.
IF I RECALL CORRECTLY, IT'S CALLED "ZOLTRAAK" IN YOUR DEMONIC MAGIC SYSTEM.
THIS IS ZOLTRAAK?
DON'T BE ABSURD.
WE DEMONS LEARNED TO RESIST SPELLS LIKE ZOLTRAAK OVER HALF A CENTURY AGO.

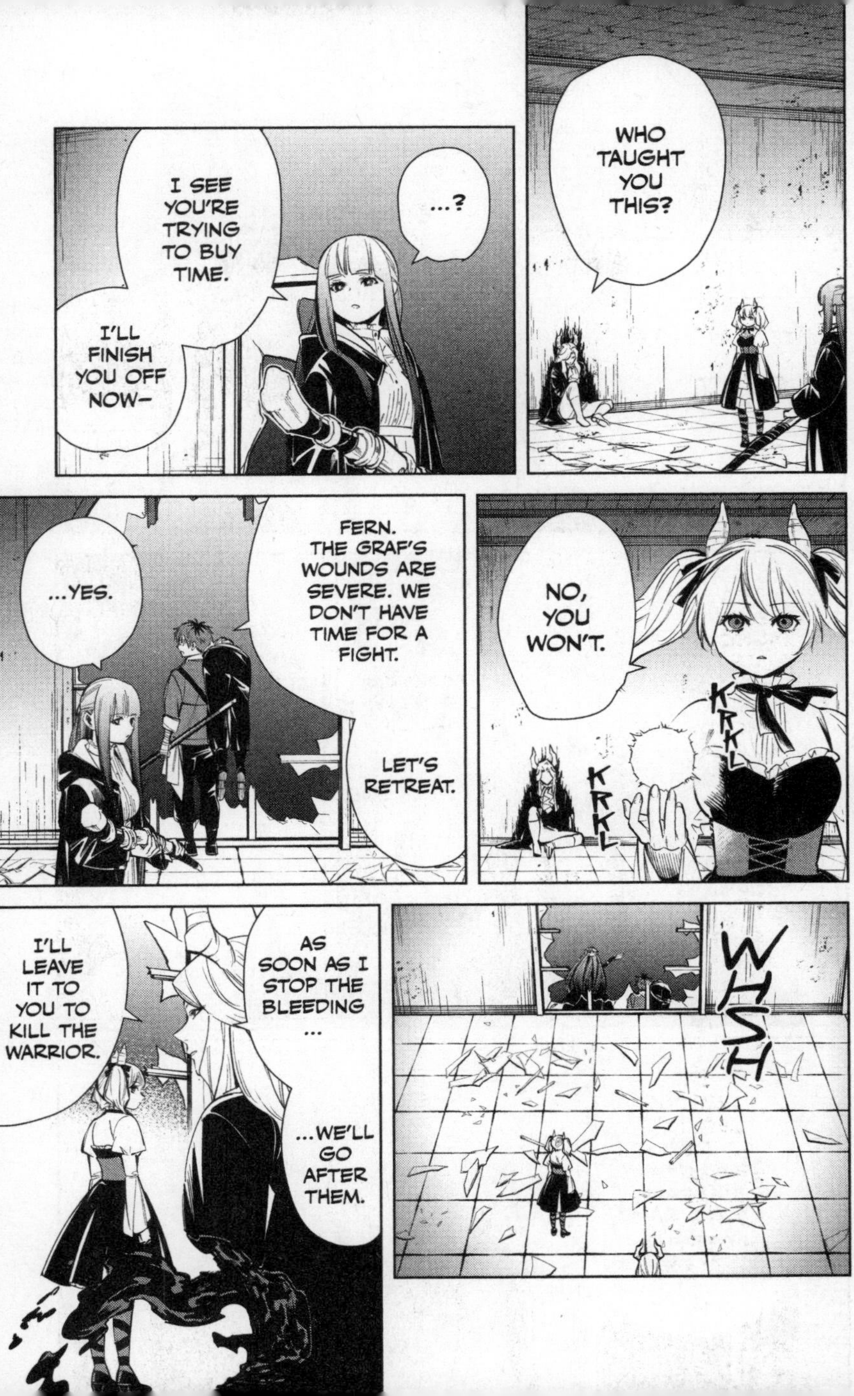
WHO TAUGHT YOU THIS?
...?
I SEE YOU'RE TRYING TO BUY TIME.
I'LL FINISH YOU OFF NOW—
NO, YOU WON'T.
KRKL
KRKL
FERN. THE GRAF'S WOUNDS ARE SEVERE. WE DON'T HAVE TIME FOR A FIGHT.
LET'S RETREAT.
...YES.
WHSH
AS SOON AS I STOP THE BLEEDING ...
...WE'LL GO AFTER THEM.
I'LL LEAVE IT TO YOU TO KILL THE WARRIOR.

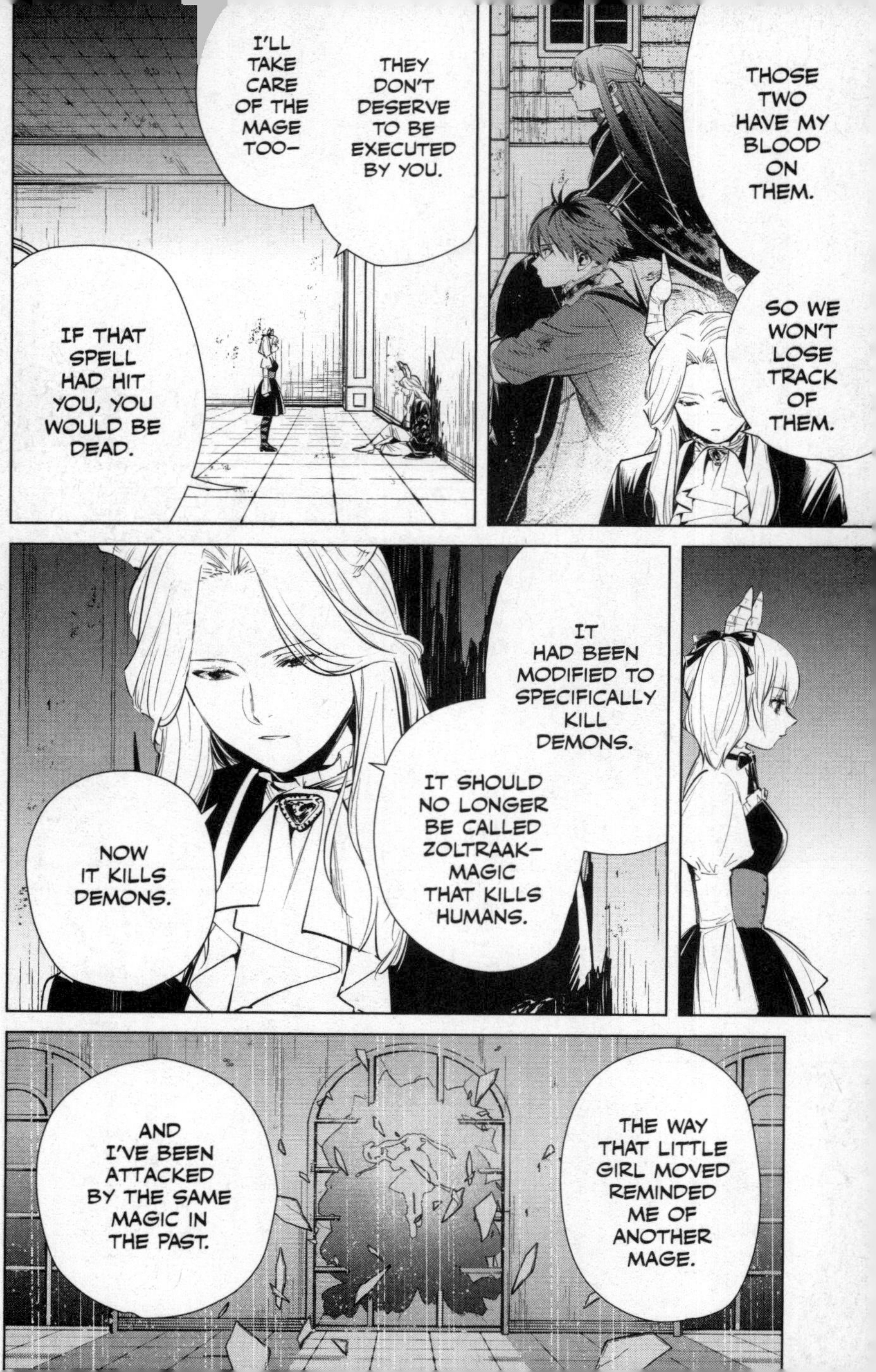
THOSE TWO HAVE MY BLOOD ON THEM.
SO WE WON'T LOSE TRACK OF THEM.
THEY DON'T DESERVE TO BE EXECUTED BY YOU.
I'LL TAKE CARE OF THE MAGE TOO–
IF THAT SPELL HAD HIT YOU, YOU WOULD BE DEAD.
IT HAD BEEN MODIFIED TO SPECIFICALLY KILL DEMONS.
IT SHOULD NO LONGER BE CALLED ZOLTRAAK–MAGIC THAT KILLS HUMANS.
NOW IT KILLS DEMONS.
THE WAY THAT LITTLE GIRL MOVED REMINDED ME OF ANOTHER MAGE.
AND I'VE BEEN ATTACKED BY THE SAME MAGIC IN THE PAST.

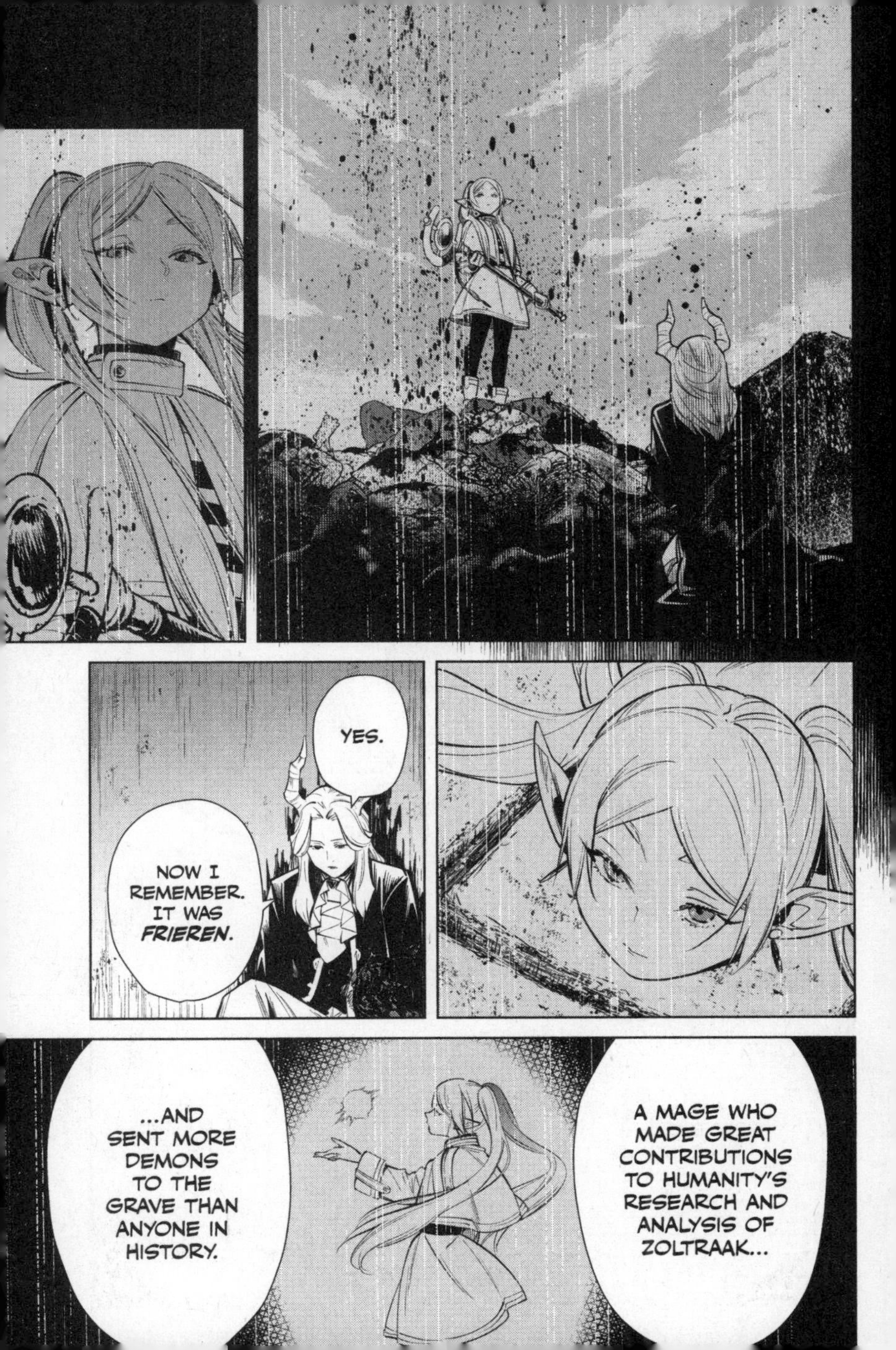
YES.
NOW I REMEMBER. IT WAS FRIEREN.
A MAGE WHO MADE GREAT CONTRIBUTIONS TO HUMANITY'S RESEARCH AND ANALYSIS OF ZOLTRAAK...
...AND SENT MORE DEMONS TO THE GRAVE THAN ANYONE IN HISTORY.

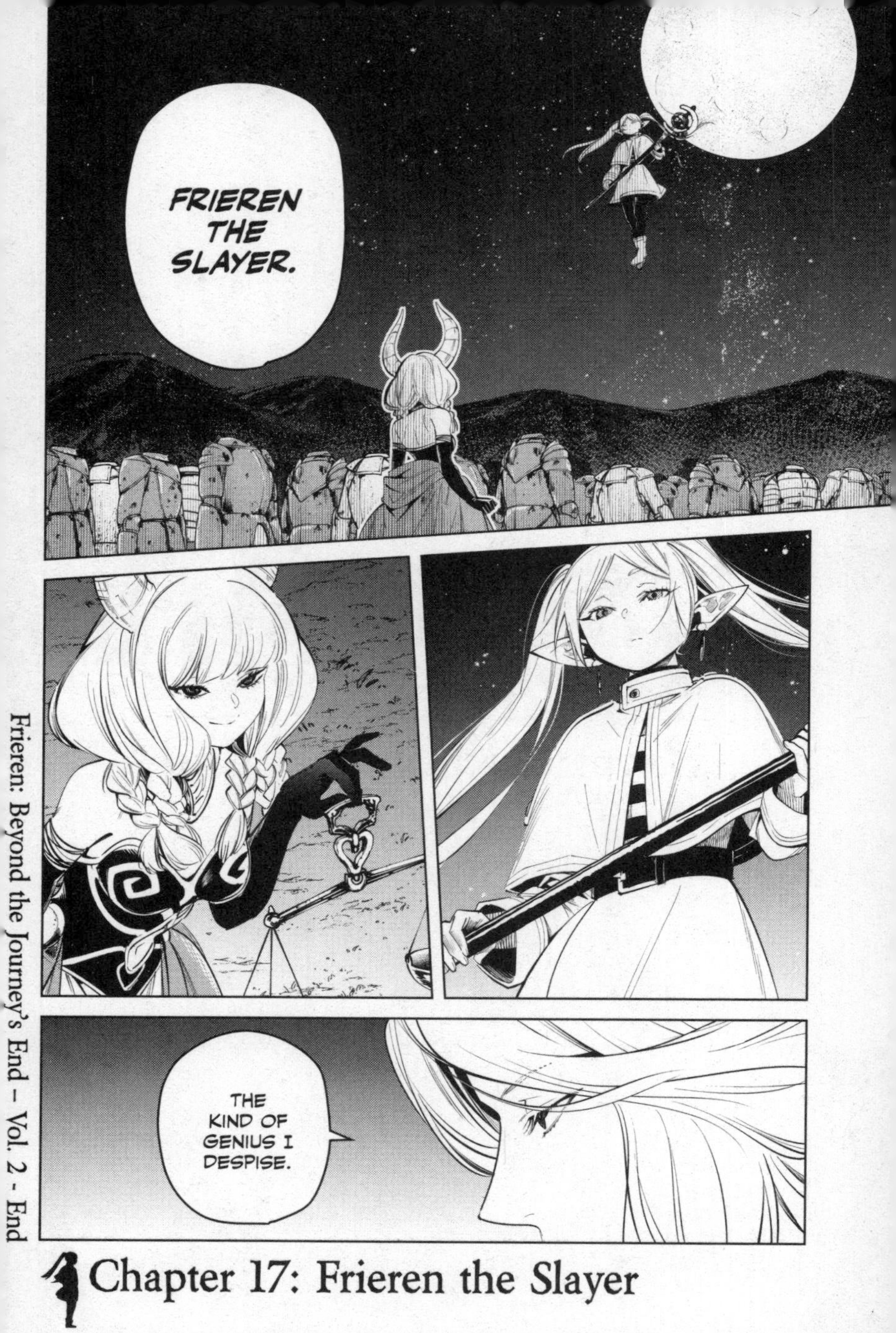
FRIEREN THE SLAYER.
THE KIND OF GENIUS I DESPISE.

Frieren: Beyond the Journey's End – Vol. 2 - End

Chapter 17: Frieren the Slayer

Frieren: Beyond Journey's End

VOLUME 2
Shonen Sunday Edition

STORY BY
KANEHITO YAMADA

ART BY
TSUKASA ABE

SOSO NO FRIEREN Vol. 2
Kanehito YAMADA, Tsukasa ABE
© 2020 Kanehito YAMADA, Tsukasa ABE
All rights reserved.
Original Japanese edition published by SHOGAKUKAN.
English translation rights in the United States of America, Canada, the United Kingdom, Ireland, Australia and New Zealand arranged with SHOGAKUKAN.

Original Cover Design: Masato ISHIZAWA + Bay Bridge Studio

Translation/Misa 'Japanese Ammo'
Touch-up Art & Lettering/Annaliese "Ace" Christman
Design/Yukiko Whitley
Editor/Mike Montesa

Printed in Canada

Published by VIZ Media, LLC
P.O. Box 77010
San Francisco, CA 94107

10 9 8 7 6 5 4 3 2 1
First printing, January 2022

VIZ MEDIA
viz.com

SHONEN SUNDAY
shonensunday.com

Frieren

Beyond Journey's End